Fodo

The Czech Republic and Slovakia

"When it comes to information on regional history, what to see and do, and shopping, these guides are exhaustive."

—*USAir Magazine*

"Usable, sophisticated restaurant coverage, with an emphasis on good value."

—Andy Birsh, *Gourmet Magazine* columnist

"Valuable because of their comprehensiveness."

—*Minneapolis Star-Tribune*

"Fodor's always delivers high quality...thoughtfully presented...thorough."

—*Houston Post*

"An excellent choice for those who want everything under one cover."

—*Washington Post*

Reprinted from *Fodor's Eastern and Central Europe*

Fodor's Travel Publications, Inc.
New York • Toronto • London • Sydney • Auckland
http://www.fodors.com/

Fodor's The Czech Republic and Slovakia

Editors: Matthew Lore and Rebecca Miller

Editorial Contributors: Steven K. Amsterdam, Robert Andrews, Mark Baker, Christopher Billy, Robert Blake, David Brown, Audra Epstein, Janet Foley, Laura M. Kidder, Ky Krauthamer, Martha Lagace, Heidi Sarna, Helayne Schiff, Mary Ellen Schultz, M. T. Schwartzman (Gold Guide editor), Timea Špitková, Dinah Spritzer, Julie Tomasz

Creative Director: Fabrizio La Rocca

Associate Art Director: Guide Caroti

Photo Researcher: Jolie Novak

Cartographer: David Lindroth, Inc.

Cover Photograph: Bruno Barbey/Magnum Photos

Text Design: Between the Covers

Copyright

Third Edition

ISBN 0–679–03000–X

Special Sales

Fodor's Travel Publications are available at special discounts for bulk purchases for sales promotions or premiums. Special editions, including personalized covers, excerpts of existing guides, and corporate imprints, can be created in large quantities for special needs. For more information, contact your local bookseller or write to Special Marketing, Fodor's Travel Publications, 201 East 50th Street, New York, NY 10022. Inquiries from Canada should be directed to your local Canadian bookseller or sent to Random House of Canada, Ltd., Marketing Department, 1265 Aerowood Drive, Mississauga, Ontario L4W 1B9. Inquiries from the United Kingdom should be sent to Fodor's Travel Publications, 20 Vauxhall Bridge Road, London SW1V 2SA, England.

PRINTED IN THE UNITED STATES OF AMERICA

10 9 8 7 6 5 4 3 2 1

CONTENTS

ON THE ROAD WITH FODOR'S

WE'RE ALWAYS THRILLED to get letters from readers, especially one like this:

It took us an hour to decide what book to buy and we now know we picked the best one. Your book was wonderful, easy to follow, very accurate, and good on pointing out eating places, informal as well as formal. When we saw other people using your book, we would look at each other and smile.

Our editors and writers are deeply committed to making every Fodor's guide "the best one"—not only accurate but always charming, brimming with sound recommendations and solid ideas, right on the mark in describing restaurants and hotels, and full of fascinating facts that make you view what you've traveled to see in a rich new light.

About Our Writers

Our success in achieving our goals—and in helping to make your trip the best of all possible vacations—is a credit to the hard work of our extraordinary writers and editors. A few of them deserve special mention:

The update of the Czech Republic chapter is the work of two writers, **Ky Krauthamer** and **Martha Lagace**. A resident of Prague since 1992, Ky is the assistant features editor of the weekly *Prague Post*; he has also contributed to *Fodor's Pocket Prague, Fodor's Europe,* and *Fodor's Affordable Europe.* Martha is an editor on the arts and entertainment desk of the *Prague Post*. She grew up in New England, Montana, and Canada, and was a freelance journalist in New York City and Paris before moving to Prague in the spring of 1991. She has also contributed to *Fodor's Pocket Prague.*

Our Slovakia updater, **Timea Špitková,** is a Slovak-born Canadian journalist and a travel writer. Though her home is Toronto, she has spent years working and living overseas especially in South America and Eastern Europe. In 1993, after completing her master's degree in Russian and East European Studies at the University of Toronto, she moved to Prague, where she writes on Slovak and Czech issues for local and foreign newspapers and magazines.

New this Year

This year we've reformatted our guides to make them easier to use. Each chapter of Fodor's *The Czech Republic and Slovakia* begins with brand-new recommended itineraries to help you decide what to see in the time you have. There are also brand-new walking and driving tours and highlights of each country's particular pleasures and pastimes. You may also notice our fresh graphics. More readable and more helpful than ever? We think so—and we hope you do, too.

On the Web

Check out Fodor's Web site (http://www.fodors.com/), where you'll find travel information on major destinations around the world and an ever-changing array of interactive features.

How to Use this Book

Organization

Up front is the **Gold Guide.** Its first section, **Important Contacts A to Z,** gives addresses and telephone numbers of organizations and companies that offer destination-related services and detailed information and publications. **Smart Travel Tips A to Z,** the Gold Guide's second section, gives specific information on how to accomplish what you need to in the Czech Republic and Slovakia as well as tips on savvy traveling. Both sections are in alphabetical order by topic.

Each chapter begins with a synopsis of the country's pleasures and pastimes, followed by an exploring section with recommended itineraries and tips on when to visit. Depending on how much time you have, you can mix and match itineraries from both chapters to create a complete vacation. Chapters are then broken into major regions and cities, with recommended walking or driving tours. Within each region, towns are covered in logical geographical order, while attractive stretches of road and minor points of interest between them are indicated by the designation En Route; all restaurants and lodgings are grouped together within town sections. Within each major city, sights are covered alphabetically. Throughout, Off the Beaten Path sights appear after the sights or towns from which they are most easily accessible. City-specific and regional A to Z sections follow each major subsection and cover getting there, getting around, and helpful contacts and resources. A countrywide A to Z section—an expanded version of the regional A to Zs—appears at the end of each chapter.

At the end of the book you'll find Portraits, which includes a chronology and suggestions for pretrip reading, both fiction and nonfiction. There is also a helpful vocabulary section covering key phrases in Czech.

Icons and Symbols

★ Our special recommendations
✕ Restaurant
🏠 Lodging establishment
✕🏠 Lodging establishment whose restaurant warrants a detour
⚠ Campgrounds
♻ Good for kids (rubber duckie)
☞ Sends you to another section of the guide for more information
✉ Address
☎ Telephone number
FAX Fax number
☉ Opening and closing times
💰 Admission prices (those we give apply only to adults; substantially reduced fees are almost always available for children, students, and senior citizens)

Numbers in white and black circles (e.g., ❷ and ②) that appear on the maps, in the margins, and within the tours correspond to one another.

Dining and Lodging

The restaurants and lodgings we list are the cream of the crop in each price range. Price charts appear in the Pleasures and Pastimes section that follows each chapter introduction.

Hotel Facilities

We always list the facilities that are available—but we don't specify whether they cost extra. When pricing accommodations, always ask what's included.

Restaurant Reservations and Dress Codes

Reservations are always a good idea; we note only when they're essential or when they are not accepted. Book as far ahead as you can, and reconfirm when you get to town. Unless otherwise noted, the restaurants listed are open daily for lunch and dinner. We mention dress only when men are required to wear a jacket or a jacket and tie. Look for an overview of local habits in the Pleasures and Pastimes section that follows each chapter introduction.

Credit Cards

The following abbreviations are used: **AE,** American Express; **D,** Discover; **DC,** Diners Club; **MC,** MasterCard; and **V,** Visa.

Please Write to Us

You can use this book in the confidence that all prices and opening times are based on information supplied to us at press time; Fodor's cannot accept responsibility for any errors. Time inevitably brings changes, so always confirm information when it matters—especially if you're making a detour to visit a specific place. In addition, when making reservations be sure to mention if you have a disability or are traveling with children, if you prefer a private bath or a certain type of bed, or if you have specific dietary needs or any other concerns.

Were the restaurants we recommended as described? Did our hotel picks exceed your expectations? Did you find a museum we recommended a waste of time? If you have complaints, we'll look into them and revise our entries when the facts warrant it. If you've discovered a special place that we haven't included, we'll pass the information along to our correspondents and have them check it out. So send your feedback, positive *and* negative, to The Czech Republic and Slovakia editor at 201 East 50th Street, New York, New York 10022—and have a wonderful trip!

Karen Cure
Editorial Director

Europe

ICELAND
Reykjavík

NORWAY
Bergen

NORTHERN
IRELAND

SCOTLAND
Edinburgh

North
Sea

Skagerr

Belfast

IRELAND
Irish
Sea

DENMARK

Dublin

UNITED
KINGDOM

Hamburg

WALES

ENGLAND

NETHERLANDS
Amsterdam

Cardiff

The Hague

London

Rotterdam

GER

English Channel

Brussels

Bonn

ATLANTIC
OCEAN

BELGIUM

LUXEMBOURG

Frankfurt

Paris

FRANCE

Zürich

Mun

Bern

SWITZERLAND

Lyon

LIECHTENST

Milan

Ver

Monte
Carlo

Marseille

Nice

MONACO

Florence

PORTUGAL

Madrid

ANDORRA

Corsica

Lisbon

SPAIN

Barcelona

Sardinia

Seville

Granada

Balearic
Islands

Tyrrhen

Gibraltar

Mediterranean Sea

MOROCCO

ALGERIA

0   400 miles

TUNISIA

0   600 km

World Time Zones

Numbers below vertical bands relate each zone to Greenwich Mean Time (0 hrs.).
Local times frequently differ from these general indications,
as indicated by light-face numbers on map.

Algiers, **29**	Berlin, **34**	Delhi, **48**	Istanbul, **40**
Anchorage, **3**	Bogotá, **19**	Denver, **8**	Jerusalem, **42**
Athens, **41**	Budapest, **37**	Djakarta, **53**	Johannesburg, **44**
Auckland, **1**	Buenos Aires, **24**	Dublin, **26**	Lima, **20**
Baghdad, **46**	Caracas, **22**	Edmonton, **7**	Lisbon, **28**
Bangkok, **50**	Chicago, **9**	Hong Kong, **56**	London
Beijing, **54**	Copenhagen, **33**	Honolulu, **2**	(Greenwich), **27**
	Dallas, **10**		Los Angeles, **6**
			Madrid, **38**
			Manila, **57**

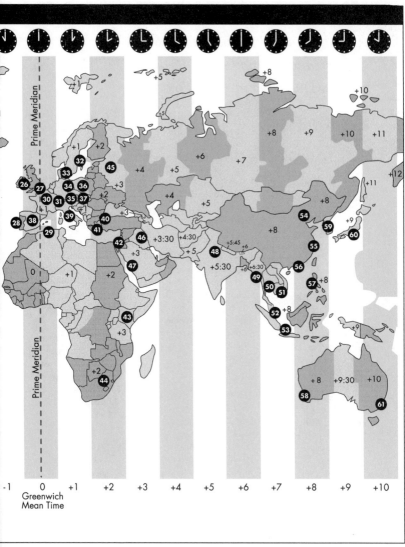

IMPORTANT CONTACTS A TO Z

*An Alphabetical Listing of Publications,
Organizations, and Companies that Will Help You
Before, During, and After Your Trip*

A

AIR TRAVEL

The major gateways to the Czech Republic and Slovakia are **Ruzyně Airport** (⊠ About 20 mi northwest of Prague, ☎ 02/367760) and Slovakia's **Ivanka Airport** near Bratislava (☎ 07/522–3003).

FLYING TIME

From New York, a nonstop flight to Prague takes 9–10 hours; with a stopover, the journey takes at least 12–13 hours. From Montréal nonstop it is 7½ hours; from Los Angeles, 16 hours. The trip from New York to Bratislava (with a stopover in Prague) takes 11–12 hours. From Montréal it is 8½ hours; from Los Angeles, 17 hours.

CARRIERS

Czech Airlines (ČSA, ☎ 212/682–5833) is the only airline that has nonstop flights to both Prague and Bratislava from the United States. For connecting flights aboard U.S. carriers, contact **Continental** (☎ 800/231–0856); **Delta** (☎ 800/241–4141); and **United** (☎ 800/538–2929). You'll need to change planes in Europe, and a European airline may operate the last leg of your flight into Prague or Bratislava.

FROM THE U.K

Carriers from the United Kingdom include **British Airways** (☎ 0181/897–4000 or 0345/222111 outside London), and **Czech Airlines** (☎ 0171/255–1898).

COMPLAINTS

To register complaints about charter and scheduled airlines, contact the U.S. Department of Transportation's **Aviation Consumer Protection Division** (⊠ C-75, Washington, DC 20590, ☎ 202/366–2220). Complaints about lost baggage or ticketing problems and concerns about safety may also be logged with the **Federal Aviation Administration (FAA) Consumer Hotline** (☎ 800/322–7873).

CONSOLIDATORS

For the names of reputable air-ticket consolidators, contact the **United States Air Consolidators Association** (⊠ 925 L St., Suite 220, Sacramento, CA 95814, ☎ 916/441–4166, FAX 916/441–3520). For discount air-ticketing agencies, *see* Discounts & Deals, *below.*

DISCOUNT PASSES

See Air Travel *in* Smart Tips A to Z, *below.*

PUBLICATIONS

For general information about charter carriers, ask for the Department of Transportation's free brochure **"Plane Talk: Public Charter Flights"** (⊠ Aviation Consumer Protection Division, C-75, Washington, DC 20590, ☎ 202/366–2220). The Department of Transportation also publishes a 58-page booklet, **"Fly Rights,"** available from the Consumer Information Center (⊠ Supt. of Documents, Dept. 136C, Pueblo, CO 81009; $1.75).

For other tips, consult the Consumers Union's monthly **"Consumer Reports Travel Letter"** (⊠ Box 53629, Boulder, CO 80322, ☎ 800/234–1970; $39 1st year).

WITHIN THE CZECH REPUBLIC

Air Ostrava (⊠ Prague, ☎ 02/2403–2731) is a small private airline that links Prague, Ostrava, and Brno.

WITHIN SLOVAKIA

ČSA links Bratislava with Poprad (Tatras) and Košice. Make reservations through Satur offices abroad or ČSA in Bratislava (☎ 07/311205).

B

BETTER BUSINESS BUREAU

For local contacts in the hometown of a tour operator you may be considering, consult the **Council of Better Busi-**

ness Bureaus (✉ 4200 Wilson Blvd., Suite 800, Arlington, VA 22203, ☎ 703/276–0100, FAX 703/525–8277).

C

CAR RENTAL

The major car-rental companies in the Czech Republic are **Avis** (☎ 800/331–1084; in Canada, 800/879–2847), **Budget** (☎ 800/472–3325; in the U.K., 0800/181181), **Dollar** (☎ 800/800–6000; in the U.K., 0990/565656, where it is known as Eurodollar), **Hertz** (☎ 800/654–3001; in Canada, 800/263–0600; in the U.K., 0345/555888), and **National InterRent** (sometimes known as Europcar InterRent outside North America; ☎ 800/227–3876; in the U.K., 0345/222–525). Rates in Prague are $37 a day and $287 a week for an economy car with unlimited mileage. This does not include tax on car rentals, which is 5%. In the Czech Republic, the state-run **Pragocar** offers Western makes for as much as $400–$900 per week. Smaller local companies, on the other hand, can rent cars built in the former Czechoslovakia for as low as $130 per week.

In addition to local companies, **Hertz** (☞ *above*) and **Europcar InterRent** (☞ *above*) both operate in Slovakia. As in the Czech Republic, prices in Slovakia vary greatly, with smaller local companies often offering lower rates than the majors (☞ Car Rentals

in the A to Z sections for Prague, the Czech Republic, and Slovakia).

See Car Rental Surcharges *in* Smart Travel Tips, *below* for additional surcharge information.

RENTAL WHOLESALERS

Contact **Auto Europe** (☎ 207/828–2525 or 800/223–5555).

CHILDREN & TRAVEL

FLYING

Look into **"Flying with Baby"** (✉ Third Street Press, Box 261250, Littleton, CO 80163, ☎ 303/595–5959; $4.95 includes shipping), cowritten by a flight attendant. **"Kids and Teens in Flight,"** free from the U.S. Department of Transportation's Aviation Consumer Protection Division (✉ C-75, Washington, DC 20590, ☎ 202/366–2220), offers tips on children flying alone. Every two years the February issue of *Family Travel Times* (☞ Know-How, *below*) details children's services on three dozen airlines. **"Flying Alone, Handy Advice for Kids Traveling Solo"** is available free from the American Automobile Association (✉ AAA, send stamped, self-addressed, legal-size envelope: Flying Alone, Mail Stop 800, 1000 AAA Dr., Heathrow, FL 32746).

KNOW-HOW

Family Travel Times, published quarterly by Travel with Your Children (✉ TWYCH, 40 5th Ave., New York, NY 10011, ☎ 212/

477–5524; $40 per year), covers destinations, types of vacations, and modes of travel.

LODGING

Young visitors to the Czech Republic will enjoy staying at one of Prague's picturesque floating "botels." For further information contact **Čedok.**

CUSTOMS

U.S. CITIZENS

The **U.S. Customs Service** (✉ Box 7407, Washington, DC 20044, ☎ 202/927–6724) can answer questions on duty-free limits and publishes a helpful brochure, "Know Before You Go." For information on registering foreign-made articles, call 202/927–0540 or write to the U.S. Customs Service (✉ Resource Management, 1301 Constitution Ave. NW, Washington DC, 20229).

COMPLAINTS➤ Note the inspector's badge number and write to the commissioner's office (✉ 1301 Constitution Ave. NW, Washington, DC 20229).

CANADIANS

Contact **Revenue Canada** (✉ 2265 St. Laurent Blvd. S, Ottawa, Ontario K1G 4K3, ☎ 613/993–0534) for a copy of the free brochure **"I Declare/Je Déclare"** and for details on duty-free limits. For recorded information (within Canada only), call 800/461–9999.

U.K. CITIZENS

HM Customs and Excise (✉ Dorset House,

Stamford St., London SE1 9NG, ☎ 0171/202–4227) can answer questions about U.K. customs regulations and publishes a free pamphlet, **"A Guide for Travellers,"** detailing standard procedures and import rules.

D

DISABILITIES & ACCESSIBILITY

COMPLAINTS

To register complaints under the provisions of the Americans with Disabilities Act, contact the U.S. Department of Justice's **Disability Rights Section** (⌧ Box 66738, Washington, DC 20035, ☎ 202/514–0301 or 800/514–0301, FAX 202/307–1198, TTY 202/514–0383 or 800/514–0383). For airline-related problems, contact the U.S. Department of Transportation's **Aviation Consumer Protection Division** (☞ Air Travel, *above*). For complaints about surface transportation, contact the Department of Transportation's **Civil Rights Office** (⌧ 400 7th St., SW, Room 10215, Washington DC, 20590 ☎ 202/366–4648).

ORGANIZATIONS

TRAVELERS WITH HEARING IMPAIRMENTS➤ The **American Academy of Otolaryngology** (⌧ 1 Prince St., Alexandria, VA 22314, ☎ 703/836–4444, FAX 703/683–5100, TTY 703/519–1585) publishes a brochure, "Travel Tips for Hearing Impaired People."

TRAVELERS WITH MOBILITY PROBLEMS➤ Contact

Mobility International USA (⌧ Box 10767, Eugene, OR 97440, ☎ and TTY 541/343–1284, FAX 541/343–6812), the U.S. branch of a Belgium-based organization (☞ *below*) with affiliates in 30 countries; **MossRehab Hospital Travel Information Service** (☎ 215/456–9600, TTY 215/456–9602), a telephone information resource for travelers with physical disabilities; the **Society for the Advancement of Travel for the Handicapped** (⌧ 347 5th Ave., Suite 610, New York, NY 10016, ☎ 212/447–7284, FAX 212/725–8253; membership $45); and **Travelin' Talk** (⌧ Box 3534, Clarksville, TN 37043, ☎ 615/552–6670, FAX 615/552–1182), which provides local contacts worldwide for travelers with disabilities.

TRAVELERS WITH VISION IMPAIRMENTS➤ Contact the **American Council of the Blind** (⌧ 1155 15th St. NW, Suite 720, Washington, DC 20005, ☎ 202/467–5081, FAX 202/467–5085) for a list of travelers' resources or the **American Foundation for the Blind** (⌧ 11 Penn Plaza, Suite 300, New York, NY 10001, ☎ 212/502–7600 or 800/232–5463, TTY 212/502–7662), which provides general advice and publishes "Access to Art" ($19.95), a directory of museums that accommodate travelers with vision impairments.

IN THE U.K.

Contact the **Royal Association for Disability and Rehabilitation**

(⌧ RADAR, 12 City Forum, 250 City Rd., London EC1V 8AF, ☎ 0171/250–3222) or **Mobility International** (⌧ Rue de Manchester 25, B-1080 Brussels, Belgium, ☎ 00–322–410–6297, FAX 00–322–410–6874), an international travel-information clearinghouse for people with disabilities.

PUBLICATIONS

Several publications for travelers with disabilities are available from the **Consumer Information Center** (⌧ Box 100, Pueblo, CO 81009, ☎ 719/948–3334). Call or write for its free catalog of current titles. The Society for the Advancement of Travel for the Handicapped (☞ Organizations, *above*) publishes the quarterly magazine **"Access to Travel"** ($13 for 1-year subscription).

The 500-page **Travelin' Talk Directory** (⌧ Box 3534, Clarksville, TN 37043, ☎ 615/552–6670, FAX 615/552–1182; $35) lists people and organizations who help travelers with disabilities. For travel agents worldwide, consult the **Directory of Travel Agencies for the Disabled** (⌧ Twin Peaks Press, Box 129, Vancouver, WA 98666, ☎ 360/694–2462 or 800/637–2256, FAX 360/696–3210; $19.95 plus $3 shipping).

TRAVEL AGENCIES & TOUR OPERATORS

The Americans with Disabilities Act requires that all travel firms serve the needs of all travelers. That said, you should note that some agencies and operators specialize in making travel arrangements for individuals and groups with disabilities, among them is **Access Adventures** (⊠ 206 Chestnut Ridge Rd., Rochester, NY 14624, ☎ 716/889–9096), run by a former physical-rehab counselor.

TRAVELERS WITH MOBILITY PROBLEMS➤ Contact **Hinsdale Travel Service** (⊠ 201 E. Ogden Ave., Suite 100, Hinsdale, IL 60521, ☎ 630/325–1335), a travel agency that benefits from the advice of wheelchair traveler Janice Perkins; and **Wheelchair Journeys** (⊠ 16979 Redmond Way, Redmond, WA 98052, ☎ 206/885–2210 or 800/313–4751), which can handle arrangements worldwide.

TRAVELERS WITH DEVELOPMENTAL DISABILITIES➤ Contact the nonprofit **New Directions** (⊠ 5276 Hollister Ave., Suite 207, Santa Barbara, CA 93111, ☎ 805/967–2841).

TRAVEL GEAR

The **Magellan's** catalog (☎ 800/962–4943, FAX 805/568–5406), includes a section devoted to products designed for travelers with disabilities.

DISCOUNTS & DEALS

AIRFARES

For the lowest airfares to the Czech Republic, call 800/FLY-4-LESS.

CLUBS

Contact **Entertainment Travel Editions** (⊠ Box 1068, Trumbull, CT 06611, ☎ 800/445–

4137; $28–$53, depending on destination), **Great American Traveler** (⊠ Box 27965, Salt Lake City, UT 84127, ☎ 800/548–2812; $49.95 per year), **Moment's Notice Discount Travel Club** (⊠ 7301 New Utrecht Ave., Brooklyn, NY 11204, ☎ 718/234–6295; $25 per year, single or family), **Privilege Card International** (⊠ 3391 Peachtree Rd. NE, Suite 110, Atlanta, GA 30326, ☎ 404/262–0222 or 800/236–9732; $74.95 per year), **Travelers Advantage** (⊠ CUC Travel Service, 49 Music Sq. W, Nashville, TN 37203, ☎ 800/548–1116 or 800/648–4037; $49 per year, single or family), or **Worldwide Discount Travel Club** (⊠ 1674 Meridian Ave., Miami Beach, FL 33139, ☎ 305/534–2082; $50 per year for family, $40 single).

HOTEL ROOMS

For hotel room rates guaranteed in U.S. dollars, call **Steigenberger Reservation Service** (☎ 800/223–5652).

PASSES

See Train Travel, *below, and* Air Travel *in* Smart Tips A to Z, *below.*

PUBLICATIONS

Consult *The Frugal Globetrotter,* by Bruce Northam (⊠ Fulcrum Publishing, 350 Indiana St., Suite 350, Golden, CO 80401, ☎ 800/992–2908; $16.95 plus $4 shipping). For publications that tell how to find the lowest prices on plane tickets, *see* Air Travel, *above.*

STUDENTS

Members of Hostelling International–American Youth Hostels (☞ Students, *below*) are eligible for discounts on car rentals, admissions to attractions, and other selected travel expenses.

GAY & LESBIAN TRAVEL

ORGANIZATIONS

The **International Gay Travel Association** (⊠ Box 4974, Key West, FL 33041, ☎ 800/448–8550, FAX 305/296–6633), a consortium of more than 1,000 travel companies, can supply names of gay-friendly travel agents, tour operators, and accommodations.

PUBLICATIONS

The 16-page monthly newsletter **"Out & About"** (⊠ 8 W. 19th St., Suite 401, New York, NY 10011, ☎ 212/645–6922 or 800/929–2268, FAX 800/929–2215; $49 for 10 issues and quarterly calendar) covers gay-friendly resorts, hotels, cruise lines, and airlines.

TOUR OPERATORS

Toto Tours (⊠ 1326 W. Albion Ave., Suite 3W, Chicago, IL 60626, ☎ 773/274–8686 or 800/565–1241, FAX 773/274–8695) offers group tours to worldwide destinations.

TRAVEL AGENCIES

The largest agencies serving gay travelers are **Advance Travel** (⊠ 10700 Northwest Fwy., Suite 160, Houston, TX 77092, ☎ 713/682–2002 or

800/292–0500), **Club Travel** (✉ 8739 Santa Monica Blvd., West Hollywood, CA 90069, ☎ 310/358–2200 or 800/429–8747), **Islanders/Kennedy Travel** (✉ 183 W. 10th St., New York, NY 10014, ☎ 212/242–3222 or 800/988–1181), **Now Voyager** (✉ 4406 18th St., San Francisco, CA 94114, ☎ 415/626–1169 or 800/255–6951), and **Yellowbrick Road** (✉ 1500 W. Balmoral Ave., Chicago, IL 60640, ☎ 773/561–1800 or 800/642–2488). **Skylink Women's Travel** (✉ 2460 W. 3rd St., Suite 215, Santa Rosa, CA 95401, ☎ 707/570–0105 or 800/225–5759) serves lesbian travelers.

H
HEALTH

FINDING A DOCTOR

For its members, the **International Association for Medical Assistance to Travellers** (✉ IAMAT, membership free; 417 Center St., Lewiston, NY 14092, ☎ 716/754–4883; ✉ 40 Regal Rd., Guelph, Ontario N1K 1B5, ☎ 519/836–0102; ✉ 1287 St. Clair Ave. W., Toronto, Ontario M6E 1B8, ☎ 416/652–0137; ✉ 57 Voirets, 1212 Grand-Lancy, Geneva, Switzerland, no phone) publishes a worldwide directory of English-speaking physicians meeting IAMAT standards.

MEDICAL ASSISTANCE COMPANIES

The following companies are concerned

primarily with emergency medical assistance, although they may provide some insurance as part of their coverage. For a list of full-service travel insurance companies, *see* Insurance, *below.*

International SOS Assistance (✉ Box 11568, Philadelphia, PA 19116, ☎ 215/244–1500 or 800/523–8930; ✉ Box 466, Pl. Bonaventure, Montréal, Québec H5A 1C1, ☎ 514/874–7674 or 800/363–0263; ✉ 7 Old Lodge Pl., St. Margarets, Twickenham TW1 1RQ, England, ☎ 0181/744–0033), **Medex Assistance Corporation** (✉ Box 5375, Timonium, MD 21094, ☎ 410/453–6300 or 800/537–2029), **Near Travel Services** (✉ Box 1339, Calumet City, IL 60409, ☎ 708/868–6700 or 800/654–6700), **Traveler's Emergency Network** (✉ 1133 15th St. NW, Suite 400, Washington DC, 20005, ☎ 202/828–5894 or 800/275–4836, FAX 202/828–5896), **TravMed** (✉ Box 5375, Timonium, MD 21094, ☎ 410/453–6380 or 800/732–5309), or **Worldwide Assistance Services** (✉ 1133 15th St. NW, Suite 400, Washington, DC 20005, ☎ 202/331–1609 or 800/821–2828, FAX 202/828–5896).

I
INSURANCE

IN THE U.S.

Travel insurance covering baggage, health, and trip cancellation or interruptions is available from **Access Amer-**

ica (✉ 6600 W. Broad St., Richmond, VA 23230, ☎ 804/285–3300 or 800/334–7525), **Carefree Travel Insurance** (✉ Box 9366, 100 Garden City Plaza, Garden City, NY 11530, ☎ 516/294–0220 or 800/323–3149), **Tele-Trip** (✉ Mutual of Omaha Plaza, Box 31716, Omaha, NE 68131, ☎ 800/228–9792), **Travel Guard International** (✉ 1145 Clark St., Stevens Point, WI 54481, ☎ 715/345–0505 or 800/826–1300), **Travel Insured International** (✉ Box 280568, East Hartford, CT 06128, ☎ 203/528–7663 or 800/243–3174), and **Wallach & Company** (✉ 107 W. Federal St., Box 480, Middleburg, VA 22117, ☎ 540/687–3166 or 800/237–6615).

IN CANADA

Contact **Mutual of Omaha** (✉ Travel Division, 500 University Ave., Toronto, Ontario M5G 1V8, ☎ 800/465–0267 in Canada or 416/598-4083).

IN THE U.K.

The **Association of British Insurers** (✉ 51 Gresham St., London EC2V 7HQ, ☎ 0171/600–3333) gives advice by phone and publishes the free pamphlet **"Holiday Insurance and Motoring Abroad,"** which sets out typical policy provisions and costs.

L
LODGING

For information on hotel consolidators, *see* Discounts & Deals, *above.*

APARTMENT & VILLA RENTAL

Among the companies to contact are **At Home Abroad** (⌂ 405 E. 56th St., Suite 6H, New York, NY 10022, ☎ 212/421–9165, ℻ 212/752–1591), **Europa-Let/Tropical Inn-Let, Inc.** (⌂ 92 N. Main St., Ashland, OR 97520, ☎ 541/482–5806 or 800/462–4486, ℻ 541/482–0660), and **Property Rentals International** (⌂ 1008 Mansfield Crossing Rd., Richmond, VA 23236, ☎ 804/378–6054 or 800/220–3332, ℻ 804/379–2073).

M
MONEY

ATMS

For specific foreign **Cirrus** locations, call 800/424–7787; for foreign **Plus** locations, consult the Plus directory at your local bank.

CURRENCY EXCHANGE

If your bank doesn't exchange currency, contact **Thomas Cook Currency Services** (☎ 800/287–7362 for locations). **Ruesch International** (☎ 800/424–2923 for locations) can also provide you with foreign banknotes before you leave home and publishes a number of useful brochures, including a "Foreign Currency Guide" and "Foreign Exchange Tips."

WIRING FUNDS

Funds can be wired via **MoneyGram**℠ (for locations and information in the U.S. and Canada, ☎ 800/926–9400) or **Western**

Union (for agent locations or to send money using MasterCard or Visa, ☎ 800/325–6000; in Canada, 800/321–2923; in the U.K., 0800/833833; or visit the Western Union office at the nearest major post office).

P
PACKING

For strategies on packing light, get a copy of *The Packing Book,* by Judith Gilford (⌂ Ten Speed Press, Box 7123, Berkeley, CA 94707, ☎ 510/559–1600 or 800/841–2665, ℻ 510/524–4588; $7.95 plus $3.50 shipping).

PASSPORTS & VISAS

U.S. CITIZENS

For fees, documentation requirements, and other information, call the State Department's **Office of Passport Services** information line (☎ 202/647–0518).

CANADIANS

For fees, documentation requirements, and other information, call the Ministry of Foreign Affairs and International Trade's **Passport Office** (☎ 819/994–3500 or 800/567–6868).

A visa is required before entering Slovakia; it will allow one-entry during a stay of up to 30 days and is valid for 6 months from date of issue. For visa applications and information, contact the Slovak Embassy (⌂ 50 Rideau Terrace, Ottawa, Ontario K1M 2A1, ☎ 613/749–4442).

U.K. CITIZENS

For fees, documentation requirements, and to request an emergency passport, call the **London Passport Office** (☎ 0990/210410).

PHOTO HELP

The **Kodak Information Center** (☎ 800/242–2424) answers consumer questions about film and photography. The *Kodak Guide to Shooting Great Travel Pictures* (available in bookstores; or contact Fodor's Travel Publications, ☎ 800/533–6478; $16.50 plus $4 shipping) explains how to take expert travel photographs.

S
SAFETY

"Trouble-Free Travel," from the AAA, is a booklet of tips for protecting yourself and your belongings when away from home. Send a legal-size SASE to Trouble-Free Travel (⌂ Mail Stop 75, 1000 AAA Dr., Heathrow, FL 32746).

SENIOR CITIZENS

CLUBS

Sears's **Mature Outlook** (⌂ Box 10448, Des Moines, IA 50306, ☎ 800/336–6330; annual membership $14.95) includes a lifestyle/travel magazine and membership in ITC-50 travel club, which offers discounts of up to 50% at participating hotels and restaurants. (☞ Discounts & Deals *in* Smart Travel Tips A to Z).

EDUCATIONAL TRAVEL

The nonprofit **Elderhostel** (⌂ 75 Federal St., 3rd Floor, Boston, MA

02110, ☎ 617/426–7788), for people 55 and older, has offered inexpensive study programs since 1975. Courses cover everything from marine science to Greek mythology and cowboy poetry. Costs for two- to three-week international trips—including room, board, and transportation from the United States—range from $1,800 to $4,500.

ORGANIZATIONS

Contact the **American Association of Retired Persons** (✉ AARP, 601 E St. NW, Washington, DC 20049, ☎ 202/434–2277; annual dues $8 per person or couple). Its Purchase Privilege Program secures discounts for members on lodging, car rentals, and sightseeing.

HOSTELING

In the United States, contact **Hostelling International–American Youth Hostels** (✉ 733 15th St. NW, Suite 840, Washington, DC 20005, ☎ 202/783–6161, FAX 202/783–6171); in Canada, **Hostelling International–Canada** (✉ 205 Catherine St., Suite 400, Ottawa, Ontario K2P 1C3, ☎ 613/237–7884); and in the United Kingdom, the **Youth Hostel Association of England and Wales** (✉ Trevelyan House, 8 St. Stephen's Hill, St. Albans, Hertfordshire AL1 2DY, ☎ 01727/855215 or 01727/845047). Membership (in the U.S., $25; in Canada, C$26.75; in the U.K., £9.30) gives you access to 5,000 hostels in 77

countries that charge $5–$40 per person per night.

ORGANIZATIONS

A major contact is the **Council on International Educational Exchange** (✉ Mail orders only: CIEE, 205 E. 42nd St., 16th Floor, New York, NY 10017, ☎ 212/822–2600, FAX 212/822–2699, info@ciee.org). The **Educational Travel Centre** (✉ 438 N. Frances St., Madison, WI 53703, ☎ 608/256–5551 or 800/747–5551, FAX 608/256–2042) offers rail passes and low-cost airline tickets, mostly for flights that depart from Chicago.

In Canada, also contact **Travel Cuts** (✉ 187 College St., Toronto, Ontario M5T 1P7, ☎ 416/979–2406 or 800/667–2887).

PUBLICATIONS

Check out the *Berkeley Guide to Eastern Europe* (available in bookstores; or contact Fodor's Travel Publications, ☎ 800/533–6478; $19.50 plus $4 shipping).

T

The country code for both the Czech Republic and Slovakia is 42. The city code for Prague is 02; for Bratislava, 07.

For local access numbers abroad, contact **AT&T** USADirect (☎ 800/874–4000), **MCI** Call USA (☎ 800/444–4444), or **Sprint** Express (☎ 800/793–1153).

Among the companies that sell tours and packages to the Czech Republic and Slovakia, the following are nationally known, have a proven reputation, and offer plenty of options.

GROUP TOURS

SUPER-DELUXE➤ **Abercrombie & Kent** (✉ 1520 Kensington Rd., Oak Brook, IL 60521-2141, ☎ 708/954–2944 or 800/323–7308, FAX 708/954–3324) and **Travcoa** (✉ Box 2630, 2350 S.E. Bristol St., Newport Beach, CA 92660, ☎ 714/476–2800 or 800/992–2003, FAX 714/476–2538).

DELUXE➤ **Maupintour** (✉ Box 807, 1515 St. Andrews Dr., Lawrence, KS 66047, ☎ 913/843–1211 or 800/255–4266, FAX 913/843–8351) and **Tauck Tours** (✉ Box 5027, 276 Post Rd. W, Westport, CT 06881, ☎ 203/226–6911 or 800/468–2825, FAX 203/221–6828).

FIRST-CLASS➤ **Brendan Tours** (✉ 15137 Califa St., Van Nuys, CA 91411, ☎ 818/785–9696 or 800/421–8446, FAX 818/902–9876), **Cedok Travel** (✉ 10 E. 40th St., #3604, New York, NY 10016, ☎ 212/725–0948 or 800/800–8891), and **General Tours** (✉ 53 Summer St., Keene, NH 03431, ☎ 603/357–5033 or 800/221–2216, FAX 603/357–4548).

ORGANIZATIONS

The **National Tour Association** (✉ NTA,

546 E. Main St., Lexington, KY 40508, ☎ 606/226–4444 or 800/755–8687) and the **United States Tour Operators Association** (✉ USTOA, 211 E. 51st St., Suite 12B, New York, NY 10022, ☎ 212/750–7371) can provide lists of members and information on booking tours.

PACKAGES

Independent vacation packages that include round-trip airfare and hotel accommodations are available from major airlines and tour operators. Among U.S. carriers, contact **Delta Dream Vacations** (☎ 800/872–7786) and **United Vacations** (☎ 800/328–6877). Leading tour operators include **Central Holidays** (✉ 206 Central Ave., Jersey City, NJ 07307, ☎ 201/798–5777 or 800/935–5000), **DER Tours** (✉ 11933 Wilshire Blvd., Los Angeles, CA 90025, ☎ 310/479–4140 or 800/937–1235), and **General Tours** (☞ Group Tours *above*).

PUBLICATIONS

Contact the USTOA (☞ Organizations, *above*) for its **"Smart Traveler's Planning Kit."** Pamphlets in the kit include the "Worldwide Tour and Vacation Package Finder," "How to Select a Tour or Vacation Package," and information on the organization's consumer protection plan. Also get a copy of the Better Business Bureau's **"Tips on Travel Packages"** (✉ Publication 24-195, 4200 Wilson Blvd., Arlington, VA 22203; $2).

THEME TRIPS

Travel Contacts (✉ Box 173, Camberley, GU15 1YE, England, ☎ 0127/667–7217, FAX 0127/663477), which represents 150 tour operators, can satisfy just about any special interest in the Czech Republic and Slovakia.

ART AND ARCHITECTURE➤ For educational programs contact **Smithsonian Study Tours and Seminars** (✉ 1100 Jefferson Dr. SW, Room 3045, MRC 702, Washington, DC 20560, ☎ 202/357–4700, FAX 202/633–9250).

BALLOONING➤ **Buddy Bombard European Balloon Adventures** (✉ 855 Donald Ross Rd., Juno Beach, FL 33408, ☎ 407/775–0039 or 800/862–8537, FAX 407/775–7008) operates balloon holidays in Prague.

BARGE/RIVER CRUISES➤ Contact **KD River Cruises of Europe** (✉ 2500 Westchester Ave., Purchase, NY 10577, ☎ 914/696–3600 or 800/346–6525, FAX 914/696–0833) for cruises on the Elbe River between Dresden and Prague.

BEER/WINE➤ **MIR Corporation** (✉ 85 S. Washington St., #210, Seattle, WA 98104, ☎ 206/624–7289 or 800/424–7289, FAX 206/624–7360, mir@igc.apc.org) leads you to the finest beers and wines of the Czech Republic and Hungary.

BICYCLING➤ Bike tours are available from **Backroads** (✉ 1516 5th St., Berkeley, CA 94710-1740, ☎ 510/577–1555 or 800/462–2848, FAX 510/527–1444, goactive@Backroads.com) and **Uniquely Europe** (✉ 2819 1st Ave., #280, Seattle, WA 98121-1113, ☎ 206/441–8682 or 800/426–3615, FAX 206/441–8862).

HISTORY➤ History buffs should contact **Herodot Travel** (✉ 775 E. Blithedale, Box 234, Mill Valley, CA 94941, ☎ FAX 415/381–4031).

HORSEBACK RIDING➤ **FITS Equestrian** (✉ 685 Lateen Rd., Solvang, CA 93463, ☎ 805/688–9494 or 800/666–3487, FAX 805/688–2943) has tours that include the Czech Republic and Hungary.

JUDAISM➤ Jewish life in the Czech Republic is the subject of a tour from the **American Jewish Congress** (✉ 15 E. 84th St., New York, NY 10028, ☎ 212/879–4588 or 800/221–4694).

LEARNING➤ For educational programs contact **Smithsonian Study Tours and Seminars** (☞ Art and Architecture, *above*).

NATURAL HISTORY➤ **Earthwatch** (✉ Box 403, 680 Mt. Auburn St., Watertown, MA 02272, ☎ 617/926–8200 or 800/776–0188, FAX 617/926–8532, info@earthwatch.org, http://www.earthwatch.org) recruits volunteers to serve in its Earth-Corps as short-term assistants to scientists on research expeditions.

PERFORMING ARTS➤ **Dailey-Thorp Travel** (✉ 330 W. 58th St., #610, New York, NY 10019-1817, ☎ 212/307–1555 or 800/998–4677,

FAX 212/974–1420) specializes in classical music and opera programs throughout Europe, including Prague.

SPAS➤ Contact **Great Spas of the World** (⊠ 211 E. 43rd St., #1404, New York, NY 10017, ☎ 212/599–0382 or 800/826–8062).

WALKING➤ For walking and hiking tours in the Czech Republic and Slovakia, contact **Adventure Center** (⊠ 1311 63rd St., #200, Emeryville, CA 94608, ☎ 510/654–1879 or 800/227–8747, FAX 510/654–4200).

TRAIN TRAVEL

DISCOUNT PASSES

The European East Pass is available through travel agents and **Rail Europe** (⊠ 226–230 Westchester Ave., White Plains, NY 10604, ☎ 914/682–5172 or 800/438–7245; ⊠ 42087 Dundas E., Suite 105, Mississauga, Ontario, Canada, L4X 1M2, ☎ 416/602–4195), **DER Tours** (⊠ Box 1606, Des Plaines, IL 60017, ☎ 800/782–2424, FAX 800/282–7474), or **CIT Tours Corp.** (⊠ 342 Madison Ave., Suite 207, New York, NY 10173, ☎ 212/697–2100 or 800/248–8687 or 800/248–7245 in western U.S.).

Rail Europe also offers a Czech Flexipass ($69, usable only in the Czech Republic), which allows first-class travel on any 5 days within a 15-day period.

FROM THE U.K.

For timetable information on trains bound for Eastern and Central Europe, consult **Cook's European Timetable,** about £10 from Thomas Cook (⊠ 378 Strand, London WC2 ROLW, ☎ 0171/836–5200, and major branches) and at some travel agencies (where looking is free). This book does not list fares, however, so ask a travel agent.

TRAVEL GEAR

For travel apparel, appliances, personal-care items, and other travel necessities, get a free catalog from **Magellan's** (☎ 800/962–4943, FAX 805/568–5406), **Orvis Travel** (☎ 800/541–3541, FAX 540/343–7053), or **TravelSmith** (☎ 800/950–1600, FAX 415/455–0554).

ELECTRICAL CONVERTERS

Send a SASE to the **Franzus Company** (⊠ Customer Service, Dept. B50, Murtha Industrial Park, Box 142, Beacon Falls, CT 06403, ☎ 203/723–6664) for a copy of the free brochure "Foreign Electricity Is No Deep, Dark Secret."

TRAVEL AGENCIES

Čedok Travel by Viktor Corporation (⊠ 10 E. 40th St., New York, NY 10016, ☎ 212/689–9720, FAX 212/481–0597; ⊠ 49 Southwark St., London, SE1 1RU, ☎ 0171/378–6009, FAX 0171/403–2321), the former state-run travel bureau that was called simply Čedok, went private in 1995 and is now a travel agent rather than a tourist information office. Its representa-

tives can make hotel reservations, book air and rail tickets, arrange escorted tours and packages for both the Czech Republic and Slovakia, but they will *not* provide general visitor information. For general visitor information for the Czech Republic, *see* Visitor Information, *below.*

For names of reputable agencies in your area, contact the **American Society of Travel Agents** (⊠ ASTA, 1101 King St., Suite 200, Alexandria, VA 22314, ☎ 703/739–2782), the **Association of Canadian Travel Agents** (⊠ Suite 201, 1729 Bank St., Ottawa, Ontario K1V 7Z5, ☎ 613/521–0474, FAX 613/521–0805) or the **Association of British Travel Agents** (⊠ 55-57 Newman St., London W1P 4AH, ☎ 0171/637–2444, FAX 0171/637–0713).

U
U.S.
GOVERNMENT
TRAVEL BRIEFINGS

The U.S. Department of State's American Citizens Services office (⊠ Room 4811, Washington, DC 20520; enclose SASE) issues **Consular Information Sheets** on all foreign countries. These cover issues such as crime, security, political climate, and health risks as well as listing embassy locations, entry requirements, currency regulations, and providing other useful information. For the latest information, stop in at any U.S. passport office, consulate, or embassy; call the interactive hot line (☎ 202/647–5225, FAX 202/647–3000); or, with your PC's modem, tap into the department's computer bulletin board (☎ 202/647–9225).

V
VISITOR
INFORMATION

CZECH REPUBLIC

The tourist desk of the **Czech Cultural Center** (✉ 1109 Madison Ave., New York, NY 10028, ☎ 212/288–0830). **In Canada and the United Kingdom: Czech Tourist Authority** (✉ Box 198, Exchange Tower, 2 First Canadian Pl., 7th Floor, Toronto, Ontario M5X 1A6, ☎ 416/367–3432, FAX 416/367–3492; ✉ 49 Southwark St., London SE1 1RU, ☎ 0171/378–6009), a state-run information

service, dispenses brochures, maps, and the like. In the United Kingdom you can also contact the **Czech Centre** (✉ 95 Great Portland St., London W1N 5RA, ☎ 0171/291–9922, FAX 0171/436–8300).

SLOVAKIA

The Slovak Information Center (✉ 406 E. 67th St., New York, NY 10021, ☎ 212/737–3971, FAX 212/737–3454) has a walk-in information center and can also provide travel information via phone, fax, or e-mail. In Canada, contact the **Slovak Culture and Information Center** (✉ 12 Birch Ave., Toronto, Ontario M4V 1C8, ☎ 416/925–0008, FAX 416/925–0009). In the United Kingdom, contact the **Embassy of the Slovak Republic** (✉ Information Dept., 25 Kensington Palace

Gardens, London W8 4QY, ☎ 0171/243–0803, FAX 0171/727–5821).

W
WEATHER

For current conditions and forecasts, plus the local time and helpful travel tips, call the **Weather Channel Connection** (☎ 900/932–8437; 95¢ per minute) from a Touch-Tone phone.

The *International Traveler's Weather Guide* (✉ Weather Press, Box 660606, Sacramento, CA 95866, ☎ 916/974–0201 or 800/972–0201; $10.95 includes shipping), written by two meteorologists, provides month-by-month information on temperature, humidity, and precipitation in more than 175 cities worldwide.

handwritten notes:

Tourdual.com
czechcenter.com
KARLOVYVARY.CZ

CEDOK / Prague
420 2 24197 111

KV · Town info. center

420 353 232 838
            "   "   862
            "   224   097

SMART TRAVEL TIPS A TO Z

Basic Information on Traveling in the Czech Republic and Slovakia and Savvy Tips to Make Your Trip a Breeze

A

AIR TRAVEL

If time is an issue, **always look for nonstop flights,** which require no change of plane. If possible, **avoid connecting flights,** which stop at least once and can involve a change of plane, even though the flight number remains the same; if the first leg is late, the second waits.

For better service, **fly smaller or regional carriers,** which often have higher passenger satisfaction ratings. Sometimes they have such in-flight amenities as leather seats or greater legroom and they often have better food.

CUTTING COSTS

The Sunday travel section of most newspapers is a good place to look for deals. *See also* Travel Passes, *below.*

MAJOR AIRLINES➤ The least-expensive airfares from the major airlines are priced for round-trip travel and are subject to restrictions. Usually, you must **book in advance and buy the ticket within 24 hours** to get cheaper fares, and you may have to **stay over a Saturday night.** The lowest fare is subject to availability, and only a small percentage of the plane's total seats is sold at that price. It's smart to **call a number of airlines,** and when you are quoted a good price, book it on the spot—the same fare may not be available on the same flight the next day. Airlines generally allow you to change your return date for a $25 to $50 fee. If you don't use your ticket, you can apply the cost toward the purchase of a new ticket, again for a small charge. However, most low-fare tickets are nonrefundable. To get the lowest airfare, **check different routings.** If your destination has more than one gateway, **compare prices to different airports.**

FROM THE U.K.➤ To save money on flights, **look into an APEX or Super-PEX.** APEX tickets must be booked in advance and have certain restrictions. Super-PEX tickets can be purchased right at the airport.

CONSOLIDATORS➤ Consolidators buy tickets for scheduled flights at reduced rates from the airlines, then sell them at prices below the lowest available from the airlines directly—usually without advance restrictions. Sometimes you can even get your money back if you need to return the ticket. Carefully read the fine print detailing penalties for changes and cancellations. If you doubt the reliability of a consolidator, **confirm your** reservation with the airline.

ALOFT

AIRLINE FOOD➤ If you hate airline food, **ask for special meals when booking.** These can be vegetarian, low-cholesterol, or kosher, for example; commonly prepared to order in smaller quantities than standard fare, they can be tastier.

JET LAG➤ To avoid this syndrome, which occurs when travel disrupts your body's natural cycles, try to maintain a normal routine. At night, **get some sleep.** By day, move about the cabin to **stretch your legs, eat light meals, and drink water—not alcohol.**

SMOKING➤ Smoking is not allowed on flights of six hours or less within the continental United States. Smoking is also prohibited on flights within Canada. For U.S. flights longer than six hours or international flights, **contact your carrier regarding their smoking policy.** Some carriers have prohibited smoking throughout their system; others allow smoking only on certain routes or even certain departures of that route.

TRAVEL PASSES

You can **save on air travel** within Europe if you plan on traveling to and from Prague aboard Czech Airlines. As part of their Euro Flyer program, you can then buy between three and nine flight coupons, which are valid for travel to any Czech Airlines destination. At $120 each, these coupons are a good deal, and the fine print still allows you plenty of freedom.

C
CAMERAS, CAMCORDERS, & COMPUTERS

IN TRANSIT

Always **keep your film, tape, or disks out of the sun;** never put these on the dashboard of a car. Carry an extra supply of batteries, and **be prepared to turn on your camera, camcorder, or laptop computer for security personnel** to prove that it's real.

X-RAYS

Always **ask for hand inspection at security.** Such requests are virtually always honored at U.S. airports, and are usually accommodated abroad. Photographic film becomes clouded after successive exposure to airport X-ray machines. Videotape and computer disks are not harmed by X-rays, but **keep your tapes and disks away from metal detectors.**

CUSTOMS

Before departing, **register your foreign-made camera or laptop with U.S. Customs.** If your equipment is U.S.-made, call the consulate of the country you'll be visiting to find out whether

it should be registered with local customs upon arrival.

CAR RENTAL

The big drawback here is price—rentals can rival airfare for the most expensive transport alternative. The pluses are a freewheeling itinerary and lots of luggage space. One restriction to keep in mind: Renting a car in a Western European country and dropping it off in the Czech Republic or Slovakia will probably be prohibited (or prohibitively expensive).

CUTTING COSTS

To get the best deal, **book through a travel agent who is willing to shop around.** Ask your agent to **look for fly-drive packages,** which also save you money, and **ask if local taxes are included** in the rental or fly price. These can be as high as 20% in some destinations. Don't forget to find out about required deposits, cancellation penalties, drop-off charges, and the cost of any required insurance coverage.

Also **ask your travel agent about a company's customer-service record.** How has it responded to late plane arrivals and vehicle mishaps? Are there often lines at the rental counter, and—if you're traveling during a holiday period—does a confirmed reservation guarantee you a car?

Always **find out what equipment is standard** at your destination before specifying what you want; automatic

transmission and air-conditioning are usually optional—and very expensive.

Be sure to **look into wholesalers**—companies that do not own their own fleets but rent in bulk from those that do and often offer better rates than traditional car-rental operations. Prices are best during off-peak periods; rentals booked through wholesalers must be paid for before you leave the United States.

INSURANCE

When driving a rented car, you are generally responsible for any damage to or loss of the rental vehicle. Before you rent, **see what coverage you already have** under the terms of your personal auto insurance policy and credit cards.

If you do not have auto insurance or an umbrella insurance policy that covers damage to third parties, purchasing CDW or LDW is highly recommended.

Collision policies that car-rental companies sell for European rentals typically do not cover stolen vehicles. Before you buy additional coverage for theft, find out if your credit card or personal auto insurance will cover the loss.

LICENSE REQUIREMENTS

In the Czech Republic your own driver's license is acceptable. An International Driver's Permit is a good idea; it is required in Slovakia for car rentals of more than one month and in the

Czech Republic for rentals of over six months. It's available from the American or Canadian automobile associations, or, in the United Kingdom, from the AA or RAC.

SURCHARGES

Ask whether the car rental rate includes the VAT. Before you pick up a car in one city and leave it in another, **ask about drop-off charges or one-way service fees,** which can be substantial. Also **ask about surcharges applied to cars picked up at airports.** Note, too, that some rental agencies charge extra if you return the car before the time specified on your contract. To avoid a hefty refueling fee, **fill the tank just before you turn in the car**—but be aware that gas stations near the rental outlet may overcharge.

CHILDREN & TRAVEL

When traveling with children, **plan ahead** and **involve your youngsters** as you outline your trip. When packing, **include things to keep them busy** en route (☞ Children & Travel *in* Important Contacts A to Z). On sightseeing days, try to **schedule activities of special interest to your children,** like a trip to a zoo or a playground. If you **plan your itinerary around seasonal festivals,** you'll never lack for things to do. In addition, **check local newspapers for special events** mounted by public libraries, museums, and parks.

BABY-SITTING

For recommended local sitters, **check with your hotel desk.**

DRIVING

If you are renting a car, don't forget to **arrange for a car seat when you reserve.** Sometimes they're free.

FLYING

As a rule, infants under two not occupying a seat fly at greatly reduced fares and occasionally for free. If your children are two or older **ask about special children's fares.** Age limits for these fares vary among carriers. Rules also vary regarding unaccompanied minors, so again, check with your airline.

BAGGAGE➤ In general, the adult baggage allowance applies to children paying half or more of the adult fare. If you are traveling with an infant, **ask about carry-on allowances** before departure. In general, for infants charged 10% of the adult fare you are allowed one carry-on bag and a collapsible stroller, which may have to be checked; you may be limited to less if the flight is full.

SAFETY SEATS➤ According to the FAA, it's a good idea to **use safety seats aloft** for children weighing less than 40 pounds. Airline policies vary. U.S. carriers allow FAA-approved models but usually require that you buy a ticket, even if your child would otherwise ride free, since the seats must be strapped into regular seats. However, some U.S. and foreign-flag airlines

may require you to hold your baby during takeoff and landing—defeating the seat's purpose. Other foreign carriers may not allow infant seats at all, or may charge a child rather than an infant fare for their use.

FACILITIES➤ When making your reservation, **request children's meals or freestanding bassinets if you need them;** the latter are available only to those seated at the bulkhead, where there's enough legroom. If you don't need a bassinet, **think twice before requesting bulkhead seats**—the only storage space for in-flight necessities is in inconveniently distant overhead bins.

GAMES

Milton Bradley and Parker Brothers have travel versions of some of their most popular games, including Yahtzee, Trouble, Sorry, and Monopoly. Prices run $5 to $8. Look for them in the travel section of your local toy store.

LODGING

Most hotels allow children under a certain age to stay in their parents' room at no extra charge; others charge them as extra adults. Be sure to **ask about the cutoff age.**

CUSTOMS & DUTIES

To speed your clearance through customs, **keep receipts for all your purchases abroad and be ready to show the inspector what you've bought.** If you feel that you've been incorrectly or unfairly charged a duty, you can **appeal assessments in dispute.** First ask to see a supervisor. If you are still unsatisfied, **write to the port director** at your point of entry, sending your customs receipt and any other appropriate documentation. The address will be listed on your receipt. If you still don't get satisfaction, you can take your case to customs headquarters in Washington.

If you are bringing in any valuables or foreign-made equipment from home, such as cameras, it's wise to carry the original receipts with you or register the items with U.S. Customs before you leave (Form 4457). Otherwise you could end up paying duty upon your return.

IN THE CZECH REPUBLIC

You may import duty-free into the Czech Republic 250 cigarettes or the equivalent in tobacco, 1 liter of spirits, 2 liters of wine, and gifts valued at up to 1,000 Kčs (approximately $35).

IN SLOVAKIA

You may import duty-free into Slovakia only articles for your own usage.

IN THE U.S.

You may bring home $400 worth of foreign goods duty-free if you've been out of the country for at least 48 hours and haven't already used the $400 allowance, or any part of it, in the past 30 days.

Travelers 21 or older may bring back 1 liter of alcohol duty-free, provided the beverage laws of the state through which they reenter the United States allow it. In addition, regardless of their age, they are allowed 100 non-Cuban cigars and 200 cigarettes. Antiques, which the U.S. Customs Service defines as objects more than 100 years old, are duty-free. Original works of art done entirely by hand are also duty-free. These include, but are not limited to, paintings, drawings, and sculptures.

Duty-free, travelers may mail packages valued at up to $200 to themselves and up to $100 to others, with a limit of one parcel per addressee per day (and no alcohol or tobacco products or perfume valued at more than $5); on the outside, the package must be labeled as being either for personal use or an unsolicited gift, and a list of its contents and their retail value must be attached. Mailed items do not affect your duty-free allowance on your return.

IN CANADA

If you've been out of Canada for at least seven days, you may bring in C$500 worth of goods duty-free. If you've been away for fewer than seven days but for more than 48 hours, the duty-free allowance drops to C$200; if your trip lasts between 24 and 48 hours, the allowance is C$50. You cannot pool allowances with family

members. Goods claimed under the C$500 exemption may follow you by mail; those claimed under the lesser exemptions must accompany you.

Alcohol and tobacco products may be included in the seven-day and 48-hour exemptions but not in the 24-hour exemption. If you meet the age requirements of the province or territory through which you reenter Canada, you may bring in, duty-free, 1.14 liters (40 imperial ounces) of wine or liquor or 24 12-ounce cans or bottles of beer or ale. If you are 16 or older, you may bring in, duty-free, 200 cigarettes, 50 cigars or cigarillos, and 400 tobacco sticks or 400 grams of manufactured tobacco. Alcohol and tobacco must accompany you on your return.

An unlimited number of gifts with a value of up to C$60 each may be mailed to Canada duty-free. These do not affect your duty-free allowance on your return. Label the package "Unsolicited Gift— Value Under $60." Alcohol and tobacco are excluded.

IN THE U.K.

From countries outside the EU, including the Czech Republic and Slovakia, you may import, duty-free, 200 cigarettes, 100 cigarillos, 50 cigars, or 250 grams of tobacco; 1 liter of spirits or 2 liters of fortified or sparkling wine or liqueurs; 2 liters of still table wine; 60 milliliters of perfume; 250 milliliters of toilet water; plus £136 worth of other goods, including gifts and souvenirs.

D

DISABILITIES & ACCESSIBILITY

Provisions for handicapped travelers in the Czech Republic and Slovakia are extremely limited; traveling with a nondisabled companion is probably the best solution. While many hotels, especially large American or international chains, offer some wheelchair-accessible rooms, special facilities at museums, restaurants, and on public transportation are difficult to find.

When discussing accessibility with an operator or reservationist, ask hard questions. Are there any stairs, inside *or* out? Are there grab bars next to the toilet *and* in the shower/tub? How wide is the doorway to the room? To the bathroom? For the most extensive facilities, meeting the latest legal specifications, **opt for newer accommodations,** which more often have been designed with access in mind. Older properties or ships must usually be retrofitted and may offer more limited facilities as a result. Be sure to **discuss your needs before booking.**

DISCOUNTS & DEALS

You shouldn't have to pay for a discount. In fact, you may already be eligible for all kinds of savings. Here are some time-honored strategies for getting the best deal.

LOOK IN YOUR WALLET

When you **use your credit card to make travel purchases,** you may get free travel-accident insurance, collision damage insurance, medical or legal assistance, depending on the card and bank that issued it. American Express, Visa, and MasterCard provide one or more of these services, so **get a copy of your card's travel benefits.** If you are a member of the AAA or an oil-company-sponsored road-assistance plan, always **ask hotel or car-rental reservationists for auto-club discounts.** Some clubs offer additional discounts on tours, cruises, or admission to attractions. And don't forget that auto-club membership entitles you to free maps and trip-planning services.

SENIORS CITIZENS & STUDENTS

As a senior-citizen traveler, you may be eligible for special rates, but you should mention your senior-citizen status up front. If you're a student or under 26, you can also get discounts, especially if you have an official ID card (☞ Senior-Citizen Discounts *and* Students on the Road, *below*).

DIAL FOR DOLLARS

To save money, **look into "1-800" discount reservations services,** which often have lower rates. These services use their buying power to get a better price on hotels, airline tickets, and sometimes even car rentals. When booking a room, always **call the hotel's local toll-free number** (if one is available) rather than the central reservations number—you'll often get a better price. Ask the reservationist about special packages or corporate rates, which are usually available even if you're not traveling on business.

JOIN A CLUB?

Discount clubs can be a legitimate source of savings, but you must use the participating hotels and visit the participating attractions in order to realize any benefits. Remember, too, that you have to pay a fee to join, so **determine whether you'll save enough to warrant your membership fee.** Before booking with a club, **make sure the hotel or other supplier isn't offering a better deal.**

GET A GUARANTEE

When shopping for the best deal on hotels and car rentals, **look for guaranteed exchange rates,** which protect you against a falling dollar. With your rate locked in, you won't pay more even if the price goes up in the local currency.

DRIVING

The plus side of driving is an itinerary free from the constraints of bus and train schedules and lots of trunk room for extra baggage. The negatives are many, however (☞ Car Rental, *above*), not the least of which are some shabbily maintained secondary roads, the risk of theft and vandalism, and difficulty finding gas. However, car travel does make it much easier to get to out-of-the-way monasteries and other sights not easily accessible by public transport. Good road maps are usually available.

A few words of caution: When traveling in the Czech Republic and Slovakia, **do not drive if you have any alcohol whatsoever in your body.** Penalties are fierce, and the blood-alcohol limit is practically zero.

ROADS & GASOLINE

In the Czech Republic and Slovakia, main roads are built to a fairly high standard. There are now quite substantial stretches of highway on main routes, and a lot of rebuilding is being done. Gas stations are fewer than they are in the West, sited at intervals of about 48 kilometers (30 miles) along main routes and on the outskirts of large towns. Very few stations remain open after 9:30 PM. At least two grades of gasoline are sold, usually 90–93 octane (regular) and 94–98 octane (super).

For additional information about driving in the two countries, *see* Getting Around by Car *in* the A to Z section at the end of each country chapter.

H
HEALTH

You may gain weight, but there are few seri-

ous health hazards for the traveler in the Czech Republic and Slovakia. Tap water tastes bad but is generally drinkable; when it runs rusty out of the tap or the aroma of chlorine is overpowering, it might help to have some iodine tablets or bottled water handy. Vegetarians and those on special diets may have a problem with the heavy local cuisine, which is based almost exclusively on pork and beef. To keep your vitamin intake above the danger levels, buy fresh fruits and vegetables at seasonal street markets—regular grocery stores often don't sell them.

SHOTS & MEDICATIONS

No vaccinations are required for entry into the Czech Republic or Slovakia, but selective vaccinations are recommended by the International Association for Medical Assistance to Travellers. Those traveling in forested areas should consider vaccinating themselves against Central European, or tick-borne, encephalitis. Schedule vaccinations well in advance of departure because some require several doses, and others may cause uncomfortable side effects.

I
INSURANCE

Travel insurance can protect your monetary investment, replace your luggage and its contents, or provide for medical coverage should you fall ill during your trip. Most

tour operators, travel agents, and insurance agents sell specialized health-and-accident, flight, trip-cancellation, and luggage insurance as well as comprehensive policies with some or all of these coverages. Comprehensive policies may also reimburse you for delays due to weather—an important consideration if you're traveling during the winter months. Some health-insurance policies do not cover preexisting conditions, but waivers may be available in specific cases. Coverage is sold by the companies listed in Important Contacts A to Z; these companies act as the policy's administrators. The actual insurance is usually underwritten by a well-known name, such as The Travelers or Continental Insurance.

Before you make any purchase, **review your existing health and homeowner's policies** to find out whether they cover expenses incurred while traveling.

BAGGAGE

Airline liability for baggage is limited to $1,250 per person on domestic flights. On international flights, it amounts to $9.07 per pound or $20 per kilogram for checked baggage (roughly $640 per 70-pound bag) and $400 per passenger for unchecked baggage. Insurance for losses exceeding the terms of your airline ticket can be bought directly from the airline at check-in for about $10 per $1,000 of coverage; note that it excludes a rather extensive list of items, shown on your airline ticket.

COMPREHENSIVE

Comprehensive insurance policies include all the coverages described above plus some that may not be available in more specific policies. If you have purchased an expensive vacation, especially one that involves travel abroad, comprehensive insurance is a must; **look for policies that include trip delay insurance,** which will protect you in the event that weather problems cause you to miss your flight, tour, or cruise. A few insurers will also sell you a waiver for preexisting medical conditions. Some of the companies that offer both these features are Access America, Carefree Travel, Travel Insured International, and Travel Guard (☞ Important Contacts A to Z).

FLIGHT

You should **think twice before buying flight insurance.** Often purchased as a last-minute impulse at the airport, it pays a lump sum when a plane crashes, either to a beneficiary if the insured dies or sometimes to a surviving passenger who loses his or her eyesight or a limb. Supplementing the airlines' coverage described in the limits-of-liability paragraphs on your ticket, it's expensive and basically unnecessary. Charging an airline ticket to a major credit card often automatically provides you with coverage that may also extend to

travel by bus, train, and ship.

HEALTH

Medicare generally does not cover health care costs outside the United States; nor do many privately issued policies. If your own health insurance policy does not cover you outside the United States, **consider buying supplemental medical coverage.** It can reimburse you for $1,000–$150,000 worth of medical and/or dental expenses incurred as a result of an accident or illness during a trip. These policies also may include a personal-accident, or death-and-dismemberment, provision, which pays a lump sum ranging from $15,000 to $500,000 to your beneficiaries if you die or to you if you lose one or more limbs or your eyesight, and a medical-assistance provision, which may either reimburse you for the cost of referrals, evacuation, or repatriation and other services, or automatically enroll you as a member of a particular medical-assistance company. (☞ Health *in* Important Contacts A to Z.)

TRIP

Without insurance, you will lose all or most of your money if you cancel your trip regardless of the reason. Especially if your airline ticket, cruise, or package tour is nonrefundable and cannot be changed, it's essential that you **buy trip-cancellation-and-interruption insurance.** When considering how much coverage you

need, look for a policy that will cover the cost of your trip plus the nondiscounted price of a one-way airline ticket should you need to return home early. Read the fine print carefully, especially sections that define "family member" and "preexisting medical conditions." Also **consider default or bankruptcy insurance,** which protects you against a supplier's failure to deliver. Be aware, however, that if you buy such a policy from a travel agency, tour operator, airline, or cruise line, it may not cover default by the firm in question.

U.K. TRAVELERS

You can buy an annual travel insurance policy valid for most vacations during the year in which it's purchased. If you are pregnant or have a preexisting medical condition, make sure you're covered before buying such a policy.

L

LANGUAGE

Czech and Slovak are Slovic languages closely related to each other and to Polish; they are also virtually incomprehensible to the non-speaker. If you do happen to speak one or the other, you will be understood in both countries. Though English is gaining popularity among young people, German is still the most useful language for tourists.

LODGING

If your experience of the former Czechoslovakia is limited to

Prague, you may be pleasantly surprised. There are Baroque mansions-turned-guest houses and elegant high-rise resorts, not to mention bed-and-breakfast inns presided over by matronly babushkas. Now that Communism is a thing of the past, there seems to be more interest in maintaining and up-grading facilities (though, inevitably, there are exceptions).

Outside major cities, hotels and inns are more rustic than elegant. Standards of service generally do not suffer, but in most rural areas the definition of "lux-ury" includes little more than a television and a private bathroom. In some instances, you may have no choice but to stay in one of the cement high-rise hotels that scar the countries' skylines. It's hard to say why Communists re-quired their hotels to be as big and impersonal as possible, but they did, and it may take a few more years to exorcise or "beautify" these ubiquitous monsters.

In rural Eastern Europe, you may have difficulty parting with more than $25–$30 per night for lodgings. Reservations are vital if you plan to visit Prague during the summer season. Reser-vations are a good idea but aren't imperative if you plan to strike out into the countryside.

APARTMENT & VILLA RENTAL

If you want a home base that's roomy enough for a family and comes with cooking facilities, **consider** **taking a furnished rental.** This can also save you money, but not always—some rentals are luxury properties (economical only when your party is large). Home-exchange directories list rentals—often second homes owned by prospective house swappers—and some services search for a house or apartment for you (even a castle if that's your fancy) and handle the paperwork. Some send an illustrated catalog; others send photographs only of specific properties, sometimes at a charge; up-front registration fees may apply.

HOME EXCHANGE

If you would like to find a house, an apart-ment, or some other type of vacation prop-erty to exchange for your own while on holiday, **become a member of a home-exchange organization,** which will send you its updated listings of available exchanges for a year, and will include your own listing in at least one of them. Arrangements for the actual exchange are made by the two parties involved, not by the organization.

M
MAIL

For specific information on postal rates and receiving mail, *see* Mail *in* the A to Z section at the end of each country chapter.

MEDICAL ASSISTANCE

No one plans to get sick while traveling, but it happens, so **consider** **signing up with a medi-cal assistance company.** These outfits provide referrals, emergency evacuation or repatria-tion, 24-hour telephone hot lines for medical consultation, cash for emergencies, and other personal and legal assistance. They also dispatch medical per-sonnel and arrange for the relay of medical records. Coverage varies by plan, so **read the fine print carefully.**

MONEY

In addition to the information below, for country-specific infor-mation about all issues relating to money, *see* Money and Expenses *in* the A to Z section at the end of each country chapter.

ATMS

CASH ADVANCES> Before leaving home, **make sure that your credit cards have been programmed for ATM use in the Czech Repub-lic and Slovakia.** Note that Discover is ac-cepted mostly in the United States. Local bank cards often do not work overseas either; **ask your bank about a MasterCard/Cirrus or Visa debit card,** which works like a bank card but can be used at any ATM displaying a MasterCard/Cirrus or Visa logo.

TRANSACTION FEES> Although fees charged for ATM transactions may be higher abroad than at home, Cirrus and Plus exchange rates are excellent, because they are based on wholesale rates offered only by major banks.

THE GOLD GUIDE / SMART TRAVEL TIPS

EXCHANGING CURRENCY

For the most favorable rates, **change money at banks.** You won't do as well at exchange booths in airports or rail and bus stations, in hotels, in restaurants, or in stores, although you may find their hours more convenient. To avoid lines at airport exchange booths, **get a small amount of the local currency before you leave home.**

TAXES

If you shop in the Czech Republic or Slovakia, **get a value-added tax (VAT) refund.** At press time, the basic VAT rate in the Czech Republic was 22%, applied to most consumer goods. A 5% rate applies to most services and some goods, including fuel and most food. In Slovakia, VAT rates were 6% and 25%. The 6% rate was applied to most food and some services, including car rentals; the 25% rate was applied to most consumer goods and some services.

TRAVELER'S CHECKS

Whether or not to buy traveler's checks depends on where you are headed; **take cash to rural areas and small towns, traveler's checks to cities.** The most widely recognized checks are issued by American Express, Citicorp, Thomas Cook, and Visa. These are sold by major commercial banks for 1%–3% of the checks' face value—it pays to **shop around.** Both American Express and Thomas Cook issue checks that can be countersigned and used by either you or your traveling companion. So you won't be left with excess foreign currency, **buy a few checks in small denominations** to cash toward the end of your trip. Before leaving home, **contact your issuer for information on where to cash your checks** without incurring a transaction fee. Record the numbers of all your checks, and keep this listing in a separate place, crossing off the numbers of checks you have cashed.

WIRING MONEY

For a fee of 3%–10%, depending on the amount of the transaction, you can have money sent to you from home through Money-Gram[SM] or Western Union (☞ Money *in* Important Contacts A to Z). The transferred funds and the service fee can be charged to a MasterCard or Visa account.

P

PACKING FOR THE CZECH REPUBLIC & SLOVAKIA

Don't worry about packing lots of formal clothing. Fashion was all but nonexistent under 40 years of Communist rule, and Western dress of any kind is considered stylish. A sports jacket for men, and a dress or pants for women, is appropriate for an evening out. Everywhere else, you'll feel comfortable in casual corduroys or jeans. The Czech Republic and Slovakia have all the extremes of an inland climate, so plan accordingly. In the higher elevations winter can last until April, and even in summer the evenings will be on the cool side.

Many areas are best seen on foot, so take a pair of sturdy walking shoes and be prepared to use them. High heels will present considerable problems on the cobblestone streets of Prague. If you plan to visit the mountains, make sure the shoes have good traction and ankle support, as some trails can be quite challenging.

Many items that you take for granted at home are occasionally unavailable or of questionable quality. Take your own toiletries and personal-hygiene products with you. Few places provide sports equipment for rent; an alternative to bringing your own equipment would be to buy what you need locally and take it home with you. In general, sporting goods are relatively cheap and of good quality.

Bring an extra pair of eyeglasses or contact lenses in your carry-on luggage. Contact lens wearers should bring enough saline and disinfecting solution with them, as they are expensive and in short supply. If you have a health problem, **pack enough medication** to last the trip or have your doctor write you a prescription using the drug's generic name, because brand names vary from country to country (you'll then

need a duplicate pre-
scription from a local
doctor). It's important
that you **don't put
prescription drugs or
valuables in luggage to
be checked,** for it could
go astray. To avoid
problems with customs
officials, carry medica-
tions in the original
packaging. Also, don't
forget the addresses of
offices that handle
refunds of lost traveler's
checks.

ELECTRICITY

To use your U.S.-pur-
chased electric-powered
equipment, **bring a
converter and an
adapter.** The electrical
current in the Czech
Republic and Slovakia
is 220 volts, 50 cycles
alternating current
(AC); wall outlets
generally take plugs
with three round
prongs.

If your appliances are
dual-voltage, you'll need
only an adapter. Hotels
sometimes have 110-
volt outlets for low-
wattage appliances near
the sink, marked FOR
SHAVERS ONLY; don't use
them for high-wattage
appliances like blow-
dryers. If your laptop
computer is older, carry
a converter; new laptops
operate equally well on
110 and 220 volts, so
you need only an
adapter.

LUGGAGE

Airline baggage al-
lowances depend on the
airline, the route, and
the class of your ticket;
ask in advance. In
general, on domestic
flights and on interna-
tional flights between
the United States and
foreign destinations,
you are entitled to

check two bags. A third
piece may be brought
on board, but it must fit
easily under the seat in
front of you or in the
overhead compartment.
In the United States, the
FAA gives airlines
broad latitude regard-
ing carry-on
allowances, and they
tend to tailor them to
different aircraft and
operational conditions.
Charges for excess,
oversize, or overweight
pieces vary.

If you are flying be-
tween two foreign
destinations, note that
baggage allowances may
be determined not by
piece but by weight—
generally 88 pounds (40
kilograms) in first class,
66 pounds (30 kilo-
grams) in business class,
and 44 pounds (20
kilograms) in economy.
If your flight between
two cities abroad *con-
nects* with your transat-
lantic or transpacific
flight, the piece method
still applies.

SAFEGUARDING YOUR
LUGGAGE➤ Before
leaving home, **itemize
your bags' contents** and
their worth, and label
them with your name,
address, and phone
number. (If you use
your home address,
cover it so that poten-
tial thieves can't see it
readily.) Inside each
bag, **pack a copy of
your itinerary.** At check-
in, **make sure that each
bag is correctly tagged**
with the destination
airport's three-letter
code. If your bags arrive
damaged—or fail to
arrive at all—file a
written report with the
airline before leaving
the airport.

**PASSPORTS &
VISAS**

If you don't already
have one, **get a pass-
port.** It is advisable that
you **leave one photo-
copy of your passport's
data page** with some-
one at home and keep
another with you,
separated from your
passport, while travel-
ing. If you lose your
passport, promptly call
the nearest embassy or
consulate and the local
police; having the data
page information can
speed replacement.

U.S. CITIZENS

All U.S. citizens, even
infants, need only a
valid passport to enter
the Czech Republic and
Slovakia for stays of up
to 30 days. Application
forms for both first-
time and renewal pass-
ports are available at
any of the 13 U.S.
Passport Agency offices
and at some post offices
and courthouses. Pass-
ports are usually mailed
within four weeks;
allow five weeks or
more in spring and
summer.

CANADIANS

You need only a valid
passport to enter the
Czech Republic for
stays of up to 180 days.
Passport application
forms are available at
28 regional passport
offices, as well as post
offices and travel agen-
cies. Whether for a first
or a renewal passport,
you must apply in
person. Children under
16 may be included on
a parent's passport but
must have their own to
travel alone. Passports
are valid for five years
and are usually mailed

within two to three weeks of application.

A visa is required before entering Slovakia. For more information, *see* Passports & Visas *in* Important Contacts A to Z.

U.K. CITIZENS

Citizens of the United Kingdom need only a valid passport to enter the Czech Republic or Slovakia for stays of up to 30 days. Applications for new and renewal passports are available from main post offices and at the passport offices in Belfast, Glasgow, Liverpool, London, Newport, and Peterborough. You may apply in person at all passport offices, or by mail to all except the London office. Children under 16 may travel on an accompanying parent's passport. All passports are valid for 10 years. Allow a month for processing.

S

SENIOR-CITIZEN DISCOUNTS

To qualify for age-related discounts, **mention your senior-citizen status up front** when booking hotel reservations, not when checking out, and before you're seated in restaurants, not when paying the bill. Note that discounts may be limited to certain menus, days, or hours. When renting a car, **ask about promotional car-rental discounts**—they can net even lower costs than your senior-citizen discount.

STUDENTS ON THE ROAD

To save money, **look into deals available through student-oriented travel agencies.** To qualify, you'll need to have a bona fide student ID card. Members of international student groups are also eligible (☞ Students *in* Important Contacts A to Z).

T

TELEPHONES

LONG-DISTANCE

The long-distance services of AT&T, MCI, and Sprint make calling home relatively convenient, but in many hotels you may find it impossible to dial the access number. The hotel operator may also refuse to make the connection. Instead, the hotel will charge you a premium rate—as much as 400% more than a calling card—for calls placed from your hotel room. To avoid such price gouging, travel with more than one company's long-distance calling card—a hotel may block Sprint but not MCI. If the hotel operator claims that you cannot use any phone card, ask to be connected to an international operator, who will help you to access your phone card. You can also dial the international operator yourself. If none of this works, try calling your phone company collect in the United States. If collect calls are also blocked, call from a pay phone in the hotel lobby. Before you go, **find out the local access codes** for your destinations.

TOUR OPERATORS

A package or tour to the Czech Republic and Slovakia can make your vacation less expensive and more hassle-free. Firms that sell tours and packages reserve airline seats, hotel rooms, and rental cars in bulk and pass some of the savings on to you. In addition, the best operators have local representatives available to help you at your destination.

A GOOD DEAL?

The more your package or tour includes, the better you can predict the ultimate cost of your vacation. Make sure you know exactly what is covered, and **beware of hidden costs.** Are taxes, tips, and service charges included? Transfers and baggage handling? Entertainment and excursions? These can add up.

Most packages and tours are rated deluxe, first-class superior, first class, tourist, or budget. The key difference is usually accommodations. If the package or tour you are considering is priced lower than in your wildest dreams, **be skeptical.** Also, **make sure your travel agent knows the accommodations** and other services. Ask about the hotel's location, room size, beds, and whether it has a pool, room service, or programs for children, if you care about these. Has your agent been there in person or sent others you can contact?

BUYER BEWARE

Each year a number of consumers are stranded

or lose their money when operators—even very large ones with excellent reputations—go out of business. To avoid becoming one of them, take the time to **check out the operator**—find out how long the company has been in business and ask several agents about its reputation. Next, **don't book unless the firm has a consumer-protection program.** Members of the USTOA and the NTA are required to set aside funds for the sole purpose of covering your payments and travel arrangements in case of default. Nonmember operators may instead carry insurance; look for the details in the operator's brochure—and for the name of an underwriter with a solid reputation. Note: When it comes to tour operators, **don't trust escrow accounts.** Although there are laws governing those of charter-flight operators, no governmental body prevents tour operators from raiding the till.

Next, **contact your local Better Business Bureau and the attorney general's offices** in both your own state and the operator's; have any complaints been filed? Finally, **pay with a major credit card.** Then you can cancel payment, provided that you can document your complaint. Always **consider trip-cancellation insurance** (☞ Insurance, *above*).

BIG VS. SMALL➤ Operators that handle several hundred thousand travelers per year can use their purchasing power to give you a good price. Their high volume may also indicate financial stability. But some small companies provide more personalized service; because they tend to specialize, they may also be more knowledgeable about a given area.

USING AN AGENT

Travel agents are excellent resources. In fact, large operators accept bookings made only through travel agents. But it's good to **collect brochures from several agencies** because some agents' suggestions may be skewed by promotional relationships with tour and package firms that reward them for volume sales. If you have a special interest, **find an agent with expertise in that area;** ASTA can provide leads in the United States. (Don't rely solely on your agent, though; agents may be unaware of small-niche operators, and some special-interest travel companies only sell direct.)

SINGLE TRAVELERS

Prices are usually quoted per person, based on two sharing a room. If traveling solo, you may be required to pay the full double-occupancy rate. Some operators eliminate this surcharge if you agree to be matched up with a roommate of the same sex, even if one is not found by departure time.

TRAIN TRAVEL

To save money, **look into rail passes** (☞ Train Travel *in* Important Contacts A to Z). But be aware that if you don't plan to cover many miles, you may come out ahead by buying individual tickets.

You can **use the East Pass** on the national rail networks of Austria, the Czech Republic, Hungary, Poland, and Slovakia. You can choose between 5 days of unlimited first-class travel within a 15-day period for $195 or 10 days of first-class travel within a one-month period for $299.

You can also **combine the East Pass with a national rail pass.** The Bulgarian Flexipass costs $70 for three days of unlimited first-class travel within a one-month period. A pass for the Czech Republic costs $69 for five days of train travel within a 15-day period. In Austria, the Austrian Rail Pass permits four days of unlimited train travel within a 10-day period for $111 in second-class or $165 in first class. The Hungarian Flexipass costs $55 for five days of unlimited first-class train travel within a 15-day period or $69 for ten days within a one-month period. The RomanianPass costs $60 for three days of first-class train travel in a 15-day period.

Many travelers assume that rail passes guarantee them seats on the trains they wish to ride. Not so. You need to **book seats ahead even if you are using a rail pass;** seat reservations are required on some European trains, particularly high-speed trains, and are a good idea on trains that may be crowded—particularly in summer on popular routes. You will also need a reservation if you purchase sleeping accommodations.

Although standards have improved during the past few years, on the whole they are far short of what is acceptable in the West. Trains are very busy and it is rare to find one running less than full or almost so. All six countries operate their own dining, buffet, and refreshment services. Always crowded, they tend to open and close at the whim of the staff. Couchette cars are second-class only and can be little more than a hard bunk without springs and adequate bed linen.

Although trains are usually crowded and aren't always comfortable, traveling by rail is very inexpensive (it's much cheaper than renting a car in this part of Europe). The rail network is extensive, though trains can be infuriatingly slow. You'll invariably enjoy interesting and friendly traveling company, however; most Czechs and Slovaks are eager to hear about the West and to discuss the enormous changes in their own countries.

FROM THE U.K.

There are no direct trains from London. You can take a direct train from Frankfurt to Prague (daily) or from Berlin to Warsaw or via Dresden to Prague (three times a day).

Vienna is a good starting point for Prague, Brno, or Bratislava. There are three trains a day from Vienna's Franz Josefsbahnhof to Prague via Třeboň and Tábor (5½ hours) and one from the Südbahnhof (South Station) via Brno (5 hours). Bratislava can be reached from Vienna by a 67-minute shuttle service that runs every two hours during the day. You should check out times and routes before leaving.

TRAVEL GEAR

Travel catalogs specialize in useful items that can **save space when packing** and make life on the road more convenient. Compact alarm clocks, travel irons, travel wallets, and personal-care kits are among the most common items you'll find. They also carry dual-voltage appliances, currency converters and foreign-language phrase books. Some catalogs even carry miniature coffeemakers and water purifiers.

U
U.S.
GOVERNMENT

The U.S. government can be an excellent source of travel information. Some of this is free and some is available for a nominal charge. When planning your trip, **find out what government materials are available.** For just a couple of dollars, you can get a variety of publications from the Consumer Information

Center in Pueblo, Colorado. Free consumer information also is available from individual government agencies, such as the Department of Transportation or the U.S. Customs Service. For specific titles, *see* the appropriate publications entry *in* Important Contacts A to Z, *above.*

W
WHEN TO GO

The tourist season in both countries generally runs from April or May through October; spring and fall combine good weather with a more bearable level of tourism. The ski season lasts from mid-December through March. Outside of the mountain resorts you will encounter few other visitors; you'll have the opportunity to see the region covered in snow, but many of the sights are closed, and it can get very, very cold. If you're not a skier, try visiting the Giant Mountain of Bohemia in late spring or fall; the colors are dazzling and you'll have the hotels and restaurants pretty much to yourself. Bear in mind that many attractions are closed November through March.

Prague is beautiful year-round, but avoid mid-summer (especially July and August) and the Christmas and Easter holidays, when the two cities are choked with visitors. Bratislava is best visited in the temperate months of spring and autumn.

Climate

The following are the average daily maximum and minimum temperatures for major cities in the region.

PRAGUE

Jan.	36F	2C	May	66F	19C	Sept.	68F	20C
	25	– 4		46	8		50	10
Feb.	37F	3C	June	72F	22C	Oct.	55F	13C
	27	– 3		52	11		41	5
Mar.	46F	8C	July	75F	24C	Nov.	46F	8C
	32	0		55	13		36	2
Apr.	58F	14C	Aug.	73F	23C	Dec.	37F	3C
	39	4		55	13		28	– 2

BRATISLAVA

Jan.	36F	2C	May	70F	21C	Sept.	72F	22C
	27	– 3		52	11		54	12
Feb.	39F	4C	June	75F	24C	Oct.	59F	15C
	28	– 2		57	14		45	7
Mar.	48F	9C	July	79F	26C	Nov.	46F	8C
	34	1		61	16		37	3
Apr.	61F	16C	Aug.	79F	26C	Dec.	39F	4C
	43	6		61	16		32	0

THE GOLD GUIDE / SMART TRAVEL TIPS

1 Destination: The Czech Republic and Slovakia

WHAT'S WHERE

Czech Republic

Planted firmly in the heart of Central Europe—Prague is some 250 miles north*west* of Vienna—the Czech Republic is culturally and historically more closely linked to Western, particularly Germanic, culture than any of its other former Eastern bloc brethren. Encompassing some 79,000 square kilometers (30,500 square miles), the Czech Republic is made up of the regions of Bohemia in the west (sharing long borders with Germany and Austria) and Moravia in the east. Moravia's White Carpathian mountains (Biele Karpaty) form the border with the young Slovak Republic, which broke its 74-year-old union with the Czechs in 1993. With a population of 1,212,000, the Czech Republic is one of the most densely populated countries of Eastern/Central Europe.

The capital city of **Prague** sits on the Vltava (Moldau) River, roughly in the middle of Bohemian territory. A stunning city of human dimensions, Prague offers the traveler a lesson in almost all of the major architectural styles of Western Europe; relatively unscathed by major wars, most of Prague's buildings are remarkably well preserved. **Southern Bohemia** is dotted with several walled towns, many of which played important roles in the Hussite religious wars of the 15th century. The two most notable towns are **Tábor** and **Český Krumlov. Western Bohemia,** especially the far western hills near the German border, remains justly famous for its mineral springs and spa towns, in particular **Karlovy Vary, Mariánské Lázně,** and **Františkovy Lázně. Northern Bohemia,** with its rolling hills, and, on the frontier with Poland, the **Krkonoše** (White Mountains), is a hiker's and camper's delight.

Slovakia

Having declared its independence from the Czech Republic in 1993, the smaller and more agrarian Slovak Republic has been struggling to revive its economic life and adjust to new post–Cold War realities. The 49,000 square kilometers (19,000 square miles) of Slovak territory is both less urbanized and less industrialized than that of the country's Moravian and Bohemian neighbors to the west. **Bratislava,** the capital, lies on the Danube in the southwestern corner of the country, just a few miles from both the Austrian and Hungarian borders. sIts small Old Town is charming and contains several buildings and churches of interest (especially to those concerned with the history of the Austrio-Hungarian Empire). Slovakia's real assets, however, are to the north and east. **Central Slovakia,** a hilly region crossed by hiking trails, is rich in folklore and medieval history. The **High Tatra Mountains** attract skiers, campers, and mountaineers from across Europe; these days they are a real meeting ground for tourists from east and west. The relatively undiscovered **Eastern Slovakia** lures travelers with its country lanes—watch out for herds of sheep and gaggles of geese—fairy-tale villages, castles, and wooden churches.

NEW AND NOTEWORTHY

Czech Republic

The Czech Republic continues along its path of economic and cultural revitalization—a path that began with the peaceful revolution of 1989 and accelerated following the breakup of the Czechoslovak state in 1993. Far from hurting the country, the Czech–Slovak split has freed officials to concentrate on the rapid economic changes of Bohemia and Moravia. Their goal is incorporation into the European Union (EU) by the year 2000. Tourism remains one of the brightest economic sectors, and visitors from the West will find the country is still affordable. Everywhere, castles, palaces, and dusty old museums are spiffing themselves up and throwing open their doors to visitors.

One tangible impact of the country's economic reforms has been an acceleration in the pace of architectural renovations. Many hotels, old private houses, and churches have new fixtures and fresh coats of paint. One such face-lift occurred in the Staroměstské náměstí (Old Town Square), one of the jewels of the "new" Prague, lined by such landmarks as the Týn Church and the Old Town Hall. Brightly painted facades and gleaming shop fronts now fan out from Old Town Square; the change will astonish visitors who last saw the city even as recently as the early 1990s.

The number of hotels—both large and small—and restaurants keeps pace with the increasing number of visitors. Restaurants that offer Cajun, Mexican, vegetarian, and other exotic fare now sit beside those that serve the traditional fare of pork and dumplings.

Prague's cultural life continues to thrive. The city is a classical-music lover's dream, with a plethora of concerts from which to choose almost every hour of the day in high season. Opera fans should also not be disappointed. The annual mid-May–early June Prague Spring Music Festival, which even before the collapse of the Communist government was one of the great events on the European calendar, attracts record numbers of music lovers.

Slovakia

Slovakia has undergone a metamorphosis since its breakup with the Czech Republic in the beginning of 1993. Although riddled with political havoc, Slovakia has taken positive strides toward economic growth and stability, exceeding many expectations along the way. Unfortunately, the government's habit of testing the limits of democracy has forced the EU to mildly reprimand Slovakia on more than one occasion. Still, the country continues steadily along the path to economic and democratic restructuring, with the goal of incorporation into the EU by the year 2000.

Slovakia has retained the former Czechoslovakia's policy of encouraging tourism; visitors from the United States and United Kingdom do not need visas, although Canadians entering the country will continue to require a visa for the foreseeable future. Those entering Slovakia from the Czech Republic should be prepared to show a passport. In addition, Czech money is no longer valid in Slovakia (and vice versa), although it can be easily converted in either country.

New hotels, pensions, and restaurants are springing up all over the country, but not fast enough to eliminate the shabby government-owned establishments that still

dominate certain parts of the scene. Almost all cities now have pensions, often housed in beautifully renovated historic buildings; they are a nice alternative to the larger hotels. Keep an eye out for the new chain of Slovak restaurants called Slovenská Reštauracia where you can get typical Slovak food in a lovely rustic environment at dirt-cheap prices. Private entrepreneurs have caught on quickly to these successful establishments, making carbon copies of the restaurants and charging higher prices. But for anyone arriving from Western or Central Europe, the difference will be negligible.

Hotel operators in the High Tatras report slower seasons than in the past, as the Eastern bloc clientele on which they've relied for more than 40 years begins to sample the more exotic climes of Spain and France. But interest in the Tatras is sure to grow as Western Europeans and North Americans discover their charm. Eastern Slovakia, known for its natural beauty and unusual architecture, remains uncharted territory and can now offer accommodation that's up to Western standards.

FODOR'S CHOICE

Castles and Churches

Czech Republic

⭐**Chrám svatého Víta, Prague Castle, Prague.** Soaring above the castle walls and dominating the city at its feet, St. Vitus Cathedral is among the most beautiful sights in Europe.

⭐**Chrám svaté Barbory, Kutná Hora, Bohemia.** Arguably the best example of the Gothic impulse in Bohemia, St. Barbara's Cathedral lifts the spirit and gives the town of Kutná Hora its unmistakable skyline.

⭐**Týn Church, Staré Město, Prague.** The gold-tipped spires of this 15th-century cathedral beckon people from all corners of Prague to the center of Old Town Square.

⭐**Vranov Castle, Vranov, Moravia.** Perched on bluff overlooking the Austrian border, this dramatic castle flaunts Gothic, Renaissance, and Baroque details.

Slovakia

★**Dóm svätej Alžbety, Košice.** Inside this 15th-century Gothic cathedral—the largest in Slovakia—stands a monumental wood carving: the 35-foot Altar of the Holy Elizabeth.

★**Kostol svätého Jakuba, Levoča.** The most impressive memorial to Gothic art in Eastern Europe; front and center on the main altar is wood-carver Pavol of Levoča's breathtaking masterpiece, *The Last Supper.*

★**Krásna Hôrka, Krásnohradské Podhradie.** Visible from miles around, this hilltop fairy-tale castle is one of Slovakia's best-preserved fortifications from the Middle Ages.

★**Wooden churches of Eastern Slovakia.** Even the nails are made of wood in these handsome Byzantine and Baroque structures. Religious paintings and icons line the interior walls of many.

Dining

Czech Republic

★**V Zátiši, Prague.** Situated in one of the city's oldest and calmest squares—the restaurant's name means "in a quiet corner"—this refined dining room offers tantalizing international specialties served with care. *$$$$*

★**Lobkovická, Prague.** An atmospheric 17th-century wine bar with an imaginative menu. *$$$*

Slovakia

★**Kláštorná vináreň, Bratislava.** Sample the best of the happy—and spicy—merger of Hungarian and Slovak cuisines at this dark, intimate monastery wine cellar not far from the banks of the Danube. *$$$*

★**Restaurant Koliba, Starý Smokovec.** This charming, rustic spot on the slopes of the Tatra Mountains serves up grilled specialties to the accompaniment of Gypsy folk music. *$$*

★**Slovenská Reštauracia, Poprad.** Here you'll find the very best of Eastern Slovakian comfort food served in a convivial village-style atmosphere. *$*

Lodging

Czech Republic

★**Dvořák, Karlovy Vary, Bohemia.** This elegant hotel right in the center of a beautiful spa town has all the modern amenities but plenty of Old World charm. *$$$$*

★**Růže, Český Krumlov, Bohemia.** Some rooms in this refurbished monastery on a hill that faces Krumlov Castle afford stunning views of the loveliest of Bohemian towns. *$$$*

★**U Páva, Prague.** A rare find among Prague's hotels, this little inn has a splendid location on a charming, gas-lit street; friendly service; and rooms with individual character and homey comfort. *$$$*

★**Bican Pension, Tábor, Bohemia.** This lovely family-run pension dates from the 14th century but has all the modern conveniences. Its cool cellar lounge provides a perfect retreat on scorching summer days. *$$*

Slovakia

★**Danube, Bratislava.** This gleaming French-run hotel on the banks of the Danube has a sterling reputation. *$$$$*

★**Grandhotel Praha, Tatranská Lomnica.** This multiturreted mansion in the foothills of the Tatras has retained the elegance and gentility of an earlier age. *$$$*

★**Arkada Hotel, Levoča.** The bright, comfortable rooms in this jewel of an antique boutique hotel belie the building's 13th-century origins. *$$*

Museums

Czech Republic

★**Národní galérie (National Gallery), Prague.** Spread among a half-dozen branches around the city, the National Gallery's collections span most major periods of European art, from medieval and Baroque masters to a controversial new display of 20th-century Czech works.

★**The Jewish Museum of Prague.** Actually a collection of several must-see sights and exhibits, Prague's "Jewish Museum" includes the dramatic and unforgettable Old Jewish Cemetery and several synagogues.

★**Theresienstadt Memorial Museum, Terezín, Bohemia.** The grounds and buildings of the most notorious Nazi concentration camp on Czech territory have been preserved as a testament to the horrible legacy of the Holocaust.

Slovakia

★**Museum of Jewish Culture in Slovakia, Bratislava.** Housed in a mid-17th-century Renaissance mansion, this exhibition covers the history of Jews in Slovakia from the time of the Great Moravian Empire to the present.

★**Šariš Icon Museum, Bardejov.** This is a captivating collection of Russian Orthodox artwork from the region's churches.

★**Warhol Family Museum of Modern Art, Medzilaborce.** Here you'll find Andy Warhol silkscreens, including two from the famous Campbell's Soup series, as well as portraits of Lenin and singer Billie Holiday.

Towns and Villages

Czech Republic

★**Český Krumlov, Bohemia.** The repainted facades and the new shops and pensions that crowd the lanes have banished much of Krumlov's old charming decay, but the hard-earned dignity of the houses and the sweet melancholy of the streetscapes abide in this lovely southern Bohemian town.

★**Telč, Moravia.** The perfectly preserved town square, clustered with superb examples of Gothic, Renaissance, and Baroque architecture, resembles a scene from a fairy tale.

Slovakia

★**Ždiar, High Tatras.** This tiny mountain village is notable for its enchanting, vibrantly painted wooden houses built in traditional peasant designs.

★**Špania Dolina, Central Slovakia.** Set in the midst of the Low Tatras, this beautiful village is renowned for its lacemaking; if you arrive in summer you'll see older women making tablecloths and lace on their front porches.

★**Levoča, Eastern Slovakia.** The medieval capital of the Spiš region seems frozen in time; between the 14th and 17th centuries it flourished as an important center of trade, crafts, and art.

FESTIVALS AND SEASONAL EVENTS

Czech Republic

The Czech government publishes an annual "Calendar of Tourist Events" in English, available from Čedok or the Prague Information Service. Visitor Information offices can provide you with exact dates and additional information.

WINTER

DEC.➤ **Christmas fairs and programs** take place in most towns and cities; among those particularly worth catching are: **Christmas in Valašsko,** in Rožnov pod Radhoštěm (✉ Valašsko Open-Air Museum, Palackého 147, Rožnov pod Radhoštěm, ☎ 0651/54331), and the **Arrival of Lady Winter Festival** in Prachatice (✉ Cultural and Information Service of Prachatice, 383 01 Prachatice, ☎ 0338/21427).

MAR.➤ **Prague City of Music Festival; Czech Alpine Skiing Championships** (✉ Tourist Information Center, Box 24, 543 51 Špindlerův Mlýn, ☎ 0438/93330).

SPRING

APR.➤ **Brno's International Consumer Goods Fair** (✉

Brno Fairs and Exhibitions, Výstaviště 1, Box 491, 660 91 Brno, ☎ 05/4115–1111); **Easter Spiritual Music Festival,** also in Brno (✉ City of Brno Culture Department, Zelný trh 12, 601 67 Brno, ☎ 05/4221–1982); the massive **Flora Flower Show** (✉ Flora, Wolkerova 17, 771 11 Olomouc, ☎ 068/414021).

MAY➤ **Prague Spring Music Festival** (✉ Hellichova 18, 118 00 Prague 1, ☎ 02/533473); **Prague Marathon; Prague Writers' Festival** (✉ Viola Theater, Národní 7, Prague 1, ☎ 02/2422–0844) offers dramatic readings by major writers from around the world; **International Childrens' Film Festival** (Zlín).

SUMMER

JUNE➤ **Prague International Film Festival; Smetana National Opera Festival** in the composer's hometown (✉ Smetana's Litomyšl Foundation, 570 01 Litomyšl, ☎ 0464/4580); **International Festival of Mime** (Mariánské Lázně); **Festival of World Records and Curiosities** (Pelhřimov).

JULY➤ **Prague Summer Culture Festival; Karlovy Vary Film Festival.**

AUG.➤ **Chopin Festival** (Mariánské Lázně); **Baroque Opera Festival** (Valtice); **Český Krumlov's International Music Festival** (✉ AUVITEX, 381 01 Český Krumlov, ☎ 0337/4275).

AUTUMN

SEPT.➤ **Brno's International Engineering Fair** (✉ Brno Fairs and Exhibitions, Výstaviště 1, Box 491, 660 91 Brno, ☎ 05/4115–1111); **Smetana International Music Festival** (✉ Studio-Forum Praha, Prvomájová 12, 153 00 Prague 5, ☎ 02/643–7560); **Mikulov Vintage Wine Festival; Prague Autumn International Music Festival** (✉ Sekaninova 26, 120 00 Prague 2, ☎ 02/692–7470); **Brno Beer Days; Mělník Vintage Wine Festival.**

OCT.➤ **AghaRTA International Jazz Festival** (Prague); **Velká Pardubická Steeplechase,** considered to be one of Europe's toughest racing events (✉ Horse Race Association, JSC, Pražská 607, 530 02 Pardubice, ☎ 040/30096); **Festival of 20th Century Music** (✉ Festa Arts Agency, Dlouhá 10, 110 00 Prague 1, ☎ 02/232–1086).

Slovakia

In addition to the events noted below, many villages also host annual folklore festivals, usually on a weekend in late summer or early fall. These often take place in the town center and are filled with singing, dancing, and drinking. The Slovak Ministry of Economy puts out an annual calendar of events in English, available in travel agencies and tourist information centers.

WINTER

MAR.➢ **Musical Spring** (Bardejov); **Folk Song Festival** (Liptovský Mikuláš).

SUMMER

JUNE➢ **International Folklore Festival** (Košice).

SPRING

APR.➢ The **International Festival of Ghosts and Phantoms** is held every year at the end of April in the striking castle in Bojnice.

MAY➢ **Košice Musical Spring** takes place in May.

AUTUMN

SEPT.➢ **Puppeteers' Festival** (Banská Bystrica).

OCT.➢ **Bratislava Music Festival** attracts national and international musicians to venues throughout the capital late in the month.

2 The Czech Republic

Faster and with greater success than any other former Soviet-bloc country, the Czech Republic has matured into a showcase democracy that offers visitors some of Central Europe's most alluring attractions. The "hundred-spired" capital city of Prague—one of the world's best-preserved architectural cityscapes— offers cultural performances, dining, and shopping as distinctive as any other world-class city's. In the countryside beyond, medieval castles perch quietly near lost-in-time baroque and Renaissance villages. Pine forests and gentle green mountains beckon outdoor enthusiasts with a multitude of pleasures.

AVICTIM OF ENFORCED OBSCURITY throughout much of the 20th century, the Czech Republic, comprising the provinces of Bohemia and Moravia (but no longer Slovakia), is once again in the spotlight. In a world where revolution was synonymous with violence, and in a country where truth was quashed by the tanks of Eastern bloc socialism, in November 1989 Václav Havel's sonorous voice proclaimed the victory of the "Velvet Revolution" to enthusiastic crowds on Wenceslas Square and preached the value of "living in truth." Recording the dramatic events of the time, television cameras panned across Prague's glorious skyline and fired the world's imagination with the image of political renewal superimposed on somber Gothic and voluptuous baroque.

By Mark Baker

Updated by
Ky Krauthamer
and Martha
Lagace

Travelers have rediscovered the country, and Czechs and Moravians have rediscovered the world. Not so long ago, the visitor was unhindered by crowds of tourists but had to struggle with a creeping sensation of melancholy and neglect that threatened to eclipse the city's beauty. Combined with a truly frustrating lack of services in every branch of the tourist industry, a trip to Czechoslovakia was always an adventure in the full sense of the word.

At least on the surface, the atmosphere is changing rapidly. The stagnant "normalization" of the Husák era, which froze the city out of the developments of the late 20th century, is giving way to the dynamic and the cosmopolitan. The revolution brought enthusiasm, bustle, and such conveniences as English-language newspapers, attentive hotels, and, occasionally, restaurants that will try to find a seat for you even if you don't have a reservation.

The revolution inspired one other thing: nationalism. Unable to unite on a common course of economic renewal, Czechs and Slovaks peacefully agreed to dissolve their 74-year-old federal state on January 1, 1993. Though the division was greeted with sadness by outsiders, visitors to either country are not likely to notice much difference save the hassle of an extra border and the need now to change money when traveling back and forth. This chapter covers the Czech Republic and its constituent provinces of Bohemia and Moravia. Slovakia is covered in a separate chapter (☞ Chapter 3).

The drab remnants of socialist reality are still omnipresent on the back roads of Bohemia and Moravia. But many of the changes made by the Communists were superficial—adding ugliness but leaving the society's core more or less intact. The colors are less jarring, not designed to attract the moneyed eye; the fittings are as they always were, not adapted to the needs of a new world.

The experience of visiting the Czech Republic still involves stepping back in time. Even in Prague, now deluged by tourists during the summer months, the sense of history—stretching back through centuries of wars, empires, and monuments to everyday life—remains uncluttered by the trappings of modernity. The peculiar melancholy of Central Europe, less tainted now by the oppressive political realities of the postwar era, still lurks in narrow streets and forgotten corners. Crumbling facades, dilapidated palaces, and treacherous cobbled streets both shock and enchant the visitor used to a world where what remains of history has been spruced up for tourist eyes.

The strange, Old World, and at times frustratingly bureaucratic atmosphere of the Czech Republic is not all a product of the communist era. Many of the small rituals that impinge on the visitor are actually remnants of the Hapsburg Empire and are also to be found, perhaps to a lesser degree, in Vienna and Budapest. The *šatná* (coatroom), for example, plays a vivid role in any visit to a restaurant or theater at any time of year other than summer. Even in the coldest weather, coats must be given with a few coins to the attendant, usually an old lady with a sharp eye for ignorant or disobedient tourists. The attendant often also plays a role in controlling the rest room; the entrance fee entitles the visitor to a small roll of paper, ceremoniously kept on the attendant's table. Another odd institution associated with this part of the world is the *Tabák-Trafik,* the little store that sells two things connected for no apparent reason: tobacco products and public-transportation tickets.

Outside the capital, for those willing to put up with the inconveniences of shabby hotels and mediocre restaurants, the sense of rediscovering a neglected world is even stronger. And the range is startling, from imperial spas, with their graceful colonnades and dilapidated villas, to the hundreds of arcaded town squares, modestly displaying the passing of time with each splendid layer of once-contemporary style. Gothic towers, Renaissance facades, baroque interiors, and aging modern supermarkets merge. Between the man-made sights, the visitor is rewarded with glorious mountain ranges and fertile rolling countryside laced with carp ponds and forests.

The key to enjoying the country is to relax. There is no point in demanding high levels of service or quality. And for the budget-conscious traveler, this is Central Europe at its most beautiful, at prices that are several times below those of Austria and even Hungary.

Pleasures and Pastimes

Castles and Châteaus
More than 2,000 castles, manor houses, and châteaus collectively form a precious and not-to-be-missed part of the country's cultural and historical heritage. Grim ruins glower from craggy hilltops and fantastical Gothic castles guard ancient trade routes. Hundreds of noble houses—Renaissance, baroque, Empire, and their many compounds—dot the countryside. Their former bourgeois and aristocratic owners were expelled in the anti-German reaction of 1945–46 or forced out by the Communists. Many of their valuable old seats now stand in near ruin, though some have been returned to the original owners while others remain in state hands. While not one, perhaps, will ever be as it once was, more sights than ever before are open to the public. Picture galleries, rooms full of historic furniture, exquisite medieval stonework, and baroque chapels—all speak of a vanished way of life whose remnants survive in every town and village of Bohemia and Moravia.

Dining
The quality of restaurant cuisine in the Czech Republic remains uneven, but many excellent private restaurants have sprung up in Prague in recent years. The traditional dishes—roast pork or duck with dumplings, or broiled meat with sauce—can be light and tasty when well prepared. Often in smaller towns the hotel restaurant is still the only dining option available.

Restaurants generally fall into three categories. A *pivnice,* or beer hall, usually offers a simple menu of goulash or pork with dumplings at very low prices. In the congenial atmosphere, you can expect to share a table. More attractive (and more expensive) are the *vinárna* (wine cellars) and *restaurace* (restaurants), which serve a full range of dishes. Wine cellars, some occupying Romanesque basements, can be a real treat, and you should certainly seek them out. A fourth dining option, the *lahůdky* (snack bar or deli), is the quickest and cheapest option.

Lunch, usually eaten between noon and 2, is the main meal for Czechs and offers the best deal for tourists. Many restaurants put out a special luncheon menu (*denní lístek*), usually printed only in Czech, with more appetizing selections at better prices. If you don't see it, ask your waiter. Dinner is usually served from 5 until 9 or 10, but don't wait too long to eat. First of all, most Czechs eat only a light meal or a cold plate of meat and cheese in the evening. Second, restaurant cooks frequently knock off early on slow nights, and the later you arrive, the more likely it is that the kitchen will be closed. In general, dinner menus do not differ substantially from lunch offerings, except the prices are higher.

CATEGORY	PRAGUE*	OTHER AREAS*
$$$$	over $25	over $20
$$$	$15–$25	$10–$20
$$	$7–$15	$5–$10
$	under $7	under $5

*per person for a three-course meal, excluding wine and tip

Hiking

The Czech Republic is a hiker's paradise, with 40,000 kilometers (25,000 miles) of well-kept, marked, and signposted trails both in the mountainous regions and leading through beautiful countryside from town to town. The best areas for ambitious mountain walkers are the Beskydy range in northern Moravia and the Krkonoše range (Giant Mountains) in northern Bohemia. The rolling Šumava Hills of southern Bohemia are excellent for less ambitious walkers. You'll find the colored markings denoting trails on trees, fences, walls, rocks, and elsewhere. The main paths are marked in red, others in blue and green, while the least important trails are marked in yellow. Hiking maps covering the entire country can be found in almost any bookstore; look for the large-scale *Soubor turistických* maps.

Lodging

The number of hotels and pensions has increased dramatically throughout the Czech Republic, in step with the influx of tourists. Finding a suitable room should pose no problem, although it is highly recommended that you book ahead during the peak tourist season (July and August, and the Christmas and Easter holidays). Hotel prices, in general, remain high. This is especially true in Prague and in the spa towns of western Bohemia. Better value can often be found at private pensions and with individual homeowners offering rooms to let. In the outlying towns, the best strategy is to inquire at the local tourist information office or simply fan out around the town and look for room-for-rent signs on houses (usually in German: ZIMMER FREI or PRIVAT ZIMMER).

Outside Prague and the major tourist centers, hotels tend to fall into two categories: the old-fashioned hotel on the main square, with rooms above a restaurant, no private bathrooms, and a price lower than you can imagine; or the modern, impersonal, and often ugly high-rise with all the basic facilities and a reasonable price. Nevertheless, you'll rarely find a room that is not clean, and some hotels (of both varieties) can be quite pleasant. Hostels are understood to mean dormitory rooms and are probably best avoided. In the mountainous areas you can often find little *chaty* (chalets), where pleasant surroundings compensate for a lack of basic amenities. *Autokempink* parks (campsites) generally have a few bungalows.

The Czech Republic's official hotel classification now follows the international star system. These ratings correspond closely to our cate-

12

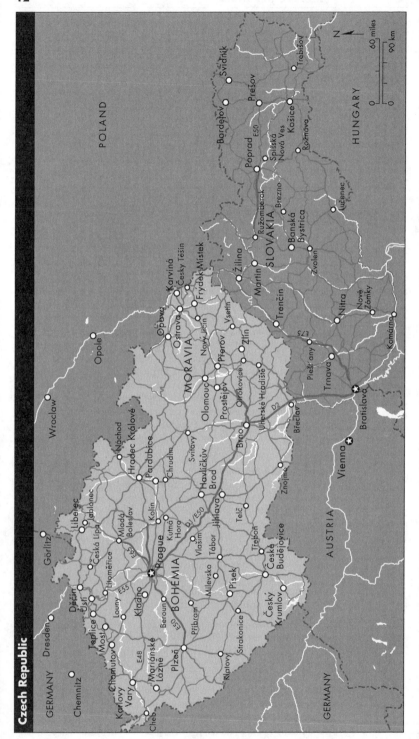

Czech Republic

gories as follows: deluxe or five-star plus four-star ($$$$); three-star ($$$); two-star ($$). The $ category will most often be met by private rooms. Often you can book rooms—both at hotels and in private homes—through Čedok or visitor bureaus. Otherwise, try calling or writing the hotel directly.

The prices quoted below are for double rooms during high season, generally not including breakfast. At certain periods, such as Easter or during festivals, prices can jump 15%–25%; as a rule, always ask the price before taking a room.

As for camping, there are hundreds of sites for tents and trailers throughout the country, but most are open only in summer (May to mid-September). You can get a map from Čedok of all the sites, with addresses, opening times, and facilities. Camping outside official sites is prohibited. Some campgrounds also offer bungalows. Campsites are divided into Categories A and B according to facilities, but both have hot water and toilets.

CATEGORY	PRAGUE*	OTHER AREAS*
$$$$	over $200	over $100
$$$	$100–$200	$50–$100
$$	$50–$100	$25–$50
$	under $50	under $25

All prices are for a standard double room during peak season.

Outdoor Activities and Sports

Bicycling: Czechs are avid cyclists. The flatter areas of southern Bohemia and Moravia are ideal for biking. Outside the larger towns, quieter roads stretch out for miles. The hillier terrain of northern Bohemia makes it popular with mountain-biking enthusiasts. Not many places rent bikes, though. Inquire at Čedok or at your hotel for rental information. **Boating and Sailing:** The country's main boating area is the enormous series of dams and reservoirs along the Vltava south of Prague. The most popular lake is Slapy, where it is possible to rent small paddleboats as well as to relax and swim on a hot day. If you have your own kayak, you can test your skills on one of the excellent rivers near Český Krumlov. **Skiing:** The two main skiing areas in the Czech Republic are the Krkonoše range in northern Bohemia and the Šumava hills of southern Bohemia (lifts at both operate from January through March). In the former, you'll find a number of organizations renting skis—although supplies may be limited. Both places are also good for cross-country skiing.

Shopping

In Prague, Karlovy Vary, and elsewhere in Bohemia, look for elegant and unusual crystal and porcelain. Bohemia is also renowned for the quality and deep-red color of its garnets; keep an eye out for beautiful garnet rings and brooches, set in either gold or silver. You can also find excellent ceramics, especially in Moravia, as well as other folk artifacts, such as printed textiles, lace, hand-knit sweaters, and painted eggs. There are attractive crafts stores throughout the Czech Republic. Karlovy Vary is blessed with a variety of unique items to buy, including the strange pipelike drinking mugs used in the spas; roses; vases left to petrify in the mineral-laden water; and *oplatky*, crispy wafers sometimes covered with chocolate. Here you'll also find *Becherovka*, a tasty herbal aperitif that makes a nice gift to take home.

Wine

Best known as a nation of beer makers, the Czechs also produce quite drinkable wines: peppy, fruity whites and mild, versatile reds. Southern Moravia, with comparatively warm summers and rich soil, grows the bulk of the wine harvest; look for the Mikulov and Znojmo regional designations. Favorite white varietals are **Müller Thurgau,** with a fine muscat bouquet and light flavor that go well with fish and veal, and **Neuburské,** yellow-green in color and with a dry, smoky bouquet, delicious with roasts. **Rulandské bílé,** a semidry Burgundy-like white, has a flowery bouquet and full-bodied flavor. It's a good complement to poultry and veal. The dry, smooth flavor of **Ryzlink Rýnský** (the Rhine Riesling grape) is best enjoyed with cold entrées and fish. **Veltlínské zelené,** distinguished by its beautiful light-green color, also goes well with cold entrées.

Belying the notion that northerly climes are more auspicious for white than red grapes, northern Bohemia's scant few hundred acres of vineyards produce reliable reds and the occasional jewel. The leading wineries are found in the towns of Roudnice and Mělník, near the confluence of the Vltava and Labe (Elbe) rivers. **Frankovka,** fiery red and slightly acidic, is well suited to game and grilled meats. **Rulandské červené,** cherry red in color and flavor, makes an excellent dry companion to poultry and game. **Vavřinecké,** the country's favorite red, dark and slightly sweet, also stands up well to red meats.

Exploring the Czech Republic

Great Itineraries

IF YOU HAVE 3 DAYS

Numbers in the text correspond to numbers in the margin and on the maps.

Make Prague your base. This will allow you plenty of time to explore the beauties and wonders of the Old Town and Hradčany, as well as to make a day trip to one of the country's fascinating smaller cities: the splendid spa town of **Karlovy Vary** ⑨, nestled in the western Bohemia hills, makes a good one-day destination.

IF YOU HAVE 5 DAYS

Plan to spend three full days exploring Prague. You could easily spend a day each in the Old Town, Malá Strana, and the castle and the other two days visiting the well-preserved medieval mining town of **Kutná Hora** ㉙ and the unforgettable concentration camp **Terezín** ㉟. Or you could spend a day amid the Renaissance charm of **Český Krumlov** ㉥.

When to Tour

Prague is beautiful year-round, but avoid midsummer (especially July and August) and the Christmas and Easter holidays, when the city is overrun with tourists. Spring and fall generally combine good weather with a more bearable level of tourism. During the winter months you'll encounter few other visitors and have the opportunity to see Prague breathtakingly covered in snow, but it can get very cold. The same guidelines generally apply to traveling in the rest of Bohemia and Moravia, although even in August, the peak of the high season, the number of visitors to these areas is far smaller than in Prague. The Giant Mountains of Bohemia come into their own in winter (December–February), when skiers from all over the country crowd the slopes and resorts. If you're not a skier, try visiting the mountains in late spring (May or June) or fall, when the colors are dazzling and you'll have the hotels and restaurants nearly to yourself. Bear in mind that many castles and museums are closed November through March.

PRAGUE

In the seven years since Prague's students took to the streets to help bring down the 40-year-old Communist regime, the city has enjoyed an unparalleled cultural renaissance. Much of the energy has come from planeloads of idealistic young Americans, but the enthusiasm has been shared in near-equal measure by their Czech counterparts and by the many newcomers who have arrived from all over the world. Amid Prague's cobblestone streets and gold-tipped spires, new galleries, cafés, and clubs teem with bright-eyed "expatriates" and perplexed locals, who must wonder how their city came to be Eastern Europe's new Left Bank. New shops and, perhaps most noticeably, scads of new restaurants have opened, expanding the city's culinary reach far beyond the traditional roast pork and dumplings. Many have something to learn in the way of presentation and service, but Praguers still marvel at a variety that was unthinkable only a few years ago.

The arts and theater are also thriving in the "new" Prague. Young playwrights, some writing in English, regularly stage their own works. Weekly poetry readings are standing room only. The city's dozen or so rock clubs are jammed nightly; bands play everything from metal and psychedelic to garage and grunge.

All of this frenetic activity plays well against a stunning backdrop of towering churches and centuries-old bridges and alleyways. Prague achieved much of its present glory in the 14th century, during the long reign of Charles IV, king of Bohemia and Moravia and Holy Roman Emperor. It was Charles who established a university in the city and laid out the New Town (Nové Město), charting Prague's growth.

During the 15th century, the city's development was hampered by the Hussite Wars, a series of crusades launched by the Holy Roman Empire to subdue the fiercely independent Czech noblemen. The Czechs were eventually defeated in 1620 at the Battle of White Mountain (Bílá Hora) near Prague and were ruled by the Hapsburg family for the next 300 years. Under the Hapsburgs, Prague became a German-speaking city and an important administrative center, but it was forced to play second fiddle to the monarchy's capital of Vienna. Much of the Lesser Town (Malá Strana), across the river, was built up at this time, becoming home to Austrian nobility and its baroque tastes.

Prague regained its status as a national capital in 1918, with the creation of the modern Czechoslovak state, and quickly asserted itself in the interwar period as a vital cultural center. Although the city escaped World War II essentially intact, it and the rest of Czechoslovakia fell under the political and cultural domination of the Soviet Union until the 1989 popular uprisings. The election of dissident playwright Václav Havel to the post of national president set the stage for the city's renaissance, which has since proceeded at a dizzying, quite Bohemian rate.

Exploring Prague

The spine of the city is the river Vltava (also known as the Moldau), which runs through the city from south to north with a single sharp curve to the east. Prague originally comprised five independent towns, represented today by its main historic districts: **Hradčany** (Castle Area), **Malá Strana** (Lesser Quarter), **Staré Město** (Old Town), **Nové Město** (New Town), and **Josefov** (the Jewish Quarter).

Hradčany, the seat of Czech royalty for hundreds of years, has as its center the **Pražský Hrad** (Prague Castle), which overlooks the city from its hilltop west of the Vltava. Steps lead down from Hradčany to Malá Strana, an area dense with ornate mansions built by 17th- and 18th-century nobility.

Karlův Most (Charles Bridge) connects Malá Strana with Staré Město. Just a few blocks east of the bridge is the focal point of the Old Town, **Staroměstské náměstí** (Old Town Square). Staré Město is bounded by the curving Vltava and three large commercial avenues: **Revoluční** to the east, **Na příkopě** to the southeast, and **Národní třída** to the south.

Beyond lies the Nové Město; several blocks south is **Karlovo náměstí,** the city's largest square. Roughly 1 kilometer (½ mile) farther south is **Vyšehrad,** an ancient castle high above the river.

On a promontory to the east of Wenceslas Square stretches **Vinohrady,** once the favored neighborhood of well-to-do Czechs; below Vinohrady lie the crumbling neighborhoods of **Žižkov** to the north and **Nusle** to the south. On the west bank of the Vltava south and east of Hradčany lie many older residential neighborhoods and enormous parks. About 3 kilometers (2 miles) from the center in every direction, Communist-era housing projects begin their unsightly sprawl.

The Old Town

A GOOD WALK

Numbers in the text correspond to numbers in the margin and on the Prague map.

Václavské náměstí (Wenceslas Square) ①, marked by the **Statue of St. Wenceslas** ② and convenient to hotels and transportation, is an excellent place to begin a tour of the Old Town (Staré Město). A long, gently sloping boulevard rather than a square in the usual sense, Václavské náměstí is bounded at the top (the southern end) by the **Národní Muzeum** (Czech National Museum) ③ and at the bottom by the pedestrian shopping areas of **Národní třída** and **Na příkopě.** Today Wenceslas Square comprises Prague's liveliest street scene. Don't miss the dense maze of arcades tucked away from the street in buildings that line both sides. You'll find an odd assortment of cafés, discos, ice cream parlors, and movie houses, all seemingly unfazed by the passage of time. At night the square changes character somewhat as dance music pours out from the crowded discos and leather-jacketed cronies crowd around the taxi stands. One eye-catching building on the square is the **Hotel Europa** ④, at No. 25, a riot of art nouveau that recalls the glamorous world of turn-of-the-century Prague.

To begin the approach to the Old Town proper, walk past the tall, art-deco Koruna complex and turn right onto the handsome pedestrian zone called **Na příkopě.** Turn left onto Havířská ulice and follow this small alley to the glittering green-and-cream splendor of the newly renovated **Stavovské Divadlo** (Estates Theater) ⑤.

Return to Na příkopě, turn left, and continue to the end of the street. On weekdays between 8 AM and 5 PM, it's well worth taking a peek at the stunning interior of the **Živnostenská banka** (Merchants' Bank) ⑥, at No. 20.

Na příkopě ends abruptly at the **Náměstí Republiky** (Republic Square) ⑦, an important New Town transportation hub (with a metro stop). The severe Depression-era facade of the **Česka Národní banka** (Czech National Bank; ⊠ Na příkopě 30) makes the building look more like a fortress than the nation's central bank. Close by stands the stately **Prašná brána** (Powder Tower), its festive Gothic spires looming above the square. Adjacent to the dignified Powder Tower, the **Obecní dům** (Municipal House), under reconstruction until 1997, looks decidedly decadent.

Walk through the arch at the base of the Powder Tower and down the formal **Celetná ulice,** the first leg of the so-called Royal Way. Monarchs favored this route primarily for its stunning entry into **Staroměstské**

náměstí (Old Town Square) and because the houses along Celetná were among the city's finest, providing a suitable backdrop to the coronation procession. The pink **Sixt House** ⑧, at Celetná 2, sports one of the street's handsomest, if restrained, baroque facades.

Staroměstské náměstí (Old Town Square) ⑨, at the end of Celetná, is dazzling, thanks partly to the double-spired **Týn Church** (Kostel Panny Marie před Týnem) ⑩, which rises over the square from behind a row of patrician houses. To the immediate left of Týn Church is **U Zvonů** (No. 13), a baroque structure that has been stripped down to its original Gothic elements.

A short walk away stands the gorgeous pink-and-ocher **Palác Kinských** (Kinský Palace). At this end of the square, you can't help noticing the expressive **Jan Hus monument** ⑪. Opposite the Týn Church is the Gothic **Staroměstská radnice** (Old Town Hall) ⑫, which with its impressive 200-foot tower, gives the square its sense of importance. As the hour approaches, join the crowds milling below the tower's 15th-century **astronomical clock** for a brief but spooky spectacle taken straight from the Middle Ages, every hour on the hour.

Walk north along the edge of the small park beside Town Hall to reach the baroque **Kostel svatého Mikuláše** (Church of St. Nicholas) ⑬, not to be confused with the Lesser Town's St. Nicholas Church, on the other side of the river (☞ A Good Walk *in* Charles Bridge and Malá Strana, *below*).

Franz Kafka's birthplace is just to the left of St. Nicholas on U radnice. A small plaque can be found on the side of the house. Continue southwest from Old Town Square until you come to **Malé náměstí** (Small Square) ⑭, a nearly perfect ensemble of facades dating from the Middle Ages. Look for tiny **Karlova ulice,** which begins in the southwest corner of Malé náměstí, and take another quick right to stay on it (watch the signs—this medieval street seems designed to confound the visitor). Turn left at the T intersection where Karlova seems to end in front of the Středočeská Galérie and continue left down the quieter Husova Street (if you want to go on directly to A Good Walk 3, veer to the right for the Charles Bridge and the other side of the river). Pause and inspect the exotic **Clam-Gallas palota** (Clam-Gallas Palace) ⑮, at Husova 20. You'll recognize it easily: Look for the Titans in the doorway holding up what must be a very heavy baroque facade.

Return to the T and continue down Husova. For a glimpse of a less successful baroque reconstruction, take a close look at the **Kostel svatého Jiljí** (Church of St. Giles) ⑯, across from No. 7.

Continue walking along Husova třída to Na Perštýně and turn right at tiny Betlémská ulice. The alley opens up onto a quiet square of the same name (Betlémská náměstí) and upon the most revered of all Hussite churches in Prague, the **Betlémská kaple** (Bethlehem Chapel) ⑰.

Return to Na Perštýně and continue walking to the right. As you near the back of the buildings of the busy **Národní třída** (National Boulevard), turn left at Martinská ulice. At the end of the street, the forlorn but majestic church **Kostel svatého Martina ve zdi** (St. Martin-in-the-Wall) ⑱ stands like a postwar ruin. Walk around the church to the left and through a little archway of apartments onto the bustling Národní třída. To the left, a five-minute walk away, lies Wenceslas Square and the starting point of the walk.

TIMING

Now that Prague is such a popular travel destination, the Wenceslas Square and Old Town Square areas are busy with activity around-the-clock almost all year round. Visitors in search of a little peace and quiet will find the streets at their most subdued on early weekend summer mornings or right after a sudden downpour; otherwise, expect to share Prague's pleasures. The streets in this walking tour are reasonably close together and can be covered in half a day, or in a full day if you have more time.

SIGHTS TO SEE

⑰ **Betlémská kaple** (Bethlehem Chapel). The church's elegant simplicity is in stark contrast to the diverting Gothic and baroque of the rest of the city. The original structure dates from the end of the 14th century, and Jan Hus himself was a regular preacher here from 1402 until his death in 1415. After the Thirty Years' War the church fell into the hands of the Jesuits and was finally demolished in 1786. Excavations carried out after World War I uncovered the original portal and three windows, and the entire church was reconstructed during the 1950s. Although little remains of the first church, some remnants of Hus's teachings can still be read on the inside walls. ⊠ *Betlémské nám. 5.* ▨ *Admission charged.* ☉ *Apr.–Sept., daily 9–6; Oct.–Mar., daily 9–5.*

Celetná ulice (Celetna Street). Most of the facades indicate the buildings are from the 17th or 18th century, but appearances are deceiving: Many of the houses in fact have foundations dating from the 12th century or earlier. **Sixt House**, at Celetná 2, dates from the 12th century— ⑧ its Romanesque vaults are still visible in the wine restaurant in the basement.

⑮ **Clam-Gallas palota** (Clam-Gallas Palace). The palace dates from 1713 and is the work of Johann Bernhard Fischer von Erlach, the famed Viennese architectural virtuoso of the day. Enter the building (push past the guard as if you know what you're doing) for a glimpse of the finely carved staircase, the work of the master himself, and of the Italian frescoes featuring Apollo that surround it. The Gallas family was prominent during the 18th century but has long since died out. The building now houses the municipal archives and is rarely open to visitors. ⊠ *Husova 20.*

Franz Kafka's birthplace. For years this memorial to Kafka's birth (July 3, 1883) was the only public acknowledgment of the writer's stature in world literature, reflecting the traditionally ambiguous attitude of the Czech government to his work. The Communists were always too uncomfortable with Kafka's themes of bureaucracy and alienation to sing his praises too loudly, if at all. As a German and a Jew, moreover, Kafka could easily be dismissed as standing outside the mainstream of Czech literature. Following the 1989 revolution, however, Kafka's popularity soared, and his works are now widely available in Czech. A fascinating little museum has been set up in the house of his birth. ⊠ *U radnice 5.* ▨ *20 Kč.* ☉ *Tues.–Sat. 10–6 (until 7 in summer).*

④ **Hotel Europa.** An art-nouveau gem, it has elegant stained glass and mosaics in the café and restaurant. The terrace, serving drinks in the summer, is an excellent spot for people-watching. ⊠ *Václavské nám. 25.*

⑪ **Jan Hus monument.** Few memorials have elicited as much controversy as this one, which was dedicated in July 1915, exactly 500 years after Hus was burned at the stake in Constance, Germany. Some maintain that the monument's Secessionist style (the inscription seems to come right from turn-of-the-century Vienna) clashes with the Gothic and baroque of the square. Others dispute the romantic depiction of Hus, who appears here in flowing garb as tall and bearded. The real Hus, historians maintain, was short and had a baby face. Still, no one can take issue with the influence of this fiery preacher, whose ability to transform doctrinal disputes, both literally and metaphorically, into the language of the common man made him into a religious and national symbol for the Czechs. ⊠ *Staroměstské nám.*

Karlova ulice. The character of Karlova ulice has changed in recent years to meet the growing number of tourists. Galleries and gift shops now occupy almost every storefront. But the cobblestones, narrow alleys, and crumbling gables still make it easy to imagine what life was like 400 years ago.

⑯ **Kostel svatého Jiljí** (Church of St. Giles). This baroque church was another important outpost of Czech Protestantism in the 16th century. The exterior is a powerful example of Gothic architecture, including the buttresses and a characteristic portal; the interior, surprisingly, is baroque, dating from the 17th century. ⊠ *Across from Husova 7.*

⑱ **Kostel svatého Martina ve zdi** (St. Martin-in-the-Wall). It was here in 1414 that Holy Communion was first given to the Bohemian laity—with both bread and wine, in defiance of the Catholic custom of the time, which dictated that only bread was to be offered to the masses, with wine reserved for the priests and clergy. From then on, the chalice came to symbolize the Hussite movement.

⑬ **Kostel svatého Mikuláše** (Church of St. Nicholas). Designed in the 18th century by Prague's own master of late baroque, Kilian Ignaz Dientzenhofer, this church is probably less successful than its namesake across town in capturing the style's lyric exuberance. Still, Dientzenhofer utilized the limited space to create a structure that neither dominates nor retreats from the imposing square. The interior is compact, with a beautiful but small chandelier and an enormous black organ that seems to overwhelm the rear of the church. The church often hosts afternoon and evening concerts.

⑭ **Malé náměstí** (Small Square). Note the Renaissance iron fountain dating from 1560 in the center of the square. The sgraffito on the house at No. 3 is not as old (1890) as it looks, but here and there you can find authentic Gothic portals and Renaissance sgraffiti that betray the square's true age.

Na příkopě. The name means "at the moat," harking back to the time when the street was indeed a moat separating the Old Town on the left from the New Town on the right. Today the pedestrian zone Na příkopě is prime shopping territory, its smaller boutiques considered far more elegant than the motley collection of stores on Wenceslas Square. But don't expect much real elegance here: After 40 years of Communist orthodoxy in the fashion world, it will be many years before the boutiques really can match Western European standards.

⑦ **Náměstí Republiky** (Republic Square). Although an important New Town transportation hub (with a metro stop), the square has never really come together as a vital public space, perhaps because of its jarring architectural eclecticism. Taken one by one, each building is interesting in its own right, but the ensemble is less than the sum of the parts.

③ **Národní Muzeum** (Czech National Museum). This imposing structure, designed by Prague architect Josef Schulz and built between 1885 and 1890, does not come into its own until it is bathed in nighttime lighting. By day the grandiose edifice seems an inappropriate venue for a musty collection of stones and bones, minerals, and coins. This museum is only for dedicated fans of the genre. ⊠ *Václavské nám. 68,* ☎ *02/2423–0485.* 🎫 *40 Kč.* ☉ *Daily 9–5; closed 1st Tues. of month.*

Obecní dům (Municipal House). When reconstruction ends, this building should return to its former glory as a center for concerts and fash-

Exploring Prague

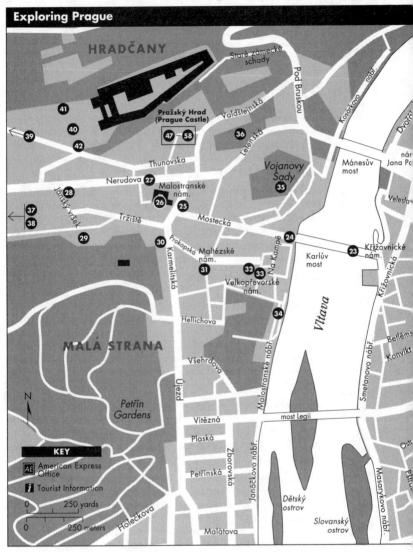

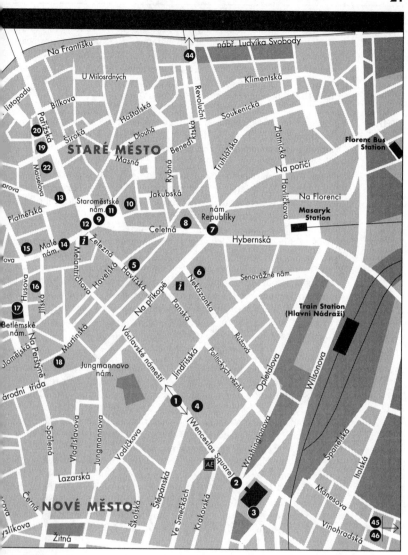

Zahrada
Valdštejnského
paláca, **36**
Židovské hřbitovy, **46**
Živnostenská banka, **6**

ionable restaurants. The style, mature art nouveau, recalls the lengths the Czech middle classes went to at the turn of the century to imitate Paris, then the epitome of style and glamour. Much of the interior bears the work of the art-nouveau master Alfons Mucha and other leading Czech artists. Mucha decorated the main Hall of the Lord Mayor upstairs, with impressive, magical frescoes depicting Czech history. The beautiful Smetana Hall is on the second floor.

<table>
<tr><td>NEED A
BREAK?</td><td>If you prefer subtle elegance, head around the corner to the café at Hotel Paříž (⊠ U Obecního domu 1, ☎ 2422–2151), a Jugendstil jewel tucked away on a relatively quiet street.</td></tr>
</table>

Palác Kinských (Kinský Palace). Built in 1765, this is considered one of Prague's finest late-baroque structures. With its exaggerated pink overlay and numerous statues, the facade looks extreme when contrasted with the more staid baroque elements of other nearby buildings. The palace once housed a German school (where Franz Kafka was a student for nine misery-laden years) and presently contains the National Gallery's graphics collection. The main exhibition room is on the second floor; exhibits change every few months and are usually worth seeing. It was from this building that Communist leader Klement Gottwald, flanked by his comrade Clementis, first addressed the crowds after seizing power in February 1948—an event recounted in the first chapter of Milan Kundera's novel *The Book of Laughter and Forgetting.* ⊠ *Staroměstské nám. 12.* 🎫 *20 Kč.* ☉ *Tues.–Sun. 10–6.*

Prašná brána (Powder Tower). Construction of the tower, one of the city's 13 original gates, was begun by King Vladislav II of Jagiello in 1475. At the time, the kings of Bohemia maintained their royal residence next door (on the site of the current Obecní dům, the Municipal House), and the tower was intended to be the grandest gate of all. But Vladislav was and thus heartily disliked by the rebellious Czech citizens of Prague. Nine years after he assumed power, fearing for his life, he moved the royal court across the river to Prague Castle. Work on the tower was abandoned, and the half-finished structure was used for storing gunpowder—hence its odd name—until the end of the 17th century. The oldest part of the tower is the base; the golden spires were not added until the end of the last century. The climb to the top affords a striking view of the Old Town and Prague Castle in the distance. ⊠ *Nám. Republiky.* 🎫 *20 Kč.* ☉ *Apr.–Oct., daily 9–6.*

★ ❾ **Staroměstské náměstí** (Old Town Square). Dazzling. Long the heart of the Old Town, the square grew to its present proportions when the city's original marketplace was moved away from the river in the 12th century. Its shape and appearance have changed little over the years. During the day the square has a festive atmosphere as musicians vie for the favor of onlookers, hefty young men in medieval outfits mint coins, and artists display renditions of Prague street scenes. If you come back to the square at night, the unlit shadowy towers of the Týn Church (to your right as you enter the square) rise ominously over the glowing baroque facades. The crowds thin out, and the ghosts of the square's stormy past return.

During the 15th century the square was the focal point of conflict between Czech Hussites and German Catholics. In 1422 the radical Hussite preacher Jan Želivský was executed here for his part in storming the New Town's town hall. Three Catholic consuls and seven German citizens were thrown out of the window in the ensuing fray—the first of Prague's many famous defenestrations. Within a few years, the

Hussites had taken over the town, expelled the Germans, and set up their own administration.

⑫ **Staroměstská radnice** (Old Town Hall). As you walk toward the building from the Hus monument, look for the 27 white crosses on the ground just in front of the Town Hall. These mark the spot where 27 Bohemian noblemen were killed by the Hapsburgs in 1621 during the dark days following the defeat of the Czechs at the Battle of White Mountain. The grotesque spectacle, designed to quash any further national or religious opposition, took some five hours to complete, as the men were put to the sword or hanged one by one.

The Town Hall has served as the center of administration for the Old Town since 1338, when King Johann of Luxembourg first granted the city council the right to a permanent location. Walk around the structure to the left and you'll see it's actually a series of houses jutting into the square; they were purchased over the years and successively added to the complex. The most interesting is the **U Minuty,** the corner building to the left of the clock tower, with its 16th-century Renaissance sgraffiti of biblical and classical motifs.

The impressive 200-foot **Town Hall Tower** was first built in the 14th century and given its current late-Gothic appearance around 1500 by the master Matyáš Rejsek. For a rare view of the Old Town and its maze of crooked streets and alleyways, climb to the top of the tower. The climb is not strenuous, but steep stairs at the top unfortunately prevent people with disabilities from enjoying the view. Enter through the door to the left of the tower.

Just before the hour, look to the upper part of the **astronomical clock,** where a skeleton begins by tolling a death knell and turning an hourglass upside down. The Twelve Apostles parade momentarily, and then a cockerel flaps its wings and crows, piercing the air as the hour finally strikes, solemnly. To the right of the skeleton, the dreaded Turk nods his head, seemingly hinting at another invasion like those of the 16th and 17th centuries. Immediately after the hour, guided tours in English and German (German only in winter) of the Town Hall depart from the main desk inside. However, the only notable features inside are the fine Renaissance ceilings and the Gothic Council Room. ⊠ *Staroměstské nám.* ☎ *To all sights 20 Kč.* ☉ *Daily 9–6 (until 5 in winter).*

NEED A BREAK? Staroměstské náměstí is a convenient spot for refreshments. **Tchibo,** at No. 6 (☎ 2481–1026), has tasty sandwiches and pastries, excellent coffee, and an outdoor terrace in season.

---

❷ **Statue of St. Wenceslas.** In 1848 citizens protested Hapsburg rule at this statue in front of the National Museum. In 1939 residents gathered to oppose Hitler's takeover of Bohemia and Moravia. It was here also, in 1969, that the student Jan Palach set himself on fire to protest the bloody invasion of his country by the Soviet Union and other Warsaw Pact countries in August of the previous year. The invasion ended the "Prague Spring," a cultural and political movement emphasizing free expression, which was supported by Alexander Dubček, the popular leader at the time. Although Dubček never intended to dismantle Communist authority completely, his political and economic reforms proved too daring for fellow comrades in the rest of Eastern Europe. In the months following the invasion, conservatives loyal to the Soviet Union were installed in all influential positions. The subsequent two decades were a period of cultural stagnation. Thousands of residents left the country or went underground; many more resigned themselves to lives of minimal expectations and small pleasures. ⊠ *Václavské nám.*

⑤ Stavovské Divadlo (Estates Theater). Built in the 1780s in the classical style and reopened in 1991 after years of renovation, the handsome theater was for many years a beacon of Czech-language culture in a city long dominated by the German variety. It is probably best known as the site of the world premiere of Mozart's opera *Don Giovanni* in October 1787, with the composer himself conducting. Prague audiences were quick to acknowledge Mozart's genius: The opera was an instant hit here, though it flopped nearly everywhere else in Europe. Mozart wrote most of the opera's second act in Prague at the Villa Bertramka, where he was a frequent guest. ⊠ *Ovocný trh.*

★ **⑩ Týn Church** (Kostel Panny Marie před Týnem). Construction of its twin jet-black spires, which still jar the eye, was begun by King Jiří of Poděbrad in 1461, during the heyday of the Hussites. Jiří had a gilded chalice, the symbol of the Hussites, proudly displayed on the front gable between the two towers. Following the defeat of the Hussites by the Catholic Hapsburgs, the chalice was removed and eventually replaced by a Madonna. As a final blow, the chalice was melted down and made into the Madonna's glimmering halo (you still can see it by walking into the center of the square and looking up between the spires). The entrance to Týn Church is through the arcades, under the house at No. 604.

Although the exterior of Týn Church is one of the best examples of Prague Gothic (in part the work of Peter Parler, architect of the Charles Bridge and St. Vitus Cathedral), much of the interior, including the tall nave, was rebuilt in the baroque style in the 17th century. Some Gothic pieces remain, however: Look to the left of the main altar for a beautifully preserved set of early Gothic carvings. The main altar itself was painted by Karel Şkréta, a luminary of the Czech Baroque. Before leaving the church, look for the grave marker (tucked away to the right of the main altar) of the great Danish astronomer Tycho Brahe, who came to Prague as "Imperial Mathematicus" in 1599 under Rudolf II. As a scientist, Tycho had a place in history that is assured: Johannes Kepler (another resident of the Prague court) used Tycho's observations to formulate his laws of planetary motion. But it is myth that has endeared Tycho to the hearts of Prague residents: The robust Dane, who was apparently fond of duels, lost part of his nose in one (take a closer look at the marker). He quickly had a wax nose fashioned for everyday use but preferred to parade around on holidays and festive occasions sporting a bright silver one. ⊠ *Celetná 5.*

U Zvonů. This baroque-cum-Gothic structure occasionally hosts concerts and art exhibitions. The exhibitions change frequently, and it's worth stopping by to see what's on. ⊠ *Celetná 13.*

❶ Václavské náměstí (Wenceslas Square). Visitors may recognize this spot from their television sets, for it was here that some 500,000 students and citizens gathered in the heady days of November 1989 to protest the policies of the former Communist regime. The government capitulated after a week of demonstrations, without a shot fired or the loss of a single life, bringing to power the first democratic government in 40 years (under playwright-president Václav Havel). Today this peaceful transfer of power is proudly referred to as the "Velvet" or "Gentle" Revolution (*něžná revolucia*). It was only fitting that the 1989 revolution should take place on Wenceslas Square. Throughout much of Czech history, the square has served as the focal point for popular discontent. Although Wenceslas Square was first laid out by Charles IV in 1348 as the center of the New Town (Nové Město), few buildings of architectural merit line the square today.

6 **Živnostenská banka** (Merchants' Bank). The style, a tasteful example of 19th-century exuberance, reflected the city's growing prosperity at the time. Ignore the guards and walk up the decorated stairs to the beautiful main banking room (note, however, that taking photos is forbidden). ⊠ *Na příkopě 20.*

The Jewish Ghetto

Prague's Jews survived centuries of discrimination, but two unrelated events of modern times have left their historic ghetto little more than a collection of museums. Around 1900, city officials decided for hygienic purposes to raze the ghetto and pave over its crooked streets. Only the synagogues, the town hall, and a few other buildings survived this early attempt at urban renewal. The second event was the Holocaust. Under Nazi occupation, a staggering percentage of the city's Jews were deported or murdered in concentration camps. Of the 35,000 Jews living in the ghetto before World War II, only about 1,200 returned to resettle the neighborhood after the war.

A GOOD WALK

To reach **Josefov,** the Jewish ghetto, leave Staroměstské námměsti (Old Town Square) via the handsome Pařížská and head north toward the river and the Hotel Inter-Continental. The festive atmosphere changes suddenly as you enter the area of the ghetto. The buildings are lower here, and older; the mood is hushed. Treasures and artifacts of the ghetto are now the property of the **Státní židovské muzeum** (State Jewish Museum), a complex comprising the Old Jewish Cemetery and the collections of the remaining individual synagogues. On Červená ulice is the **Vysoká synagóga** (High Synagogue) ⑲; adjacent, at Maislova 18, is the **Židovská radnice** (Jewish Town Hall), now home to the Jewish Community Center. The **Staronová synagóga** (Old-New Synagogue) ⑳ across the street at Červená 2 is the oldest standing synagogue in Europe.

Continue along Červená ulice, which becomes the little street **U starého hřbitova** (At the Old Cemetery) beyond Maislova ulice. At the bend in the road lies the Jewish ghetto's most astonishing sight, the **Starý židovský hřbitov** (Old Jewish Cemetery) ㉑. Just to the right of the cemetery entrance is the **Obřadní síň** (Ceremony Hall), which houses a moving exhibition of drawings made by children held at the Nazi concentration camp at Terezín (Theresienstadt), in northern Bohemia. If you were to continue in the other direction through the cemetery, you would come to the **Pinkasova synagóga** (Pinkas Synagogue), a handsome Gothic structure. Return to Maislova ulice via U starého hřbitova and turn right in the direction of the Old Town once again, crossing Široká ulice. Look in at the enormous collection of silver articles of worship in the **Maislova synagóga** (Maisel Synagogue) ㉒.

TIMING

The Jewish ghetto is one of the most popular visitor destinations in Prague, especially in the height of summer, when its tiny streets are jammed to bursting with tourists almost all the time. The best time to savor any of these sights without any crowds and distractions would be early morning when the museums and cemetery first open. The area itself is very compact and a basic walk-through should take only half a day. Travelers who'd like to linger in the museums could easily spend two days or more exploring this area.

SIGHTS TO SEE

㉒ **Maislova synagóga** (Maisel Synagogue). This houses a huge number of silver articles of worship confiscated by the Nazis from synagogues throughout Central Europe. Here you'll find the State Jewish Museum's finest collection of Torah wrappers and mantles, silver pointers, breastplates, spice boxes, candleholders (the eight-branched *Hanukkiah* and the seven-branched menorah), and Levite washing sets. ⊠ *Maislova 10.* ☞ *For admission information to this and other synagogues, see entry under Státní židovské muzeum.*

Obřadní síň (Ceremony Hall). It now houses drawings made by children at the Nazi concentration camp Terezín. During the early years of the war the Nazis used the camp for propaganda purposes to demonstrate their "humanity" toward the Jews, and prisoners were given relative freedom to lead "normal" lives. Transports to death camps in Poland began in earnest in the final months of the war, however, and many thousands of Terezín prisoners, including many of these children, eventually perished. ☞ *For admission information to the hall, see entry under Státní židovské muzeum.*

Pařížská Street. The buildings on this street date from the end of the 19th century, and their elegant facades reflect the prosperity of the Czech middle classes at the time. Here and there you can spot the influence of the Viennese Jugendstil, with its emphasis on mosaics, geometric forms, and gold inlay. The look is fresh against the busier 19th-century revival facades of most of the other structures.

Pinkasova synagóga (Pinkas Synagogue). Further testimony to the appalling crimes perpetrated against the Jews during World War II can be seen in this newly renovated synagogue. The names of 77,297 Bohemian and Moravian Jews murdered by the Nazis were inscribed in rows on the walls inside (many of the names, sadly, have been destroyed by water damage). The building's foundation dates from the 11th century. Enter the synagogue from Široká Street on the other side of the cemetery, or through the cemetery. ☞ *For admission information to this and other synagogues, see entry under Státní židovské muzeum.*

㉕ Staronová synagóga (Old-New Synagogue). Dating from the mid-13th century, it is one of the most important works of early Gothic in Prague. The odd name recalls the legend that the synagogue was built on the site of an ancient Jewish temple and that stones from the temple were used to build the present structure. The synagogue has not only survived fires and the razing of the ghetto at the end of the last century but also emerged from the Nazi occupation intact; it is still in active use. The oldest part of the synagogue is the entrance, with its vault supported by two pillars. The grille at the center of the hall dates from the 15th century. Note that men are required to cover their heads inside and that during services men and women sit apart. ⊠ *Červená 2.*

★ ㉑ Starý židovský hřbitov (Old Jewish Cemetery). An unforgettable sight, this melancholy space not far from the busy city was, from the 14th century to 1787, the final resting place for all Jews living in Prague. Some 12,000 graves in all are piled atop one another in 12 layers. Walk the paths amid the gravestones. The relief symbols represent the name or profession of the deceased. The oldest marked grave belongs to the poet Avigdor Kara, who died in 1439. The best-known marker is probably that of Jehuda ben Bezalel, the famed Rabbi Loew, who is credited with having created the mythical Golem in 1573. Even today, small scraps of paper bearing wishes are stuffed into the cracks of the rabbi's tomb in the hope he will grant them. Loew's grave lies just a few steps from the entrance, near the western wall of the cemetery.

Státní židovské muzeum (State Jewish Museum). All the synagogues and the Old Jewish Cemetery are under the auspices of this museum. In a bit of irony, the holdings are vast thanks to Hitler, who had planned to open a museum here documenting the life and practices of what he had hoped would be an "extinct" people. The cemetery and most of the synagogues are open to the public. Each synagogue specializes in certain artifacts, and you can buy tickets for all the buildings at either Maislova synagóga, Pinkasova synagóga, Vysoká synagóga, or in front of the Old Jewish Cemetery. ☎ 02/231–0681. ✉ *Combined ticket to Jewish Museum collections and Old Jewish Cemetery 270 Kč; museum collections only, 150 Kč; Old Jewish Cemetery only, 120 Kč. ☉ Apr.–May, Sun.–Fri. 9–6; June–Oct., Sun.–Fri. 9–6:30; Nov.–Mar., Sun.–Fri. 9–4:30; closed Jewish holidays.*

⑲ **Vysoká synagóga** (High Synagogue). This striking building features rich Torah mantles and silver. It was ordered built in the second half of the 16th century by the banker and businessman Mordecai Maisel (☞ Jewish Town Hall, *below*) and was expanded at the end of the 17th century. ⊠ *Červená ul. (enter at No. 101). ✉ For admission information to this and other synagogues, see entry under Státní židovské muzeum.*

★ **Židovská radnice** (Jewish Town Hall). The hall was the creation of Mordecai Maisel, an influential Jewish leader at the end of the 16th century. It was restored in the 18th century and given its clock and bell tower at that time. A second clock, with Hebrew numbers, keeps time counterclockwise. Now home to the Jewish Community Center, the building also houses Prague's only kosher restaurant, Shalom. ⊠ *Maislova 18.*

Charles Bridge and Malá Strana

A GOOD WALK

Prague's **Malá Strana** (the so-called Lesser Quarter, or Little Town) is not for the methodical traveler. Its charm lies in the tiny lanes, the sudden blasts of bombastic architecture, and the soul-stirring views that emerge for a second before disappearing behind the sloping roofs.

Begin the tour on the Old Town side of **Karlův most** (Charles Bridge) ㉓, which you can reach by foot in about 10 minutes from the Old Town Square. Rising above it is the majestic **Old Town Bridge Tower**; the climb of 138 steps is worth the effort for the views it affords of the Old Town and, across the river, of Malá Strana and Prague Castle.

It's worth pausing to take a closer look at some of the statues as you walk across Charles Bridge toward Malá Strana. Approaching Malá Strana, you'll see the Kampa Island below you, separated from the Lesser Town by an arm of the Vltava known as Čertovka (Devil's Stream).

By now you are almost at the end of the bridge. In front of you is the striking conjunction of the two **Malá Strana bridge towers** ㉔, one Gothic, the other Romanesque. Together they frame the baroque flamboyance of St. Nicholas Church in the distance. At night this is an absolutely wondrous sight. If you didn't climb the tower on the Old Town side of the bridge, it's worth scrambling up the wooden stairs inside the Gothic tower **Mostecká věž** for the views over the roofs of the Malá Strana and of the Old Town across the river.

Walk under the gateway of the towers into the little uphill street called **Mostecká ulice.** You have now entered the **Malá Strana** (Lesser Quarter). Follow Mostecká ulice up to the rectangular **Malostranské náměstí** (Lesser Quarter Square) ㉕, now the district's traffic hub rather than its heart. On the left side of the square stands **Chrám svatého Mikuláše** (St. Nicholas Church) ㉖.

Nerudova ulice ㉗ runs up from the square toward Prague Castle. Lined with gorgeous houses (and in recent years an ever-larger number of places to spend money), it's sometimes burdened with the moniker "Prague's most beautiful street." A tiny passageway at No. 13, on the left-hand side as you go up, leads to **Tržiště ulice** and the **Schönbornský palác** ㉙, once Franz Kafka's home, now the Embassy of the United States. The street winds down to the quarter's noisy main street, **Karmelitská,** where the famous "Infant of Prague" resides in the **Kostel Panny Marie vítězné.** Tiny **Prokopská ulice** leads off of Karmelitská, past the former Church of St. Procopius, now converted, oddly, into an apartment block, and into **Maltézské náměstí** ㉛, a characteristically noble compound. Nearby, **Velkopřevorské náměstí** ㉜ boasts even grander palaces.

A tiny bridge at the cramped square's lower end takes you across the little backwater called Čertovka to **Kampa Island** ㉞ and its broad lawns, cafés, and river views. Winding your way underneath the Charles Bridge and along the street **U lužického semináře** brings you to a quiet walled garden, **Vojanovy sady** ㉟. Another, more formal garden, with an unbeatable view of Prague Castle looming above, the **Zahrada Valdštejnského paláca** ㊱ hides itself off busy Letenská ulice near the Malostranská metro station.

TIMING

The area is at its best in the evening, when the softer light hides the crumbling facades and brings you into a world of glimmering beauty. The basic walk described here could take as little as half a day—longer if you'd like to explore the area's lovely nooks and crannies.

SIGHTS TO SEE

㉘ **Bretfeld palác** (Bretfeld Palace). It's worth taking a quick look at this rococo house on the corner of Nerudova ulice and Jánský vršek. The relief of St. Nicholas on the facade is the work of Ignaz Platzer, but the building is valued more for its historical associations than for its architecture: This is where Mozart, his lyricist partner Lorenzo da Ponte, and the aging but still infamous philanderer and music lover Casanova stayed at the time of the world premiere of *Don Giovanni* in 1787. The Malá Strana gained a new connection with Mozart when its streets were used to represent 18th-century Vienna in the filming of Miloš Forman's *Amadeus.* ✉ *Nerudova 33.*

The archway at Nerudova 13, more or less opposite the Santini-designed **Kostel Panny Marie ustavičné pomoci u Kajetánů** (Church of Our Lady of Perpetual Help at the Theatines), hides one of the many winding passageways that give the Malá Strana its enchantingly ghostly character at night. Follow the dogleg curve downhill, past two restaurants, vine-covered walls, and some broken-down houses. The alleyway really comes into its own only in the dark, the dim lighting hiding the grime and highlighting the mystery.

★ ㉖ **Chrám svatého Mikuláše** (St. Nicholas Church). With its dynamic curves, this church is one of the purest and most ambitious examples of high baroque. The celebrated architect Christoph Dientzenhofer began the Jesuit church in 1704 on the site of one of the more active Hussite churches of 15th-century Prague. Work on the building was taken over by his son Kilian Ignaz Dientzenhofer, who built the dome and presbytery; Anselmo Lurago completed the whole in 1755 by adding the bell tower. The juxtaposition of the broad, full-bodied dome with the slender bell tower is one of the many striking architectural contrasts that mark the Prague skyline. Inside, the vast pink-and-green space is impossible to take in with a single glance; every corner bristles with movement, guiding the eye first to the dramatic statues, then to the hectic frescoes, and on to the shining faux-marble pillars. Many of the statues are the work of Ignaz Platzer; they constitute his last blaze of success. When the centralizing and secularizing reforms of Joseph II toward the end of the 18th century brought an end to the flamboyant baroque era, Platzer's workshop was forced to declare bankruptcy. ⊠ *Malostranské nám.* 🎫 *20 Kč.* ⊙ *Daily 9–4 (until 5 or 6 in summer).*

㉞ Kampa Island. Prague's largest island is cut off from the "mainland" by the narrow Čertovka streamlet. The name Čertovka translates as Devil's Stream and reputedly refers to a cranky old lady who once lived on Maltese Square (given the river's present filthy state, however, the name is ironically appropriate). The unusually well-kept lawns of the **Kampa Gardens** that occupy much of the island are one of the few places in Prague where sitting on the grass is openly tolerated. If it's a warm day, spread out a blanket and bask for a while in the sunshine. The row of benches that line the river to the left is also a popular spot from which to contemplate the city. At night this stretch along the river is especially romantic.

★ ㉓ Karlův most (Charles Bridge). The view from the foot of the bridge on the Old Town side is nothing short of breathtaking, encompassing the towers and domes of Malá Strana and the soaring spires of St. Vitus Cathedral to the northwest. This heavenly vision, one of the most beautiful in Europe, changes subtly in perspective as you walk across the bridge, attended by the host of baroque saints that decorate the bridge's peaceful Gothic stones. At night its drama is spellbinding: St. Vitus Cathedral lit in a ghostly green, the castle in monumental yellow, and the Church of St. Nicholas in a voluptuous pink, all viewed through the menacing silhouettes of the bowed statues and the Gothic towers. If you do nothing else in Prague, you must visit the Charles Bridge at night. During the day the pedestrian bridge buzzes with activity. Street musicians vie with artisans hawking jewelry, paintings, and glass for the hearts and wallets of the passing multitude. At night the crowds thin out a little, the musicians multiply, and the bridge becomes a long block party—nearly everyone brings a bottle.

When the Přemyslide princes set up residence in Prague in the 10th century, there was a ford across the Vltava at this point, a vital link along one of Europe's major trading routes. After several wooden bridges and the first stone bridge had washed away in floods, Charles IV appointed the 27-year-old German Peter Parler, the architect of St. Vitus Cathedral, to build a new structure in 1357. After 1620, following the defeat of Czech Protestants by Catholic Hapsburgs at the Battle of White Mountain, the bridge and its adornment became caught up in the Catholic-Hussite (Protestant) conflict. The many baroque statues that began to appear in the late 17th century, commissioned by Catholics, eventually came to symbolize the totality of the Austrian (hence Catholic) triumph. The Czech writer Milan Kundera sees the statues from this perspective: "The thousands of saints looking out from all sides, threatening you, following you, hypnotizing you, are the raging hordes of occupiers who invaded Bohemia three hundred and fifty years ago to tear the people's faith and language from their hearts."

The religious conflict is less obvious nowadays, leaving only the artistic tension between baroque and Gothic that gives the bridge its allure. It's worth pausing to take a closer look at some of the statues as you walk toward Malá Strana. The third on the right, a brass crucifix with Hebrew lettering in gold, was mounted on the location of a wooden cross destroyed in the battle with the Swedes (the golden lettering was reputedly financed by a Jew accused of defiling the cross). The eighth statue on the right, St. John of Nepomuk, is the oldest of all; it was designed by Johann Brokoff in 1683. On the left-hand side, sticking out from the bridge between the 9th and 10th statues (the latter has a wonderfully expressive vanquished Satan), stands a Roland statue. This knightly figure, bearing the coat of arms of the Old Town, was once a reminder that this part of the bridge belonged to the Old Town before Prague became a unified city in 1784.

In the eyes of most art historians, the most valuable statue is the 12th, on the left. Mathias Braun's statue of St. Luitgarde depicts the blind saint kissing Christ's wounds. The most compelling grouping, however, is the second from the end on the left, a work of Ferdinand Maximilien Brokov from 1714. Here the saints are incidental; the main attraction is the Turk, his face expressing extreme boredom while guarding Christians imprisoned in the cage at his side. When the statue was erected, just 29 years after the second Turkish invasion of Vienna, it scandalized the Prague public, who smeared the statue with mud.

Kostel Panny Marie vítězné (Church of Our Lady Victorious). Just down the street from the ☞ **Vrtbovský palác,** this comfortably ramshackle church makes the unlikely home of one of Prague's best-known religious artifacts, the *Pražské Jezulátko* (Infant Jesus of Prague). Originally brought to Prague from Spain in the 16th century, this tiny porcelain doll (now bathed in neon lighting straight out of Las Vegas) is renowned worldwide for showering miracles on anyone willing to kneel before it and pray. Nuns from a nearby convent arrive at dawn each day to change the infant's clothes; pieces of the doll's extensive wardrobe have been sent by believers from around the world. ⊠ *Karmelitská 9a.* 🎟 *Free.*

㉝ Lennon Peace Wall. Amid the pompous display of baroque finery stands a peculiar monument to the passive rebellion of Czech youth against the strictures of the former Communist regime. Under the Communists, Western rock music was officially discouraged, and students adopted the former Beatle as a symbol of resistance. Paintings of John Lennon and lyrics from his songs in Czech and English began to appear on the wall sometime in the 1980s. Even today, long after the Communists have departed, new graffiti still turns up regularly. It's not clear how long the police or the owners of the wall will continue to tolerate the massive amount of writing (which has started to spread to other walls around the neighborhood), but the volume of writing suggests that the Lennon myth continues to endure.

Malá Strana (Lesser Quarter). One of Prague's most exquisite neighborhoods, Malá Strana was established in 1257 and for years was home to the merchants and craftsmen who served the royal court.

㉔ Malá Strana bridge towers. The lower, Romanesque tower formed a part of the earlier wooden and stone bridges, and its present appearance stems from a renovation in 1591. The Gothic tower, **Mostecká věž,** was added to the bridge a few decades after its completion. ⊠ *Mostecká ul.* 🎟 *20 Kč.* ⊗ *Apr.–Oct., daily 9–6.*

㉕ Malostranské náměstí (Lesser Quarter Square). The arcaded houses on the left, dating from the 16th and 17th centuries, exhibit a mix of baroque and Renaissance elements.

㉛ Maltézské náměstí (Maltese Square). Peaceful and grandiose, this square was named for the Knights of Malta. In the middle is a sculpture depicting John the Baptist. This work, by Ferdinand Brokov, was erected in 1715 to commemorate the end of a plague. The relief on the far side shows Salome engrossed in her dance of the seven veils while John is being decapitated. There are two intricately decorated palaces on this square: to the right the rococo Turba Palace, now the Japanese Embassy, and at the bottom the Nostitz Palace, the Dutch Embassy.

27 **Nerudova ulice.** This steep little street used to be the last leg of the Royal Way, walked by the king before his coronation, and it is still the best way to get to Prague Castle. It was named for the 19th-century Czech journalist and poet Jan Neruda (after whom Chilean poet Pablo Neruda renamed himself). Until Joseph II's administrative reforms in the late 18th century, house numbering was unknown in Prague. Each house bore a name, depicted on the facade, and these are particularly prominent on Nerudova ulice. House No. 6, U červeného orla (At the Red Eagle), proudly displays a faded painting of a red eagle. Number 12 is known as U tří housliček (At the Three Violins). In the early 18th century, three generations of the Edlinger violin-making family lived here. Joseph II's scheme numbered each house according to its position in Prague's separate "towns" (here Malá Strana) rather than according to its sequence on the street. The red plates record these original house numbers; the blue ones are the numbers used in addresses today—except, oddly enough, in some of the newer suburbs—while, to confuse the tourist, many architectural guides refer to the old red number plates.

NEED A BREAK?

Nerudova ulice is filled with little restaurants and snack bars and offers something for everyone. **U zeleného čaje,** at No. 19, is a fragrant little tearoom, offering fruit and herbal teas as well as light salads and sweets. **U Kocoura** at No. 2 is a traditional pub that hasn't caved in to touristic niceties.

Two palaces break the unity of the burghers' houses on Nerudova ulice. Both were designed by the adventurous baroque architect Giovanni Santini, one of the Italian builders most in demand by wealthy nobles of the early 18th century. The **Morzin Palace,** on the left at No. 5, is now the Romanian Embassy. The fascinating facade, with an allegory of night and day, was created in 1713 and is the work of F. M. Brokov of Charles Bridge statue fame. Across the street at No. 20 is the **Thun-Hohenstein Palace,** now the Italian Embassy. The gateway with two enormous eagles (the emblem of the Kolovrat family, who owned the building at the time) is the work of the other great Charles Bridge statue sculptor, Mathias Braun. Santini himself lived at No. 14, the so-called **Valkoun House.**

Old Town Bridge Tower. This was where Peter Parler (the architect of St. Vitus Cathedral) began his bridge building. The carved facades he designed for the sides of the bridge were destroyed by Swedish soldiers in 1648, at the end of the Thirty Years' War. The sculptures facing the square, however, are still intact; they depict an old and gout-ridden Charles IV with his son, who later became Wenceslas IV. 🎫 *20 Kč.* ⊘ *Daily 9–7.*

29 **Schönbornský palác** (Schönborn Palace). Franz Kafka had an apartment in this massive baroque building at the top of **Tržiště ulice** from March through August 1917, after moving out from Zlatá ulička (Golden Lane) (☞ Prague Castle, *below*). The U.S. Embassy now occupies this prime location. If you look through the gates, you can see the beautiful formal gardens rising up to the Petřín hill; they are unfortunately not open to the public. ✉ *Tržiště at Vlašská.*

U tří pštrosů (the Three Ostriches). The original building stems from the 16th century, when one of the early owners was a supplier of ostrich feathers to the royal court and had the house's three unmistakable emblems painted on the facade. The top floors and curlicue gables were early baroque additions from the 17th century. The ancient inn functions as a hotel to this day. It was the site of the first coffeehouse in Prague, opened by the Armenian Deodat Damajian in 1714. ⊠ *Dražického nám. 12.*

NEED A
BREAK?
At the corner of Na Kampě, right next to the arches of the Charles Bridge, the small stand-up café **Bistro Bruncvík** serves hot wine and coffee in winter and cold drinks in summer. Its slices of pizza are also satisfying.

㉜ Velkopřevorské náměstí (Grand Priory Square). The palace fronting the square is considered one of the finest baroque buildings in the Malá Strana, though it is now part of the Embassy of the Knights of Malta and no longer open to the public. Opposite is the flamboyant orange-and-white stucco facade of the Buquoy Palace, built in 1719 by Giovanni Santini and the present home of the French Embassy. From the street you can glimpse an enormous twinkling chandelier through the window, but this is about all you'll get to see of the elegant interior.

㉟ Vojanovy sady. Once the gardens of the Monastery of the Discalced Carmelites, later taken over by the Order of the English Virgins and now part of the Ministry of Finance, this walled garden, with its weeping willows, fruit trees, and benches, makes another peaceful haven in summer. Exhibitions of modern sculptures are often held here, contrasting sharply with the two baroque chapels and the graceful Ignaz Platzer statue of John of Nepomuk standing on a fish at the entrance. The park is surrounded by the high walls of the old monastery and new Ministry of Finance buildings, with only an occasional glimpse of a tower or spire to remind you that you're in Prague. ⊠ *U lužického semináře, between Letenská and Míšeňská Sts.* ⊙ *Daily 8–5 (until 7 in summer).*

㉚ Vrtbovský palác (Vrtba Palace and Gardens). An unobtrusive door on noisy Karmelitská hides the entranceway to an intimate courtyard. Walk between the two Renaissance houses, the one to the left built in 1575, the one to the right in 1591. The owner of the latter house was one of the 27 Bohemian nobles executed by the Hapsburgs in 1621 before the Old Town Hall. The house was given as confiscated property to Count Sezima of Vrtba, who bought the neighboring property and turned the buildings into a late-Renaissance palace. The Vrtbovská zahrada (Vrtba Gardens), created a century later, boasts one of the best views over the Malá Strana rooftops and is a fascinating oasis from the tourist beat. Unfortunately, the gardens are perpetually closed for renovation, even though there is no sign of work in progress. The powerful stone figure of Atlas that caps the entranceway dates from 1720 and is the work of Mathias Braun. ⊠ *Karmelitská ul. 25.*

OFF THE
BEATEN PATH
VILLA BERTRAMKA – Mozart fans won't want to pass up a visit to this villa, where the great composer lived while in Prague. The small, well-organized museum is packed with memorabilia, including the program from that exciting night in 1787 when *Don Giovanni* had its world premiere in Prague. Also on hand is one of the master's pianos. Take Tram No. 12 from Karmelitská south to the Anděl metro station (or ride Metro Line B), walk down Plzeňská ulice a few hundred yards, and take a left at Mozartova ulice. ⊠ *Mozartova ul. 169, Smíchov,* ⊙ *02/543893.* 🎟 *60Kč.* ⊙ *Daily 10–5.*

★ **㊱ Zahrada Valdštejnského paláce** (Wallenstein Palace Gardens). Albrecht von Wallenstein, onetime owner of the house and gardens, began a meteoric military career in 1624 when the Austrian emperor Ferdinand II retained him to save the empire from the Swedes and Protestants during the Thirty Years' War. Wallenstein, wealthy by marriage, offered to raise 20,000 men at his own cost and lead them personally. Ferdinand II accepted and showered Wallenstein with confiscated land and titles. Wallenstein's first acquisition was this enormous area. Having knocked down 23 houses, a brick factory, and three gardens, in 1623 he began to build his magnificent palace with its idiosyncratic high-walled gardens and superb Renaissance *sala terrena*. Walking around the formal paths, you'll come across numerous statues, an unusual fountain with a woman spouting water from her breasts, and a lava-stone grotto along the wall. Most of the palace itself is earmarked to serve the Czech Senate. The only part open to the public, the cavernous *Jízdárna,* or riding school (not to be confused with the Prague Castle Riding School), hosts occasional art exhibitions. ⊠ *Garden entrance at Letenská 10.* ✆ *Free.* ☉ *May–Sept., daily 9–7.*

The Castle District

To the west of Prague Castle is the residential **Hradčany** (Castle District), the town that during the early 14th century emerged out of a collection of monasteries and churches. The concentration of history packed into one small area makes Prague Castle and the Castle District challenging objects for visitors not versed in the ups and downs of Bohemian kings, religious uprisings, wars, and oppression. The picturesque area surrounding Prague Castle, with its breathtaking vistas of the Old Town and Malá Strana, is ideal for just wandering; but the castle itself, with its convoluted history and architecture, is difficult to appreciate fully without investing a little more time.

A GOOD WALK

Begin on **Nerudova ulice** ㉗, which runs east–west a few hundred yards south of Prague Castle. At the western foot of the street, look for a flight of stone steps guarded by two saintly statues. The stairs lead up to Loretánská ulice, affording panoramic views of St. Nicholas Church and Malá Strana. At the top of the steps, turn left and walk a couple hundred yards until you come to a dusty elongated square named **Pohořelec** ㉟. Go through the inconspicuous gateway at No. 8 and up the steps, and you'll find yourself in the courtyard of one of the city's richest monasteries, the **Strahovský klášter** ㊳.

Retrace your steps to Loretánské náměstí, which is flanked by the feminine curves of the baroque **Loreto Church** ㊴. Across the road, the 29 half pillars of the **Černínský palác** now mask the Czech Ministry of Foreign Affairs. At the bottom of Loretánské náměstí, a little lane trails to the left into the area known as **Nový Svět**; the name means "new world," though the district is as Old World as they come. Turn right onto the street Nový Svět. Around the corner you get a tantalizing view of the cathedral through the trees. Walk past the Austrian Embassy to Kanovnická ulice, a winding street lined with the dignified but melancholy **Kostel svatého Jana Nepomuckého.** At the top of the street on the left, the rounded, Renaissance corner house **Martinický palác** (Martinic Palace) catches the eye with its detailed sgraffito drawings. Martinic Palace opens onto **Hradčanské náměstí** ㊵ with its grandiose gathering of Renaissance and baroque palaces. To the left of the bright yellow Archbishop's Palace on the square is an alleyway leading down to the **Národní galérie** ㊶ and its collections of European art. Across the square, the handsome sgraffito sweep of **Schwarzenberský palác** (Schwarzenberg Palace) ㊷ beckons; this is the building you saw from the back side at the beginning of the tour.

TIMING

Brisk-paced sightseers could zip through Hradčany in an hour, but to do it justice, allow at least an hour just for ambling and admiring the passing buildings and views of the city. The Strahov Monastery's halls need about a half hour to take in, and the Loreto Church and its treasures at least that length of time. The National Gallery in the Šternberský palá deserves at least a couple of hours.

SIGHTS TO SEE

Černínský palác (Chernin Palace). While the Loreto Church represents the softer side of the Counter-Reformation, this ungainly, overbearing structure seems to stand for the harsh political fate that met the Czechs after their defeat at the battle of Bílá Hora in 1620. During World War II it was the seat of the occupying German government.

㊵ Hradčanské náměstí (Hradčany Square). With its fabulous mixture of baroque and Renaissance housing, topped by the castle itself, the square featured prominently (ironically, disguised as Vienna) in the film *Amadeus,* directed by the then-exiled Czech director Miloš Forman. The house at No. 7 was the set for Mozart's residence, where the composer was haunted by the masked figure he thought was his father. Forman used the flamboyant rococo **Arcibiskupský palác** (Archbishop's Palace), at the top of the square on the left, as the Viennese archbishop's palace. The plush interior, shown off in the film, is open to the public only on Maundy Thursday.

㊴ Loreto Church. The church's seductive lines were a conscious move on the part of Counter-Reformation Jesuits in the 17th century who wanted to build up the cult of Mary and attract the largely Protestant Bohemians back to the church. According to legend, angels had carried Mary's house in Nazareth and dropped it in a patch of laurel trees in Ancona, Italy; known as *Loreto* (from the Latin for laurel), it immediately became a center of pilgrimage. The Prague Loreto was one of many re-creations of this scene across Europe, and it worked: Pilgrims came in droves. The graceful facade, with its voluptuous tower, was built in 1720 by Kilian Ignaz Dientzenhofer, the architect of the two St. Nicholas churches in Prague. Most spectacular of all is a small exhibition upstairs displaying the religious treasures presented to Mary in thanks for various services, including a monstrance studded with 6,500 diamonds. ⊠ *Loretánské nám. 7,* ☎ *02/2451–0789.* ▣ *30 Kč.* ☉ *Tues.–Sun. 9–12:15 and 1–4:30.*

★ ㊶ Národní galérie (National Gallery); housed in the 18th-century Šternberský palác (Sternberg Palace). You'll need at least an hour to view the palace's impressive art collection—one collection in Prague you should not miss. On the first floor there's an exhibition of icons and other religious art from the 3rd through the 14th centuries. Up a second flight of steps is an entire room full of Cranachs and an assortment of paintings by Holbein, Dürer, Brueghel, Van Dyck, Canaletto, and Rubens. Other branches of the National Gallery are scattered around town, notably, the modern art collections in the Veletržní palác (☞ Letná and Holešovice, *below*). ⊠ *Hradčanské nám. 15,* ☎ *02/2451–0594.* ▣ *50 Kč.* ☉ *Tues.–Sun. 10–6.*

Nový Svět. This picturesque, winding little alley, with facades from the 17th and 18th centuries, once housed Prague's poorest residents; now many of the homes are used as artists' studios. The last house on the street, No. 1, was the home of the Danish-born astronomer Tycho Brahe. Living so close to the Loreto, so the story goes, Tycho was constantly disturbed during his nightly stargazing by the church bells. He ended up complaining to his patron, Emperor Rudolf II, who instructed the Capuchin monks to finish their services before the first star appeared in the sky.

③ **Pohořelec** (Scene of Fire) suffered tragic fires in 1420, 1541, and 1741. The 1541 calamity sparked into life on Malostranské náměstí and spread up the hill, ravaging much of Malá Strana and the castle as it raged. Many Gothic houses burned down, opening up large plots for the Renaissance and especially the Baroque houses and palaces that dominate the quarter's architectural face.

㊷ **Schwarzenberský palác** (Schwarzenberg Palace). This boxy palace with its extravagant sgraffito facade was built for the Lobkowicz family between 1545 and 1563; today it houses the **Vojenské historické muzeum** (Military History Museum), one of the largest of its kind in Europe. Of more general interest are the jousting tournaments held in the courtyard in summer. ⊠ *Hradčanské nám. 2.* 🖼 *20 Kč.* ☉ *Apr.–Oct., Tues.–Sun. 10–6.*

★ **㊳** **Strahovský klášter** (Strahov Monastery). Founded by the Premonstratensian order in 1140, the monastery remained in their hands until 1952, when the Communists abolished all religious orders and turned the entire complex into the **Památník národního písemnictví** (Museum of National Literature). The major building of interest is the **Strahov Library,** with its collection of early Czech manuscripts, the 10th-century Strahov New Testament, and the collected works of famed Danish astronomer Tycho Brahe. Also of note is the late-18th-century **Philosophical Hall.** Engulfing its ceilings is a startling sky-blue fresco completed by the Austrian painter Franz Anton Maulbertsch in just six months. The fresco depicts an unusual cast of characters, including Socrates' nagging wife Xanthippe, Greek astronomer Thales with his trusty telescope, and a collection of Greek philosophers mingling with Descartes, Diderot, and Voltaire. ⊠ *Strahovské nádvoří 1/132.* 🖼 *20 Kč.* ☉ *Daily 9–noon and 1–5.*

OFF THE
BEATEN PATH

PETŘÍN – For a superb view of the city—from a mostly undiscovered, tourist-free perch—stroll over from the Strahov Monastery along the paths toward Prague's own miniature version of the Eiffel Tower. The tower and its breathtaking view, the hall of mirrors, and the seemingly abandoned church are beautifully peaceful and well worth an afternoon's wandering. You can also walk up from Karmelitská ulice or Újezd down in Malá Strana or ride the funicular railway from U lanové dráhy ulice, off Újezd. Regular public-transportation tickets are valid. For the descent, take the funicular or meander on foot down through the stations of the cross on the pathways leading back to Malá Strana.

Prague Castle

A GOOD WALK

Numbers in the text correspond to numbers in the margin and on the Prague Castle (Pražský hrad) map.

Despite its monolithic presence, Pražský hrad (Prague Castle) is a collection of buildings dating from the 10th to the 20th centuries, all linked by internal courtyards. The most important structures are **Chrám svatého Víta** (St. Vitus Cathedral) ㊾, clearly visible soaring above the castle walls, and the **Královský palác** (Royal Palace) ㊿, the official residence of kings and presidents and still the center of political power in the Czech Republic. The castle is compact and easy to navigate in. Visitors can easily design a walking tour to fit their interests and the time they have for sightseeing. Be forewarned: In summer, St. Vitus Cathedral and Golden Lane take the brunt of the heavy sightseeing traffic, while all of the castle is hugely popular.

The castle is at its mysterious best in early morning and late evening, and it is incomparable when it snows. You can charge through the castle in 10 minutes, but that would be criminal. The cathedral deserves an hour, as does the Royal Palace, while you can easily spend an entire day taking in the many other museums and their architectural details, the views of the city, and the hidden nooks of the castle.

54 Bazilika svatého Jiří (St. George's Basilica). This church was originally built in the 10th century by Prince Vratislav I, the father of Prince (and St.) Wenceslas. It was dedicated to St. George (of dragon fame), who it was believed would be more agreeable to the still largely pagan people. The outside was remodeled during early baroque times, although the striking rusty-red color is in keeping with the look of the Romanesque edifice. The interior, following substantial renovation, looks more or less as it did in the 12th century and is the best-preserved Romanesque relic in the country. The effect is at once barnlike and peaceful, the warm golden yellow of the stone walls and the small triplet arched windows exuding a sense of enduring harmony. The house-shaped, painted tomb at the front of the church holds the remains of the founder, Vratislav I. Up the steps, in a chapel to the right, is the tomb Parler designed for St. Ludmila, the grandmother of St. Wenceslas. ⊠ *Náměstí U sv. Jiří.*

49 Castle Information Office. Empress Maria Theresa's court architect, Nicolò Pacassi, received the imperial approval to remake the castle in the 1760s. The castle took heavy damage from Prussian shelling during the War of the Austrian Succession in 1757. The **Druhé nádvoří** (Second Courtyard) was the main victim of his attempts at imparting classical grandeur to what had been a picturesque collection of Gothic and Renaissance styles. Except for the view of the spires of St. Vitus Cathedral towering above the palace, there's little for the eye to feast upon here. The main reason to come is to visit the main castle information office for entrance tickets, headphones for listening to recorded tours, tickets to cultural events, and changing money. ⊠ *Druhé nádvoří.* 🎫 *Tickets (80 Kč, valid for 3 consecutive days) give admission to older parts of St. Vitus Cathedral, Royal Palace, St. George's Basilica, and Mihulka Tower.* ☉ *These sites open Nov.–Mar., daily 9–5; Apr.–Oct., daily 9–4. Castle gardens Apr.–Oct., Tues.–Sun. 10–6 (free admission).*

The Second Courtyard also houses the reliquary of Charles IV inside the **Kaple svatého Kříže** (Chapel of the Holy Cross). Displays include Gothic silver busts of the major Bohemian patron saints and bones and vestments that supposedly belonged to various saints.

Built in the late-16th and early 17th centuries, the Second Courtyard was part of a reconstruction program commissioned by Rudolf II, under whom Prague enjoyed a period of unparalleled cultural development. Once the Prague court was established, the emperor gathered around him some of the world's best craftsmen, artists, and scientists, including the brilliant astronomers Johannes Kepler and Tycho Brahe.

Rudolf also amassed a large collection of art, surveying instruments, and coins. The bulk of the collection was looted by the Swedes and Hapsburgs during the Thirty Years' War or auctioned off during the 18th century, but a small part of the collection was rediscovered in unused castle rooms in the 1960s. It used to be displayed, and will be again when slow-moving repairs are completed, in the **Obrazárna** (Picture Gallery), on the left side of the Second Courtyard. The passageway at the gallery entrance forms the northern entrance to the castle and leads out over a luxurious ravine known as the **Jelení příkop** (Stag Moat).

Prague Castle (Pražský hrad)

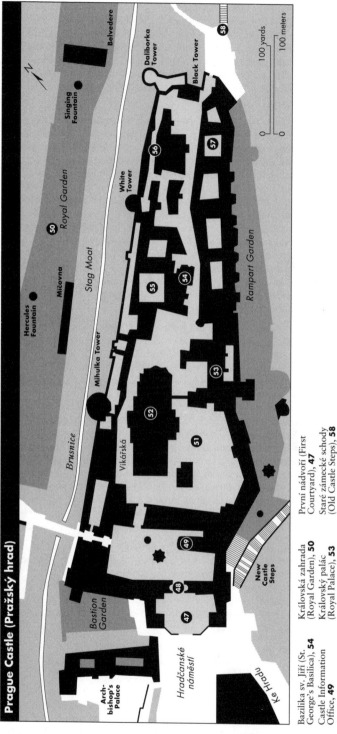

Bazilika sv. Jiří (St.
George's Basilica), **54**

Castle Information
Office, **49**

Chrám sv. Víta (St.
Vitus Cathedral), **52**

Klášter sv. Jiří (St.
George's Convent), **55**

Královská zahrada
(Royal Garden), **50**

Královský palác
(Royal Palace), **53**

Lobkovický palác,
(Lobkowicz Palace) **57**

Matyášova brána
(Matthias Gate), **48**

První nádvoří (First
Courtyard), **47**

Staré zámecké schody
(Old Castle Steps), **58**

Třetí Nádvoří (Third
Courtyard), **51**

Zlatá ulička (Golden
Lane), **56**

★ ⑤ **Chrám svatého Víta** (St. Vitus Cathedral). With its graceful, soaring towers, this Gothic cathedral—among the most beautiful in Europe—is the spiritual heart of Prague Castle, the city itself, and all of the Czech Republic. It has a long and complicated history, beginning in the 10th century and continuing to its completion in 1929. If you want to hear its history in depth, English-speaking guided tours of the cathedral and the Royal Palace (☞ *below*) can be arranged at the information office in the castle's Second Courtyard.

Once you enter the cathedral, pause to take in the vast but delicate beauty of the Gothic and neo-Gothic interior glowing in the colorful light that filters through the startlingly brilliant stained-glass windows. This back half, including the western facade and the two towers you can see from outside, was not completed until 1929, following the initiative of the Union for the Completion of the Cathedral set up in the last days of the 19th century. Don't let the neo-Gothic delusion keep you from examining this new section. The six stained-glass windows to your left and right and the large rose window behind are modern masterpieces. Take a good look at the third window up on the left. The familiar art-nouveau flamboyance, depicting the blessing of the 9th-century St. Cyril and St. Methodius (missionaries to the Slavs and creators of the Cyrillic alphabet), is the work of the Czech father of the style, Alfons Mucha. He achieved the subtle coloring by painting rather than staining the glass.

If you walk halfway up the right-hand aisle (and you've bought a Prague Castle sightseeing ticket, which permits you to enter the older parts of the cathedral (☞ Castle Information Office, *above*), you will find the exquisitely ornate **Chapel of St. Válav (Wenceslas)**. With a 14th-century tomb holding the saint's remains, this square chapel is the ancient heart of the cathedral. Wenceslas (the "good king" of Christmas-carol fame) was a determined Christian in an era of widespread paganism. In 925, as prince of Bohemia, he founded a rotunda church dedicated to St. Vitus on this site. But the prince's brother, Boleslav, was impatient to take power and ambushed Wenceslas four years later near a church at Stará Boleslav, northeast of Prague. Wenceslas was originally buried in that church, but his grave produced so many miracles that he rapidly became a symbol of piety for the common people, something that greatly irritated the new Prince Boleslav. In 931 Boleslav was finally forced to honor his brother by reburying the body in the St. Vitus Rotunda. Shortly afterward, Wenceslas was canonized.

The rotunda was replaced by a Romanesque basilica in the late 11th century. Work was begun on the existing building in 1344, on the initiative of the man who was later to become Charles IV. For the first few years the chief architect was the Frenchman Mathias d'Arras, but after his death in 1352, the work was continued by the 22-year-old German architect Peter Parler, who went on to build the Charles Bridge and many other Prague treasures.

The small door in the back of the chapel leads to the **Crown Chamber,** the repository of the Bohemian crown jewels. It remains locked with seven keys held by seven different people and is definitely not open to the public.

A little beyond the Wenceslas Chapel on the same side, stairs lead down to the underground **royal crypt,** interesting primarily for the information it provides about the cathedral's history. As you descend the stairs, on the right you'll see parts of the old Romanesque basilica. A little farther, in a niche to the left, are portions of the foundations of the rotunda. Moving around into the second room, you'll find a rather eclectic group of royal remains ensconced in new sarcophagi dating from the 1930s. In the center is Charles IV, who died in 1378. Rudolf II, patron of Renaissance Prague, is entombed at the rear in the original tin coffin. To his right is Maria Amalia, the only child of Maria Theresa to reside in Prague. Ascending the wooden steps back into the cathedral, you'll come to the white-marble **Royal Mausoleum**, atop which lie stone statues of the first two Hapsburg kings to rule in Bohemia, Ferdinand I and Maximilian II.

The cathedral's **Royal Oratory** was used by the kings and their families when attending mass. Built in 1493, the work is a perfect example of late Gothic, laced on the outside with a stone network of gnarled branches very similar in pattern to the ceiling vaulting in the Royal Palace (☞ *below*). The oratory is connected to the palace by an elevated covered walkway, which you can see from outside.

From here you can't fail to catch sight of the ornate silver **sarcophagus of St. John of Nepomuk**, designed by the famous Viennese architect Fischer von Erlach. According to legend, when Nepomuk's body was exhumed in 1721 to be reinterred, the tongue was found to be still intact and pumping with blood. These strange tales sadly served a highly political purpose. The Catholic Church and the Hapsburgs were seeking a new folk hero to replace the protestant Jan Hus, whom they despised. The late Father Nepomuk was sainted and reburied a few years later with great ceremony in the 3,700-pound silver tomb, replete with angels and cherubim; the tongue was enshrined in its own reliquary.

The eight chapels around the back of the cathedral are the work of the original architect, Mathias d'Arras. A number of old tombstones, including some badly worn grave markers of medieval royalty, can be seen within, amid furnishings from later periods. Opposite the wooden relief, depicting the looting of the cathedral by Protestants in 1619, is the **Wallenstein Chapel**. Since the last century, it has housed the Gothic tombstones of its two architects, Mathias d'Arras and Peter Parler, who died in 1352 and 1399, respectively. If you look up to the balcony, you can just make out the busts of these two men, designed by Parler's workshop. The other busts around the triforium depict various Czech kings.

The Hussite wars in the 15th century put an end to the first phase of the cathedral's construction. During the short era of illusory peace before the Thirty Years' War, lack of money laid to rest any idea of finishing the building, and the cathedral was closed by a wall built across from the Wenceslas Chapel. Not until the 20th century was the western side of the cathedral, with its two towers, completed according to Parler's original plans. ⊠ *St. Vitus Cathedral.* ☜ *Free admission to the western part. Chapels, crypt, and tower accessible with castle-wide ticket.* ⊙ *May–Sept., daily 9–5; Oct.–Apr., daily 9–4.*

⑤ **Klášter svatého Jiří** (St. George's Convent). The first convent in Bohemia, founded in 973 next to the even older St. George's Basilica, now houses the Old Bohemian Collection of the **Czech National Gallery**. The museum runs through the history of Czech art from the early Middle Ages, with exhibits that include religious statues, icons, and triptychs, to the rather more secular themes of the Mannerist school and the voluptuous work of the court painters of Rudolf II. ⊠ *Nám. U sv. Jiří,* ☎ *02/2451–0695.* ☜ *50 Kč.* ⊙ *Tues.–Sun. 10–6.*

⑤ **Královská zahrada** (Royal Garden). This peaceful swath of greenery affords an unusually lovely view of St. Vitus Cathedral and the castle's walls and bastions. Originally laid out in the 16th century, it endured devastation in war, neglect in times of peace, and many redesigns, reaching its present parklike form early this century. Luckily, its Renaissance treasures survive. The garden front of the **Míčovna** (Ball Game Hall), built by Bonifaz Wohlmut in 1568, is completely covered by a dense tangle of allegorical sgraffiti; it was restored in the 1970s after fading to near invisibility.

The **Královský letohrádek** (Royal Summer Palace, also known as the Belvedere), at the garden's eastern end, deserves its usual description as "one of the most beautiful Renaissance structures north of the Alps." Italian architects began it; Wohlmut finished it off in the 1560s with a copper roof like an upturned boat's keel riding above the graceful arcades of the ground floor. In the 18th and 19th centuries, military engineers tested artillery in the interior, which had already lost its rich furnishings to Swedish soldiers during their siege of the city in 1648. The Renaissance-style *giardinetto* (little garden) adjoining the summer palace centers around another masterwork, the Italian-designed, Czech-cast *Singing Fountain*, which resonates to the sound of falling water. ⊠ *Garden entrances from U Prašného mostu ul. and Mariánské hradby ul. near Chotkovy Sady Park.* 🖼 *Free.* ☉ *Apr.–Oct., Tues.–Sun. 10–5:45.*

❸ Královský palác (Royal Palace). There are two main points of interest inside the externally nondescript palace. The first is the **Vladislavský sál** (Vladislav Hall), the largest secular Gothic interior space in Central Europe. The enormous hall was completed in 1493 by Benedict Ried, who was to late-Bohemian Gothic what Peter Parler was to the earlier version. The room imparts a sense of space and light, softened by the sensuous lines of the vaulted ceilings and brought to a dignified close by the simple oblong form of the early Renaissance windows, a style that was just beginning to make inroads in Central Europe. In its heyday, the hall was the site of jousting tournaments, festive markets, banquets, and coronations. In more recent times, it has been used to inaugurate presidents, from the Communist Klement Gottwald in 1948 to Václav Havel in 1990.

From the front of the hall, turn right into the rooms of the **Česká kancelář** (Bohemian Chancellery). This wing was built by the same Benedict Ried only 10 years after the hall was completed, but it shows a much stronger Renaissance influence. Pass through the Renaissance portal into the last chamber of the chancellery. This room was the site of the second defenestration of Prague, in 1618, an event that marked the beginning of the Bohemian rebellion and, ultimately, of the Thirty Years' War. This peculiarly Bohemian method of expressing protest (throwing someone out a window) had first been used in 1419 in the New Town Hall, an event that led to the Hussite wars. Two hundred years later the same conflict was reexpressed in terms of Hapsburg-backed Catholics versus Bohemian Protestants. Rudolf II had reached an uneasy agreement with the Bohemian nobles, allowing them religious freedom in exchange for financial support. But his successor, Ferdinand II, was a rabid opponent of Protestantism and disregarded Rudolf's tolerant "Letter of Majesty." Enraged, the Protestant nobles stormed the castle and chancellery and threw two Catholic officials and their secretary, for good measure, out the window. Legend has it they landed on a mound of horse dung and escaped unharmed, an event the Jesuits interpreted as a miracle. The square window in question is on the left as you enter the room.

At the back of the Vladislav Hall, a staircase leads up to a gallery of the **All Saints' Chapel.** Little remains of Peter Parler's original work, but the church contains some fine works of art. The large room to the left of the staircase is the **Stará sněmovna** (council chamber), where the Bohemian nobles met with the king in a kind of prototype parliament. Portraits of the Hapsburg rulers line the walls. The descent from Vladislav Hall toward what remains of the **Romanesque palace** is by way of a wide, shallow set of steps. This **Riders' Staircase** was the entranceway for knights who came for the jousting tournaments. ⊠ *Royal Palace, Třetí nádvoří.*

57 **Lobkovický palác** (Lobkowicz Palace). From the beginning of the 17th century until the 1940s, this building was the residence of the powerful Catholic Lobkowicz family. It was to this house that the two defenestrated officials escaped after landing on the dung hill in 1618. During the 1970s the building was restored to its early baroque appearance and now houses the permanent exhibition "Monuments of the Czech National Past." If you want to get a chronological understanding of Czech history from the beginnings of the Great Moravian Empire in the 9th century to the Czech national uprising in 1848, this is the place. Copies of the crown jewels are on display here; but it is the rich collection of illuminated Bibles, old musical instruments, coins, weapons, royal decrees, paintings, and statues that makes the museum well worth visiting. Detailed information on the exhibits is available in English. ⊠ *Jiřská ul.* 🖼 *30 Kč.* ☉ *Tues.–Sun. 9–5.*

48 **Matyášova brána** (Matthias Gate). Built in 1614, the stone gate once stood alone in front of the moats and bridges that surrounded the castle. Under the Hapsburgs, the gate survived by being grafted as a relief onto the palace building. As you go through it, notice the ceremonial white-marble entrance halls on either side, which lead up to President Václav Havel's reception rooms (only rarely open to the public).

47 **První nádvoří** (First Courtyard). The main entrance to Prague Castle from Hradčanské náměstí is a little disappointing. Going through the wrought-iron gate, guarded at ground level by pristine Czech soldiers and from above by the ferocious *Battling Titans* (a copy of Ignaz Platzer's original 18th-century statues), you'll enter this courtyard, built on the site of old moats and gates that once separated the castle from the surrounding buildings and thus protected the vulnerable western flank. The courtyard is one of the more recent additions to the castle, designed by Maria Theresa's court architect, Nicolò Pacassi, in the 1760s. Today it forms part of the presidential office complex. Pacassi's reconstruction was intended to unify the eclectic collection of buildings that made up the castle. From a distance, the effect is monumental. As you move farther into the castle, large parts appear to be relatively new, while in reality they cover splendid Gothic and Romanesque interiors.

58 **Staré zámecké schody** (Old Castle Steps). Unending lines of tourists pass by dozens of trinket sellers and, in recent years, more and more beggars as they troop up and down this long walled staircase. It starts from the castle's Black Tower and comes out just above the Malostranská metro station. There you can catch the subway or take a tram toward Malostranské náměstí.

51 **Třetí nádvoří** (Third Courtyard). The contrast between the cool, dark interior of the cathedral and the brightly colored Pacassi facades of the Third Courtyard just outside is startling. The courtyard's clean lines are the work of Slovenian architect Josip Plečnik in the 1930s, but the modern look is a deception. Plečnik's paving was intended to cover an underground world of wooden houses, streets, and walls dating from the 9th through the 12th centuries—rediscovered when the cathedral was completed. Since these are not open to the public, we are left with the modern structure (supplemented recently by an exchange office). Plečnik did add a few eclectic features to catch the eye: a granite obelisk to commemorate the fallen of the First World War, a black-marble pedestal for the Gothic statue of St. George (the original is in the museum at St. George's Convent), and the peculiar golden ball topping the eagle fountain near the eastern end of the courtyard.

56 **Zlatá ulička** (Golden Lane). An enchanting collection of tiny, ancient, brightly colored houses crouches under the fortification wall looking remarkably like a Disney set for *Snow White and the Seven Dwarfs*. Legend has it that these were the lodgings of the international group of alchemists whom Rudolf II brought to the court to produce gold. The truth is a little less romantic: The houses were built during the 16th century for the castle guards, who supplemented their income by practicing various crafts outside the jurisdiction of the powerful guilds. By the early 20th century, Golden Lane had become the home of poor artists and writers. Franz Kafka, who lived at No. 22 in 1916 and 1917, described the house on first sight as "so small, so dirty, impossible to live in and lacking everything necessary." But he soon came to love the place. As he wrote to his fiancée: "Life here is something special . . . to close out the world not just by shutting the door to a room or apartment but to the whole house, to step out into the snow of the silent lane." The lane now houses tiny stores selling books, music, and crafts.

Letná and Holešovice

From above the Vltava's left bank, the large grassy plateau called Letná affords one of the classic views of the Old Town and the many bridges crossing the river. Beer gardens, tennis, and Frisbee attract people of all ages, while amateur soccer players emulate the professionals of Prague's top team, Sparta, which plays in the stadium just across the road. Ten minutes' walk from Letná, down into the residential neighborhood of Holešovice, brings you to a massive, gray-blue pile of a building that might have been designed by a young postmodernist architect. In fact it dates to the 1920s, and the cool exterior gives no hint of the cavernous halls within or of the treasures of Czech and French modern art that line its corridors. Just north along Dukelských hrdinů Street, Stromovka—a royal hunting preserve turned gracious park—offers quiet strolls under huge old oaks and chestnuts.

Numbers in the margin correspond to numbers on the Prague map.

43 **Letenské sady** (Letna Gardens). Come to this large, shady park for an unforgettable view from on high of Prague's bridges. From the enormous cement pedestal at the center of the park, the largest statue of Stalin in Eastern Europe once beckoned to citizens on the Old Town Square far below. The statue was ripped down in the 1960s, when Stalinism was finally discredited. The walks and grass that stretch out behind the pedestal are perfect for relaxing on a warm afternoon. On sunny Sundays expatriates often meet up here to play ultimate Frisbee. ⊠ *Prague 7. To get to Letna, cross the Čechův Bridge, opposite the Hotel Inter-Continental, and climb the stairs.*

44 **Veletržní palác Museum of Modern Art.** The National Gallery's newest museum, housed in a trade-fair hall in the Holešovice neighborhood, set off a furor when it opened in 1995. The lighting, the exhibit design, the unused empty spaces in the building's two enormous halls, even the selection of paintings and sculpture—all came under critics' scrutiny. The negative voices couldn't deny, though, that the palace—itself a key work of constructivist architecture—serves a vital purpose in making permanently accessible hundreds of pieces of 20th-century Czech art. Much of the collections languished in storage for decades, either because some cultural commissar forbade its public display or for simple lack of exhibition space. The collection of 19th- and 20th-century French art, including an important group of early cubist paintings by Picasso and Braque, is also here, moved from the Šternberský Palace (☞ The Castle District, *above*). ⊠ *Veletržní at Dukelských hrdinů, Prague 7.* 🗔 *80 Kč.* ☉ *Tues.–Sun. 10–6.*

OFF THE
BEATEN PATH **ZOOLOGICKÁ ZAHRADA –** Prague's small but delightful zoo is north of the city in Troja, under the shadow of the Troja Castle. Take the metro Line C to Nádraží Holešovice and change to Bus 112. ⊠ *U trojského zámku 3, Prague 7,* ☎ *02/688-0480.* 🗔 *30 Kč.* ☉ *May–Sept., daily 9–6; Oct.–Apr., daily 9–4.*

Vinohrady

From Riegrovy sady and its sweeping view of the city from above the National Museum, the elegant residential neighborhood called Vinohrady extends its streets of eclectic apartment houses and villas eastward and southward. The pastel-tinted ranks of turn-of-the-century apartment houses—many crumbling after years of neglect—are slowly but unstoppably being transformed into upscale flats, slick offices, eternally packed new restaurants, and a range of shops unthinkable only a half decade ago. Much of the development lies on or near Vinohradská, the main street, which extends from the top of Wenceslas Square to a belt of enormous cemeteries about two miles eastward. Yet the flavor of daily life persists: Smoky old pubs still ply their trade on the quiet side streets; the stately theater, Divadlo na Vinohradech, keeps putting on excellent shows as it has for decades; and on the squares and in the parks nearly everyone still practices Prague's favorite form of outdoor exercise—walking the dog.

45 **Kostel Nejsvětějšího Srdce Páně** (Church of the Most Sacred Heart). If you've had your fill of Romanesque, Gothic, and baroque, take the metro to the Jiřího z Poděbrad station (Line A) for a look at a startling art-deco edifice. Designed in 1927 by Slovenian architect Josip Plečnik (the same architect commissioned to update Prague Castle), the church resembles a luxury ocean liner more than a place of worship. The effect was conscious; during the 1920s and '30s, the avant-garde imitated mammoth objects of modern technology. Plečnik used many modern elements on the inside: Notice the hanging speakers, seemingly designed to bring the word of God directly to the ears of each worshiper. You may be able to find someone at the back entrance of the church who will let you walk up the long ramp into the fascinating glass clock tower. ⊠ *Nám. Jiřího z Poděbrad, Prague 3.*

46 **Židovské hřbitovy** (New Jewish Cemetery). Tens of thousands of Czechs find eternal rest in Vinohrady's cemeteries. The modest **tombstone of Franz Kafka** in the newest of the city's half-dozen Jewish cemeteries, situated where Vinohrady's elegance peters out into more mundane districts, seems grossly inadequate to Kafka's stature but oddly in proportion to his own modest ambitions. The cemetery is usually open for visitors, although guards sometimes inexplicably seal off the grounds. Turn right at the main cemetery gate and follow the wall for about 100 yards. Dr. Franz Kafka's thin, white tombstone lies at the front of Section 21. ⊠ *Vinohradská at Jana Želivského, Prague 3 (metro station Želivského).* 🗔 *Free.* ☉ *Summer, Sun.–Thurs. 8–5; winter Sun.–Thurs. 9–4 (closes at 3 on Sun. in winter).*

A much smaller, but older, Jewish burial ground huddles at the foot of the soaring rocket ship–like television tower that broke ground in the last years of communism and used to be dubbed, in mockery, "Big Brother's Finger." The cemetery once spread where the tower now stands, but Jewish community leaders agreed, or were pressured, into letting it be dug up and the most historic tombstones crammed into one corner of the large square. The stones date back as far as the 17th century; a little neoclassical mausoleum stands forlornly just outside the fence. The cemetery gate is almost never unlocked. ⊠ *Fibichova at Kubelíkova, Prague 3.*

Dining

Dining choices in Prague have increased greatly in the past year as hundreds of new places have opened to cope with the increased tourist demand. Quality and price vary widely, though. Be wary of tourist traps; cross-check prices of foreign-language menus with Czech versions. Also ask if there is a *denní lístek* (daily menu). These menus, usually written only in Czech, generally list cheaper and often fresher selections (though many places provide daily menus for the midday meal only).

The crush of visitors has placed tremendous strain on the more popular restaurants. The upshot: Reservations are nearly always required; this is especially true during peak tourist periods. If you don't have reservations, try arriving a little before standard meal times: 11:30 AM for lunch or 5:30 PM for dinner.

For a cheaper and quicker alternative to the sit-down establishments listed below, try a light meal at one of the city's growing number of street stands and fast-food places. Look for stands offering *párky* (hot dogs) or *smažený syr* (fried cheese). McDonald's, with several locations in the city, heads the list of Western imports. For more exotic fare, try a gyro (made from pork) at the stand on the Staroměstské náměstí or the very good vegetarian fare at **Country Life** (⊠ Melantrichova ul. 15, ☎ 02/2421–3366), open Sunday to Friday. The German coffeemaker **Tchibo** has teamed up with a local bakery and now offers tasty sandwiches and excellent coffee at convenient locations on the Staroměstské náměstí and at the top of Wenceslas Square.

Old Town

$$$$ ✕ **Potomac.** Chef Jörn Heinrich lends imagination and creativity to Potomac's fresh imported ingredients, and discerning diners can't ask for anything more. The two-pepper soup proves a superb starter for main courses of grilled sea bass, and beef fillet with roasted cashews, green beans, and kidney beans. ⊠ *Renaissance Hotel, V celnici 7, Prague 1 (near Námûstí Republiky),* ☎ 02/2182–2431. *Jacket required. AE, DC, MC, V.*

$$$$ ✕ **V Zátiši.** White walls and casual grace accentuate the subtle flavors
★ of smoked salmon, plaice, beef Wellington, and other non-Czech specialties. Order the house *Rulandské červené,* a fruity Moravian red wine that meets the exacting standards of the food. In behavior unusual for the city, the benign waiters fairly fall over each other to serve diners. ⊠ *Liliová 1, Betlémské nám., Staré Město,* ☎ 02/2422–8977. *AE, DC, MC, V.*

$$$ ✕ **Fakhreldine.** This elegant Lebanese restaurant, crowded with diplomats who know where to find the real thing, has an excellent range of Middle Eastern appetizers and main courses. For a moderately priced meal, try several appetizers—hummus and garlic yogurt, perhaps—instead of a main course. ⊠ *Klimentská 48, Prague 1,* ☎ 02/232–7970. *AE, DC, MC, V.*

$$ ✕ **U Rychtáře** (The Landlord's). A contender for best Italian restaurant in Prague, there's plenty to tempt here, from 20 pasta dishes to nine pizzas, fish courses, and flavorful omelets. Especially tasty are the linguine with chicken breast, ginger, shallots, and parsley; and farfalle with broccoli and pepper sauce. The classic Italian desserts, *tiramisù* and *tartuffo*, are crafted with love. ⊠ *Dlouhá 2, Prague 1, ☎ 02/232–7207. AE, MC, DC, V.*

$ ✕ **Kogo Pizzeria-Caffeteria.** This is an appealing, laid-back place that serves divine cappuccino and reasonably priced Italian food with hints of Mediterranean fare. Recommended are blue-cheese pasta, and Kogo pizza (ham, peppers, basil, and Niva cheese). ⊠ *Havelská 27, Prague 1, no phone. No credit cards.*

$ ✕ **Profit.** The unfortunate name masks a clean, spacious pub that serves such excellent Czech standbys as goulash and pork with dumplings and sauerkraut at astonishingly reasonable prices. The central location could hardly be better. ⊠ *Betlémské nám. 8, Staré Město, ☎ 02/2422–2776. No credit cards.*

New Town (Nové Město)

$$$$ ✕ **Parnas.** The first choice for visiting dignitaries and businesspeople blessed with expense accounts, Parnas has creative, freshly prepared cuisine, more nouvelle than Bohemian, served in an opulent 1920s setting. Window seats afford stunning views of Prague Castle. There is a small, mostly Czech vintage wine list and a fine selection of appetizers and desserts (the chocolate mousse is a must). ⊠ *Smetanovo nábřeží 2, Nové Město, ☎ 02/2422–7614. Jacket required. AE, DC, MC, V.*

$$$$ ✕ **Taj Mahal.** Authentic Indian food in Prague? It's not as far-fetched as it once was. Specialties of northern and southern India are the focus at Taj Mahal, and the tandoori chicken is divine. ⊠ *Krétova 10, Prague 1 (near metro Muzeum), ☎ 02/2422–5566. AE, MC, V.*

$$$ ✕ **Cerberus.** Traditional Czech cooking is raised to an uncommonly high level at this New Town restaurant. The Bohemian staples of pork, duck, rabbit, and game are prepared and presented (by an attentive staff) as haute cuisine. Despite the modern decor, the ambience is warm and intimate. ⊠ *Soukenická 19, Nové Město, ☎ 02/231–0985. AE, MC, V.*

$$ ✕ **Bella Napoli.** Come here for real Italian food at a price-to-quality
★ ratio that's hard to beat in Prague. Ignore the faux Italian interior and the alabaster Venus de Milos astride shopping-mall fountains and head straight for the 65 Kč antipasto bar, which will distract you with fresh olives, eggplant, squid, and mozzarella. For your main course, go with any of a dozen superb pasta dishes or splurge with shrimp or chicken parmigiana. The Italian-American chef hails from Brooklyn and knows his stuff. ⊠ *V jámě 8, Nové Město, ☎ 02/2422–7315. No credit cards.*

$$ ✕ **Dolly Bell.** Whimsically designed, the upside-down tables hanging
★ from the ceiling provide a clever counterpoint to the huge selection of Yugoslav dishes, with an emphasis on meat and seafood. Especially worth sampling are the cornbread with Balkan cheese, cheese pie, and meat-filled pastry. ⊠ *Neklanova 20, Prague 2, ☎ 02/298–815. AE, DC, MC, V.*

$$ ✕ **Na Zvonařce.** This bright beer hall supplements traditional Czech dishes—mostly pork, beer, and more pork—with some innovative Czech and international choices, all at unbeatably cheap prices. Noteworthy entrées include juicy fried chicken and English roast beef; fruit dumplings for dessert are a rare treat. The service may be slow, but that simply allows time to commune with a tankard of ale on the outside terrace during the summer. ⊠ *Šafaříkova 1, Prague 2, ☎ 02/691–1311. No credit cards.*

$$ ✕ **Pezinok.** Slovak cooking is hard to find in Prague, and this cozy wine restaurant is still the best in town. Heavy furnishings and subdued lighting add an oddly formal touch. Order à la carte (the set menus are overpriced) and choose from homemade sausages or *halušky,* boiled noodles

46

Prague Dining and Lodging

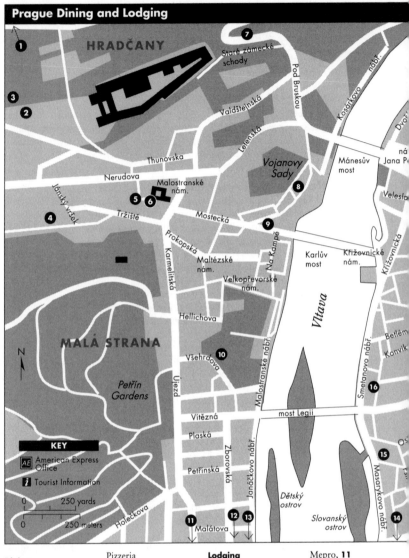

Dining
Bella Napoli, **35**
Cerberus, **24**
Dolly Bell, **14**
Fakhreldine, **25**
Kogo Pizzeria-
Caffeteria, **20**
Lobkovická, **4**
Myslivna, **40**
Na Zvonařce, **39**
Parnas, **16**
Penguin's, **12**
Pezinok, **34**

Pizzeria
Coloseum, **33**
Potomac, **29**
Profit, **18**
Rusalka, **15**
Taj Mahal, **38**
U Mecenáše, **5**
U Počtů, **7**
U Rychtáře, **21**
U Tří Zlatých Hvězd, **6**
U Zlaté Hrušky, **2**
V Krakovské, **37**
V Zátiši, **19**

Lodging
Apollo, **22**
Astra, **41**
Axa, **28**
Balkan, **13**
City Hotel Moráň, **36**
Diplomat, **1**
Grand Hotel
Bohemia, **31**
Harmony, **27**
Kampa, **10**

Mepro, **11**
Meteor Plaza, **30**
Opera, **26**
Palace, **32**
Pension Louda, **23**
Pension Unitas, **17**
Pension U Raka, **3**
U Páva, **8**
U Tří Pštrosů, **9**

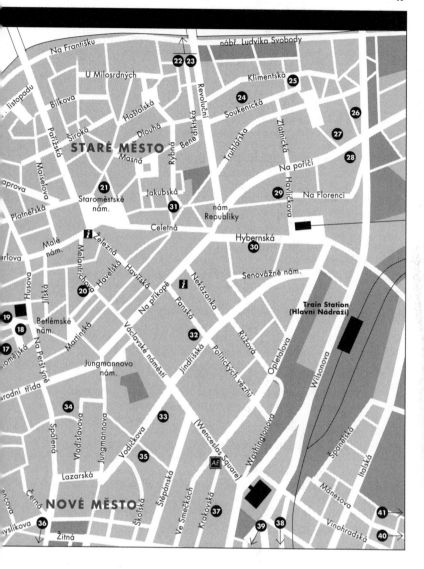

served with tangy sheep's cheese. The restaurant's full-bodied wines
come from the Slovak town for which the restaurant is named.
⊠ *Purkyňova 4, Nové Město,* ☎ *02/291996. AE, DC, MC, V.*

$$ ✕ **Rusalka.** This quiet, cozy nook is the perfect pre- or post-theater
dining spot, named after Dvořák's beloved opera, and it's right behind
the National Theater. International specialties are presented with flair:
Try the spicy Japanese chicken soup and chicken in sage and farfalle.
⊠ *Na struze 1/277, Prague 1,* ☎ *02/2491–5876. AE, MC, V.*

$$ ✕ **V Krakovské.** At this clean, proper pub close to the major tourist
sights, the food is traditional and hearty; this is the place to try Bo-
hemian duck, washed down with a dark beer from Domažlice in western Bohemia. ⊠ *Krakovská 20, Nové Město,* ☎ *02/261–537. No credit
cards.*

 $ ✕ **Pizzeria Coloseum.** Delicious pizza to satisfy all tastes, and the lo-
cation can't be beat: right off Wenceslas Square. The picnic tables
makes this an ideal spot for an informal lunch or dinner. There's a salad
bar, too. ⊠ *Vodiākova 32, Prague 1,* ☎ *02/2421–4914. AE, V.*

Malá Strana

$$$$ ✕ **U Mecenáše.** A fetching Renaissance inn from the 17th century, with
dark, high-backed benches in the front room and cozy, elegant sofas
and chairs in back, this is the place to splurge: From the aperitifs to
the steaks and the cognac (swirled lovingly in oversize glasses), the presentation is seamless. ⊠ *Malostranské nám. 10, Malá Strana,* ☎ *02/
533881. Jacket required. AE, DC, MC, V.*

$$$ ✕ **Lobkovická.** This dignified *vinárna* (wine hall) set inside a 17th-cen-
 ★ tury town palace serves some of Prague's most imaginative dishes.
Chicken breast with crabmeat and curry sauce is an excellent main dish
and typical of the kitchen's innovative approach to sauces and spices.
Deep-red carpeting sets the perfect mood for enjoying bottles of Mora-
vian wine brought from the musty depths of the restaurant's wine cel-
lar. ⊠ *Vlašská 17, Malá Strana,* ☎ *02/530185. Jacket and tie. AE, DC,
MC, V.*

$$ ✕ **U Tří Zlatých Hvězd** (the Three Golden Stars). A perfect spot for a
romantic evening, the cuisine is hearty, classic Czech with thoughtful
European touches. Recommended are rose of smoked salmon with dill
mayonnaise as a starter, followed by roast duck Bohemian style with
apples, bacon, dumplings, and red cabbage. ⊠ *Malostranské nám. 8,
Prague 1,* ☎ FAX *02/539660. AE, DC, MC, V.*

Hradčany

$$$$ ✕ **U Zlaté Hrušky.** At this bustling bistro perched on one of Prague's
prettiest cobblestone streets, slide into one of the cozy dark-wood
booths and let the cheerful staff advise on wines and specials. Duck
and carp are house favorites. After dinner, stroll to the castle for an
unforgettable panorama. ⊠ *Nový Svět 3, Hradčany,* ☎ *02/531133.
Jacket and tie. AE, DC, MC, V.*

Vinohrady

$$ ✕ **Myslivna.** The name means "hunting lodge," and the cooks at this
far-flung neighborhood eatery certainly know their way around veni-
son, quail, and boar. Attentive staff can advise on wines: Try Vavřin-
ecké, a hearty red that holds its own with any beast. The stuffed quail
and the leg of venison with walnuts both get high marks. A cab from
the city center to Myslivna should cost under 200 Kč. ⊠ *Jagellonska
21, Prague 3,* ☎ *02/6270209. AE, V.*

Letná, Holešovice

$$ ✕ **U Počtů.** Superior, discreet service, a relative rarity in Prague, heightens the pleasure of dining at this charmingly old-fashioned restaurant. Midnight garlic soup and chicken livers in wine sauce are flawlessly rendered, and grilled trout is delicious. ⊠ *Milády Horakové 47, Prague 7,* ☎ *02/370085. MC, V.*

Smíchov

$$ ✕ **Penguin's.** The emphasis at this popular eatery is on classic Czech and international dishes, served in an elegant mauve-and-matte-black setting. Try any of the steaks or the chicken breast with potatoes. The penguin in the name refers to the Pittsburgh variety, of hockey fame—the owner's favorite team. ⊠ *Zborovská 5, Prague 5,* ☎ *02/545660. No credit cards.*

Lodging

Visitors are frequently disappointed by the city's lodging options. Hotel owners were quick to raise prices after 1989, when tourists first began flocking to Prague, but they have been much, much slower in raising their facilities to Western standards. In most of the $$$$ and $$$ hotels, you can expect to find a restaurant and an exchange bureau on or near the premises. Bills are paid in Czech crowns, though some hotels still insist you pay in hard (that is, Western) currency; be certain to inquire *before* making a reservation. During the summer season reservations are absolutely imperative; the remainder of the year they are highly recommended.

A cheaper and often more interesting alternative to Prague's generally mediocre hotels are private rooms and apartments. Prague is full of travel agencies offering such accommodations; sacrificing a little privacy is the only drawback. The biggest room-finding service is probably **AVE** (☎ 02/2422–3226), with offices in the main train station (⊠ Hlavní nádraží) and at Holešovice station (⊠ Nádraží Holešovice). Both offices are open daily from 7 AM to 10 PM. Their Ruzyně Airport office is open from 7 AM to 9 PM. Prices start at around $15 per person per night. Insist on a room in the city center, however, or you may find yourself in a dreary, far-flung suburb. Other helpful room-finding agencies include **Hello Ltd.** (⊠ Senovážné nám. 3, Nové Město, ☎ 02/2421–2741) and **City of Prague Accommodation Service** (⊠ Haštalské nám. 8, Staré Město, ☎ 02/231–0202, FAX 02/2481–0603), which is open daily 8–8, until 10 in summer. Čedok and Prague Information Service (PIS) offices can also help in locating private accommodations. If all else fails, just take a walk through the Old Town: The number of places advertising ACCOMMODATION (often written in German as UNTERKUNFT) is astounding.

$$$$ 🏨 **Diplomat.** This sprawling complex opened in 1990 and remains one ★ of the best business hotels in town. Even though it's in the suburbs, the Diplomat is convenient to the airport and, via the metro, to the city center. The modern rooms may not exude much character, but they are tastefully furnished and quite comfortable. Hotel staff members are competent and many are bilingual. Guests have access to a pool, sauna, and fitness center. ⊠ *Evropská 15, 160 00 Prague 6,* ☎ *02/2439–4111,* FAX *02/2439–4215. 387 rooms with bath. 2 restaurants, bar, pool, sauna, health club, nightclub, conference room. AE, DC, MC, V.*

$$$$ 🏨 **Grand Hotel Bohemia.** This beautifully refurbished art-nouveau town palace is just a stone's throw from the Old Town Square. The Austrian owners opted for a muted, modern decor in the rooms but left the sumptuous public areas just as they were. Each room is outfitted with a fax and answering machine. ⊠ *Královdorska 4, 110 00 Prague 1,* ☎ *02/2480–4111,* 𝔽𝔸𝕏 *02/232–9545. 78 rooms with bath. Restaurant, café. AE, DC, MC, V.*

$$$$ 🏨 **Palace.** For the well-heeled, this is Prague's most coveted address—an art-nouveau town palace perched on a busy corner only a block from the very central Wenceslas Square. Renovated in 1989, the hotel's spacious, well-appointed rooms, each with a private white-marble bathroom, are fitted in velvety pinks and greens cribbed straight from an Alfons Mucha print. Two rooms are set aside for travelers with disabilities. The ground-floor buffet boasts the city's finest salad bar. ⊠ *Panská 12, 110 00 Prague 1,* ☎ *02/2409–3111,* 𝔽𝔸𝕏 *02/2422–1240. 125 rooms with bath. 2 restaurants, bar, café, snack bar, minibars, sauna, satellite TV. AE, DC, MC, V.*

$$$$ 🏨 **U Tří Pštrosů.** The location could not be better—a romantic corner in the Malá Strana only a stone's throw from the river and within arms' reach of the Charles Bridge. The airy rooms, dating back 300 years, still have their original oak-beamed ceilings and antique furniture; many also have views over the river. Massive walls keep out the noise of the crowds on the bridge. An excellent in-house restaurant serves traditional Czech dishes to guests and nonguests alike. ⊠ *Dražického nám. 12, 118 00 Prague 1,* ☎ *02/2451–0779,* 𝔽𝔸𝕏 *02/2451–0783. 18 rooms with bath. Restaurant. AE, MC, V (no credit cards in restaurant).*

$$$ 🏨 **Axa.** Funky and functional, this modernist high-rise, built in 1932, was a mainstay of the budget-hotel crowd until a makeover forced substantial price hikes. The rooms, now with color television sets and modern plumbing, are certainly improved; however, the lobby and public areas look decidedly tacky, with plastic flowers and glaring lights. ⊠ *Na poříčí 40, 113 03 Prague 1,* ☎ *02/2481–2580,* 𝔽𝔸𝕏 *02/2481–2067. 109 rooms, most with bath. Restaurant, bar, pool, exercise room, nightclub. AE, DC, MC, V.*

$$$ 🏨 **City Hotel Morán.** This 19th-century town house was tastefully renovated in 1992; now the lobby and public areas are bright and inviting, made over in an updated Jugendstil style. The modern if slightly bland rooms are a cut above the Prague standard for convenience and cleanliness; ask for one on the sixth floor for a good view of Prague Castle. ⊠ *Na Moráni 15, 120 00 Prague 2 (corner of Václavská),* ☎ *02/2491–5208,* 𝔽𝔸𝕏 *02/297533. 53 rooms, most with bath. Restaurant, bar. AE, DC, MC, V.*

$$$ 🏨 **Harmony.** This is one of the newly renovated, formerly state-owned standbys. The stern 1930s facade clashes with the bright, nouveau riche–type 1990s interior, but cheerful receptionists and big, clean rooms compensate for the aesthetic flaws. Ask for a room away from the bustle of one of Prague's busiest streets. ⊠ *Na poříčí 31, 110 00 Prague 1,* ☎ *02/232–0720,* 𝔽𝔸𝕏 *02/231–0009. 60 rooms with bath. Restaurant, snack bar. AE, DC, MC, V.*

$$$ 🏨 **Kampa.** This early baroque armory turned hotel is tucked away on
★ a leafy corner at the southern end of Malá Strana. The rooms are clean, if sparse, though the bucolic setting makes up for any discomforts. Note the late-Gothic vaulting in the massive dining room. ⊠ *Všehrdova 16, 118 00 Prague 1,* ☎ *02/2451–0409,* 𝔽𝔸𝕏 *02/2451–0377. 85 rooms with bath. Restaurant, café. AE, DC, MC, V.*

$$$ 🏨 **Meteor Plaza.** This popular Old Town hotel, operated by the Best Western chain, combines the best of New World convenience and Old World charm (Empress Maria Theresa's son, Joseph, stayed here when he was passing through in the 18th century). The setting is ideal: a newly renovated baroque building that is only five minutes on foot from downtown. There is a good, if touristy, in-house wine cellar. ⊠ *Hybernská*

6, 110 00 Prague 1, ☏ 02/2422–0664, ℻ 02/2421–3005. 86 rooms
with bath. Restaurant, business center. AE, DC, MC, V.

$$$ ▣ **Pension U Raka.** This private guest house offers the peace and co-
★ ziness of an alpine lodge, plus a quiet location on the ancient, wind-
ing streets of Nový Svět, just behind the Loreto Church and a 10-minute
walk from Prague Castle. The dark-wood building has only five rooms,
but if you can get a reservation (try at least a month in advance), you
will gain a wonderful base for exploring Prague. ⊠ Černínská ul.
10/93, 118 00 Prague 1, ☏ 02/351453 or 02/2051–1100, ℻ 02/353074
or 02/2051–0511. 5 rooms with bath. AE, DC, MC, V.

$$$ ▣ **U Páva.** This neoclassical inn, on a quiet gaslit street in Malá Strana,
★ offers upstairs suites that afford an unforgettable view of Prague Cas-
tle. Best of all, the U Páva is small and intimate—the perfect escape
for those who've had their fill of cement high-rise resorts. The staff is
courteous and helpful, while the reception and public areas are elegant
and discreet. ⊠ U lužického semináře 32, 118 00 Prague 1, ☏ 02/2451–
0922, ℻ 02/533379. 11 rooms with bath. Restaurant, bar. AE, DC,
MC, V.

$$ ▣ **Apollo.** This is a standard, no-frills, square-box hotel where clean
rooms come at a fair price. Its primary flaw is its location: roughly 20
minutes by metro or bus from the city center. ⊠ Kubišova 23, 182 00
Prague 8 (metro Holešovice, Line C, then Tram 5, 17, or 25 to the
Hercovka stop), ☏ 02/688–0628, ℻ 02/688–4570. 35 rooms with
bath. AE, MC, V.

$$ ▣ **Astra.** The location best serves drivers coming in to town from the
east, although the nearby metro station makes this modern hotel easy
to reach from the center. It's good value at the price. ⊠ Mukařovská
1740/18, 100 00 Prague 10 (from metro station Skalka, Line A, walk
south on Na padesátém about 5 mins to Mukařovská), ☏ 02/781–
3595, ℻ 02/781–0765. 50 rooms with bath. Restaurant, in-room satellite TVs, nightclub. AE, DC, MC, V.

$$ ▣ **Mepro.** Standard rooms and service and a reasonably central loca-
tion make this small hotel worth considering. The Smíchov neighbor-
hood offers a good range of restaurants (for one, the U Mikuláše
Dačického wine tavern, across the street from the hotel) and nice
strolls along the river or up the Petřín hill. ⊠ Viktora Huga 3, 150 00
Prague 5, ☏ 02/549167, ℻ 02/561–8587. 26 rooms with bath. Snack
bar, in-room satellite TVs. AE, MC, V.

$$ ▣ **Opera.** Once the lodging of choice for divas performing at the
nearby State Theater, the Opera greatly declined under the Commu-
nists. New owners, however, are working hard to restore the hotel's
former luster. Until then, the clean (but smallish) rooms, friendly staff,
and fin-de-siècle charm are still reason enough to recommend it. Rooms
without bath are half price. ⊠ Těšnov 13, 110 00 Prague 1, ☏ 02/
231–5609, ℻ 02/231–1477. 66 rooms, some with bath. Restaurant,
bar. AE, DC, MC, V.

$ ▣ **Balkan.** One of the few central hotels that can compete in cost with
private rooms, the spartan Balkan is on a busy street, not far from
Malá Strana and the National Theater. ⊠ Svornosti 28, 150 00 Prague
5, ☏ ℻ 02/540777. 24 rooms with bath. Breakfast not included.
Restaurant. AE.

$ ▣ **Pension Louda.** The friendly owners of this family-run guest house,
★ set in a suburb roughly 20 minutes by tram from the city center, go
out of their way to make you feel welcome. The large, spotless rooms
are an unbelievable bargain, and the hilltop location offers a stunning
view of greater Prague. ⊠ Kubišova 10, 182 00 Prague 8 (metro
Holešovice, Line C, then Tram 5, 17, or 25 to the Hercovka stop),
☏ 02/688–1491, ℻ 02/688–1488. 9 rooms with bath. No credit cards.

$ ⛫ **Pension Unitas.** Operated by the Christian charity Unitas in an Old Town convent, the spartan rooms at this well-run establishment used to serve as interrogation cells for the Communist secret police. Conditions are much more comfortable nowadays, if far from luxurious. Alcohol and tobacco are not permitted. ⊠ *Bartolomějská 9, 110 00 Prague 1,* ☎ *02/232–7700,* 🗏 *02/232–7709. 40 rooms, none with bath. AE, MC, V.*

Nightlife and the Arts

Nightlife

CABARET

For adult stage entertainment (with some nudity) try the **Lucerna Bar** (⊠ Štěpánská ul. 61, at Wenceslas Sq.) or **Varieté Praga** (⊠ Vodičkova ul. 30, ☎ 02/2421–5945).

DISCOS

Dance clubs come and go with predictable regularity. The longtime favorite is **Radost FX** (⊠ Bělehradská 120, Prague 2, ☎ 02/251210), featuring imported DJs playing the latest dance music and techno from London. The café on the ground floor is open all night and serves wholesome vegetarian food. Two popular discos for dancing the night away with fellow tourists are **Lávká** (⊠ Novotného lávká 1, near the Charles Bridge), featuring open-air dancing by the bridge on summer nights, and the **Corona Club and Latin Café** (⊠ Novotného lávká, Prague 1), which highlights Latin, Gypsy, and other dance-friendly live music. Discos catering to a very young crowd blast sound onto lower Wenceslas Square.

JAZZ CLUBS

Jazz gained notoriety under the Communists as a subtle form of protest, and the city still has some great jazz clubs, featuring everything from swing to blues and modern. **Reduta** (⊠ Národní 20, ☎ 02/2491–2246) features a full program of local and international musicians. **AghaRTA** (⊠ Krakovská 5, ☎ 02/2421–2914) offers a variety of jazz acts in an intimate café/nightclub atmosphere. Music starts around 9 PM, but come earlier to get a seat. Check posters around town or any of the English-language newspapers for current listings.

PUBS, BARS, AND LOUNGES

Bars or lounges are not traditional Prague fixtures; social life, of the drinking variety, usually takes place in pubs (pivnice or *hospody*), which are liberally sprinkled throughout the city's neighborhoods. Tourists are welcome to join in the evening ritual of sitting around large tables and talking, smoking, and drinking beer. Before venturing in, however, it's best to familiarize yourself with a few points of pub etiquette. Always ask if a chair is free before sitting down. To order a beer (*pivo*), do not wave the waiter down or shout across the room; he will usually assume you want beer and bring it over to you without asking. He will also bring subsequent rounds to the table without asking. To refuse, just shake your head or say no thanks. At the end of the evening, usually around 10:30 or 11:00, the waiter will come to tally the bill. Some of the most popular pubs in the city center include **U Medvídků** (⊠ Na Perštýně 7), **U Vejvodů** (⊠ Jilská 4), and **U Zlatého Tygra** (⊠ Husova ul. 17). All can get impossibly crowded.

One of the oddest phenomena of Prague's post-1989 renaissance is the sight of travelers and tour groups from the United States, Britain, Australia, and even Japan descending on this city to experience the life of— American expatriates. There are a handful of bars guaranteed to ooze Yanks and other native English speakers. **Jo's Bar** (⊠ Malostranské nám. 7) is a haven for younger expats, serving bottled beer, mixed drinks, and good Mexican food. The **James Joyce Pub** (⊠ Liliová 10) is authentically Irish, with Guinness on tap and excellent food. **U Malého Glena** puts on live jazz, folk, and rock (⊠ Karmelitská 23, ☎ 02/535–8115). The major hotels also run their own bars and nightclubs. The **Piano Bar** (⊠ Hotel Palace, Panská ul. 12) is the most pleasant of the lot; jacket and tie are suggested.

ROCK CLUBS

Prague's rock scene is thriving. Hard-rock enthusiasts should check out the **Rock Café** (⊠ Národní 20, ☎ 02/2491–4416) or **Strahov 007** (⊠ Near Strahov Stadium; take Bus 218 2 stops from Anděl metro station). **RC Bunkr** (⊠ Lodecká 2, ☎ 02/2481–0665) was the first post-revolutionary underground club. The **Malostranska Beseda** (⊠ Malostranské nám. 21, ☎ 02/539024) and the **Belmondo Revival Club** (⊠ Bubenská 1, Prague 7, ☎ 02/791–4854) are dependable bets for sometimes bizarre, but always good, musical acts from around the country.

The Arts

Prague's cultural flair is legendary, though performances are usually booked far in advance by all sorts of Praguers. The concierge at your hotel may be able to reserve tickets for you. Otherwise, for the cheapest tickets go directly to the theater box office a few days in advance or immediately before a performance. The biggest ticket agency, **Tiketpro,** has outlets all over town and accepts credit cards (main branch at ⊠ Štěpánská 61, Lucerna passage, ☎ 02/2481–4020). **Bohemia Ticket International** (⊠ Na příkopě 16, ☎ 02/2421–5031; ⊠ Václavské nám. 25, ☎ 02/2422–7253) sells tickets for major cultural events, though at semi-inflated prices. Tickets can also be purchased at **American Express** (⊠ Václavské nám. 56).

For details of cultural events, look for the English-language newspaper the *Prague Post* or the monthly *Velvet* magazine, or the monthly *Prague Guide,* available at hotels and tourist offices.

FILM

If a film was made in the United States or Britain, the chances are good that it will be shown with Czech subtitles rather than dubbed. (Film titles, however, are usually translated into Czech, so your only clue to the movie's country of origin may be the poster used in advertisements.) Popular cinemas are **Blaník** (⊠ Václavské nám. 56, ☎ 02/2421–6698), **Hvěda** (⊠ Václavské nám 38, ☎ 02/264545), **Praha** (⊠ Václavské nám. 17, ☎ 02/262035), and **Světozor** (⊠ Vodičkova ul. 39, ☎ 02/263616). Prague's English-language publications carry film reviews and full timetables.

MUSIC

Classical concerts are held all over the city throughout the year. The best orchestral venues are the resplendent art-nouveau **Obecní dům** (⊠ Smetana Hall, Nám. Republiky 5, scheduled to reopen in the spring of 1997), home of the Prague Symphony Orchestra, and **Dvořák Hall** (⊠ In the Rudolfinum, nám. Jana Palacha, ☎ 02/2489–3111). The latter concert hall is home to one of Central Europe's best orchestras, the Czech Philharmonic, which has been racked in recent years by bitter disputes among players, conductors, and management but still plays sublimely.

Performances also are held regularly in the **Garden on the Ramparts** below Prague Castle (where the music comes with a view), the two **churches of St. Nicholas** (on Old Town Square and Malostranské náměstí), the **Church of Sts. Simon and Jude** (⊠ Dušní ul., in the Old Town, near the Hotel Inter-Continental), the **Church of St. James**

(⊠ Malá Štupartská, near Old Town Square), the **Zrcadlová kaple** (⊠ Mirror Chapel, Klementinum, Mariánské náměstí, Old Town), the **Lobkowicz Palace** at Prague Castle, and plenty more palaces and churches. Dozens of classical ensembles survive off the tourist-concert trade at these and many other venues. The standard of performance ranges from adequate to superb, though the programs tend to take few risks. Serious fans of baroque music have the opportunity to hear works of little-known Bohemian composers at these concerts. Some of the best chamber ensembles are the **Talich Chamber Orchestra,** the **Guarneri Trio,** the **Wihan Quartet,** the **Czech Piano Trio,** and the **Agon** contemporary music group.

Concerts at the **Villa Bertramka** (⊠ Mozartova ul. 169, Smíchov, ☎ 02/543893) emphasize the music of Mozart and his contemporaries (☞ Off the Beaten Path *in* Charles Bridge and Malá Strana, *above*).

Fans of organ music will be delighted by the number of recitals held in Prague's historic halls and churches. Popular programs are offered at **St. Vitus Cathedral** in Hradčany, **U Křižovníků** near the Charles Bridge, the **Church of St. Nicholas** in Malá Strana, and **St. James's Church** on Malá Štupartská in the Old Town, where the organ plays amid a complement of baroque statuary.

OPERA AND BALLET

The Czech Republic has a strong operatic tradition, and performances at the **Národní divadlo** (⊠ National Theater, Národní třída 2, ☎ 02/2491–2673) and the **Statní Opera Praha** (⊠ State Opera House, Wilsonova 4, ☎ 02/265353), near the top of Wenceslas Square, can be excellent. It's always worthwhile to buy a cheap ticket (for as little as 10 Kč) just to take a look at these stunning 19th-century halls; appropriate attire is recommended. Now, unlike the Communist period, operas are almost always sung in their original tongue, and the repertoire offers plenty of Italian favorites and the Czech national composers Janáček, Dvořák, and Smetana. The historic **Stavovské divadlo** (⊠ Estates' Theater, Ovocný trh. 1, ☎ 02/2421–5001), where *Don Giovanni* premiered in the 18th century, plays host to a mix of operas and dramatic works. Simultaneous translation into English via a microwave transmitter and headsets is usually offered at drama performances. The National and State theaters also occasionally have ballets.

PUPPET SHOWS

This traditional form of Czech popular entertainment has been given new life thanks to the productions mounted at the **National Marionette Theater** (⊠ Žatecká 1) and the **Magic Theater of the Baroque World** (⊠ Celetná 13). Traditionally, children and adults alike enjoy the hilarity and pathos of these performances.

THEATER

Theater thrives in the Czech Republic as a vibrant art form. A dozen or so professional companies play in Prague to ever-packed houses; the language barrier can't obscure the players' artistry. Tourist-friendly, nonverbal theater abounds as well, notably Black Theater, a melding of live acting, mime, video, and stage trickery, which continues to draw crowds despite signs of fatigue. The famous **Laterna Magika** (Magic Lantern) puts on a similar extravaganza (⊠ Národní třída 4, ☎ 02/2491–4129). Performances usually begin at 7 or 7:30 PM. Several English-language theater groups operate sporadically in Prague; pick up a copy of the *Prague Post* for complete listings.

Outdoor Activities and Sports

Fitness Clubs

The best fitness clubs in town are at the **Forum Hotel** (⊠ Kongresova ul. 1, ☎ 02/6119–1111; Vyšehrad metro station), the **Hilton Hotel** (⊠ Pobřežní 1, ☎ 02/2484–1111; Florenc metro station), and the **AXA Hotel** (⊠ Na Poříčí 12, ☎ 2481–2580; Florenc metro station). All three are open to nonresidents, but call first to inquire about rates.

Golf

You can golf year-round at Prague's only course, located outside the city at the **Stop Motel** (⊠ Plzeňská ul. 215, ☎ 02/523251). Take a taxi to the motel or Tram 7 to the end of the line.

Jogging

The best place for jogging is the **Letenské sady,** the large park across the river from the Hotel Inter-Continental. Cross the Svatopluka Çecha Bridge, climb the stairs, and turn to the right for a good, long run far away from the car fumes. The **Riegrový sady,** a park in Vinohrady behind the main train station, is also nice, but it is small and a bit out of the way.

Spectator Sports

Prague plays host to a wide variety of spectator sports, including world-class ice hockey, handball, tennis, and swimming. Most events, however, are held at irregular intervals. The best place to find out what's going on (and where) is the weekly sports page of the *Prague Post,* or you can inquire at your hotel.

SOCCER

National and international matches are played regularly at the Sparta Stadium in Holešovice, behind the Letenské Sady (☞ Jogging, *above*). To reach the stadium, take Tram 1, 25, or 26 to the Sparta stop.

Swimming

The best public swimming pool in Prague is at the **Podolí Swimming Stadium** in Podolí, easily reached from the city center via Tram 3 or 17. The indoor pool is 50 meters long, and the complex also includes two open-air pools, a sauna, a steam bath, and a wild-ride water slide. (A word of warning: Podolí, for all its attractions, is notorious as a local hot spot of petty thievery; don't entrust any valuables to the lockers—it's best to either check them in the safe with the *vrátnice* (superintendent) or better yet, don't bring them at all.) The pool at the **Hilton Hotel** is smaller, but the location is more convenient (☞ Fitness Clubs, *above*). Another pool to try is in the **Hotel Olšanka** (⊠ Táboritská 23, Prague 3, ☎ 6709–2111).

Tennis

There are public courts at the **Strahov Stadium** in Břevnov. Take Tram 8 to the end from the Hradčanská metro stop and change to Bus 143, 149, or 217. The **Hilton Hotel** (☞ Fitness Clubs, *above*) has two indoor courts available for public use.

Shopping

Despite the relative shortage of quality clothes—Prague has a long way to go before it can match shopping meccas Paris and Rome—the capital is a great place to pick up gifts and souvenirs. Bohemian crystal and porcelain deservedly enjoy a worldwide reputation for quality, and plenty of shops offer excellent bargains. The local market for antiques and artworks is still relatively undeveloped, while dozens of antiquarian bookstores can yield some excellent finds, particularly German and Czech books and graphics. Another bargain is recorded music: CD prices are about half what you would pay in the West.

Shopping Districts

The major shopping areas are **Národní třída,** running past Můstek to Na příkopě, and the area around **Staroměstské náměstí** (Old Town Square). **Pařížská ulice, Karlova ulice** (on the way to the Charles Bridge), and the area just south of **Josefov** (the Jewish Quarter) are also good places to find boutiques and antiques shops. In the Malá Strana, try **Nerudova ulice,** the street that runs up to the Castle Hill district.

Department Stores

These are not always well stocked and often have everything except the one item you're looking for, but a stroll through one may yield some interesting finds and bargains. The best are **Kotva** (⊠ Nám. Republiky 8), **Tesco** (⊠ Národní třída 26), **Bílá Labut'** (⊠ Na poříčí 23), and **Krone** (⊠ Václavské nám. 21).

Street Markets

For fruits and vegetables, the best street market in central Prague is on **Havelská ulice** in the Old Town. Arrive early in the day if you want something a bit more exotic than tomatoes and cucumbers. The best market for nonfood items is the flea market in **Holešovice,** north of the city center, although there isn't really much of interest here outside of cheap tobacco and electronics products. Take the metro Line C to the Vltavská station and then ride any tram heading east (running to the left as you exit the metro station). Exit at the first stop and follow the crowds.

Specialty Stores

ANTIQUES

Starožitnosti (antiques shops) are everywhere in Prague, but you'll need a sharp eye to distinguish truly valuable pieces from merely interesting ones. Many dealers carry old glassware and vases. Antique jewelry, many pieces featuring garnets, is also popular. Remember to retain your receipts as proof of legitimate purchases, otherwise you may have difficulty bringing antiques out of the country. Comparison shop at stores along Karlova ulice in the Old Town. Also check in and around the streets of the former Jewish ghetto for shops specializing in Jewish antiques and artifacts. **Art Program** (⊠ Nerudova ul. 28) in the Malá Strana has an especially beautiful collection of art-deco jewelry and glassware.

BOOKS AND PRINTS

It's hard to imagine a more beautiful bookstore than **U Karlova Mostu** (⊠ Karlova ul. 2, Staré Město, ☎ 02/2422–9205), with its impressive selection of old maps, prints, and rare books.

One shop that comes close in appeal to U Karlova Mostu is **Antikvariát Karel Křenek** (⊠ Celetná 31, ☎ 02/231–4734), near the Powder Tower in the Old Town. It stocks prints and graphics from the 1920s and '30s, in addition to a small collection of English books.

If you'd just like a good read, be sure to check out the **Globe Bookstore and Coffeehouse** (⊠ Janovského 14, Prague 7, ☎ 02/6671–2610), which is one of Prague's meccas for the local English-speaking community.

U Knihomola Bookstore and Café (⊠ Mánesova 79, Prague 2, ☎ 02/627–7770) is a close contender to the Globe for the best place to find the latest in English literature, plus it stocks the best selection of new

English-language art books and guidebooks. It's near the metro stop Jiřího z Poděbrad.

CRYSTAL AND PORCELAIN

Moser (⊠ Na příkopě 12, ☎ 02/2421–1293), the flagship store for the world-famous Karlovy Vary glassmaker, is the first address for stylish, high-quality lead crystal and china. Even if you're not in the market to buy, stop by the store simply to browse through the elegant wood-paneled salesrooms on the second floor. The staff will gladly pack goods for traveling. **Bohemia** (⊠ Pařížska 2, ☎ 02/2481–1023) carries a wide selection of porcelain from Karlovy Vary. If you still can not find anything, have no fear: There is a crystal shop on just about every street in central Prague.

FOOD

Specialty food stores have been slow to catch on in Prague. **Fruits de France** (⊠ Jindřišská 9, Nové Město, ☎ 02/2422–0304) stocks Prague's freshest fruits and vegetables imported directly from France at Western prices. The bakeries at the **Krone** and **Kotva** department stores sell surprisingly delicious breads and pastries. Both stores also have large, well-stocked basement grocery stores.

FUN THINGS FOR CHILDREN

Children enjoy the beautiful watercolor and colored-chalk sets available in nearly every stationery store at rock-bottom prices. The Czechs are also master illustrators, and the books they've made for young "pre-readers" are some of the world's loveliest. Many stores also offer unique wooden toys, sure to delight any young child. For these, look in at **Obchod Vším Možným** (⊠ Nerudova 45, ☎ 02/536941). For older children and teens, it's worth considering a Czech or Eastern European watch, telescope, or set of binoculars. The quality/price ratio is unbeatable.

JEWELRY

The **Granát** shop at Dlouhá 30 in the Old Town has a comprehensive selection of garnet jewelry, plus contemporary and traditional pieces set in gold and silver. Several shops specializing in gold jewelry line Wenceslas Square.

MUSICAL INSTRUMENTS

Melodia (⊠ Jungmannova nám. 17, ☎ 02/2422–2500) carries a complete range of quality musical instruments at reasonable prices. **Capriccio** (⊠ Újezd 15, Prague 1, ☎ 02/532507) is a great place to find sheet music of all kinds.

SPORTS EQUIPMENT

Adidas has an outlet at Na Příkopě 8. Department stores also sometimes carry medium-quality sports equipment.

Prague A to Z

Arriving and Departing

BY BUS

The Czech complex of regional bus lines known collectively as **ČSAD** operates its dense network from the sprawling main bus station on Křižíkova (metro stop: Florenc, Lines B or C). For information about routes and schedules call 02/2421–1060, consult the confusingly displayed timetables posted at the station, or visit the information window, situated at the bus unloading area (☉ Mon.–Fri. 6–7:45, Sat. 6–4, Sun. 8–6). The helpful private travel agency Tourbus, in the pedestrian overpass above the station, dispenses bus information daily until 8 PM.

If the ticket windows are closed, you can usually buy a ticket from the driver.

Prague is well served by major roads and highways from anywhere in the country. On arriving in the city, simply follow the signs to CENTRUM (city center). During the day, traffic can be heavy, especially on the approach to Wenceslas Square. Pay particular attention to the trams, which enjoy the right-of-way in every situation. Note that parts of the historic center of Prague, including Wenceslas Square itself, are closed to private vehicles.

Parking is permitted in the center of town, including on Wenceslas Square, with a voucher from one of the major hotels, on a growing number of streets with parking meters, or in the few small lots within walking distance of the historic center. An underground lot is at Náměstí Jana Palacha, near Old Town Square.

Ruzyně Airport: Twenty kilometers (12 miles) northwest of the downtown area, the airport is small but easily negotiated; allow yourself plenty of time when departing Prague because the airport is still too small to handle the large numbers of travelers who move through it, and you may encounter long lines at customs and check-in.

ČSA (the Czech national carrier) offers direct flights all over the world from Ruzyně. Major airlines with offices in Prague are **Air France** (☎ 02/2422–7164), **Alitalia** (☎ 02/2481–0079, 232–5966), **Austrian Airlines** (☎ 02/231–3378), **British Airways** (☎ 02/232–9020), **ČSA** (☎ 02/2010–4111), **Delta** (☎ 02/267141), **KLM** (☎ 02/2422–8678), **Lufthansa** (☎ 02/2481–1007), **SAS** (☎ 02/2421–4749), and **Swissair** (☎ 02/2481–2111).

Between the Airport and Downtown: The Cedaz minibus shuttle links the airport with Náměstí Republiky (a square just off the Old Town). It runs hourly, more often at peak periods, between 6 AM and 9:30 PM daily and makes an intermediate stop at the Dejvická metro station. The one-way fare is 60 Kč. Regular municipal bus service (Bus 119) also connects the airport and the Dejvická metro stop; the fare is 10 Kč. From Dejvická you can take a subway to the city center. To reach Wenceslas Square, get off at the Můstek station.

Taxis offer the easiest and most convenient way of getting downtown. The trip is a straight shot down Evropská Boulevard and takes approximately 20 minutes. The road is not usually busy, but anticipate an additional 20 minutes during rush hour (7 AM–9 AM and 3 PM–6 PM). The ride costs about 300 Kč.

International trains arrive at and depart from either the main station, **Hlavní nádraží,** Wilsonova ulice, about 500 yards east of Wenceslas Square; or the suburban **Nádraží Holešovice,** (☎ 02/2461–5865), about 2 kilometers (1½ miles) north of the city center. This is an unending source of confusion—always make certain you know which station your train is using. For train times, consult timetables in stations or get in line at the information offices upstairs at the main station, open daily 6 AM–10 PM, or downstairs near the exits (⊠ Under the ČD Centrum sign), or call 2422–4200. The Čedok office at Na příkopě 18 (☎ 02/2419–7111) also provides train information and issues tickets.

Wenceslas Square is a convenient five-minute walk from the main station, or you can take the subway one stop to Muzeum. A taxi ride from the main station to the center will cost about 50 Kč. To reach the city center from Nádraží Holešovice, take the subway (Line C) four stops to Muzeum.

Getting Around

To see Prague properly, there is no alternative to walking, especially since much of the city center is off-limits to automobiles. And the walking couldn't be more pleasant—most of it along the beautiful bridges and cobblestone streets of the city's historic core. Before venturing out, however, be sure you have a good map.

BY BUS AND TRAM

Prague's extensive bus and streetcar network allows for fast, efficient travel throughout the city. Tickets are the same as those used for the metro, although you validate them at machines inside the bus or streetcar. Tickets (*jizdenky*) can be bought at hotels, newsstands, and from dispensing machines in the metro stations. The price of a ticket increased in 1996 from 6 Kč to 10 Kč; the new tickets permit one hour's travel throughout the metro, tram, and bus network, rather than the current one ticket–one ride system. You can also buy a one-day pass allowing unlimited use of the system for 50 Kč, a two-day pass for 85 Kč, a three-day pass for 110 Kč, and a five-day pass for 170 Kč. The passes can be purchased at the main metro stations and at some newsstands. A refurbished old tram, No. 91, plies a route in the Old Town and Lesser Quarter on summer weekends. Trams 50–59 and Buses 500 and above run all night, after the metro shuts down at midnight. All night-tram routes intersect at the corner of Lazarská and Spálená streets in the New Town near the Národní Třída metro station.

BY SUBWAY

Prague's subway system, the metro, is clean and reliable. Trains run daily from 5 AM to midnight. Validate the tickets at the orange machines before descending the escalators; each ticket is good for 60 minutes of uninterrupted travel. Trains are patrolled often; the fine for riding without a valid ticket is 200 Kč. Beware of pickpockets, who often operate in large groups, on crowded trams and metro cars.

BY TAXI

Dishonest taxi drivers are the shame of the nation. Luckily visitors do not need to rely on taxis for trips within the city center (it's usually easier to walk or take the subway). Typical scams include drivers doctoring the meter or simply failing to turn the meter on and then demanding an exorbitant sum at the end of the ride. In an honest cab, the meter will start at 10 Kč and increase by 12 Kč per kilometer (½ mile) or 1 Kč per minute at rest. Most rides within town should cost no more than 80 Kč–100 Kč. To minimize the chances of getting ripped off, avoid taxi stands in Wenceslas Square and other heavily touristed areas. The best alternative is to phone for a taxi in advance. Some reputable firms are **AAA Taxi** (☎ 02/3399) and **Sedop** (☎ 02/6731–4184). Many firms have English-speaking operators.

Contacts and Resources

CAR RENTALS

The following rental agencies are based in Prague:

Alamo Rent a Car (✉ Elišky Krásnohorské 2/10, Prague 7, ☎ 370187 or 0601281–260). **Avis** (✉ Elišky Krásnohorské 9, Prague 7, ☎ 02/231–5515). **Budget** (✉ Hotel Inter-Continental, ☎ 02/2488–9995). **Esocar** (✉ Husitská 58, Prague 3, ☎ 02/278888). **Hertz** (✉ Karlovo nám. 28, Prague 2, ☎ 297836 or 290122).

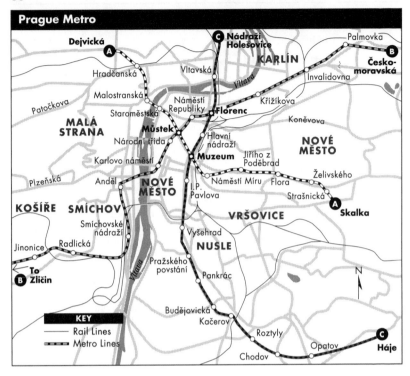

Prague Metro

United States (✉ Tržiště 15, Malá Strana, ☎ 02/2451–0847). **British** (✉ Thunovská ul. 14, Malá Strana, ☎ 02/2451–0439). **Canadian** (✉ Mickiewiczova ul. 6, Hradčany, ☎ 02/2431–1108).

Police (☎ 158). **Ambulance** (☎ 155). **Medical emergencies: Foreigners' Department of Na Homolce Hospital** (✉ Roentgenova 2, Prague 5, weekdays ☎ 02/5292–2146, evenings and weekends ☎ 02/520022 or 02/5292–2191); **First Medical Clinic of Prague** (✉ Vyšehradská 35, Prague 2, ☎ 02/292286, 298978; 24-hr emergency ☎ 02/0601–225050, mobile phone). Be prepared to pay in cash for medical treatment, whether you are insured or not. **Dentists** (✉ Vladislavova 22, Prague 1, ☎ 02/2422–7663 for 24-hr emergency service).

Lost credit cards: American Express (☎ 02/2421–9992); Diners Club, Visa (☎ 02/2412–5353); MasterCard (☎ 02/2442–3135).

In the central city these are too numerous to list. *See* Shopping, *above*, for a few recommended bookstores a bit off the tourist routes. Street vendors on Wenceslas Square and Na příkopě carry leading foreign newspapers and periodicals. For hiking maps and auto atlases, try the **Jan Kanzelsberger** bookstore on Wenceslas Square (✉ Václavské nám. 42, ☎ 02/2421–7335).

Čedok's (☎ 02/231–8949) three-hour "Historical Prague" tour (🚌 490 Kč), offered year-round, is a combination bus-walking venture that covers all the major sights. It departs daily at 10 AM and 2 PM from the Čedok office at Pařížská 6 (near the Inter-Continental Hotel). Between May and October, "Panoramic Prague" (🚌 300 Kč), an abbreviated version of the above tour, departs Wednesday, Friday, and Saturday at 11 AM from the Čedok office at Na příkopě 18. On Friday Čedok also offers "Prague on Foot," a slower-paced, three-hour walking tour that departs at 9:30 AM from Na příkopě 18. The price is 290 Kč. More tours are offered, especially in summer, and the above schedule may well vary according to demand. Prices may also go up in high season.

Many private firms now offer combination bus-walking tours of the city that typically last two or three hours and cost 300 Kč–400 Kč or more. For more information, address inquiries to any of the dozen operators with booths on Wenceslas Square, Staroměstské náměstí (near the Jan Hus monument), or Náměstí Republiky (near the Obecní Dům).

Personal Guides: You can contact the Čedok office at Bilkova 6 (☎ 02/231–8255) to arrange a personalized walking tour. Times and itineraries are negotiable; prices start at around 500 Kč per hour.

LATE-NIGHT PHARMACIES
There are two 24-hour pharmacies close to the city's center, both called **Lékárna** (⊠ Štefánikova 6, Prague 5, ☎ 02/537039; ⊠ Belgická 37, Prague 2, ☎ 02/258189).

TRAVEL AGENCIES
American Express (Václavské nám. 56, ☎ 02/2422–9883, FAX 02/2422–7708); **Thomas Cook** (Národní třída 28, ☎ 02/2110–5272).

For low-price bus tickets to just about anywhere in Europe, try **Bohemia Tour** (⊠ Zlatnická 7) or **Čedok**'s main office (⊠ Na příkopě).

VISITOR INFORMATION
Čedok, the ubiquitous travel agency, is the first stop for general tourist information and city maps. Čedok will also exchange money, arrange guided tours, and book passage on airlines, buses, and trains. You can pay for Čedok services, including booking rail tickets, with any major credit card. Note limited weekend hours. ⊠ *Main office: Na příkopě 18,* ☎ *02/2419–7111,* FAX *02/2422–5339.* ☉ *Weekdays 8:30–6, Sat. 9–1. Other downtown offices: Rytířská 16 and Pařížská 6.*

The **Prague Information Service (PIS)** (⊠ Staroměstské nám. 22; Na příkopě 20) is generally less helpful than Čedok but offers city maps and general tourist information and arranges group and individual tours. It can also exchange money and help in obtaining tickets for cultural events.

The **Czech Tourist Authority** (⊠ Národní třída 37, ☎ FAX 02/2421–1458) can provide information on tourism outside Prague but does not sell tickets or book accommodations.

To find out what's on for the month and to get the latest tips for shopping, dining, and entertainment, consult Prague's weekly English-language newspaper, the *Prague Post*. It prints comprehensive entertainment listings and can be bought at most downtown newsstands as well as in major North American and European cities. The monthly *Prague Guide,* available at newsstands and tourist offices for 25 Kč, provides a good overview of major cultural events and has listings of restaurants, hotels, and organizations offering traveler assistance.

SOUTHERN BOHEMIA

With Prague at its heart, and Germany and the former Austro-Hungarian Empire on its mountainous borders, the kingdom of Bohemia was for centuries buffeted by religious and national conflicts, invasions, and wars. But its position also meant that Bohemia benefited from the cultural wealth and diversity of Central Europe. The result is a glorious array of castles, walled cities, and spa towns set in a gentle rolling landscape, boasting a past that would be difficult to match in any other provincial area of Central Europe.

Southern Bohemia (separate sections on the northern and western areas follow) is particularly famous for its involvement in the Hussite religious wars of the 15th century, which revolved around the town of Tábor. But the area also has more than its fair share of well-preserved and stunning walled towns, built up through the ages by generations of the noble families of the day, who left behind layers of Gothic, Renaissance, and baroque architecture (particularly notable in Çeský Krumlov). Farther north and an easy drive east of Prague is the old silver-mining town of Kutná Hora, once a rival to Prague for the royal residence.

The major towns of southern Bohemia offer some of the best accommodations in the Czech Republic. (This is also true of western Bohemia; ☞ *below*.) Towns with private rooms available are noted below; here, as in many parts of Bohemia, the only real options for dining are the restaurants and cafés at the larger hotels and resorts.

Numbers in the margin correspond to numbers on the Bohemia map.

Kutná Hora

59 *70 km (44 mi) east of Prague.*

The approach to Kutná Hora looks much as it has for centuries. The long economic decline of this town, once Prague's chief rival in Bohemia for wealth and beauty, spared it the postwar construction that has blighted the outskirts of so many other Czech cities. Though it is undeniably beautiful, with an intact Gothic and baroque townscape, Kutná Hora can leave one feeling a bit melancholy. The town owes its illustrious past to silver, discovered here during the 12th century. For some 400 years the mines were worked with consummate efficiency, the wealth going to support grand projects throughout Bohemia. Charles IV used the silver to finance his transformation of Prague from a market town into the worthy capital of the Holy Roman Empire during the 14th century. As the silver began to run out during the 16th and 17th centuries, however, Kutná Hora's importance faded. What remains is the paradox you see today: poor inhabitants dwarfed by the splendors of the Middle Ages.

★ Forget the town center for a moment and walk to the **Chrám svaté Barbory** (St. Barbara's Cathedral), a 10-minute stroll from the main Palackého náměstí along Barborská ulice. The approach to the cathedral, overlooking the river, is magnificent. Statues line the road, and the baroque houses vie with each other for attention. In the distance, the netted vaulting of the cathedral resembles a large, magnificent tent more than a religious center; the effect gives the cathedral a cheerier look than that of the dignified Gothic towers of Prague. St. Barbara's is undoubtedly Kutná Hora's masterpiece and a high point of the Gothic style in Bohemia. Built in the 14th and 15th centuries, it drew on the talents of the Peter Parler workshop as well as on other Gothic luminaries, such as Matthias Rejsek and Benedikt Ried.

St. Barbara is the patron saint of miners, and silver-mining themes dominate the interior. Gothic frescoes depict angels carrying shields with mining symbols. The town's other major occupation, minting, can be seen in frescoes in the **Mintner's Chapel**. A statue of a miner, donning the characteristic smock and dating from 1700, stands proudly in the

Bohemia

Dresden

Bautzen

Görlitz

Löbau

Freiberg

Pirna

Zittau

Chemnitz

Děčín   13   Nový Bor

Spindlerův
Mlýn   **79**

Ústí nad
Labem   Liberec   Jablonec

Teplice

Litvínov   Mimoň

Vrchlabí

Most   Litoměřice   **77**   Doksy   Turnov

Vejprty   Chomutov   **76** Terezín   Nová Pakn

Ohře   Mělník   Mladá

Kraslice   Elbe   **78**   Boleslav

Františkovy
Lázně   **68**   Ostrov   Zatec   Louny   Zlonice   Neratovice   Jičín

70   Karlovy Vary   Veltrusy Château   **75**   Celákovice   Poděbrady

Sokolov   Bochov   and Gardens   Roztoky

69   Bečov   Lidice   Prague   Labe

Cheb   **71**   **72**   Toužim   Kralovice   Beroun   **74**   Rudná   Kolín   **59**

**Mariánské
Lázně**   **Teplá**   Berounka   Říčany   Uhlířské   Kutná
Hora

Plana   Zdice   333   Janovice

Tachov   **Plzeň**   **73**   **Konopiště**   Zbraslavice

Bor   Stříbro   Rokycany   **61**   **60**

Dobřany   Příbram   Sedlčany   **Český
Šternberk**

Horšovský   Nepomuk   Vltava

Domažlice   Milevsko

Klatovy   Horažďovice   **Písek**   **62**   Pelhřimov

Cham   Sušice   **67**   Soběslav   Kamenice

Strakonice   Veselí

Vimperk   Vodňany   Třeboň   Jindr.
Hradec   **63**

Regen   Hluboká nad Vltavou   **66**

Deggendorf   **České Budějovice**   Borovany

**Český
Krumlov**   **65**   Trhové Sviny

Passau   vod. nádrž
Lipno   Kaplice   Gmünd

GERMANY   **Rožmberk
nad Vltavou**   **64**   Freistadt

AUSTRIA   Stadl-Paura   N

0   20 miles
0   30 km

nave. But the main attraction of the interior is the vaulting itself—attributed to Ried (also responsible for the fabulous vaulting in Prague Castle's Vladislav Hall)—which carries the eye effortlessly upward. ⊠ *Barborská ul.* ☎ *20 Kč.* ☉ *Tues.–Sun. 9–noon and 2–4.*

The romantic view over the town from the cathedral area, marked by the visibly tilting 260-foot tower of St. James Church, is impressive, and few modern buildings intrude. As you descend into town, the **Hrádek** (Little Castle), on your right along Barborská ulice, was once part of the town's fortifications and now houses a museum of mining and coin production and a claustrophobic medieval mine tunnel. ⊠ *Barborská ul.* ☎ *20 Kč.* ☉ *Apr.–Oct., Tues.–Sun. 9–noon and 1–5.*

NEED A
BREAK? The **Café U Hrádku** is a pleasant place to stop for refreshments or a light home-cooked meal. Lamps and furnishings from the 1920s add a period touch. ⊠ *Barborská ul. 33,* ☎ *0327/4277.* ☉ *Tues.–Sun. 10–5. No credit cards.*

You'll easily find the **Vlašský dvůr** (Italian Court), the old mint, by following the signs through town. Coins were first minted here in 1300, struck by Italian artisans brought in from Florence—hence the mint's odd name. It was here that the famed Prague groschen, one of the most widely circulated coins of the Middle Ages, was minted until 1726, and here, too, that the Bohemian kings stayed on their frequent visits. Something of the court's former wealth can be glimpsed in the formal Gothic interiors of the chapel and tower rooms. A **coin museum,** open in spring and summer, allows you to see the small, silvery groschen being struck and gives you a chance to buy replicas. Small wooden triptychs can be purchased in the chapel. ⊠ *Havlíčkovo nám.* ☎ *30 Kč.* ☉ *Apr.–Oct., daily 10–6; Nov.–Mar., daily 10–4.*

If the door to the **Chrám svatého Jakuba** (St. James Church) next door is open, peek inside. Originally a Gothic church dating from the early 1400s, the structure was almost entirely transformed into baroque during the 17th and 18th centuries. The characteristic onion dome on the tower was added in 1737. The paintings on the wall include works of the best baroque Czech masters; the *Pietà* is by the 17th-century painter Karel Škréta. Pause to admire the simple Gothic beauty of the 12-sided **kamenná kašna** (stone fountain) at Rejskovo náměstí, just off Husova ulice. This unique work, some 500 years old, is supposedly the creation of Rejsek, one of the architects of St. Barbara's.

Before leaving the city, stop in the nearby suburb of Sedlec for a bone-chilling sight: a chapel decorated with the bones of some 40,000 people. The All Saints' Cemetery Chapel, or **Bone Church,** at the site of the former Sedlec Monastery, came into being in the 14th century, when development forced the clearing of a nearby graveyard. Monks of the Cistercian order came up with the bright idea of using the bones for decoration; the most recent creations date from the end of the last century. ☎ *20 Kč.* ☉ *Daily 9–noon and 2–4.*

Lodging

$$$ 🏨 **Medínek.** This is one of the few hotels in town with modern conveniences, so book in advance or risk being squeezed out by German and Austrian tour groups. The location, on the main square, puts you at an easy stroll from the sights, and the ground-floor restaurant offers decent Czech cooking in an atmosphere more pleasant than that found in the local beer halls. Yet, as with many of the hotels built during the 1960s and 1970s, the modern architecture blights the surrounding square. ⊠ *Palackého nám. 316, 284 01 Kutná Hora,* ☎ *0327/*

2741, ⟨FAX⟩ *0327/2743. 90 rooms, some with bath. Restaurant, café. AE, MC, V.*

$$ ⊡ **U Hrnčíře.** This is a picturesque little inn situated next to a potter's shop near the town center. The quaintness doesn't make up for the very standard, plain rooms, but the friendly staff gives the hotel a decidedly homey feel. The restaurant in the back garden features a beautiful view overlooking the valley. ⊠ *Barborská 24, 284 01 Kutná Hora,* ☎ *0327/2113. 5 rooms with bath. Restaurant. AE, MC, V.*

Český Šternberk

60 *40 km (24 mi) from Kutná Hora, 24 km (15 mi) from Benešov.*

At night this 13th-century castle looks positively evil, occupying a forested knoll over the Sázava River. By daylight, the structure, last renovated in the 17th century, is less haunting but still impressive. Although the castle became the property of the Czechoslovak state following the Communist coup, Count Šternberk (the former owner) was permitted to occupy it until his death in 1966 as a reward for not cowering to the occupying German forces. Ownership returned to the Šternberk family in 1991. In season, you can tour some of the rooms fitted out with period furniture (mostly rococo); little of the early Gothic has survived the many renovations. ⊠ *Český Šternberk,* ☎ *0303/55101.* ⌨ *75 Kč.* ☉ *May–June and Sept., Tues.–Sun. 9–5; July–Aug., Tues.–Sun. 9–6; Apr. and Oct., weekends 9–4.*

Konopiště

61 *25 km (15 mi) west of Český Šternberk, 45 km (27 mi) southeast of Prague.*

Given its remote location, Český Šternberk is ill equipped for a meal or an overnight stay. Instead, continue on to the superior facilities of Konopiště (via the industrial town of Benešov). Konopiště is best known for its 14th-century castle, which served six centuries later as the residence of the former heir to the Austrian crown, Franz Ferdinand d'Este. Scorned by the Austrian nobility for having married a commoner, Franz Ferdinand wanted an impressive summer residence to win back the envy of his peers, and he spared no expense in restoring the castle to its original Gothic form, filling its 82 rooms with outlandish paintings, statues, and curiosities. Franz Ferdinand's dream came to a fateful end in 1914 when he was assassinated at Sarajevo, an event that precipitated World War I. The Austrian defeat in the war ultimately led to the fall of the Hapsburgs. Ironically, the destiny of the Austrian Empire had been sealed at the castle a month before the assassination, when Austrian emperor Franz Joseph I met with Germany's Kaiser Wilhelm II and agreed to join forces with him in the event of war.

★ To visit **Zámek Konopiště** (Konopiště Castle), start from the Konopiště Motel, about a kilometer (½ mile) off Route 3, and walk straight for about 2 kilometers (1 mile) along the trail through the woods. Before long, the rounded, neo-Gothic towers appear through the trees, and you reach the formal garden with its almost mystical circle of classical statues. Built by the wealthy Beneschau family, the castle dates from around 1300 and for centuries served as a bastion of the nobility in their struggle for power with the king. In what must have been a great affront to royal authority at the end of the 14th century, Catholic nobles actually captured the weak King Wenceslas (Václav) IV in Prague and held him prisoner in the smaller of the two rounded towers. To this day the tower is known affectionately as the Václavka. Several of the rooms, reflecting the archduke's extravagant taste and lifestyle, are open to the public during the tourism season. A valuable collection of weapons from the 16th to 18th centuries can be seen in the Weapons Hall on the third floor. Less easy to miss are the hundreds of stuffed animals, rather macabre monuments to the archduke's obsession with hunting. ⊠ *Zá mek Konopiště, Benešov, about 3 km (2 mi) west of train and bus stations on red- or yellow-marked paths).* ☎ *Each tour 90–200 Kč.* ⊙ *Apr. and Oct., Tues.–Sun. 9–3; May–Aug., Tues.–Sun. 9–5; Sept., Tues.–Sun. 9–4.*

Dining and Lodging

$$$$ ✕ **Stodola.** It's a little cabin, next to the Konopiště Motel, with a reputation as one of the best exemplars of Bohemian-style grilled meats, chicken, and fish dishes. The live folk music in the evenings is romantic rather than obtrusive; the wines and service are excellent. ⊠ *Benešov,* ☎ *0301/22732. No lunch. AE, MC, V.*

$$$ 🏨 **Konopiště Motel.** Long a favorite with diplomats in Prague, who come for the fresh air and outdoor sports, the motel is about 2 kilometers (1 mile) from Konopiště Castle, on a small road about a kilometer from the main Prague–Tabor highway (Route 3). The rooms are small but well appointed (ask for one away from the main road). The castle and gardens are an easy 20-minute walk through the woods; a campground is nearby. ⊠ *256 01 Benešov,* ☎ *0301/22732,* 🖷 *0301/22053. 40 rooms with bath. 2 restaurants, in-room satellite TV, minigolf, parking. Breakfast not included. AE, DC, MC, V.*

Tábor

62 *40 km (25 mi) south of Konopiště down Route 3.*

It's hard to believe this dusty Czech town was built to receive Christ on his return to Earth in the Second Coming. But that's what the Hussites intended when they flocked here by the thousands in 1420 to construct a society modeled on the communities of the early Christians. Tábor's fascinating history is unique among Czech towns. It started out not as a mercantile or administrative center but as a combination utopia and fortress.

Following the execution of Jan Hus, a vociferous religious reformer who railed against the Catholic Church and the nobility, reform priests drawing on the support of poor workers and peasants took to the hills of southern Bohemia. These hilltop congregations soon grew into permanent settlements, wholly outside the feudal order. The most important settlement, on the Lužnice River, became known in 1420 as Tábor. Tábor quickly evolved into the symbolic and spiritual center of the Hussites (now called Taborites) and, together with Prague, served as the bulwark of the reform movement.

The early 1420s in Tábor were heady days for religious reformers. Private property was denounced, and the many poor who made the pilgrimage to Tábor were required to leave their possessions at the town gates. Some sects rejected the doctrine of transubstantiation (the belief that the Eucharist becomes the Body and Blood of Christ), making Holy Communion into a bawdy, secular feast of bread and wine. Still other reformers considered themselves superior to Christ—who by dying had shown himself to be merely mortal. Few, however, felt obliged to work for a living, and the Taborites had to rely increasingly on raids of neighboring villages for survival.

War fever in Tábor at the time ran high, and the town became one of the focal points of the ensuing Hussite wars (1419–34), which pitted reformers against an array of foreign crusaders, Catholics, and noblemen. Under the brilliant military leadership of Jan Žižka, the Taborites enjoyed early successes, but the forces of the established church proved too mighty in the end. Žižka was killed in 1424, and the Hussite uprising ended at the rout of Lipany 10 years later. But even after the fall, many of the town's citizens resisted recatholicization. Fittingly, following the Battle of White Mountain in 1620 (the final defeat for the Czech Protestants), Tábor was the last city to succumb to the conquering Hapsburgs.

Begin a walking tour of the town at the **Žižkovo náměstí** (Žižka Square), named for the gifted Hussite military leader. A large bronze statue of Žižka from the 19th century dominates the square, serving as a reminder of the town's fiery past. The stone tables in front of the Gothic town hall and the house at No. 6 date from the 15th century and were used by the Hussites to give daily Communion to the faithful. Follow the tiny streets around the square, which seemingly lead nowhere. They curve around, branch off, and then stop; few lead back to the main square. The confusing street plan was purposely laid during the 15th century to thwart incoming invasions.

The **Museum of the Hussite Movement,** just behind the town hall, documents the history of the reformers. Note the elaborate network of tunnels carved by the Hussites below the Old Town for protection in case of attack. ⊠ *Křivkova ul. 31.* 🖼 *20 Kč.* ☺ *Daily 8:30–5; closed weekends Nov.–Mar. and Mon. Apr.–Oct.*

Leave the square along **Pražská ulice,** a main route to the newer part of town, and note the beautiful Renaissance facades from the 16th century. Turn right at Divadelní and head to the Lužnice River to see the remaining walls and fortifications of the 15th century, irrefutable evidence of the town's vital function as a stronghold. **Kotnov hrad** (Kotnov Castle), rising above the river in the distance to the right, dates from the 13th century and was part of the earliest fortifications. The large pond to the northeast of Tábor was created as a reservoir in 1492; since it was used for baptism, the fervent Taborites named the lake Jordan.

Lodging

$$ 🏨 **Palcát.** A 10-minute walk from the Old Town Square, the slightly rundown Palcát is quite a contrast. The architecture is overwhelmingly drab, but the rooms, though plain, are bright and comfortable; those on the upper floors have a dazzling view of the Old Town. ⊠ *Tř. 9, Května 2467, 390 01 Tábor,* ☎ *0361/252901,* 𝔽𝔸𝕏 *0361/252905. 65 rooms with shower. Restaurant, bar, café, conference hall. Breakfast included. AE, MC, V.*

$–$$ 🏨 **Bican Pension.** Highly recommended. This lovely family-run pen-
★ sion is sure to inspire you to linger in Tábor. The staff couldn't be nicer, nor could the view from either side of the pension: One side faces the Old Town, the other offers a soothing view of the river and the rolling landscape beyond. The premises date from the 14th century, and the Bicans will gladly oblige with a minitour of the house's own catacombs. The chilly basement lounge is a godsend on sweltering summer days. ⊠ *Hradební 189/16, 390 01 Tábor,* ☎ *0361/252109. 6 rooms with bath. Lounge, sauna, use of kitchen. Breakfast included. No credit cards.*

Třeboň

63 *48 km (28 mi) south of Tábor.*

Amid a plethora of ponds rests another jewel of a town with a far different historical heritage than Tábor's. Třeboň was settled during the 13th century by the Wittkowitzes (later called the Rosenbergs), once

Bohemia's noblest family. From 1316 to the end of the 16th century, the dynasty dominated southern Bohemia. You can see their emblem, a five-petaled rose, on castles, doorways, and coats of arms all over the region. The Rosenbergs' wealth was based on silver and real estate. Their official residence was 40 kilometers (25 miles) to the southwest, in Český Krumlov, but Třeboň was an important second residence and repository of the family archives.

Thanks to the Rosenberg family, this unlikely landlocked town has become the center of the Czech Republic's fishing industry. During the 15th and 16th centuries, the Rosenbergs peppered the countryside with 6,000 enormous ponds, partly to drain the land and partly to breed fish. Carp breeding is still big business, and if you are in the area in the late autumn, you may be lucky enough to witness the great carp harvests, when tens of thousands of the glittering fish are netted. The largest pond, bearing the Rosenberg name, lies just north of Třeboň. The **Rybník Svět** (Svět Pond) is closest to town, along the southern edge. Join the locals on a warm afternoon for a stroll along its banks and enjoy the mild breezes.

Begin a walking tour of Třeboň from the park outside the town walls, with the Svět Pond at your back. From here, the simple sgraffito Renaissance exterior of the castle, with its deep turrets, is highly impressive. The intact town walls, built during the 16th century, are among the best in the Czech Republic. Continue along the park, turning left at the first of the three gates into town. An 18th-century brewery, still producing outstanding beer, is off to the right. First brewed in 1379, as the redbrick tower proudly boasts, beer enjoys nearly as long a tradition here as in Plzeň or České Budějovice. Continue straight ahead to arrive at the main square, with its familiar collection of arcaded Renaissance and baroque houses. Look for the **Bílý Koníček** (Little White Horse), the best-preserved Renaissance house on the square, dating from 1544. The large rectangular gable on the roof is composed of numerous tiny towers.

The entrance to **Zámek Třeboň** (Třeboň Château) lies at the southwest corner of the square. From here it looks plain and sober, with its stark white walls, but the rooms (open to the public) are sumptuous recreations of 16th-century life. The castle also houses a permanent exhibition of pond building. The last of the Rosenbergs died in 1611, and the castle eventually became the property of the Schwarzenberg family, who built their family tomb in a grand park on the other side of Svět Pond. It is now a monumental neo-Gothic destination for Sunday-afternoon picnickers. ⊠ *Zámek Třeboň,* ☎ *0333/721193.* ≤ *40 Kč.* ⊙ *Apr. and Oct., weekends 9–4; May and Sept., Tues.–Sun. 9–4; June–Aug., Tues.–Sun. 9–5.*

In the **Augustine Monastery,** adjacent to the castle, take a look at the famous Altar of the Masters of Wittingau, dating from the late 14th century. The altar was removed in 1781 from St. Giles Church (Chrám svatého Jiljí), on Husova třída. The paintings themselves, the most famous example of Bohemian Gothic art, are now in the National Gallery in Prague.

NEED A BREAK?   Before leaving Třeboň, sample some of the excellent local beer at the **Bílý Koníček** (☎ 0333/2818), now a modest hotel and restaurant on the square. You can also get a variety of nonalcoholic beverages as well as good local dishes at reasonable prices.

Lodging

$ 🏨 **Bílý Koníček.** This old-style hotel occupies one of the most striking Renaissance buildings on the main square. With the nearby Zlatá Hvězda being remodeled, it's a very acceptable alternative. The rooms fail to measure up to the splendid facade but are suitably clean. ⌧ *Masarykovo nám. 97, 379 01 Třeboň,* ☎ *0333/721213,* ℻ *0333/721136. 10 rooms with bath. Restaurant. Breakfast not included. V.*

Swimming

You can swim in most of the larger carp ponds around town. The Svět Pond is particularly appealing because of its little sandy beaches, although these are generally crowded in summer.

Rožmberk nad Vltavou

★ ⑥⑤ *60 km (36 mi) southwest of Třeboň.*

This little village, just a few kilometers from the former Iron Curtain, was forgotten in the postwar years. It seems like a ghost town, especially at night with the darkened **Rosenberg hrad** (Rosenberg Castle) keeping lonely vigil atop the hill overlooking the Vltava River. A barely visible German sign, WIRTSCHAFT ZUM GOLDENEN BÄREN (Inn at the Golden Bear), on the battered facade of a beer hall across the bridge, adds to the feeling of abandonment, as if nothing has happened here in decades. Take a moment to enjoy the silence and walk up the hill to the castle. The slender tower, the Jakobinka, dates from the 13th century, when the Rosenberg family built the original structure. Most of the exterior, however, is neo-Gothic from the last century. In summer you can tour some of the rooms, admiring the weapons and Bohemian paintings. From the castle gates, the Romanesque-Gothic church below, standing beside the lone figure of St. Christopher on the bridge, looks especially solemn. ⌧ *Rožmberk nad Vltavou,* ☎ *0337/9838.* 🎟 *50 Kč.* ☉ *Apr. and Oct., weekends 9–3; May and Sept., Tues.–Sun. 9–3:15; June–Aug., Tues.–Sun. 9–4:15.*

Český Krumlov

★ ⑥⑤ *22 km (13 mi) north of Rožmberk nad Vltavou.*

Český Krumlov, the official residence of the Rosenbergs for some 300 years, is an eye-opener: None of the surrounding towns or villages, with their open squares and mixtures of old and new buildings, will prepare you for the beauty of the Old Town. Here the Vltava works its wonders as nowhere else but in Prague itself, swirling in a nearly complete circle around the town. Across the river stands the proud castle, rivaling any in the country in size and splendor.

For the moment, Český Krumlov's beauty is still intact, even though the dilapidated buildings that lend the town its unique atmosphere are slowly metamorphosizing into boutiques and expensive pensions. In peak months, when visitors from Austria and Germany pack the streets, the existing facilities for visitors can be woefully overburdened. But overlook any minor inconveniences and enjoy a rare, unspoiled trip through time.

Begin a tour of the Old Town from the main **Svornosti náměstí.** The square itself is disappointing; the arcades hide the richness of the buildings' architecture. The **town hall,** at No. 1, built in 1580, is memorable for its Renaissance friezes and Gothic arcades. Tiny alleys fan out from the square in all directions. Horní ulice begins just opposite the Hotel Krumlov. A quick visit to the **Městské muzeum** (City Mu-

seum) at No. 152 is a good way to familiarize yourself with the rise
and fall of the Rosenberg dynasty.

Just opposite the museum, at No. 154, are the Renaissance facades,
complete with lively sgraffiti, of the former **Jesuit school**—now the semi-
luxurious Růže Hotel Český Krumlov, which owes its abundance of
Renaissance detailing to its location on the main trading routes to Italy
and Bavaria—a perfect site for absorbing incoming fashions. The
tower of the nearby late-Gothic **St. Vitus Church,** built in the late
1400s, rises from its position on Kostelní ulice to offset the larger, older
tower of the castle across the river. The view over the Old Town and
castle is at its most spectacular from here.

To get to **Krumlov hrad** (Krumlov Castle), make your way from St. Vitus
to the main street, Radniční, via either Masná or Kostelní ulice, both
of which form a big ring around the square. Cross the peaceful Vltava
and enter at one of two gates along the Latrán. The oldest and most
striking part of the castle is the round 12th-century tower, renovated,
like the rest of the building in the 16th century, to look something like
a minaret, with its delicately arcaded Renaissance balcony. The tower
is part of the old border fortifications, guarding the Bohemian frontiers from Austrian incursion.

The castle passed out of the Rosenbergs' hands when the last of the
line, the dissolute Petr Vok, sold castle and town to Rudolf II in 1601
to pay off his debts. The castle's Renaissance and baroque features and
its most sumptuous furnishings were added later by the Eggenberg and
Schwarzenberg families.

As you enter the castle area, look into the old moats, where two playful brown bears now reside—unlikely to be of much help in protecting the castle from attack. In season, the castle rooms are open to the
public. The **Hall of Masks** is the most impressive interior, with its richly
detailed 18th-century frescoes. After proceeding through a series of courtyards, you'll come to a wonderfully romantic elevated passageway with
spectacular views of the huddled houses of the Old Town. The Austrian expressionist painter Egon Schiele often stayed in Český Krumlov
in the early years of this century and liked to paint this particular view
over the river. He called his now famous Krumlov series *The Dead Town.*
From the river down below, the elevated passageway is revealed in all
its Renaissance glory as part of a network of tall arches, looking like
a particularly elaborate Roman viaduct. On top runs a narrow three-
story residential block (still inhabited), dressed in gray-and-white Renaissance stripes. At the end of the passageway you'll come to the
luxuriously appointed castle gardens (open only in summer). In the middle is an open-air theater, one of Bohemia's first such theaters and remarkable for its still-intact gold stage. Performances are held here in
July and August. ⊠ *Český Krumlov hrad,* ☎ *0337/3135.* ☞ *70 Kč.*
☉ *Apr. and Oct., Tues.–Sun. 9–noon and 1–3; May–Aug., Tues.–Sun.
9–noon and 1–5, Sept., Tues.–Sun. 9–noon and 1–4.*

The **Egon Schiele Center** exhibits the work of Schiele and other 20th-
century artists in a rambling Renaissance house near the river.
⊠ *Široká 70–72.* ☞ *100 Kč.* ☉ *Daily 10–6.*

Dining and Lodging

Český Krumlov is crammed with pensions and private rooms for rent,
many priced around $15 per person per night. The best place to look
is along the tiny Parkán ulice, which parallels the river just off the main
street. A safe bet is the house at Parkán No. 107, blessed with several
nice rooms and friendly management (☎ 0337/4396).

$ **✗ ⋈ Na louži.** Wood floors and exposed-beam ceilings lend a traditional
★ touch to this warm, inviting, family-run pub, which also has rooms
for rent upstairs. The atmosphere is cozy and the service attentive. The
quality extends to the food, which is as close to homemade as you'll
find. This is a rare treat among the inns of Bohemia. ⊠ *Kájovská 66,
381 01 Český Krumlov,* ☎ ⅋ℵ *0337/5495. 5 rooms with bath. Restaurant. No credit cards.*

$$$ **⋈ Růže.** This Renaissance monastery has been renovated and trans-
★ formed into an excellent luxury hotel, only a five-minute walk from
the main square. The rooms are spacious and clean—some also have
drop-dead views of the town below, so ask to see several before choos-
ing. The restaurant, too, is top-rate; the elegant dining room is formal
without being oppressive, and the menu draws from traditional Czech
and international cuisines. ⊠ *Horní ul. 153, 381 01 Český Krumlov,*
☎ *0337/2245,* ⅋ℵ *0337/3881. 50 rooms, most with bath. Restaurant,
nightclub. AE, MC, V.*

Nightlife and the Arts

An outdoor theater in the castle gardens in **Český Krumlov** is a popu-
lar venue for plays and concerts throughout the summer.

České Budějovice

⑥⑥ *22 km (13 mi) from Çeský Krumlov: Follow Route 159, then Route
3.*

After the glories of Çeský Krumlov, any other town would be a let-
down—and Çeské Budějovice, known as Budweis under the Hapsburgs
and famous primarily for its beer, is no exception. The major attrac-
tion of what is basically an industrial town is the enormously pro-
portioned main square, lined with arcaded houses and worth an hour
or two of wandering. To get a good view over the city, it's well worth
climbing the 360 steps up to the Renaissance gallery of the **Černá Věž**
(Black Tower), at the northeast corner of the square next to St. Nicholas
Cathedral. ▣ *10 Kč.* ☉ *Apr.–Oct., Tues.–Sun. 9–5.*

Lodging

$$$ **⋈ Gomel.** This modern high-rise, a 15-minute walk from the main square
along the road to Prague, is probably best suited to business travelers.
The rooms are plain, but the hotel does offer a reasonable range of facilities and has an English-speaking staff. ⊠ *Pražská tř. 14, 307 01
Çeské Budějovice,* ☎ *038/7311390,* ⅋ℵ *038/7311365. 180 rooms with
bath or shower. 3 restaurants, café, nightclub, conference hall. Breakfast included. AE, DC, MC, V.*

$$$ **⋈ Zvon.** Old-fashioned, well-kept, and comfortable, the Zvon has an
ideal location, right on the main town square. The rooms are bright,
and the period bathrooms have large bathtubs. The price is high, how-
ever, for the level of facilities. ⊠ *Nám. Přemysla Otakara II 28, 307
01 Çeské Budějovice,* ☎ *038/7311383,* ⅋ℵ *038/7311385. 75 rooms,
most with bath. Restaurant. Breakfast not included. AE, MC, V.*

Hluboká nad Vltavou

★ *9 km (6 mi) north of Çeské Budějovice.*

This is one of the Czech Republic's most curious castles. Although the
structure dates from the 13th century, what you see is pure 19th-cen-
tury excess, perpetrated by the wealthy Schwarzenberg family as proof
of their "good taste." If you think you've seen it somewhere before,
you're probably thinking of Windsor Castle, near London, on which

it was carefully modeled. Take a tour; 41 of the 140 rooms are open to the public. The rather pompous interior reflects the no-holds-barred tastes of the time, but many individual pieces are interesting in their own right. The wooden Renaissance ceiling in the large dining room was removed by the Schwarzenbergs from the castle at Çeský Krumlov and brought here in the 19th century. Also look for the beautiful late-baroque bookshelves in the library, holding some 12,000 books. If your interest in Czech painting wasn't satisfied in Prague, have a look at the **Aleš Art Gallery** in the Riding Hall, featuring the works of southern Bohemian painters from the Middle Ages to the present. The collection is the second largest in Bohemia. ✉ *Admission to castle and gallery 100 Kč.* ۩ *Apr.–Oct., daily (except Mon. in May, Sept., and Oct.) 9–4:30 (until 5 June–Aug.).*

In summer the castle grounds make a nice place for a stroll or a picnic. If you're in the mood for a more strenuous walk, follow the yellow trail signs 2 kilometers (1¼ miles) to the **Ohrada hunting lodge,** which houses a museum of hunting and fishing and also has a small zoo for children. ☎ *038/965340.* ۩ *Apr.–Oct., daily 9–noon and 1–4; May–Aug., daily 1–5.*

Písek

67 *60 km (37 mi) northwest of České Budějovice.*

If it weren't for Písek's 700-year-old **Gothic bridge,** peopled with baroque statues, you could easily bypass the town and continue on to Prague. After the splendors of Český Krumlov or even Třeboň, Písek's main square is admittedly plain, despite its many handsome Renaissance and baroque houses. The bridge, a five-minute walk from the main square along Karlovo ulice, was commissioned in 1254 by Přemysl Otakar II, who sought a secure crossing over the difficult Otava River for his salt shipments from nearby Prachatice. Originally one of the five major Hussite strongholds, as early as the 9th century Písek stood at the center of one of the most important trade routes to the west, linking Prague to Passau and the rest of Bavaria. The baroque statues of saints were not added until the 18th century.

Return to the town square and look for the 240-foot tower of the early Gothic **Mariánský chrám** (Church of Mary). Construction was started at about the time the bridge was built. The tower was completed in 1487 and got its baroque dome during the mid-18th century. On the inside, look for the *Madonna from Písek,* a 14th-century Gothic altar painting. On a middle pillar is a rare series of early Gothic wall paintings dating from the end of the 13th century.

OFF THE
BEATEN PATH

ZVÍKOV – If you've got room for still another castle, head for Zvíkov Castle, about 18 kilometers (11 miles) north of town. The castle, at the confluence of the Otava and Vltava rivers, is impressive for its authenticity. Unlike many other castles in Bohemia, Zvíkov survived the 18th and 19th centuries unrenovated and still looks just as it did 500 years ago. The side trip also brings you to the dams and man-made lakes of the Vltava, a major swimming and recreation area that stretches all the way back to Prague.

Southern Bohemia A to Z

Arriving and Departing

Prague is the main gateway to southern Bohemia (☞ Arriving and Departing *in* Prague A to Z, *above*). Several trains a day run from Vienna to Prague; most of these travel via Třeboň and Tábor. To drive from Vienna, take the E49 from Gmünd.

Getting Around

BY BUS

All the major sights are reachable from Prague using ČSAD's dense bus network. Service between the towns, however, is far less frequent and will require some forethought.

BY CAR

Car travel affords the greatest ease and flexibility in this region. The major road from Prague south to Tábor and Çeské Budějovice, though often crowded, is in relatively good shape.

BY TRAIN

Benešov (Konopiště), Tábor, and Třeboň all lie along the major southern line in the direction of Vienna, and train service to these cities from Prague is frequent and comfortable. Good connections also exist from Prague to Çeské Budějovice. For other destinations, you may have to combine the train and bus.

Contacts and Resources

EMERGENCIES

Police (☎ 158). **Ambulance** (☎ 155).

GUIDED TOURS

Çedok (☎ 02/2419–7111) offers several specialized tours that include visits to Çeské Budějovice, Hluboka Castle, Çeský Krumlov, Kutná Hora, and Çeský Šternberk. Çedok also offers a full-day excursion to Moser, the oldest glassworks in Central Europe, south of Prague. Prague departure points include the Çedok offices at Na příkopě 18 and Bílkova ulice 6 and the Panorama, Forum, and Hilton hotels.

VISITOR INFORMATION

Çedok is the first stop for general tourist information and city maps:

Çeské Budějovice (Çedok Çeské Budějovice, ⊠ Nám. Přemysla Otakára II 39, ☎ 038/7352127). **Çeský Krumlov** (Çedok, ⊠ Latrá 79, ☎ 0337/2189; Infocentrum, ⊠ Nám. Svornosti 1, ☎ 0337/5670). **Kutná Hora** (Kulturní a Informační Centrum, ⊠ Palackého 377, ☎ 0327/2378). **Písek (**Çedok, ⊠ Velké nám. 1, ☎ 0362/212988). **Třeboň** (Informační středisko, ⊠ Masarykovo nám. 103, ☎ 0333/721169).

WESTERN BOHEMIA

Until World War II, western Bohemia was the playground of Central Europe's rich and famous. Its three well-known spas, Karlovy Vary, Mariánské Lázně, and Františkový Lázně (better known by their German names: Karlsbad, Marienbad, and Franzensbad, respectively) were the annual haunts of everybody who was anybody—Johann Wolfgang von Goethe, Ludwig van Beethoven, Karl Marx, and England's King Edward VII, to name but a few. Although strictly "proletarianized" in the Communist era, the spas still exude a nostalgic aura of a more elegant past and, unlike most of Bohemia, offer a basic tourist infrastructure that makes dining and lodging a pleasure.

Karlovy Vary

★ ⑱ *132 km (79 mi) due west on Route 6 (E48) from Prague. By car the trip takes about two hours.*

Karlovy Vary, better known outside the Czech Republic by its German name, Karlsbad, is the most famous Bohemian spa. It is named for Emperor Charles (Karl) IV, who allegedly happened upon the springs in 1358 while on a hunting expedition. As the story goes, the emperor's hound—chasing a harried stag—fell into a boiling spring and was scalded. Charles had the water tested and, familiar with spas in Italy, ordered baths to be established in the village of Vary. The spa reached its heyday in the 19th century, when royalty came here from all over Europe for treatment. The long list of those who "took the cure" includes Goethe (no fewer than 13 times, according to a plaque on one house in the Old Town), Schiller, Beethoven, and Chopin. Even Karl Marx, when he wasn't decrying wealth and privilege, spent time at the resort and wrote some of *Das Kapital* here between 1874 and 1876.

The shabby streets of modern Karlovy Vary, though, are vivid reminders that those glory days are long over. Aside from a few superficial changes, the Communists made little new investment in the town for 40 years; many of the buildings are literally crumbling behind their beautiful facades. Today officials face the daunting tasks of financing the town's reconstruction and carving out a new role for Karlovy Vary, in an era when few people can afford to set aside weeks or months at a time for a leisurely cure. To raise some quick cash, many sanatoriums have turned to offering short-term accommodations to foreign visitors (at rather expensive rates). It's even possible at some spas to receive "treatment," including carbon-dioxide baths and massage. For most visitors, though, it's enough simply to stroll the streets and parks and allow the eyes to feast awhile on the splendors of the past.

Whether you're arriving by bus, train, or car, your first view of the town on the approach from Prague will be of the ugly new section on the banks of the Ohře River. Don't despair: Continue along the main road—following the signs to the Grandhotel Pupp—until you reach the lovely main street of the older spa area, situated gently astride the banks of the little Teplá River. The walk from the New Town to the spa area is about 20 minutes; take a taxi if you're carrying a heavy load. The **Old Town** is still largely intact. Tall 19th-century houses, boasting decorative and often eccentric facades, line the spa's proud, if dilapidated, streets. Throughout you'll see colonnades full of the healthy and the not-so-healthy sipping the spa's hot sulfuric water from odd pipe-shaped drinking cups. At night the streets fill with steam escaping from cracks in the earth, giving the town a slightly macabre feel.

Karlovy Vary's jarringly modern **Vřídlo Colonnade,** home of the spring of the same name, is the town's hottest and most dramatic spring. The Vřídlo is indeed unique, shooting its scalding water to a height of some 40 feet. Walk inside the arcade to watch the hundreds of patients here take the famed Karlsbad drinking cure. You'll recognize them promenading somnambulistically up and down, eyes glazed, clutching a drinking glass filled periodically at one of the five "sources." The waters are said to be especially effective against diseases of the digestive and urinary tracts. They're also good for the gout-ridden (which probably explains the spa's former popularity with royals!). If you want to join the crowds and take a sip, you can buy your own spouted cup from vendors within the colonnade.

Walk in the direction of the New Town, past the wooden **Market Colonnade.** Continue down the winding street until you reach the **Mill Colonnade.** This neo-Renaissance pillared hall, built in 1871–81, offers four springs bearing the romantic names of Rusalka, Libussa, Prince Wenceslas, and Millpond. If you continue down the valley, you'll soon arrive at the very elegant **Park Colonnade,** a white wrought-iron construction built in 1882 by the Viennese architectural duo of Fellner and Helmer, who sprinkled the Austro-Hungarian Empire with many such edifices during the late 19th century and who also designed the town's theater (1886), the Market Colonnade (1883), and one of the old bathhouses (1895), now a casino.

The 20th century emerges at its most disturbing a little farther along the valley across the river, in the form of the huge, bunkerlike **Thermal Hotel,** built in the late 1960s. Although the building is a monstrosity, the view of Karlovy Vary from the rooftop pool is nothing short of spectacular. Even if you don't feel like a swim, it's worth taking the winding road up to the baths for the view.

The **Imperial Sanatorium** is a perfect example of turn-of-the-century architecture, with its white facade and red-roofed tower. The Imperial was once the haunt of Europe's wealthiest financiers. Under the Communists, though, the sanatorium was used to house visiting Soviet dignitaries—a gesture of "friendship" from the Czech government. The Imperial has recently reopened as a private hotel, but it will be many years before it can again assume its former role.

You'll find the steep road **Zámecký vrch** by crossing over the little Gogol Bridge near the Hotel Otova, then following the steps leading behind the colonnade. Walk uphill until you come to the redbrick **Victorian Church,** once used by the local English community. A few blocks farther along Petra Velikeho Street, you'll come to a splendiferous **Russian Orthodox church,** once visited by Czar Peter the Great. Return to the English church and take a sharp right uphill on the redbrick road. Then turn left onto a footpath through the woods, following the signs to **Jeleni Skok** (Stag's Leap). After a while you'll see steps leading up to a bronze statue of a deer towering over the cliffs, the symbol of Karlovy Vary. From here a winding path leads up to a little red **gazebo** (Altán Jeleni Skok), opening onto a fabulous panorama of the town.

NEED A BREAK? Reward yourself for making the climb with a light meal at the nearby restaurant **Jeleni Skok.** You may have to pay an entrance fee if there is a live band (but you'll also get the opportunity to polka). If you don't want to walk up, you can drive from the church.

The **Grandhotel Pupp** is the former favorite of the Central European nobility and longtime rival of the Imperial. The Pupp's reputation was tarnished somewhat during the years of Communist rule (the hotel was renamed the Moskva-Pupp), but the hotel's former grandeur is still in evidence. Even if you're not staying here, be sure to stroll around the impressive facilities and have a drink in the elegant cocktail bar.

Diagonally across from the Grandhotel Pupp, behind a little park, is the pompous Fellner and Helmer **Imperial Spa,** now known as **Lázně I** and housing the local casino. As you walk back into town along the river, you'll pass a variety of interesting stores, including the Moser glass store and the Elefant, one of the last of a dying breed of sophisticated coffeehouses in the Czech Republic. Across the river is the Fellner and Helmer theater. Continue on to the right of the Vřídlo, where the tour began, and walk up the steps to the white **Kostel svatej Maři Magdaleny** (Church of Mary Magdalene). Designed by Kilian Dientzenhofer (architect of the two St. Nicholas churches in Prague), this church is the best of the few baroque buildings still standing in Karlovy Vary.

Dining and Lodging

$$$ ✕ **Embassy.** This cozy wine restaurant, conveniently located near the Grandhotel Pupp, serves an innovative range of pastas, seafoods, and meats: Tagliatelle with smoked salmon in cream sauce makes an excellent main course. Highlights of the varied dessert menu include plum dumplings with *fromage blanc* (white cheese). ⊠ *Nová Louka 21,* ☎ *017/23049,* ℻ *017/23146. DC.*

$$ ✕ **Karel IV.** Its location atop an old castle not far from the main colon-
★ nade affords diners the best view in town. Good renditions of tradi-
tional Czech standbys—mostly pork and beef entrées—are served in
small, secluded dining areas that are particularly intimate after sun-
set. ⊠ *Zámecký vrch 2,* ☎ *017/27255. AE, MC.*

$ ✕ **Vegetarian.** This is a tiny, mostly meat-free oasis not far from the
Hotel Thermal in the New Town. Look for a small but tempting array
of vegetarian standards and nontraditional variations of Czech dishes.
⊠ *I. P. Pavlova 25,* ☎ *017/29021. No credit cards.*

$$$$ 🏨 **Dvořák.** Consider a splurge here if you're longing for Western stan-
★ dards of service and convenience. Opened in late 1990, this Austrian-
owned hotel occupies three renovated town houses a five-minute walk
from the main spas. The staff is helpful, and the rooms are spotlessly
clean. If possible, request a room with a bay-window view of the
town. ⊠ *Nová Louka 11, 360 21 Karlovy Vary,* ☎ *017/3224145,* ℻
*017/3222814. 87 rooms with bath. Restaurant, café, in-room satellite
TVs, pool, beauty parlor, massage, sauna, exercise room. Breakfast included. AE, DC, MC, V.*

$$$$ 🏨 **Grandhotel Pupp.** This enormous 300-year-old hotel, perched on
★ the edge of the spa district, is one of Central Europe's most famous resorts. Standards and service slipped under the Communists (when the
hotel was known as the Moskva-Pupp), but the highly professional management is working hard to atone for the decades of neglect. Ask for
a room furnished in 19th-century period style. The food in the ground-
floor restaurant is passable, but the elegant setting makes the hotel worth
a splurge. ⊠ *Mírové nám. 2, 360 21 Karlovy Vary,* ☎ *017/209111,*
℻ *017/24032. 298 rooms with bath. 4 restaurants, lounge, in-room
satellite TVs, sauna, exercise room, 2 nightclubs. Breakfast included.
AE, DC, MC, V.*

$$$ 🏨 **Elwa.** Renovations have successfully integrated modern comforts
into this older, elegant spa resort located midway between the Old and
New Towns. Modern features include clean, comfortable rooms (most
with television) and an on-site fitness center. ⊠ *Zahradní 29, 360 21
Karlovy Vary,* ☎ *017/3228472,* ℻ *017/3228473. 30 rooms with
bath. Restaurant, bar, beauty parlor, health club. Breakfast included.
AE, DC, MC, V.*

Nightlife and the Arts

In Karlovy Vary, the action centers on the two nightclubs of the **Grand-
hotel Pupp.** The "little dance hall" is open daily 8 PM–1 AM. The second
club is open Wednesday through Sunday 7 PM–3 AM. **Club Propaganda**
(⊠ Jaltska 7) is Karlovy Vary's best venue for live rock and new music.

Outdoor Activities and Sports

Karlovy Vary's warm open-air pool (on top of the Thermal Hotel) of-
fers the unique experience of swimming comfortably even in the coolest
weather; the view over the town is outstanding.

Shopping

In western Bohemia, Karlovy Vary is best known to glass enthusiasts
as home of the **Moser** glass company, one of the world's leading pro-
ducers of crystal and decorative glassware. In addition to running the
flagship store at Na Příkopě 12 in Prague, the company operates an
outlet in Karlovy Vary on Stará Louka, next to the Cafe Elefant. A num-
ber of outlets for lesser-known, although also high-quality, makers of
glass and porcelain can also be found along Stará Louka.

For excellent buys in porcelain, try the **Pirkenhammer** outlet below the Hotel Atlantic (⊠ Tržiště 23).

A cheaper but nonetheless unique gift from Karlovy Vary would be a bottle of the ubiquitous bittersweet (and potent) Becherovka, a liqueur produced by the town's own Jan Becher distillery. Always appreciated as gifts are the unique pipe-shaped ceramic drinking cups used to take the drinking cure at spas. Find them at the colonnades in Karlovy Vary and Mariánské Lázně. You can also buy boxes of tasty Oplatky wafers, sometimes covered with chocolate, at shops in all of the spa towns.

Cheb

🔞 *42 km (26 mi) southwest of Karlovy Vary.*

Known for centuries by its German name of Eger, the old town of Cheb lies on the border with Germany in the far west of the Czech Republic. The town has been a fixture of Bohemia since 1322 (when the king purchased the area from German merchants), but as you walk around the beautiful medieval square, it's difficult not to think you're in Germany. The tall merchants' houses surrounding the square, with their long, red-tiled sloping roofs dotted with windows like droopy eyelids, are more Germanic in style than anything else in Bohemia. You'll also hear a lot of German on the streets—but more from the many German visitors than from the town's residents.

Germany took full possession of the town in 1938 under the terms of the notorious Munich Pact. But following World War II, virtually the entire German population was expelled, and the Czech name of Cheb was officially adopted. A more notorious German connection has emerged in the years following the 1989 revolution. Cheb has quickly become the unofficial center of prostitution for visiting Germans. Don't be startled to see young women, provocatively dressed, lining the highways and bus stops on the roads into town. The legal status of prostitution remains unsettled, and its level of toleration varies from town to town. The police have been known to crack down periodically on streetwalkers and their customers.

Begin a tour of the town in the bustling central square, **Náměstí Krále Jiřího z Poděbrad,** where the ubiquitous Vietnamese vendors have re-established its original marketplace function. The statue in the middle, similar to the Roland statues you see throughout Bohemia and attesting to the town's royal privileges, represents the town hero, Wastel of Eger. Look carefully at his right foot, and you'll see a small man holding a sword and a head—this denotes the town had its own judge and executioner.

Walk downhill from the square to see two rickety groups of timbered medieval buildings, 11 houses in all, divided by a narrow alley. The houses, forming the area known as **Špalíček,** date from the 13th century and were home to many Jewish merchants. **Židovská ulice** (Jews' Street), running uphill to the left of the Špalíček, served as the actual center of the ghetto. Note the small alley running off to the left of Židovská. This calm street, with the seemingly inappropriate name ulička Zavražděných (Lane of the Murdered), was the scene of an outrageous act of violence in 1350. Pressures had been building for some time between Jews and Christians. Incited by an anti-Semitic bishop, the townspeople finally chased the Jews into the street, closed off both ends, and massacred them. Only the name attests to the slaughter.

NEED A BREAK? Cheb's main square abounds with cafés and little restaurants, all offering a fairly uniform menu of schnitzel and sauerbraten aimed at visiting

Germans. The **Kavárna Špalíček,** nestled in the Špalíček buildings, is one of the better choices and has the added advantage of a unique architectural setting.

History buffs, particularly those interested in the Hapsburgs, will want to visit the **Chebský muzeum** (Cheb Museum) in the Pachelbel House, behind the Špalíček on the main square. It was in this house that the great general of the Thirty Years' War, Albrecht von Wallenstein (Valdštejn), was murdered in 1634 on the orders of his own emperor, the Hapsburg Ferdinand II. According to legend, Wallenstein was on his way to the Saxon border to enlist support to fight the Swedes when his own officers barged into his room and stabbed him through the heart with a stave. The stark bedroom with its four-poster bed and dark-red velvet curtains has been left as it was in his memory. The museum is also interesting in its own right: It has a section on the history of Cheb and a collection of minerals (including one discovered by Goethe). ⊠ *Nám. Krále Jiřího z Poděbrad.* ☉ *Tues.–Sun. 9–noon and 1–5.*

The **art gallery** in the bright-yellow baroque house near the top of the square, open daily 9–5, offers an excellent small collection of Gothic sculpture from western Bohemia and a well-chosen sampling of modern Czech art. One of the country's best-known private galleries of photography, **Gallery G4,** is just off the square at ⊠ *Kamenná 4.*

In the early 1820s, Goethe often stayed in the **Gabler House,** on the corner of the square at the museum. He shared a passionate interest in excavation work with the town executioner, and they both worked on the excavation of the nearby extinct volcano Komorní Hůrka. In 1791 Germany's second most famous playwright, Friedrich Schiller, lived at No. 2, at the top of the square next to the "new" town hall, where he planned his famous *Wallenstein* trilogy.

If you follow the little street on the right side of the square at the Gabler House, you will quickly reach the plain but imposing **Kostel svatého Mikuláše** (St. Nicholas Church). Construction began in 1230, when the church belonged to the Order of the Teutonic Knights. You can still see Romanesque windows under the tower; renovations throughout the centuries added an impressive Gothic portal and a baroque interior. Just inside the Gothic entrance is a wonderfully faded plaque commemorating the diamond jubilee of Hapsburg emperor Franz Josef in 1908.

From here walk down the little alley onto Kammená and turn left onto Křižovnická. Follow the road up to **Chebský hrad** (Cheb Castle), on a cliff overlooking the Ohře River. The castle was built in the late 12th century for Holy Roman Emperor Frederick Barbarossa. The square black tower was built with blocks of lava taken from the nearby Komorní Hůrka volcano; the redbrick walls were added during the 15th century. Inside the castle grounds is the carefully restored double-decker chapel, built in the 12th century. The rather dark ground floor, still in Romanesque style, was used by commoners. The bright ornate top floor, with pointed Gothic windows, was reserved for the emperor and his family and has a wooden bridge leading to the royal palace. ⊠ *Hradní ul.* ☉ *Apr. and Oct., Tues.–Sun. 9–4; May and Sept., Tues.–Sun. 9–5; June–Aug., Tues.–Sun. 9–6.*

Dining and Lodging

$$ ✕ **Eva.** Of the many restaurants opened on and around the main square since the tourism boom began in the early 1990s, the Eva is certainly one of the best. A decent array of mostly Czech and German dishes is served in a stylish, contemporary setting that is carefully maintained by a troop of attentive waiters. ⊠ *Jateční 4,* ☎ *0166/22498. No credit cards.*

Cheb's hotels have failed to keep pace with the times. For a short stay, a room in a private home is a better bet. Owners of an older home at Valdstejnova 21 offer two clean and comfortable rooms (☎ 0166/33088). Several houses along Přemysla Otakara Street north of the city have rooms available. Try the house at No. 7 (☎ 0166/22270).

$$ 🏨 **Hvězda.** This turn-of-the-century hotel was last renovated in the 1970s, which partly accounts for its present disheveled look. The location at the top of the main square is excellent, but the dilapidated facilities do not justify the prices. ⊠ *Nám. Krále Jiřího 4–6, 351 01 Cheb,* ☎ *0166/22549,* FAX *0166/22546. 38 rooms, most with bath. Restaurant, café, in-room TVs. MC, V.*

$$ 🏨 **Hradní Dvůr.** This somewhat cramped older hotel is due for a renovation; until then, the plain rooms are kept acceptably clean. The hotel's prime asset is location, on a side street that runs parallel to the main square. Request a room on the top floor, above the noisy reception area. ⊠ *Dlouhá ul. 12, 350 02 Cheb,* ☎ *0166/22006,* FAX *0166/22444. 21 rooms, some with bath. Restaurant, nightclub. AE, MC.*

Františkovy Lázně

70 *6 km (4 mi) from Cheb.*

This little spa town couldn't make a more distinct contrast to nearby Cheb's slightly seedy, hustling air and medieval streetscapes. You might like to ease the transition by walking the red-marked path from Cheb's main square, westward along the river and then north past **Komorní Hůrka.** The extinct volcano is now a tree-covered hill, but excavations on one side have laid bare the rock, and one tunnel is still open. Goethe instigated and took part in the excavations, and you can still barely make out a relief of the poet carved into the rock face.

Františkovy Lázně, or Franzensbad, the smallest of the three main Bohemian spas, isn't really in the same league as the other two (Karlovy Vary and Mariánské Lázně). Built on a more modest scale at the start of the 19th century, the town's ubiquitous kaiser-yellow buildings have been prettified after their neglect under the previous regime and now present cheerful facades, almost too bright for the few strollers. The poorly kept parks and the formal, yet human-scale neoclassical architecture retain much of their former charm. Overall, a pleasing torpor reigns in Františkovy Lázně. There is no town to speak of, just **Národní ulice,** the main street, which leads down into the spa park. The waters, whose healing properties were already known in the 16th century, are used primarily for curing infertility—hence the large number of young women wandering the grounds.

The most interesting sight in town may be the small **Spa Museum,** just off Národní ulice. There is a wonderful collection of spa antiques, including copper bathtubs and a turn-of-the-century exercise bike called a Velotrab. The guest books (*Kurbuch*) provide an insight into the cosmopolitan world of pre–World War I Central Europe. The book for 1812 contains the entry "Ludwig van Beethoven, composer from Vienna." ⊠ *Ul. Doktora Pohoreckého 8.* 🎫 *15 Kč.* ☉ *Weekdays 9–noon and 2–5; June–Sept., also open weekends 9–4.*

Exploration of the spa itself should start on Národní ulice. Wander down the street to the main spring, **Františkuv prameň,** under a little gazebo filled with brass pipes. The colonnade to the left was decorated with a bust of Lenin that was replaced in 1990 by a memorial to the American liberation of the town in April 1945. Walk along the path to the left until you come to the Lázeňská poliklinika, where you can arrange for a day's spa treatment for around 350 Kč. The park surrounding the town is good for aimless wandering, interrupted by empty pedestals for discarded statues of historical figures no longer considered worthy of memorial.

NEED A
BREAK?

Only insipid pop music (the scourge of eating and drinking places everywhere in the country) spoils the mood in the little café of the **Hotel Slovan** on Národní. The tiny gallery and lively frescoes make it a cheerful spot for cake, coffee, or alcoholic drinks.

Dining and Lodging

$$$ ✕🏨 **Slovan.** A quaint and gracious establishment—the perfect com-
★ plement to this relaxed little town. The eccentricity of the original turn-of-the-century design survived a thorough renovation during the 1970s; the airy rooms are clean and comfortable, and some come with a balcony overlooking the main street. The main-floor restaurant serves above-average Czech dishes; consider a meal here even if you're staying elsewhere. ⊠ *Národní 5, 35101 Františkovy Lázně,* ☎ *0166/942841,* 📠 *0166/942843. 25 rooms, most with bath. Restaurant, café, wine bar. DC, V.*

$$$ 🏨 **Centrum.** Renovations have left the rooms clean and well appointed if a bit sterile. Still, it is among the best-run hotels in town and only a short walk from the main park and central spas. ⊠ *Anglická 41, 351 01 Františkovy Lázně,* ☎ *0166/943156,* 📠 *0166/942843. 30 rooms with bath. Restaurant, wine bar, in-room TVs. MC, V.*

$$$ 🏨 **Tři Lilie.** Reopened in 1995 after an expensive refitting, it once accommodated the likes of Goethe, Metternich, and Hapsburg emperor Ferdinand V ("the Benign"). Though too new to have developed a style of its own, the "Three Lilies" has certainly become the best-equipped hotel in town. Spa treatments are conducted off-premises. ⊠ *Máchova at Libušina (off Národní),* ☎ *0166/942415. 31 rooms with bath. Restaurant, brasserie, café. No credit cards. Reservations are made through the town's spa management: Obchodní oddělení, Lázně Františkovy Lázně a.s., Jiráskova 17, 351 01 Františkovy Lázně,* ☎ 📠 *0166/942970.*

$$ 🏨 **Bajkal.** This is an offbeat, older hotel with acceptably clean rooms and a friendly staff. It is on the far side of the park from the main spas, roughly a 10-minute walk from the city center. The travel agency in the building also books private accommodations. ⊠ *Americká ul. 84/4, 351 01 Františkovy Lázně,* ☎ *0166/942501,* 📠 *0166/942503. 25 rooms, most with bath. Restaurant. V.*

Mariánské Lázně

★ ⓐ *30 km (18 mi) southeast of Cheb, 47 km (29 mi) south of Karlovy Vary.*

Visitors' expectations of what a spa resort should be come nearest to full reality here. It's far larger and better maintained than Františkovy Lázně and is greener and quieter than Karlovy Vary. This was the spa favored by Britain's Edward VII; Goethe and Chopin, among other luminaries, also repaired here frequently. Mark Twain, on a visit to the spa in 1892, labeled the town a "health factory" and couldn't get over how new everything looked. Indeed, at that time everything was new. The sanatoriums, all built in the middle of the last century in a confident, outrageous mixture of "neo" styles, fan out impressively around a finely groomed oblong park. Cure takers and curiosity seekers alike parade through the two stately colonnades, both placed near the top of the park. Buy a spouted drinking cup (available at the colonnades) and join the rest of the sippers taking the drinking cure. Be forewarned, though: The waters from the Rudolph, Ambrose, and Caroline springs, though harmless, all have a noticeable diuretic effect. For this reason they're used extensively in treating disorders of the kidney and bladder. Several spa hotels offer more extensive treatment for visitors, including baths and massage. Prices are usually reckoned in U.S. dollars or German marks. For more information, inquire at the main spa offices at ⊠ *Masarykova 22,* ☎ *0165/2170,* ⨳ *0165/2982.*

A stay in Mariánské Lázně, however, can be healthful even without special treatment. Special walking trails of all difficulty levels surround the resort in all directions. The best advice is simply to put on comfortable shoes, buy a hiking map, and head out. One of the country's few golf courses lies 3 or 4 kilometers (2 or 3 miles) from town to the east. Hotels can also help to arrange special activities, such as tennis and horseback riding. For the less intrepid, a simple stroll around the gardens, with a few deep breaths of the town's famous air, is enough to restore a healthy sense of perspective.

Dining and Lodging

$$ ✕ **Filip.** This bustling wine bar is where locals come to find relief from the sometimes large horde of tourists. A tasty selection of traditional Czech dishes—mainly pork, grilled meats, and steaks—is served by a friendly and efficient staff. ⊠ *Poštovní 96,* ☎ *0165/2639. No credit cards.*

$$ ✕ **Koliba.** This combination hunting lodge and wine tavern, set in the
★ woods roughly 20 minutes on foot from the spas, is an excellent alternative to the hotel restaurants in town. Grilled meats and shish kebobs, plus tankards of Moravian wine (try the cherry-red Rulandské Červené), are served with traditional gusto. ⊠ *Dusíkova, on the road to Karlovy Vary,* ☎ *0165/5169. AE, DC, MC, V.*

$ ✕ **Classic.** This small, trendy café on the main drag serves fine sandwiches and light meals throughout the day. Unusual for this part of the world, it also offers a full breakfast menu until 11 AM. ⊠ *Hlavní tř. 131/50,* ☎ *0165/2807. Reservations not accepted. AE, DC, MC, V.*

The best place to look for private lodgings is along Paleckého ulice and Hlavní třída, south of the main spa area. Private accommodations can also be found in the neighboring villages of Zádub and Závišín and along roads in the woods to the east of Mariánské Lázně.

$$$$ ⊞ **Excelsior.** This lovely older hotel is on the main street and is convenient to the spas and colonnade. The renovated rooms are clean and comfortable, and the staff is friendly and helpful. The food in the adjoining restaurant is only average, but the romantic setting provides adequate compensation. ⊠ *Hlavní tř. 121, 353 01 Mariánské Lázně,* ☎ *0165/2705 or 0165/622705,* ⨳ *0165/5346 or 0165/625346. 64 rooms with bath. Restaurant, café. AE, DC, MC, V.*

$$$$ ⊞ **Hotel Golf.** Book in advance to secure a room at this stately villa situated 3½ kilometers (2 miles) out of town on the road to Karlovy Vary. A major renovation in the 1980s left the large, open rooms with a cheery, modern look. The restaurant on the main floor is excellent, but the big draw is the 18-hole golf course on the premises, one of the few in the Czech Republic. ⊠ *Zádub 55, 353 01 Mariánské Lázně,* ☎ *0165/2651 or 0165/2652,* ⨳ *0165/2655. 25 rooms with bath. Restaurant, in-room satellite TVs, pool, golf, tennis. AE, DC, MC, V.*

$$$ ⊞ **Bohemia.** This renovated spa resort is definitely worth the splurge;
★ beautiful crystal chandeliers in the main hall set the stage for a comfortable and elegant stay. The rooms are well appointed and completely

equipped, though you may want to be really decadent and request one of the enormous suites overlooking the park. The helpful staff can arrange spa treatments and horseback riding. ⊠ *Hlavní tř. 100, 353 01 Mariánské Lázně,* ☎ *0165/3251,* FAX *0165/2943. 77 rooms with bath. Restaurant, in-room TVs and phones. AE, DC, MC, V.*

Nightlife and the Arts

Mariánske Lázně sponsors a music festival each June, with numerous concerts featuring Czech and international composers and orchestras. The town's annual Chopin festival each autumn brings in fans of the Polish composer's work from around the world.

Mariánské Lázně's **Casino Marienbad** (☎ 0165/3292) is at Anglická 336 and is open daily 6 AM–2 AM. For late-night drinks, try the **Hotel Golf** (☞ Lodging, *above*), which has a good nightclub in season.

Teplá

72 *15 km (9 mi) from Mariánské Lázně.*

It is worth making a detour to the little town of Teplá and its 800-year-old monastery, which once played an important role in Christianizing pagan Central Europe. If you don't have a car, a bus departs daily in season from Mariánské Lázně (inquire at the information office in front of the Hotel Excelsior). The sprawling monastery, founded by the Premonstratensian order of France in 1193 (the same order that established Prague's Strahov Monastery), once controlled the farms and forests for miles around. The order even owned the spa facilities at Mariánské Lázně and until 1942 used the proceeds from them to cover operating expenses. Today the complex betrays none of this earlier prosperity. Over the centuries, it was plundered dozens of times during wars and upheavals, but history reserved the severest blow for the night of April 13, 1950, when security forces employed by the Communists raided the grounds and imprisoned the brothers. The monastery's property was given to the Czech army, and for the next 28 years the buildings were used as barracks. In 1991 the government returned the monastery buildings and immediate grounds (but not the original land holdings) to the order, and the brothers began to pick up the pieces—physically and spiritually.

The most important building on the grounds from an architectural point of view is the Romanesque **basilica** (1197), with its unique triple nave. The rest of the monastery complex was originally Romanesque, but it was rebuilt in 1720 by baroque architect K. I. Dientzenhofer. There are several wall and ceiling paintings of interest here, as well as some good sculpture. The most valuable collection is in the **Nová knihovna** (New Library), where you will find illuminated hymnals and rare manuscripts, including a German translation of the New Testament that predates Luther's by some 100 years. Tours of the church and library are given daily (English notes are available). The monastery also offers short-term accommodations (inquire directly at the monastery offices on the grounds). ⊠ *Kláštor, 364 61 Teplá,* ☎ *0169/92264.* 🖃 *Monastery 80 Kč.* ☉ *Tues.–Sun. 9–3 (until 4:30 in summer).*

Plzeň

73 *92 km (55 mi) from Prague.*

The sprawling industrial city of Plzeň is hardly a tourist mecca, but it's worth stopping off for an hour or two on the way back to Prague.

Two sights here are of particular interest to beer fanatics. The first is the **Pilsner-Urquell Brewery,** to the east of the city near the railway station. Group tours of the 19th-century redbrick building are offered weekdays at 12:30 PM, during which you can taste the valuable brew, exported around the world. The beer was created in 1842 using the excellent Plzeň water, a special malt fermented on the premises, and hops grown in the region around Žatec. ⊠ *U Prazdroje,* ☎ *019/7062888.* ⊡ *50 Kč.*

NEED A
BREAK? You can continue drinking and find some cheap traditional grub at the large **Na Spilce** beer hall just inside the brewery gates. The pub is open daily from 10 AM to 10 PM.

The second stop on the beer tour is the **Pivovarské muzeum** (Brewery Museum), in a late-Gothic malt house one block northeast of the main square. ⊠ *Veleslavinova ul. 6,* ☎ *019/7235574.* ⊡ *40 Kč.* ☉ *Tues.–Sun. (daily in summer) 10–6.*

The city's architectural attractions center on the main square, **Náměstí Republiky.** The square is dominated by the enormous Gothic **Chrám svatého Bartoloměja** (Church of St. Bartholomew). Both the square and the church towers hold size records: The former is the largest in Bohemia, and the latter, at 102 meters (335 feet), the highest in the Czech Republic. The church was begun in 1297 and completed almost 200 years later. Around the square, mixed in with its good selection of stores, are a variety of other architectural jewels, including the town hall, adorned with sgraffiti and built in the Renaissance style by Italian architects during the town's heyday in the 16th century.

Dining and Lodging

$$$ ✕⊡ **Continental.** Just five minutes on foot from the main square, the fin-de-siècle Continental remains the best hotel in Pzleň, a relative compliment considering the hotel is slightly rundown and the rooms, though large, are exceedingly plain. The restaurant, however, serves dependably satisfying traditional Czech dishes. ⊠ *Zbojnická 8, 305 31 Plzeň,* ☎ *019/7236477,* 𝔽𝕏 *019/7221746. 46 rooms, 23 with bath or shower. Restaurant, café. Breakfast included. AE, DC, MC, V.*

$$$ ⊡ **Central.** This angular 1960s structure (named the Ural until 1990) is recommendable for its sunny rooms, friendly staff, and great location, right on the main square. Indeed, even such worthies as Czar Alexander of Russia stayed here in the days when the hotel was a charming inn known as the Golden Eagle. ⊠ *Nám. Republiky 33, 305 31 Plzeň,* ☎ *019/7226757,* 𝔽𝕏 *019/7226064. 77 rooms with shower. Restaurant, café, wine bar. AE, DC, MC, V.*

$$ ⊡ **Slovan.** A gracious off-white facade, sweeping stairways, and large, elegant rooms attest to the Slovan's former grandeur, and there's a pleasant, English-speaking staff to boot. The restaurant still occupies the once beautiful ballroom, but the experience is spoiled by mediocre food and the rock-music accompaniment. The Slovan's best asset may be its location, on a lovely square of its own, a short walk from the main square. ⊠ *Smetanový Sady 1, 305 31 Plzeň,* ☎ *019/7227256,* 𝔽𝕏 *019/7227012. 100 rooms, most with bath or shower. Restaurant, café. Breakfast included. AE, DC, MC, V.*

Western Bohemia A to Z

Arriving and Departing

Prague is the main gateway to western Bohemia (☞ Arriving and Departing *in* Prague A to Z, *above*). Major trains from Munich and Nürnberg stop at Cheb and some of the spa towns. It is also an easy drive across the border from Bavaria on the E48 to Cheb and from there to any of the spas.

Getting Around

Good, if slow, train service links all the major towns west of Prague. The best stretches are from Františkovy Lázně to Plzeň and from Plzeň to Prague. The Prague–Karlovy Vary run takes far longer than it should but has a romantic charm all its own. Note that most trains heading west to Germany (in the direction of Nürnberg) stop at Mariánské Lázně. Most trains leave from Prague's Hlavní nádraží (main station), but be sure to check on which station if in doubt.

Contacts and Resources

EMERGENCIES
Police (☎ 158). **Ambulance** (☎ 155).

GUIDED TOURS
Čedok (☎ 02/2419–7111) offers several specialized tours covering western Bohemia's major sights. Tour "G-O" combines a trip to Lidice in northern Bohemia (☞ *below*) with a visit to the spa town of Karlovy Vary. The trip takes a full day and departs three times weekly. Prague departure points are at the Čedok offices at Na příkopě 18 and Bílkova ulice 6, and the Panorama, Forum, and Hilton hotels.

VISITOR INFORMATION
Čedok is the first stop for general tourist information and city maps:

Cheb (✉ Májova 31, ☎ 0166/30650). **Mariánské Lázně** (✉ Třebízského 2/101, ☎ 0165/2254; Infocentrum, ✉ Hlavní 47, ☎ 0165/2474; City Service, ✉ Hlavní 626/1, ☎ 0165/3816).

NORTHERN BOHEMIA

Northern Bohemia is a paradox: While much of it was despoiled over the past 40 years by rampant, postwar industrialization, here and there you can still find areas of great natural beauty. Particularly along the Labe (Elbe River), rolling hills, perfect for walking, guard the country's northern frontiers with Germany and Poland. Hikers and campers head for the Giant Mountains (Krkonoše) on the Polish border (the only region which has good hotels); this range is not so giant, actually, though it is very pretty. As you move toward the west, the interest is more historical, in an area where the influence of Germany was felt in less pleasant ways than in the spas. You needn't drive too far to reach the Sudetenland, the German-speaking border area that was ceded to Hitler by the British and French in 1938. Indeed, the landscape here is riddled with the tragic remains of the Nazi occupation of Czech lands from 1939 to 1945. Most drastically affected was Terezín, better known as the infamous concentration camp, Theresienstadt, where the Nazis converted the redbrick fortress town into a Jewish ghetto and prison camp during World War II.

In the area around Terezín and Litoměřice, tourist amenities are practically nonexistent; if you do choose to stay overnight, you'll generally be able to find a room in a primitive inn or a rather unwelcoming modern hotel. In many parts of Bohemia the only real options for dining are the restaurants and cafés at the larger hotels and resorts.

Lidice

74 *18 km (11 mi) from Prague on Route 7 (the road to Ruzyně Airport). Head in the direction of Slaný. Turn off at the Lidice exit and follow the country road for 3 km (1¼ mi).*

The **Lidice museum and monument** are unforgettable sights. The empty field to the right, with a large cross at the bottom, is where the town of Lidice stood until 1942, when it was viciously razed by the Nazis in retribution for the assassination of German district leader Reinhard Heydrich.

The Lidice story really begins with the notorious Munich Pact of 1938, according to which the leaders of Great Britain and France permitted Hitler to occupy the largely German-speaking border regions of Czechoslovakia (the so-called Sudetenland). Less than a year later, in March 1939, Hitler used his forward position to occupy the whole of Bohemia and Moravia, making the area into a protectorate of the German Reich. To guard his new possessions, Hitler appointed ruthless Nazi Reinhard Heydrich as Reichsprotektor. Heydrich immediately implemented a campaign of terror against Jews and intellectuals while currying favor with average Czechs by raising rations and wages. As a result, the Czech army-in-exile, based in Great Britain, soon began planning Heydrich's assassination. In the spring of 1942 a small band of parachutists was flown in to carry out the task.

The assassination attempt took place just north of Prague on May 27, 1942, and Heydrich died from his injuries on June 4. Hitler immediately ordered the little mining town of Lidice, west of Prague, "removed from the face of the earth," since it was alleged (although later found untrue) that some of the assassins had been sheltered by villagers there. On the night of June 9, a Gestapo unit entered Lidice, shot the entire adult male population (199 men), and sent the 196 women to the Ravensbruck concentration camp. The 103 children in the village were sent either to Germany to be "Aryanized" or to death camps. On June 10, the entire village was razed. The assassins and their accomplices were found a week later in the Orthodox Church of Sts. Cyril and Methodius in Prague's New Town, where they committed suicide after a shoot-out with Nazi militia.

The monument to these events is a sober place. The arcades are graphic in their depiction of the deportation and slaughter of the inhabitants. The museum itself is dedicated to those killed, with photographs of each person and a short description of his or her fate. You'll also find reproductions of the German documents ordering the village's destruction, including the Gestapo's chillingly bureaucratic reports on how the massacre was carried out and the peculiar problems encountered in Aryanizing the deported children. The exhibits highlighting the international response (a suburb of Chicago was even renamed for the town) are heartwarming. An absorbing 18-minute film in Czech (worthwhile even for non-Czech speakers) tells the Lidice story. ✉ *Museum: ul. 10. června 1942.* 🎫 *20 Kč.* ☉ *Daily 9–5.*

Lidice was rebuilt after the war on the initiative of a group of miners from Birmingham, England, who called their committee "Lidice Must Live." Between New Lidice and the museum is a rose garden with some 3,000 bushes sent from all over the world. The wooden cross in the field to the right of the museum, starkly decorated with barbed wire, marks the place in Old Lidice where the men were executed. Remains of brick walls are visible here, left over from the Gestapo's dynamite and bulldozer exercise. Still, Lidice is a sad town, not a place to linger.

Veltrusy Château and Gardens

75 *25 km (15 mi) north of Prague.*

The aristocratic retreat of Veltrusy contrasts vividly with the ordinariness of nearby Kralupy, an industrial town better left unexplored. The mansion's late-baroque splendor lies hidden in a carefully laid out English park full of old and rare trees and scattered with 18th-century architectural follies. The château itself has been turned into a museum showcasing the cosmopolitan lifestyle of the imperial aristocracy, displaying Japanese and Chinese porcelain, English chandeliers, and 16th-century tapestries from Brussels. ☎ *20 Kč.* ☉ *Apr. and Oct.–Dec., weekends 9–4; May–Aug., Tues.–Sun. 8–5; Sept., Tues.–Sun. 9–5.*

Nelahozeves

2½ km (1½ mi) on foot by marked paths from Veltrusy Château. By car, the route is more circuitous: Turn right out of Veltrusy onto the highway and over the river, then make a sharp left back along the river to Nelahozeves.

Nelahozeves was the birthplace in 1841 of Antonín Dvořák, the Czech Republic's greatest composer. Dvořák's pretty corner house on the main road (No. 12), with its tidy windows and arches, has a small memorial museum. In Dvořák's time, the house was an inn run by his parents, and it was here that he learned to play the violin. ☎ *Free.* ☉ *Tues.–Thurs. and weekends 9–noon and 2–5.*

For those not enamored of the spirit of Dvořák's youth, the main attraction in town is the brooding Renaissance **chateau,** with its black-and-white sgraffito, once the residence of the powerful Lobkowitz family. The castle now houses an excellent collection of fine art. ☎ *0205/22995.* ☎ *80 Kč.* ☉ *Tues.–Sun. 10–5 (until 3 in winter).*

Terezín

76 *36 km (22 mi) from Nelahozeves on Route 8.*

★ The old garrison town of Terezín gained notoriety under the Nazis as the nefarious Nazi concentration camp **Theresienstadt,** though the enormity of Theresienstadt's role in history is difficult to grasp at first. The Czechs have put up few signs to tell you what to see; the town's buildings, parks, and buses resemble those of any of a hundred other unremarkable places, built originally by the Austrians and now inhabited by Czechs. You could easily pass through it and never learn any of the town's dark secrets.

Part of the problem is that **Malá Pevnost** (Small Fortress), the actual prison and death camp, is 2 kilometers (1¼ miles) south of Terezín. Visitors to the strange redbrick complex see the prison more or less as it was when the Nazis left it in 1945. Above the entrance to the main courtyard stands the cynical motto ARBEIT MACHT FREI (Work will make you free). Take a walk around the various rooms, still housing a sad collection of rusty bedframes, sinks, and shower units. At the far end of the fortress, opposite the main entrance, is the special wing built by the Nazis when space became tight. The windowless cells are horrific; try going into one and closing the door—and then imagine being crammed in with 14 other people. In the center of the fortress is a museum and a room where films are shown. ☎ *0416/92225.* ☎ *90 Kč.* ☉ *Daily 8–4 (until 5 in summer).*

During World War II, Terezín served as a detention center for thousands of Jews and was used by the Nazis as an elaborate prop in a nefarious propaganda ploy. The large barracks buildings around town, once used in the 18th and 19th centuries to house Austrian soldiers, became living quarters for thousands of interred Jews. But in 1942, to placate international public opinion, the Nazis cynically decided to transform the town into a showcase camp—to prove to the world their "benevolent" intentions toward the Jews. To give the place the image of a spa town, the streets were given new names such as Lake Street, Bath Street, and Park Street. Numerous elderly Jews from Germany were taken in by the deception and paid large sums of money to come to the new "retirement village." Just before the International Red Cross inspected the town in early 1944, Nazi authorities began a beautification campaign: painted the buildings, set up stores, laid out a park with benches in front of the town hall, and arranged for concerts and sports. The map just off the main square shows the town's street plan as the locations of various buildings between 1941 and 1945. The Jews here were able, with great difficulty, to establish a cultural life of their own under the limited "self-government" that was set up in the camp. The inmates created a library and a theater, and lectures and musical performances were given on a regular basis.

Once it was clear that the war was lost, however, the Nazis dropped any pretense and quickly stepped up transport of Jews to the Auschwitz death camp in Poland. Transports were not new to the ghetto; to keep the population at around 30,000, a train was sent off every few months or so "to the east" to make room for incoming groups. In the fall of 1944, these transports were increased to one every few days. In all, some 87,000 Jews were murdered in this way, and another 35,000 died from starvation or disease. The town's horrific story is told in words and pictures at the **Ghetto Museum,** just off the central park in town.

For all its history, Terezín is no place for an extended stay. Locals have chosen not to highlight the town's role during the Nazi era, and hence little provision has been made for visitors.

Litoměřice

⑦ *4 km (2½ mi) from Terezín, 70 km (42 mi) north of Prague.*

The decrepit state of the houses and streets belies this riverside town's medieval status as one of Bohemia's leading towns and a rival to Prague. It has remained largely untouched by modern development. Even today, although the food industry has established several factories in the surrounding area, much of central Litoměřice is like a living museum.

The best way to get a feel for Litoměřice is to start at the excellent **Městské muzeum** (City Museum), on the corner of the main square and Dlouhá ulice in the Old Town Hall building. The building itself deserves notice as one of the first examples of the Renaissance style in Bohemia, dating from 1537–39. Unfortunately, the museum's exhibits are described in Czech (with written commentary in German available from the ticket seller); but even if you don't understand the language, you'll find this museum fascinating. Despite its position near the old border with Germany, Litoměřice was a Czech and Hussite stronghold, and one of the museum's treasures is the brightly colored, illuminated gradual, or hymn book, depicting Hus's burning at the stake in Constance. Note also the golden chalice nearby, the old symbol of the Hussites. Farther on you come to an exquisite Renaissance pulpit and altar decorated with painted stone reliefs. On the second floor the most interesting exhibit is from the Nazi era, when Litoměřice became a part of Sudeten Germany and a border town of the German Reich, providing soldiers for nearby Theresienstadt. ⊠ *Mírové nám.* 🎟 *10 Kč.* 🕐 *Tues.–Sun. 10–5.*

After leaving the museum, stroll along the busy but decaying central square, which sports a range of architectural styles from Renaissance arcades to baroque gables and a Gothic bell tower. The town's trademark, though, is the chalice-shaped tower at No. 7, the **Chalice House,** built in the 1560s for an Utraquist patrician. The Utraquists were moderate Hussites who believed that laymen should receive wine as well as bread in the sacrament of Holy Communion. On the left-hand corner of the Old Town Hall is a replica of a small and unusual Roland statue (the original is in the museum) on a high stone pedestal. These statues, found throughout Bohemia, signify the town as a "royal free town," due all the usual privileges of such a distinction. This particular statue is unique because instead of showing the usual handsome knight, it depicts a hairy caveman wielding a club. Even in the 15th century, it seems, Czechs had a sense of humor.

NEED A BREAK?
> For an ice cream, a fruit drink, or a cup of coffee, try the little stand-up **Atropic Cafe,** next to the museum on the main square (⊠ Mírové nám). Good beer and passable Czech food are served up daily in clean surroundings at the **Pivnice Kalich** (⊠ Lidická 9), a block from the main square.

A colorful, two-story baroque house with a facade by the 18th-century Italian master-builder Octavio Broggio houses the **Galerie výtvarného umění** (Art Gallery). Its strong collection of Czech art from the Gothic to the baroque and its temporary shows of living artists, make it one of the country's best provincial art museums. ⊠ *Michalská 7.* 🎟 *16 Kč.* 🕐 *Tues.–Sun. 10–6 (until 5 in winter).*

More of Broggio's work can be seen in the facade and interior of the **All Saints' Church,** to the right of the town hall, while the church's high tower keeps its 16th-century appearance. Broggio also remade the monastery **Church of St. Jacob** (⊠ Ul. Velká Dominikánská), whose exterior sorely needs restoration. His most beautiful work, though, is the small **Kostel svatého Václava** (St. Wenceslas Chapel), squeezed into an unwieldy square to the north of town on the cathedral hill and now an Orthodox church. **Dóm svatého Štěpána** (St. Stephen's Cathedral), farther up the hill, is monumental but uninspired. Its one real treasure is a Lucas Cranach painting of St. Anthony—but unfortunately the cathedral door is often locked. There are also a number of paintings by the famed 17th-century Bohemian artist Karel Škréta.

Lodging

$$ 🏨 **Roosevelt.** The Secession-style town bathhouse was converted into a small hotel in 1994, adding to this area's limited supply of decent accommodations. On a 19th-century residential street, the Roosevelt is a couple minutes' walk from the town center. ⊠ *Rooseveltova 18, 412 01 Litoměřice,* ☎ *0416/8061,* 🖷 *0416/8062. 30 rooms with bath. Restaurant, in-room TVs. Breakfast not included. AE, MC, V.*

OFF THE BEATEN PATH
> **STŘEKOV CASTLE –** The Vltava River north of Litoměřice flows through a long, unspoiled winding valley, packed in by surrounding hills, which has something of the look of a 16th-century landscape painting. As you near heavily industrialized Ústí nad Labem, your eyes are suddenly assaulted by the towering mass of Střekov Castle, perched precariously on huge cliffs and rising abruptly above the right bank. The fortress was built in 1319 by King Johann of Luxembourg to control the rebellious no-

bles of northern Bohemia. During the 16th century it became the residence of Wenceslas of Lobkowicz, who rebuilt the castle in the Renaissance style. The lonely ruins have served to inspire many German artists and poets, including Richard Wagner, who came here on a moonlit night in the summer of 1842. But if you arrive on a dark night, about the only classic that comes to mind is Mary Shelley's *Frankenstein*. Inside there is a small historical exhibit relating to the Lobkowicz family, which owns the castle, and on winemaking. ⊠ *400 03 Ústí nad Labem,* ☎ *047/31553.* ☉ *Apr.–Oct., Tues.–Sun. 9–5.* ▣ *30 Kč.*

Mělník

78 *50 km (31 mi) south from Střekov; continue on Route 261 through the picturesque hills of the Elbe banks back through Litoměřice and on to Mělník. Follow Route 9 south about 30 km (20 mi) to return to Prague.*

If coming by car, park on the small streets just off the pretty but hard-to-find main square (head in the direction of the towers to find it). Mělník is a lively town, known best perhaps as the source of the special Ludmila wine, the country's only decent wine not produced in southern Moravia. The town's **zámek,** a smallish castle a few blocks from the main square, majestically guards the confluence of the Elbe River with two arms of the Vltava. The view here is stunning, and the sunny hillsides are covered with vineyards. As the locals tell it, Emperor Charles IV was responsible for bringing wine production to the area. Having a good eye for favorable growing conditions, he encouraged vintners from Burgundy to come here and plant their vines.

The courtyard's three dominant architectural styles, reflecting alterations to the castle over the years, fairly jump out at you. On the north side, note the typical arcaded Renaissance balconies, decorated with sgraffiti; to the west, a Gothic tract is still easy to make out. The southern wing is clearly baroque (although also decorated with arcades). Inside the castle at the back, you'll find a vinárna with mediocre food but excellent views overlooking the rivers. On the other side is a museum devoted to wine making and folk crafts. ▣ *Museum 20 Kč.* ☉ *May–Oct., Tues.–Sun. 10–5 (June–Aug. until 6).*

Lodging

$$ 🏨 **Ludmila.** Though the hotel is an inconvenient 4 kilometers (2½ miles) outside town, the Ludmila's pleasant English-speaking staff keeps the plain but cozy rooms impeccably clean, and the restaurant is better than many you will find in Mělník itself. ⊠ *Pražská 2639,* ☎ *0206/622423. 79 rooms with shower or bath. Restaurant, souvenir shop. Breakfast included. AE, MC, V.*

Špindlerův Mlýn and the Krkonoše Range

79 *To get to the Krkonoše area from Prague, take the D11 freeway 55 km (33 mi) east to Poděbrady, then via Freeway 32 through Jičín, Nová Paka (switch to Route 16), and Vrchlabí (a total distance of 152 km [91 mi]), finally reaching Špindlerův Mlýn on the stretch of Freeway 295. Excellent bus connections link Prague with the towns of Špindlerův Mlýn, Vrchlabí, and Pec pod Sněžkou.*

If you're not planning to go to the Tatras in Slovakia but nevertheless want a few days in the mountains, head for the **Krkonoše range**—the so-called Giant Mountains—near the Polish frontier. Here you'll find the most spectacular scenery in Bohemia, although it oversteps linguistic convention to call these rolling hills "giant" (the highest point is 1,602 meters, or 5,256 feet). Not only is the scenery beautiful, but the local architecture is refreshingly rural after all the towns and cities; the steep-roofed timber houses, painted in warm colors, look just right pitched against sunlit pinewoods or snowy pastures.

Dining and Lodging

$$ ✕▥ **Savoy.** This Tudor-style chalet, more than 100 years old but thor-
★ oughly renovated in the early 1980s, is rich in alpine atmosphere and very comfortable—its cozy reception area is more typical of a family inn than a large hotel. The rooms, although on the smallish side and sparsely furnished, are immaculately clean. The restaurant serves fine traditional Czech dishes in a comfortably polished setting. ⊠ *54351 Špindlerův Mlýn,* ☎ *0438/93521,* ℻ *0438/93641. 50 rooms, most with bath or shower. Restaurant, bar. Breakfast included. AE, DC, MC, V.*

$$$ ▥ **Montana.** This "modern" 1970s hotel is ill suited to the rustic set-
ting, and the rooms are more spartan than luxurious; but the service is attentive, and the staff can offer good advice for planning walks around this popular resort town. ⊠ *54351 Špindlerův Mlýn,* ☎ *0438/93551,* ℻ *0438/93556. 70 rooms with bath. Restaurant, bar, café, in-room TVs. Breakfast included. AE, DC, MC, V.*

$ ▥ **Nechanicky.** At this private, older hotel near the bridge in the cen-
ter of town, the management is working to improve the structure's some-
what tarnished appearance. The rooms are bright, clean, and well proportioned; front-facing rooms enjoy an excellent view overlooking the town. ⊠ *54351 Špindlerův Mlýn,* ☎ *0438/93263,* ℻ *0438/93315. 16 rooms with bath. Restaurant. Breakfast included. No credit cards.*

Outdoor Activities and Sports

Janské Lázně (another spa), **Pec pod Sněžkou,** and **Špindlerův Mlýn** are the principal resorts of the area, the last the most sophisticated in its accommodations and facilities. **Špindlerův Mlýn** is attractively placed astride the rippling Labe (Elbe) River, here in its formative stages. To get out and experience the mountains, a good trip is to take a bus from Špindlerův Mlýn via Janské Lázně to Pec pod Sněžkou—a deceptively long journey by road of around 50 kilometers (31 miles). From there, embark on a two-stage chairlift to the top of **Sněžka** (the area's highest peak) and then walk along a ridge overlooking the Pol-
ish countryside, eventually dropping into deep, silent pinewoods and returning to Špindlerův Mlýn. If you walk over the mountain instead of driving around it, the return trip is just 11 kilometers (7 miles)—a comfortable walk of about three to four hours. The path actually takes you into Poland at one point; you won't need a visa, but take your passport along just in case.

The source of the Labe also springs from the heights near the Polish border. From the town of **Harrachov,** walkers can reach it by a marked trail. The distance is about 10 kilometers (6 miles). From Špindlerův Mlýn, a beautiful but sometimes steep trail follows the Labe Valley up to the source near **Labská Bouda.** Allow about three hours for this walk and take good shoes and a map.

Northern Bohemia A to Z

Arriving and Departing

Prague is the gateway to northern Bohemia (☞ Arriving and Depart-
ing *in* Prague A to Z, *above*). If you are driving, the E55 leads directly into the Czech Republic from Dresden and winds down to Prague via the old spa town of Teplice.

Getting Around

Motorists driving through northern Bohemia are rewarded with a particularly picturesque drive along the Labe (Elbe) River on the way to Střekov Castle near Ústí nad Labem (☞ *above*). Train connections in the north are spotty at best; bus is the preferred means of travel. Regular train service connects Prague with Ústí nad Labem, but to reach other towns you'll have to take slower local trains or the bus.

Contacts and Resources

EMERGENCIES

Police (☎ 158). **Ambulance** (☎ 155).

GUIDED TOURS

Čedok (☎ 02/2419–7111) offers several specialized tours covering the major sights in northern Bohemia. Tour "G-O" combines a trip to Lidice with a visit to the spa town of Karlovy Vary. The trip takes a full day and departs three times weekly. Prague departure points are the Čedok offices at Na příkopě 18 and Bílkova ulice 6 and the Panorama, Forum, and Hilton hotels.

Several private companies also offer trips to Lidice and Terezín (Theresienstadt) in northern Bohemia. For the latter, try **Wittmann Tours** (☎ 02/439–6293 or 02/251235). Bus tours leave from Pařížska 28 daily at 10 AM, returning around 5 PM (950 Kč adults).

VISITOR INFORMATION

Northern Bohemia's main tourist center is in **Litoměřice**: Infocentrum (✉ Mírové nám., ☎ 0416/2136). It's open daily in summer, closed Sunday in winter.

SOUTHERN MORAVIA

Lacking the turbulent history of Bohemia to the west or the stark natural beauty of Slovakia farther east, Moravia, the easternmost province of the Czech Republic, is frequently overlooked as a travel destination. Still, although Moravia's cities do not match Prague for beauty, and its gentle mountains hardly compare with Slovakia's strikingly rugged Tatras, Moravia's colorful villages and rolling hills certainly do merit a few days of exploration. After you've seen the admittedly superior sights of Bohemia and Slovakia, come here for the good wine, the folk music, the friendly faces, and the languid pace.

Moravia has a bit of both Bohemia and Slovakia. It is closer culturally to Bohemia: The two were bound together as one kingdom for some 1,000 years, following the fall of the Great Moravian Empire (Moravia's last stab at Slavonic statehood) at the end of the 10th century. All the historical and cultural movements that swept through Bohemia, including the religious turbulence and long period of Austrian Hapsburg rule, were felt strongly here as well. But, oddly, in many ways Moravia resembles Slovakia more than its cousin to the west. The colors come alive here in a way that is seldom seen in Bohemia: The subdued earthen pinks and yellows in towns such as Telč and Mikulov suddenly erupt into the fiery reds, greens, and purples of the traditional folk costumes farther to the east. Folk music, all but gone in Bohemia, is still very much alive in Moravia. You'll hear it, ranging from the foot stomping to the tear-jerking, sung with pride by young and old alike.

Southern Moravia's highlands define the "border" with Bohemia. Here, towns such as Jihlava and Telč are virtually indistinguishable from their Bohemian counterparts. The handsome squares, with their long arcades, bear witness to the prosperity enjoyed by this part of Europe several hundred years ago. The tour then heads south along the frontier with Austria—until recently a heavily fortified expanse of the Iron Curtain. Life is just starting to return to normal in these parts, as the towns and people on both sides of the border seek to reestablish ties going back centuries. One of their common traditions is wine making; and Znojmo, Mikulov, and Valtice are to the Czech Republic what the small towns of the *Weinviertel* on the other side of the border are to Austria.

Don't expect gastronomic delights in Moravia. The food—especially outside Brno—is reasonably priced, but the choices are usually limited to roast pork, sauerkraut, and dumplings or fried pork and french fries. Moravia's hotels are only now beginning to recover from 40 years of state ownership, and excellent hotels are few and far between. In many larger towns, private rooms are preferred. In mountainous areas inquire locally about the possibility of staying in a *chata* (cabin). These are abundant and often a pleasant alternative to the faceless modern hotels. Many lack modern amenities, though, so be prepared to rough it.

Numbers in the margin correspond to numbers on the Moravia map.

Jihlava

⑧⓪ *100 km (62 mi) from Prague.*

On the Moravian side of the rolling highlands that mark the border between Bohemia and Moravia, and just off the main highway from Prague to Brno, lies the old mining town of Jihlava, a good place to begin an exploration of Moravia. If the silver mines here had held out just a few more years, the townspeople claim, Jihlava could have become a great European city—and a household name to foreign visitors. Indeed, during the 13th century, the town's enormous **main square** was one of the largest in Europe, rivaled in size only by those in Cologne and Kraków. But history can be cruel: The mines went bust during the 17th century, and the square today bears witness only to the town's once oversize ambitions.

The **Kostel svatého Ignáce** (St. Ignace Church) in the northwest corner of the square is relatively young for Jihlava, built at the end of the 17th century, but look inside to see a rare Gothic crucifix, created during the 13th century for the early Bohemian king Přemysl Otakar II. The town's most striking structure is the Gothic **Kostel svatého Jakuba** (St. James Church) to the east of the main square, down the Farní ulice. The church's exterior, with its uneven towers, is Gothic; the interior is baroque; and the font is a masterpiece of the Renaissance style, dating from 1599. Note also the baroque **Chapel of the Holy Virgin**, sandwiched between two late-Gothic chapels, with its oversize 14th-century pietà. Two other Gothic churches worth a look are the **Kostel svatého Kříža** (Church of the Holy Cross), north of the main square, and the **Minoritský kostel** (Minorite Church), to the west of the square. Just next to the latter is the last remaining of the original five medieval town gates.

Dining and Lodging

$$ ✕🏠 **Zlatá Hvězda.** Centrally located on the main square, this reconstructed old hotel in a beautiful Renaissance house is comfortable and surprisingly elegant. You're a short walk from Jihlava's restaurants and shops, though the on-site café and wine bar are among the best in town. ⊠ *Nám. Míru 32, 58601,* ☎ *066/29421,* 🆁🅰🆇 *066/29426. 17 rooms with bath. Restaurant, café, wine bar. Breakfast included. AE, MC, V.*

Moravia

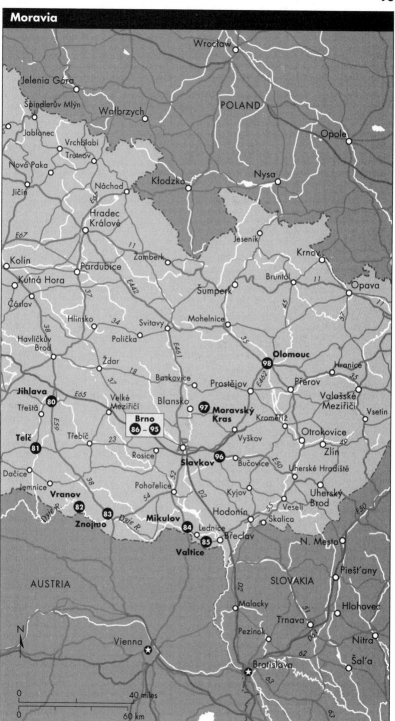

Wrocław

Jelenia Góra

Špindlerův Mlýn   Wałbrzych   POLAND

Jablonec   Vrchlabí   Opole

Nová Paka   Trutnov

Jičín   Náchod   Kłodzko   Nysa

Hradec
Králové   Jeseník   Krnov

Kolín   Žamberk   Bruntál   11   Opava
Pardubice   57
Kutná Hora   E442   37   Šumperk   45
Čáslav   11

Hlinsko   34   Svitavy   Mohelnice   35
Havlíčkův   Polička   Olomouc
Brod   E461   98   Hranice   35
Žďar   18   Přerov
Jihlava   E65   37   Baskovice   Prostějov   E462   Valašské
80   Velké   Blansko   Meziříčí
Třeštá   Meziříčí   97   Moravský   Kroměříž   Vsetín
Telč   E59   Třebíč   23   Brno   Kras   Vyškov   Otrokovice
81   86 – 95   Zlín   49
Dačice   Rosice   Slavkov   96   Bučovice   E50
Jemnice   Vranov   38   Pohořelice   Kyjov   Uherské Hradiště
82   83   Dyje R.   02   Uherský
Znojmo   Mikulov   Hodonín   55   Veselí   Brod
84   Lednice   Skalica   E50
85   Břeclav   N. Mesto
Valtice

AUSTRIA   SLOVAKIA   Piešťany

02   Malacky   Hlohovec
N   Trnava   51
Pezinok   Nitra
Vienna   62   Šaľa
Bratislava   63

0   40 miles
0   60 km

Telč

★ ⑧ *30 km (19 mi) to the south from Jihlava, via Route 406.*

The little town of Telč has an even more impressive main square than that of Jihlava. But what strikes the eye most here is not its size but the unified style of the buildings. On the lowest levels are beautifully vaulted Gothic halls, just above are Renaissance floors and facades, and all of it is crowned with rich baroque gables. The square is so perfect you feel more as if you've entered a film set rather than a living town. The town allegedly owes its architectural unity to Zacharias of Neuhaus, for whom the main square is now named. During the 16th century, so the story goes, the wealthy Zacharias had the castle—originally a small fort overlooking the Bohemian border with Hungary—rebuilt in the Renaissance style. But the contrast between the new castle and the town's rather ordinary buildings was so great that Zacharias had the square rebuilt to match the castle's splendor. Luckily for architecture fans, the Neuhaus dynasty died out shortly thereafter, and succeeding nobles had little interest in refashioning the town according to the vogue of the day.

It's best to approach Telč's main square on foot. If you've come by car, park outside the main walls on the side south of town and walk through the **Great Gate,** part of the original fortifications dating to the 13th century. The tiny Palackého ulice takes you past the 160-foot Romanesque tower of the **Kostel svatého Ducha** (Church of the Holy Ghost) on your right. This is the oldest standing structure in Telč, dating from the first quarter of the 13th century. As you walk up Palackého ulice, the **square** unfolds nobly in front of you, with the castle at the top and beautiful houses, bathed in pastel reds and golds, gracing both sides. If you're a fan of Renaissance reliefs, note the black-and-white sgraffito corner house at No. 15, which dates from the middle of the 16th century. The house at No. 61, across from the Černý Orel Hotel, is also noteworthy for its fine detail.

At the northern end of the square, the **château** forms a complex with the former **Jesuit college** and **St. James Church.** The château, originally Gothic, was built during the 14th century, when Telč first gained importance as a town bordering the old Hungarian kingdom. It was given its current Renaissance appearance by Italian masters between 1553 and 1568. In season, you can tour the castle and admire the rich Renaissance interiors, equally as impressive as the Italian palaces on which the château was modeled. Given the reputation of nobles for lively banquets lasting for hours, the sgraffito relief in the dining room depicting gluttony (in addition to the six other deadly sins) seems odd indeed. Other interesting rooms with sgraffiti include the Treasury, the Armory, and the Blue and Gold chambers.

NEED A
BREAK?   The restaurant of the **Černý Orel** Hotel on the main square is a good place to have coffee or a meal; the hotel itself is a fine place to spend the night (☞ *below*). If you're looking for sweets, you can get good homemade cakes at a little private café, **Cukrárna u Matěje,** at Na baště 2 (no phone).

Dining and Lodging

$$ ✕🖽 **Černý Orel.** Here you'll get a very rare treat: an older, refined hotel
★   that combines modern amenities in a traditional setting. The public areas are functional but elegant, and the basic but inviting rooms are well balanced and comfortably furnished. The hotel, with its baroque facade, is a perfect foil to the handsome main square outside; ask for a room overlooking it. Even if you don't stay here, take a meal at the hotel restau-

In case you want to see the world.

At American Express, we're here to make your journey a smooth one. So we have over 1,700 travel service locations in over 120 countries ready to help. What else would you expect from the world's largest travel agency?

do more

Travel

http://www.americanexpress.com/travel

In case you want to be welcomed there.

We're here to see that you're always welcomed at establishments everywhere. That's why millions of people carry the American Express® Card – for peace of mind, confidence, and security, around the world or just around the corner.

do more

Cards

In case you're running low.

We're here to help with more than 118,000 Express Cash locations around the world. In order to enroll, just call American Express before you start your vacation.

do more

Express Cash

And just in case.

We're here with American Express® Travelers Cheques and Cheques *for Two.*® They're the safest way to carry money on your vacation and the surest way to get a refund, practically anywhere, anytime.

Another way we help you...

do more

Travelers Cheques

rant, one of the best in town. ⊠ *Nám. Zachariase z Hradce 7, 588 56 Telč,* ☎ ⅋ *066/962220. 30 rooms, most with bath. Restaurant, wine bar, 24-hour exchange. Breakfast included. AE, DC, MC, V.*

$$ 🏨 **Telč.** This is a slightly upscale alternative to the Černý Orel, even though the bright, polished appearance of the reception area doesn't quite carry over to the functional but pleasant rooms. Some rooms open up onto a pleasant courtyard. The location, in a corner of the main square, is ideal. ⊠ *Na Můstku 37, 588 56 Telč,* ☎ *066/962109,* ⅋ *066/96887. 10 rooms with bath. Restaurant. Breakfast included. AE, MC, V.*

Vranov

82 *55 km (34 mi) southeast of Telč.*

Leave Telč and continue farther south into the heart of Moravian wine country. Follow the signs first to the picturesque little town of **Dačice,** then along Route 408 through **Jemnice,** and finally to the chain of recreation areas along the man-made lakes of the **Dyje (Thaya) River.** Turn right at Šumná and follow the signs to the little town of Vranov, nestled snugly between hill and river.

As a swimming and boating center for southern Moravia, Vranov would be a good place to stop in its own right. But what makes the
★ town truly noteworthy is the enormous and colorful **Vranov Castle,** rising 200 feet from a rocky promontory. For nearly 1,000 years, this was the border between Bohemia and Austria and therefore worthy of a fortress of these dimensions. You'll either love or hate this proud mongrel of a building, as its multicolored Gothic, Renaissance, and baroque elements vie for your attention. In the foreground, the solemn Renaissance tower rises over some Gothic fortifications. The structure is shored up on its left by a golden baroque church, with a beautiful pink-and-white baroque dome to the back. Each unit is spectacular, but the overall effect of so many styles mixed together is jarring.

Take your eyes off the castle's motley exterior and tour its mostly baroque (and more harmonious) interior. The most impressive room is certainly the 43-foot-high elliptical **Hall of Ancestors,** the work of the Viennese master Johann Bernhard Fischer von Erlach (builder of the Clam-Gallas Palace in Prague and the Hofburg in Vienna). The frescoes, added by the Salzburg painter Johann Michael Rottmayr, depict scenes from Greek mythology. Look inside the **castle church** as well. The rotunda, altar, and organ were designed by Fischer von Erlach at the end of the 17th century. ☎ *0624/97215.* 🎫 *50 Kč.* ☉ *Apr.–May, weekends 9– 6; June–Oct., Tues.–Sun. 9–6.*

Znojmo

83 *20 km (12 mi) east of Vranov. Follow Route 408 and turn right on the busier Route 38.*

Znojmo enjoys a long history as an important frontier town between Austria and Bohemia and is the cultural center of southern Moravia. The Přemyslide prince Břetislav I had already built a fortress here in the 11th century, and in 1226 Znojmo became the first Moravian town (ahead of Brno) to receive town rights from the king. But, alas, modern Znojmo, with its many factories and high-rises, isn't really a place for lingering. Plan on spending no more than a few hours walking through the Old Town, admiring the views over the Dyje River, and visiting the remaining fortifications and churches that stand between the New Town and the river.

Znojmo's tumbledown **main square,** now usually filled with peddlers selling everything from butter to cheap souvenirs, isn't what it used to be when it was crowned by Moravia's most beautiful **town hall.** Unfortunately, the 14th-century building was destroyed in 1945, just before the end of the war, and all that remains of the original structure is the 250-foot Gothic tower you see at the top of the square—looking admittedly forlorn astride the modern department store that now occupies the space.

For a cheerier sight, follow the rundown Zelinářská ulice, which trails from behind the Town Hall Tower to the southwest in the direction of the Old Town and the river. The grand, Gothic **Kostel svatého Mikuláše** (St. Nicholas Church), on the tiny Old Town square (Staré Město), dates from 1338, but its neo-Gothic tower was not added until the last century, when the original had to be pulled down. If you can get into the church (it's often locked), look for the impressive sacraments house, which was built around 1500 in late-Gothic style.

The curious, two-layered **Kostel svatého Václava** (St. Wenceslas Church), built at the end of the 15th century, stands just behind St. Nicholas. The upper level of this tiny white church is dedicated to St. Anne, the lower level to St. Martin. Farther to the west, along the medieval ramparts that separate the town from the river, stands the original 11th-century **Rotunda svatej Kateřiny** (St. Catherine's Rotunda), still in remarkably good condition. Step inside to see a rare cycle of restored frescoes from 1134 depicting various members of the early Přemyslide dynasty.

The **Jihomoravské Muzeum** (South Moravian Museum), just across the way in the former town castle, houses an extensive collection of artifacts from the area, dating from the Stone Age to the present. Unless you're a big fan of museums, though, there's little point in making a special visit to this one; and unless you can read Czech, you'll have difficulty making sense of the collection. ⊠ *Přemyslovců ul. 6,* ☎ *0625/224961.* ⌧ *10 Kč.* ☉ *Tues.–Sun. 9–5; closed weekends in winter.*

Dining and Lodging

Znojmo's other claims to fame have endeared the town to the hearts (and palates) of Czechs everywhere. The first is the Znojmo gherkin, first cultivated in the 16th century. You'll find this tasty accompaniment to meals at restaurants all over the country. Just look for the *Znojmo* prefix—as in *Znojemský guláš,* a tasty stew spiced with pickles. Znojmo's other treat is wine. As the center of the Moravian wine industry, this is an excellent place to pick up a few bottles of your favorite grape at any grocery or beverage store. But don't expect to learn much about a wine from its label: Oddly, you'll search in vain for the vintage or even the name of the vineyard on labels, and about the only information you can gather is the name of the grape and the city in which the wine was bottled. The best towns to look for, in addition to Znojmo, are Mikulov and Valtice. Some of the best varieties of grapes are Rulandské and Vavřinecké (for red) and Ryslink and Müller Thurgau (for white).

\$\$ ☷ **Pension Inka.** Rather than stay in a hotel, you might consider staying in this tiny, family-run pension not far from the center of town. The facilities are modest, but the rooms are bright and well kept. The kitchen is available for the use of guests. ⊠ *Jarošova ul. 27, 669 02 Znojmo,* ☎ *0624/224059. 3 rooms with bath. No credit cards.*

\$ ☷ **Pension Havelka.** Though it is tiny, the charms of this family-run
★   pension's tastefully folksy furnishings and ideal location in the center

of Old Town can only be topped by its friendly, obliging management. They'll gladly set you up at one of the family's two other pensions if this one happens to be full. ✉ *Nám. Mikulásské 3, 669 02 Znojmo,* ☎ FAX *0624/220138. 2 rooms with shared bath. Restaurant, café, use of kitchen. Breakfast included. No credit cards.*

Mikulov

84 *Leave Znojmo by heading northeast on Route 54 in the direction of Pohořelice. Make a right turn when you see signs to Mikulov, eventually arriving in town along Route 52 after a semicircuitous drive of 54 km (34 mi).*

Mikulov is known today chiefly as the border crossing on the Vienna–Brno road. If you want to leave the Czech Republic for a day to stock up on Western supplies, this is the place to do it. The nearest Austrian town, Poysdorf, is just 7 kilometers (4½ miles) away.

In many ways, Mikulov is the quintessential Moravian town. The soft pastel pinks and yellows of its buildings look almost mystical in the afternoon sunshine against the greens of the surrounding hills. But aside from the busy wine industry, not much goes on here. The main sight is the striking **château,** which dominates the tiny main square and surrounding area. The château started out as the Gothic residence of the noble Liechtenstein family in the 13th century and was given its current baroque appearance some 400 years later. The most famous resident was Napoléon, who stayed here in 1805 while negotiating peace terms with the Austrians after winning the battle of Austerlitz (Slavkov, near Brno). Sixty-one years later, Bismarck used the castle to sign a peace treaty with Austria. The castle's darkest days came at the end of World War II, when retreating Nazi SS units set the town on fire. In season, take a walk from the main square up around the side of the castle into the **museum** of wine making. The most remarkable exhibit is a wine cask made in 1643, with a capacity of more than 22,000 gallons. This was used for collecting the vintner's obligatory tithe. 🎟 *20 Kč.* ☉ *Apr.–Oct., Tues.–Sun. 9–4 (9–5 in summer).*

If you happen to arrive at grape-harvesting time in October, head for one of the many private *sklípeks* (wine cellars) built into the hills surrounding the town. The tradition in these parts is simply to knock on the door; more often than not, you'll be invited in by the owner to taste a recent vintage.

Dining and Lodging

$$$ ✕🏨 **Rohatý Krokodýl.** This is a prim, nicely renovated hotel on a quaint
★ street in the Old Town. The standards and facilities are the best in Mikulov, particularly the ground-floor restaurant, which serves a typical but delicately prepared selection of traditional Czech dishes. ✉ *Husova 8, 692 00 Mikulov,* ☎ *0625/2692,* FAX *0625/3887. 13 rooms with bath. Restaurant. Breakfast included. MC, V.*

Shopping

The secret of Moravian wine is only now beginning to extend beyond the country's borders. A vintage bottle from one of the smaller but still excellent vineyards in Bzenec, Velké Pavlovice, or Hodonín would be appreciated by any wine connoisseur.

Valtice

85 *9 km (6 mi) to the east of Mikulov along Route 414.*

This small town would be wholly nondescript except for the fascinating **château,** just off the main street, built by the Liechtenstein family in the 19th century. Next to the town's dusty streets, with their dilapidated postwar storefronts, the castle looks positively grand, a glorious if slightly overexuberant holdover from a long-lost era. But the best news of all is that you can also spend the night there if you like. Unusual for the country, the left wing of the castle has been converted into the Hubertus Hotel. The rooms aren't luxurious, but the setting is inspiring (especially if the standard high-rise hotels are getting you down). The castle boasts some 365 windows, painted ceilings, and much ornate woodwork. A small museum on the ground floor demonstrates how the town and castle have changed over the years according to aristocratic and political whim. Even if you're just passing through, enjoy a drink on the terrace behind the hotel, an ideal spot in which to relax on a warm afternoon. The Valtice winery is behind and to the right of the castle, but it is not open to the public. ☎ 0627/94423. 🎫 *Chateau 60 Kč.* ☉ *Apr.–Oct., Tues.–Sun. 9–4.*

Dining and Lodging

$$ ✕🏨 **Hubertus.** This comfortable hotel, tucked away in one wing of a
★ neo-Renaissance palace, is not hard to find. Just look for the only palace in town; the hotel is on the left-hand side. Though the rooms are neither palatial nor furnished in period style, they are nevertheless generously proportioned and comfortable. The restaurant, with garden terrace, serves reasonable Moravian cooking and good wine. Book ahead in summer, as the hotel is popular with Austrians who like to slip across the border for an impromptu holiday. ✉ *Zámek, 69142,* ☎ *0627/94537,* 🖷 *0627/94538. 62 rooms, 13 with bath. Restaurant, wine bar. Breakfast included. AE, MC, V.*

NEED A   The little mountain town of Pavlov, a short drive or bus ride from Mikulov
BREAK?   or Valtice, has several wine cellars built into the hills and makes for a
                 good refreshment stop. At **U Venuše** (✉ Česká 27), be sure to sample
                 some of the owner's wine, which comes from his private *sklípek* across
                 the lake in Strachotín. After dinner, stroll around the village, perched romantically overlooking a man-made lake.

Lednice

7 km (4½ mi) northwest of Valtice.

The Liechtenstein family peppered the countryside with neoclassical temples and follies, such as Lednice, throughout the 19th century as a display of their wealth and taste. An abandoned summer palace lies just to the north of Valtice, not far from the tiny town of **Hlohovec.** In winter you can walk or skate across the adjoining Hlohovec Pond to the golden-yellow building; otherwise follow the tiny lane to Hlohovec, just off Route 422 outside Valtice. Emblazoned across the front of the palace is the German slogan ZWISCHEN ÖSTERREICH UND MÄHREN (Between Austria and Moravia), another reminder of the proximity of the border and the long history that these areas share.

The extravagantly neo-Gothic château at **Lednice,** though obviously in disrepair, affords stunning views of the surrounding grounds and ponds. Be sure to tour the sumptuous interior; particularly resplendent with the afternoon sunshine streaming through the windows are the blue-and-green silk wallcoverings embossed with the Moravian eagle in the formal dining room and bay-windowed drawing room. The grounds, now a pleasant park open to the public, even boast a 200-foot minaret and a massive greenhouse filled with exotic flora. ✉

Zámek, ☎ *0627/98306.* ✉ *90 Kč.* ☉ *Apr.–Oct., Tues.–Sun. 9–4 (until 6 in summer).*

Dolní Věstonice

18 km (11 mi) northwest from Lednice.

From Lednice, follow the Dyje River to the northwest through the villages of Bulhary and Milovice and on to the tiny town of Dolní Věstonice, perched alongside another giant artificial lake. Although the town has little going for it today, some 20,000 to 30,000 years ago the area was home to a thriving prehistoric settlement, judging from ivory and graves found here by archaeologists in 1950. Some of the world's earliest ceramics were also discovered, among them a curvaceous figurine of ash and clay that has become known as the Venus of Věstonice. The original is kept in Brno, but you can see replicas, real mammoth bones, and much else of archaeological interest at the excellent **museum** in the center of town along the main road. ✉ *20 Kč.* ☉ *Apr.–Sept., Tues.–Sun. 8–noon and 1–4.*

Outdoor Activities and Sports

For walking enthusiasts, the **Pavlovské vrchy** (Pavlov Hills), where the settlement was found, offers a challenging climb. Start out by ascending the **Děvín Peak** (1,800 feet), just south of Dolní Věstonice. A series of paths then follows the ridges the 10 kilometers (6 miles) to Mikulov.

Southern Moravia A to Z

Arriving and Departing

BY BUS

Bus connections from Prague to Jihlava are excellent and inexpensive, and, in lieu of a car, the best way to get to Moravia. Southern Moravian destinations are also well served from Bratislava and other points in Slovakia.

BY CAR

Southern Moravia is within easy driving distance of Prague, Bratislava, and eastern Slovakia. Jihlava, the starting point for touring the region, is 124 kilometers (78 miles) southeast of Prague along the excellent D1 freeway. Southern Moravia is also easily reached by car from Austria; there are major border crossings at Háté (below Znojmo) and Mikulov.

Getting Around

☞ Getting Around *in* Czech Republic A to Z, *below.*

Contacts and Resources

EMERGENCIES

Police (☎ 158). **Ambulance** (☎ 155). **Breakdowns** (☎ 154 or 123 [in some areas 0123]).

VISITOR INFORMATION

Telč (✉ Nám. Zachariáše z Hradce 10).

BRNO

Moravia's cultural and geographic center, Brno (pronounced *burrno*) grew rich in the 19th century and doesn't look or feel like any other Czech or Slovak city. Beginning with a textile industry imported from Germany, Holland, and Belgium, Brno became the industrial heartland of the Austro-Hungarian Empire during the 18th and 19th centuries—hence its nickname "Manchester of Moravia." You'll search in vain for an extensive old town; you'll also find few of the traditional arcaded storefronts that typify other historic Czech towns. What you will see instead are fine examples of Empire and neoclassical styles, their formal, geometric facades more in keeping with the conservative tastes of the 19th-century middle class.

In the early years of this century, the city became home to the best young architects working in the cubist and constructivist styles. And experimentation wasn't restricted to architecture. Leoš Janáček, an important composer of the early modern period, also lived and worked in Brno. The modern tradition continues even today, and the city is considered to have the best theater and performing arts in Moravia.

It's best to avoid Brno at trade-fair time (the biggest are in early spring and early autumn), when hotel and restaurant facilities are strained. If the hotels are booked, Čedok or the accommodation services at the town hall or main station will help you find a room.

Exploring Brno

A Good Walk

Numbers in the text correspond to numbers in the margin and on the Brno map.

Begin the walking tour at the triangular **Náměstí Svobody** (Freedom Square) ⑱ in the heart of the commercial district. Then walk up the main Masarykova ulice toward the train station and make a right through the little arcade at No. 6 to see the animated Gothic portal of the **Stará radnice** (Old Town Hall) ⑲. Leave the town hall by Pilgram's portal and turn right into the old **Zelný trh** (Cabbage Market) ⑳. On the far side of the market, dominating the square, stands the severe Renaissance **Dietrichstein Palace** ⑲ at No. 8. From the garden, walk down the stairs to the baroque **Kostel Nalezení svatého Kříže** (Church of the Holy Cross) ⑳.

Towering above the church and market is the **Chrám sv. Petra a Pavla** (Cathedral of Sts. Peter and Paul) ⑨, Brno's main church and a fixture of the skyline. The best way to get to the cathedral is to return to the Cabbage Market (via the little street off the Kapucínské náměstí), make a left at the market, and walk up the narrow Petrská ulice, which begins just to the right of the Dietrichstein Palace. Before leaving the cathedral area, stroll around the park and grounds. The view of the town from here is pretty, and the mood is restful. Continue the tour by walking down the continuation of the Petrská ulice to Biskupská ulice. Turn left at the Starobrněnská ulice and cross the busy Husova třída onto Pekařská ulice, which planners are hoping to someday transform into a lively area of boutiques and shops. At the end of the street is the Mendlovo náměstí (Mendel Square) and the **Monastery of Staré Brno** ⑨.

Continue the tour along the busy and somewhat downtrodden Úvoz ulice (in the direction of Špilberk Castle). Take the first right and climb the stairs to the calmer residential street of Pellicova. If there's a unique beauty to Brno, it's in neighborhoods such as this one, with its attractive houses, each in a different architectural style. Many houses incorporate cubist and geometric elements of the early modern period (1920s and '30s). Begin the ascent to **Špilberk hrad** (Špilberk Castle) ⑨. There is no direct path to the castle; just follow your instincts (or a detailed map) upward, and you'll get there. From the top, look over to the west at the gleaming art-deco pavilions of the Brno **Výstaviště** (exhibition grounds) ⑨ in the distance. The earliest buildings were completed in 1928, in time to hold the first cultural exhibition to celebrate the 10th anniversary of the Czech state. The grounds are now the site of annual trade fairs. Before leaving Brno, try to visit Ludwig Mies van der Rohe's **Villa Tugendhat** ⑨⑤, though you will need to travel there by car, taxi, or tram.

Timing

The tour should take two or three hours at a leisurely pace. Allow an extra hour to explore Špilberk Castle. Museum enthusiasts could easily spend a half day or more browsing the city's many collections.

Sights to See

⑨① **Chrám sv. Petra a Pavla** (Cathedral of Sts. Peter and Paul). Sadly, Sts. Peter and Paul is one church that probably looks better from a distance. The interior, a blend of baroque and Gothic, is light and tasteful but hardly overwhelming. Still, the slim neo-Gothic twin spires, added in this century to give the cathedral more of its original Gothic dignity, are a nice touch. Don't be surprised if you hear the noon bells ringing from the cathedral at 11 o'clock. The practice dates from the Thirty Years' War, when Swedish troops were massing for an attack outside the town walls. Brno's resistance had been fierce, and the Swedish commander decreed that he would give up the fight if the town could not be taken by noon the following day. The bell ringer caught wind of the decision and the next morning, just as the Swedes were preparing a final assault, rang the noon bells—an hour early. The ruse worked, and the Swedes decamped. Ever since, the midday bells have been rung an hour early as a show of gratitude. While the city escaped, the cathedral caught a Swedish cannon shot and suffered severe damage in the resulting fire. ⊠ *Petrov at Petrská.* 🖾 *Free.* ☉ *During daylight hrs, except during services.*

⑧⑨ **Dietrichstein Palace.** The building was once home to Cardinal Count Franz von Dietrichstein, who led the Catholic Counter-Reformation in Moravia following the Battle of White Mountain in 1620. Today the palace and the adjoining **Biskupský dvůr** (Bishop's Court) house the **Moravské muzeum** (Moravian Museum), with its mundane exhibits of local history, artifacts, and wildlife. To enter the Bishop's Court, walk through the little gate to the left of the Dietrichstein Palace and then through the lovely Renaissance garden. Note the arcades, the work of 16th-century Italian craftsmen. ⊠ *Zelný trh 8.* ☉ *Tues.–Sun. 9–5 (Bishop's Court closes at 5).*

⑨⓪ **Kostel Nalezení svatého Kříže** (Church of the Holy Cross). This plain-looking baroque church was formerly part of the Capuchin Monastery. If you've ever wondered what a mummy looks like without its bandages, then enter the door to the monastery's *hrobka* (crypt). In the basement are the mummified remains of some 200 nobles and monks from the late 17th and the 18th centuries, ingeniously preserved by a natural system of air circulating through vents and chimneys. The best-known mummy is Colonel František Trenck, commander of the brutal Pandour regiment of the Austrian army, who, at least in legend, spent several years in the dungeons of Špilberk Castle before finding his final rest here in 1749. Even in death the hapless colonel has not found peace—someone made off with his head several years ago. A note of caution about the crypt: The graphic displays may frighten small children, so ask at the admission desk for the small brochure (10 Kč) with pictures that preview what's to follow. ⊠ *Kapucínské nám.* 🖾 *20 Kč.* ☉ *Tues.–Sat. 9–11:45 and 2–4:30, Sun. 11–11:45 and 2–4:30.*

⑨② **Monastery of Staré Brno.** The uninspiring location seems to confirm the adage that genius can flourish anywhere, for in the 19th century this was home to Gregor Mendel, the shy monk who became the father of modern genetic research. If you recall from high-school science, it

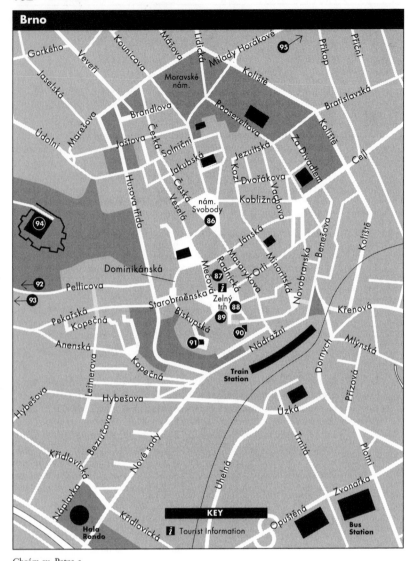

Brno

KEY

i Tourist Information

Chrám sv. Petra a
Pavla, **91**

Dietrichstein
Palace, **89**

Kostel Nalezení
svatého Kříže, **90**

Monastery of
Staré Brno, **92**

Náměstí Svobody, **86**

Špilberk hrad, **94**

Stará radnice, **87**

Villa Tugendhat, **95**

Výstaviště, **93**

Zelný trh, **88**

was Mendel's experiments with crossing pea and bean plants, from which he figured out dominant and recessive traits, that led to the first formulations of the laws of heredity. A small statue to his memory can be found in the garden behind the monastery. ⊠ *Mendlovo nám. 1.* ⊙ *Sept.–May, weekdays 8–5; June–Aug., daily 9–6.*

86 **Náměstí Svobody** (Freedom Square). The square itself is architecturally undistinguished, but here and along the adjoining streets you'll find the city's best stores and shopping opportunities. A certain air of friendly provinciality reigns here amid the hurrying crowds of shoppers and schoolchildren, and the relatively small numbers of tourists have yet to make much of an impact on the city center.

94 **Špilberk hrad** (Špilberk Castle). Once among the most feared places in the Hapsburg Empire, this fortress-cum-prison still broods over the town from behind its menacing walls. Špilberk's advantageous location was no secret to the early kings, who moved here during the 13th century from neighboring Petrov Hill. Successive rulers gradually converted the old castle into a virtually impregnable fortress. Indeed, it successfully withstood the onslaughts of Hussites, Swedes, and Prussians over the centuries; only Napoléon, in 1809, succeeded in occupying the fortress. But the castle is best known for its gruesome history as a prison for the Austro-Hungarian monarchy and, later, for the Nazis in World War II. Although tales of torture during the Austrian period are probably legendary (judicial torture had been prohibited prior to the first prisoners' arrival in 1784), conditions for the hardest offenders were hellish: shackled day and night in dark, dank catacombs and fed only bread and water. The most brutal corrections ended with the death of the harsh, rationalist ruler Joseph II in 1790. The casemates (passages within the walls of the castle) have been turned into an exhibition of the late-18th-century prison and their Nazi-era use as an air-raid shelter. Parents should note that young children can easily become lost in the spooky, dim casemates. More dangerous, the low parapets atop the castle walls near the restaurant provide little security for overcurious climbers. The castle is still being renovated, and there are plans for more displays on the German occupation during World War II. In summertime, temporary historical exhibitions are installed in the west wing. ☎ *05/4221–4145.* ⊡ *Casemates 20 Kč.* ⊙ *Tues.–Sun. 9–4:45 (until 6 June–Sept.).*

NEED A BREAK? After a long walk and a good climb, what could be better than one of the best beers you'll ever have? The **Stopkova pivnice,** at Česka 5, will set you up with one, or a soft drink, in clean, comfortable surroundings. If you're hungry, try the house goulash, a tangy mixture of sausage, beef, rice, egg, and dumpling. For something more substantial, head for the restaurant on the second floor.

87 **Stará radnice** (Old Town Hall). The oldest secular building in Brno has an important Gothic portal. The door is the work of Anton Pilgram, architect of Vienna's St. Stephen's Cathedral, and was completed in 1510; the building itself is about 200 years older. Look above the door to see a badly bent pinnacle that looks as if it wilted in the afternoon sun. This isn't the work of vandals but was apparently done by Pilgram himself out of revenge against the town. According to legend, Pilgram had been promised an excellent commission for his portal, but when he finished, the mayor and city councillors reneged on their offer. So angry was Pilgram at the duplicity, he purposely bent the pinnacle and left it poised, fittingly, over the statue of justice.

Just inside the door are the remains of two other famous Brno legends, the **Brno Dragon** and the **wagon wheel.** The dragon—a female alligator to be anatomically correct—apparently turned up at the town walls one day in the 17th century and began eating children and livestock. A gatekeeper came up with the novel idea of filling a sack with limestone and placing it inside a freshly slaughtered goat. The dragon devoured the goat, swallowing the limestone as well, and went to quench its thirst at a nearby river. The water mixed with the limestone, bursting the dragon's stomach (the scars on the dragon's stomach are still clearly visible). The story of the wagon wheel, on the other hand, concerns a bet placed some 400 years ago that a young wheelwright, Jiří Birk, couldn't chop down a tree, fashion the wood into a wheel, and roll it from his home at Lednice (33 miles away) to the town walls of Brno—all between sunup and sundown. The wheel stands as a lasting tribute to his achievement (the townspeople, however, became convinced that Jiří had enlisted the help of the devil to win the bet, so they stopped frequenting his workshop; poor Jiří died penniless).

No longer the seat of the town government, the Old Town Hall holds exhibitions and performances. To find out what's on, look for a sign on the door of the exhibition room. The view from the top of the tower is one of the best in Brno, but the climb (five flights) is strenuous. What catches the eye is not so much any single building—although the cathedral does look spectacular—but the combination of old and new that defines modern Brno. In the distance, next to the crooked roofs and baroque onion domes, a power plant looks startlingly out of place. ⊠ *Radnická ul. 8.* 🎫 *Tower 10 Kč.* ☉ *Apr.–Sept., daily 9–5.*

95   **Villa Tugendhat.** Designed by Ludwig Mies van der Rohe and completed in 1930, this austere white villa, built in the Bauhaus style, counts among the most important works of the modern period. The emphasis here is on function and the use of geometric forms, but you be the judge as to whether the house fits the neighborhood. The Tugendhat family fled before the Nazis, and their original furnishings vanished during the war or the house's subsequent heavy handed remodeling. Replicas of Mies's cool, functional designs have been installed in the downstairs living area. Some of the original exotic wood paneling and an eye-stopping onyx screen remain in place. The best way to get there is to take a taxi or Tram 3, 5, or 11 to the Dětská nemocnice stop and then walk up the unmarked Černopolní Street for 10 minutes or so. ⊠ *Černopolní 45,* ☎ *05/4521–2118.* 🎫 *80 Kč.* ☉ *Wed.–Sun. 10–5.*

93   **Výstaviště** (exhibition grounds). The earliest buildings were completed in 1928, in time to hold the first cultural exhibition to celebrate the 10th anniversary of the Czech state. The Brno-born modern architect Adolf Loos designed the interior of the 19th-century mansion on the grounds, and Bohuslav Fuchs—another modernist linked to Brno—created the City of Brno Pavilion. The enormous circular Pavilion Z dates from 1959. The grounds are now the site of annual trade fairs, and the grounds may be closed between fairs. ⊠ *Výstaviště 1,* ☎ *05/4115 3101. From main train station, take Tram 1 or 18 west to the 5th stop.*

88   **Zelný trh** (Cabbage Market). The only place where Brno begins to look like a typical Czech town, the Cabbage Market is immediately recognizable, not just for the many stands from which farmers still sell vegetables but also for the unique **Parnassus Fountain** that adorns its center. This baroque pile of rocks (you either love it or hate it) couldn't be more out of place amid the formal elegance of most of the buildings on the square. But when Johann Bernhard Fischer von Erlach created the fountain in the late 17th century, it was important for a striving town like

Brno to display its understanding of the classics and of ancient Greece. Thus, Hercules slays a three-headed dragon, while Amphitrite on top awaits the arrival of her lover—all incongruously surrounded by farmers hawking turnips and onions.

OFF THE
BEATEN PATH

MORAVSKÝ KRUMLOV – Admirers of art-nouveau meister Alfons Mucha may want to make a short detour off the main highway linking Mikulov and Brno. The town museum is the unlikely home of one of Mucha's most celebrated works, his 20-canvas *Slav Epic.* This enormous work, which tells the story of the emergence of the Slav nation, was not well received when it was completed in 1928; painters at the time were more interested in imitating modern movements and considered Mucha's representational art to be old-fashioned. Interest in Mucha's lyrical style has grown in recent years, however, and the museum annually attracts some 15,000 visitors. *Museum: ☒ Zámecká 1, ☎ 0621/2789–2225. ☺ Apr.–Oct. Tues.–Sun. 9–noon and 1–4.*

Dining and Lodging

$$$ ✕ **Černý Medvěd.** Undoubtedly Brno's most comfortable dining room, it has plush red upholstery and, weather permitting, a fire crackling on the open hearth. Wild game is the key ingredient in a menu that focuses on Czech specialties. ☒ *Jakubské nám. 1,* ☎ *05/4221–4548. MC, V.*

$$ ✕ **Baroko vinárna.** This 17th-century wine cellar housed in a Minorite monastery offers excellent cooking in a fun, if touristy, setting. Try the roast beef Slavkov, named for the site of Napoléon's triumph not far from Brno. Mystery of Magdalene is a potato pancake stuffed with pork, liver, mushrooms, and presumably anything else the cook could get his hands on. ☒ *Orlí 17,* ☎ *05/4221–1344. No credit cards. No lunch.*

$$ ✕ **Maccaroni.** Delicious pastas and pizzas (a welcome alternative to the heavy local fare) are served here in a casual, unhurried setting. Take a taxi, walk the 15 minutes from the center, or ride Tram 5 or 6 to the stop called Nemocnice u sv. Anny. ☒ *Pekařská 80,* ☎ *05/4321–4528. MC.*

$$ ✕ **Modrá Hvězda.** Liberal opening hours and a convenient location just to the west of Náměstí Svobody make this cheery restaurant a good choice for a quick lunch or off-hours snack. ☒ *Starobrněnská 20,* ☎ *05/4221–5292. AE, DC, MC, V.*

$$$$ 🏨 **Grand.** Though not really grand, this hotel, built in 1870 and thoroughly remodeled in 1988, is certainly comfortable and the best in Brno. High standards are maintained through the hotel's association with an Austrian chain. The reception and public areas are clean and modern; service is attentive; and the rooms, though small, are well appointed. Ask for a room at the back, overlooking the town, as the hotel is on a busy street opposite the railroad station. ☒ *Benešova 18/20, 657 83 Brno,* ☎ *05/4232–1287,* 🖷 *05/4221–0345. 113 rooms with bath. 3 restaurants, minibars, in-room satellite TVs, casino, nightclub. AE, DC, MC, V.*

$$$$ 🏨 **Holiday Inn.** Opened in 1993, this modern but handsome representative of the American chain has become the hotel of choice for business travelers in town for a trade fair. It has all you'd expect for the price, including a well-trained, multilingual staff, clean and well-appointed rooms, and a full range of business services. The location, at the exhibition grounds about a mile from the city center, is inconvenient for those who don't have a car. ☒ *Křížkovského 20, 603 00 Brno,* ☎ *05/4312–2111,* 🖷 *05/4115–9081. 205 rooms with bath. Restaurant, café, sauna, conference rooms. AE, DC, MC, V.*

$$$ ☒ **Pegas.** This little inn makes an excellent choice given its reasonable
★   price and central location. The plain rooms are snug and clean, and
      the staff is helpful and friendly. Even if you don't stay here, be sure to
      have a meal at the house pub-microbrewery. ☒ *Jakubská 4, 602 00
      Brno,* ☎ *05/4221–0104,* ☒ *05/4221–1232. 15 rooms with bath.
      Restaurant. AE, DC, MC, V.*

$$$ ☒ **Slavia.** The century-old Slavia, just off the main Česká ulice, was
      thoroughly renovated in 1987, giving the public areas an efficient, up-
      to-date look and leaving the rooms plain but clean. The café, with ad-
      jacent terrace, is a good place to enjoy a cool drink on a warm
      afternoon. ☒ *Solniční 15/17, 622 16 Brno,* ☎ *05/4221–5080,* ☒ *05/
      4221–1769. 81 rooms with shower or bath. Restaurant, café, mini-
      bars, parking. AE, DC, MC, V.*

$$ ☒ **U svatého Jakuba.** Little seems to have changed here for several
      decades, including the behavior of the staff (who operate on the premise
      that the customer may always be right, but should also be grateful for
      any services rendered). It used to be classed as a "moderate" hotel, but
      the cheaper establishments of the central city have vanished into the
      precapitalist past, leaving this one to keep up tradition by offering basic
      accommodation at reasonable rates. ☒ *Jakubské nám. 6, 602 00 Brno,*
      ☎ *05/4221–0795,* ☒ *05/4221–0797. 37 rooms, most with bath.
      Restaurant, wine bar. MC, V.*

Nightlife and the Arts

Brno is renowned throughout the Czech Republic for its theater and
performing arts. The two main locales for jacket-and-tie cultural events
are the **Mahen Theater** (for drama) and the modern **Janáček Theater**
(for opera and ballet). Both are slightly northwest of the center of town,
just off Rooseveltova ul. Check the schedules at the theater or pick up
a copy of *KAM,* Brno's monthly bulletin of cultural events. Buy tick-
ets directly at the theater box office 30 minutes before showtime. One
of the country's best-known fringe theater companies, **Divadlo Husa
na provázku** (Goose on a String Theater), has its home where Petrská
Street enters Zelný trh (☒ Zelný trh 9, ☎ 05/4221–0099).

For more sophisticated entertainment than talk and drink at the local
pivnice or vinárna, head for the **casinos** at the **Grand Hotel** (☒ Benešova
18/20, across from the main station, ☎ 05/4232–1287) and the **In-
ternational Hotel** (☒ Husova 16, ☎ 05/4212–2111); the tables usu-
ally stay open until 3 AM or 4 AM. Both hotels also have bars that serve
drinks until very late. The "casinos" on Náměstí Svobody are glori-
fied video gambling parlors with a mixed clientele of clueless tourists
and all-too-streetwise locals.

Klub Alterna (☒ Kounicova 48, a few blocks north of the city center)
puts on good Czech jazz and folk performers.

Shopping

Moravia produces very attractive folk pottery, painted with bright
red, orange, and yellow flower patterns. You can find these products
in stores and hotel gift shops throughout the region. For more mod-
ern art objects, including paintings, stop by **Dílo** (☒ Kobližná 4).
Merkuria (down the street at ☒ Kobližná 10) stocks a beautiful selec-
tion of crystal and porcelain from Karlovy Vary. You can buy English
paperbacks including a huge range of travel guidebooks, should Cen-
tral America suddenly seem more alluring than Central Europe, at the
Zahraniční literatura shop (☒ Nám. Svobody 18).

Brno A to Z

Arriving and Departing

BY BUS

Bus connections from Prague to Brno are excellent and inexpensive, and, in lieu of a car, the best way to get here. Buses also run daily between Brno's main bus station and Vienna's Wien-Mitte station, leaving Brno at 7:30 AM and 5:30 PM. Round-trip tickets cost about $27.

BY CAR

Brno, within easy driving distance of Prague, Bratislava, and eastern Slovakia, is 196 kilometers (122 miles) from Prague and 121 kilometers (75 miles) from Bratislava.

BY PLANE

The private carrier **Air Ostrava** links Prague with Brno and Ostrava (Prague, ☎ 02/2403–2731 or 02/0601–533003 [mobile phone]). The distances between the cities are short, however, and it's ultimately cheaper and quicker to drive or take a bus. During the two large Brno trade fairs, in April and September, foreign carriers also connect the city with Frankfurt and Vienna. These flights are usually crowded with businessmen, so you'll have to book well in advance.

BY TRAIN

Several trains daily make the three-hour run from Prague to Brno. Most use Prague's **Hlavní nádraží** (main station), but some depart from and arrive at the suburban station **Holešovice nádraží** (Holešovice station) or at **Masarykovo nádraží** (Masaryk station), on Hybernská ulice in the city center. Trains leaving Prague for Budapest and Bucharest (and some Vienna-bound trains) also frequently stop in Brno (check timetables to be sure).

Getting Around

BY BUS

The Brno bus station is a 10-minute walk behind the train station. To find it, simply go to the train station and follow the signs to ČSAD.

BY TRAIN

Comparatively good trains run frequently on the Prague–Brno–Břeclav main line.

Contacts and Resources

B&B RESERVATION AGENCIES

If you've arrived at Brno's main station and are stuck for a room, try the accommodations service on the far left of the main hall, open every day (closes at 10 AM Sun.); you can place a sports bet there too.

EMERGENCIES

Police (☎ 158). **Ambulance** (☎ 155). **Breakdowns** (☎ 154 or 123 [in some areas 0123]).

LATE-NIGHT PHARMACIES

Brno has a 24-hour pharmacy at Kobližná ulice 7.

TRAVEL AGENCIES

American Express representative (✉ Starobrněnská 20); **CKM** (youth travel bureau; ✉ Česká 11, ☎ 05/4221–2677).

VISITOR INFORMATION

Čedok (✉ Nádražní 10/12, ☎ 05/4232–1267); **Kulturní a informační Centrum** (✉ Radnická 8 [Old Town Hall], ☎ 05/4221–1090). ☞ Visitor Information *in* Czech Republic A to Z, *below.*

NORTHERN MORAVIA

Just north of Brno is the **Moravian Karst,** a beautiful wilderness area with an extensive network of caves, caverns, and underground rivers. Many caves are open to the public, and some tours even incorporate underground boat rides. Farther to the north lies Moravia's "second capital," **Olomouc,** an industrial but still charming city with a long history as a center of learning. Paradoxically, despite its location far from the Austrian border, Olomouc remained a bastion of support for the Hapsburgs and the empire at a time when cries for independence could be heard throughout Bohemia and Moravia. In 1848, when revolts everywhere threatened to bring the monarchy down, the Hapsburg family fled here for safety. Franz Joseph, who went on to personify the stodgy permanence of the empire, was even crowned here as Austrian emperor that same year.

The green foothills of the **Beskydy range** begin east of Olomouc, perfect for a day or two of walking in the mountains. Farther to the east you'll find the spectacular peaks of the Tatras, and the tour is a good jumping-off point for exploring eastern Slovakia or southern Poland. Similarly, if you're coming from Slovakia, you could easily begin in Olomouc and conduct the tour in reverse order.

Slavkov

96   *20 km (12 mi) east of Brno.*

Slavkov, better known as **Austerlitz,** was the scene of one of the great battlefields of European history, where the armies of Napoléon met and defeated the combined forces of Austrian emperor Franz II and Czar Alexander I in 1805. If you happen to have a copy of *War and Peace* handy, you will find no better account of it anywhere. Scattered about the rolling agricultural landscapes are a museum, a garden, and the memorial chapel of the impressive **Cairn of Peace.** In the town of Slavkov itself, the baroque château houses more memorabilia about the battle; it's well worth visiting. ✉ *Slavkov U Brna,* ☎ *05/941204.*

Moravský Kras

97   *30 km (19 mi) north of Brno.*

If it's scenic rather than military tourism you want, however, take a short trip north from Brno up the Svitava Valley and into the Moravský Kras (Moravian Karst), an area of limestone formations, underground stalactite caves, rivers, and tunnels. The most interesting part is near **Blansko** and includes the **Kateřinská jeskyně** (Catherine Cave), **Punkevní jeskyně** (Punkva Cave), and the celebrated **Macocha Abyss,** the deepest drop of the karst (more than 400 feet). Several caves can be visited: Try the 90-minute Punkva tour, which includes a visit to the Macocha Abyss and a boat trip along an underground river. In a controversial decision, the state turned over some of the area's tourist services to a private firm, which operates the *Eco-Express* train-on-wheels linking the Skalní Mlýn Hotel to the Punkva Cave, and the funicular from Punkva to the Macocha Abyss. ✉ *20 Kč to Kateřinská jeskyně, 60 Kč to Punkevní jedkyně, including underground boat ride.* ☉ *Daily 8–2. Funicular:* ✉ *50 Kč.* ☉ *Daily 8–5 (until 3 Oct.–Apr.).*

Hiking

Underground or on the surface, the walking is excellent in the karst, and if you miss one of the few buses running between the town of Blansko and the cave region, you may have to hoof it anyway. Try to obtain a map in Brno or from the tourist information office in Blansko, which is across the road from the train station and 300 yards from the bus station (☎ 0506/53635). It's 8 kilometers (5 miles) from the unattractive outskirts of Blansko to the Skalní Mlýn Hotel and nearby Catherine Cave, set amid thickly forested ravines. Look out for Devil's Bridge (*Čertův most*), a natural bridge high over the road just past the entrance to Catherine Cave; or follow the yellow-marked path from the cave for another couple of miles to the Macocha Abyss. Before setting out, check with the information office or at the bus station for current bus schedules; for much of the year the last bus from Skalní Mlýn back to Blansko leaves at around 3 PM.

Olomouc

★ ⑨⑧ *77 km (48 mi) northeast of Brno.*

Olomouc is a paradox—so far from Austria yet so supportive of the empire. The Hapsburgs always felt at home here, even when they were being violently opposed by Czech nationalists and Protestants throughout Bohemia and much of Moravia. During the revolutions of 1848, when the middle class from all over the Austro-Hungarian Empire seemed ready to boot the Hapsburgs out of their palace, the royal family fled to Olomouc, where they knew they could count on the population for support. The 18-year-old Franz Joseph was even crowned emperor here in 1848 because the situation in Vienna was still too turbulent.

Despite being overshadowed by Brno, Olomouc, with its proud square and prim 19th-century buildings, still retains something of a provincial imperial capital, not unlike similarly sized cities in Austria. The focal point here is the triangular **Horní náměstí** (Upper Square), marked at its center by the bright and almost flippantly colored Renaissance **radnice** (town hall) with its 220-foot tower. The tower was begun in the late 14th century and given its current appearance in 1443; the astronomical clock on the outside was built in 1422, but its inner mechanisms and modern mosaic decorations date from immediately after World War II. Be sure to look inside at the beautiful Renaissance stairway. There's also a large Gothic banquet room in the main building, with scenes from the city's history, and a late-Gothic chapel.

The eccentric **Trinity Column** in the northwest corner of the square, at more than 100 feet, is the largest of its kind in the Czech Republic and houses a tiny chapel. Four baroque fountains, depicting Hercules (1687), Caesar (1724), Neptune (1695), and Jupiter (1707), dot the main square and the adjacent **Dolní náměstí** (Lower Square) to the south, as if to reassure us that this Moravian town was well versed in the humanities.

NEED A BREAK?   The wooden paneling and floral upholstery in the **Café Mahler** recall the taste of the 1880s, when Gustav Mahler briefly lived just around the corner while working as a conductor at the theater on the other side of the Upper Square. It makes a good spot for ice cream, cake, or coffee. ⌧ *Horní nám. 11.*

Just north of the Horní náměstí, along the small Jana Opletalova ulice, stands the **Chrám svatého Mořice** (Church of St. Maurice), the town's best Gothic building. Construction began in 1412, but a fire 40 years later badly damaged the structure; its current fierce, gray exterior dates from the middle of the 16th century. The baroque organ inside, the largest in the Czech Republic, contains 2,311 pipes.

The interior of triple-domed **Kostel svatého Michala** (St. Michael's Church) casts a dramatic spell. The frescoes, the high, airy central dome, and the shades of rose, beige, and gray marble on walls and arches blend to a harmonious, if dimly glimpsed, whole. The decoration followed a 1709 fire, which came 30 years after the original construction. Architect and builder are not known, but it's surmised they are the same team that put up the Church of the Annunciation on Svatý Kopeček (Holy Hill), a popular Catholic pilgrimage site just outside Olomouc. ⊠ *Žerotínovo nám., 1 block uphill from the Upper Square along Školní ul.*

Between the main square and the **Dóm svatého Václava** (Cathedral of St. Wenceslas) lies a peaceful neighborhood given over to huge buildings, done in baroque or later styles, mostly belonging either to the university or the archbishopric. As it stands today, the cathedral is just another example of the overbearing neo-Gothic enthusiasm of the late 19th century, having passed through just about every other architectural fad since its true Gothic days. To the left of the church, however, is the entrance to the **Přemyslide Palace,** now a museum, where you can see early 16th-century wall paintings decorating the Gothic cloisters and, upstairs, a wonderful series of two- and three-arched Romanesque windows. This part of the building was used as a schoolroom some 700 years ago, and you can still make out drawings of animals engraved on the walls by early young vandals. You can get an oddly phrased English-language pamphlet to help you around the building. ⊠ *Dómská ul.* 🎫 *20 Kč.* ☉ *Tues.–Sun. 9–12:30 and 1–5.*

The **deacon's house** opposite the cathedral, now part of Palácký University, has two unusual claims to fame. Here, in 1767, the young musical prodigy Wolfgang Amadeus Mozart, age 11, spent six weeks recovering from a mild attack of chicken pox. The 16-year-old King Wenceslas III suffered a much worse fate here in 1306, when he was murdered, putting an end to the Přemyslide dynasty.

OFF THE BEATEN PATH

PŘÍBOR – Fans of dream interpretation and psychoanalysis shouldn't leave Moravia without stopping at this little town, the birthplace of Sigmund Freud. To find it, drive east out of Olomouc along Route 35, following the signs first to Lipník, then Hranice, Nový Jičín, and finally Příbor—about 50 kilometers (31 miles) in all. Park at the Náměstí Sigmunda Freuda (Sigmund Freud Square). The seemingly obvious name for the main square is actually new; the former Communist regime was not in favor of Freudians. The comfortable, middle-class house, marked with a plaque, where the doctor was born in 1856 is a short walk away along Freudova ulice. At present, the house is still inhabited, so you can't go inside. ⊠ *Freudova ul. 117.*

Lodging

$$$ 🏨 **Flora.** Don't expect luxury at this 1960s cookie-cutter high-rise, about a 15-minute walk from the town square. To its credit, the staff is attentive (English is spoken), and the pleasant if anonymous rooms are certainly adequate for a short stay. ⊠ *Krapkova ul. 34, 779 00 Olomouc,* ☎ *068/412021,* 📠 *068/412221. 175 rooms, most with bath or shower. Restaurant. AE, DC, MC, V.*

$$ 🏨 **Národní Dům.** Built in 1885 and a block from the main square, this is a better choice than the Flora for evoking a little of Olomouc's 19th-century history. The handsome building recalls the era's industriousness, as does the large, gracious café on the main floor. Standards have slipped in the intervening years, though, and signs of decline are evident. ⊠ *Třída 8. května 21, 772 00 Olomouc,* ☎ *068/522–4806,* 📠 *068/522–4808. 63 rooms, most with bath or shower. Restaurant, café, snack bar. AE, DC, MC, V.*

$$ 🏨 **U Dómu sv. Václava.** A pleasant place that well represents a new class of Czech hotel and pension, you'll find modernized fittings installed in an old, often historic, house. This pension's six small suites all have kitchenettes. It's just down the street from the sleepy Cathedral Square. ✉ *Dómská 4, 772 00 Olomouc,* ☎ *068/522–0502,* FAX *068/522– 0501. 6 rooms with bath. In-room TVs, kitchenettes. MC, V.*

Hiking and Cross-Country Skiing

The gentle, forested peaks of the **Beskydy Mountains** are popular destinations for hill walking, berry picking, and cross-country skiing; several resorts have ski lifts as well. The year-round resort town of Rožnov pod Radhoštěm has bus connections to all major cities in the country. Stay the night at one of the modest but comfortable mountain chalets in the area. You'll find a good one, the **Chata Soláň,** along the road between Rožnov and Velké Karlovice (✉ 756 06 Velké Karlovice, ☎ 0657/ 94365). The latter settlement lies at the end of a rail line from Vsetín. But be sure to take along a good map before venturing along the tiny mountain roads. Also, some roads may be closed during the winter.

Northern Moravia A to Z

Arriving and Departing

Brno is the gateway to northern Moravia, whether by bus, car, plane, or train. ☞ Arriving and Departing *in* Brno A to Z, *above.*

Getting Around

Comparatively good trains run frequently on the Prague–Olomouc–Vsetín main lines. In any event, you'll sometimes have to resort to the bus to reach the smaller, out-of-the-way places throughout northern Moravia. ☞ Getting Around *in* the Czech Republic A to Z, *below.*

Contacts and Resources

EMERGENCIES

Police (☎ 158). **Ambulance** (☎ 155). **Breakdowns** (☎ 154 or 123 [in some areas 0123]).

VISITOR INFORMATION

Olomouc: Information Center (✉ Horní nám. [Town Hall], ☎ 068/551– 3385), ☉ daily 9–7.

THE CZECH REPUBLIC A TO Z

Arriving and Departing

By Bus

Several bus companies run direct services between London and Prague. Two with almost daily service are Kingscourt Express (London, ☎ 0181/673–7500) and Eurolines, both operating out of London's Victoria Coach Station. The trip takes 20–24 hours and costs around $85 one-way.

By Car

The most convenient ferry ports for Prague are Hoek van Holland and Ostend. To reach Prague from either ferry port, drive first to Cologne (Köln) and then through either Dresden or Frankfurt.

By Plane

FROM NORTH AMERICA

All international flights to the Czech Republic fly into Prague's **Ruzyně Airport,** about 20 kilometers (12 miles) northwest of downtown. The airport is small and easy to negotiate.

ČSA (Czech Airlines), the Czech and Slovak national carrier (☎ 718/656–8439), maintains regular direct flights to Prague from New York's JFK Airport, and twice-weekly flights from Chicago, Los Angeles, and Montréal.

Several other international airlines have good connections from cities in the United States and Canada to European bases and from there to Prague. **British Airways** (☎ 800/247–9297) flies daily via London; and **SwissAir** (☎ 718/995–8400), daily via Zurich.

FLYING TIME
From New York, a nonstop flight to Prague takes 9–10 hours; with a stopover, the journey will take at least 12–13 hours. From Montreal nonstop it is 7½ hours; from Los Angeles, 16 hours.

FROM THE UNITED KINGDOM
British Airways (☎ 0171/897–4000) has daily nonstop service to Prague from London (with connections to major British cities); **ČSA** (☎ 0171/255–1898) flies five times a week nonstop from London. The flight takes around three hours.

By Train
There are no direct trains from London. You can take a direct train from Paris via Frankfurt to Prague (daily) or from Berlin via Dresden to Prague (three times a day). Vienna is a good starting point for Prague, Brno, or Bratislava. There are three trains a day from Vienna's Franz Josefsbahnhof to Prague via Třeboň and Tábor (5½ hours) and two from the Südbahnhof (South Station) via Brno (5 hours).

Getting Around

By Bus
The Czech Republic's extremely comprehensive state-run bus service, **ČSAD,** is usually much quicker than the normal trains and more frequent than express trains, unless you're going to the major cities. (The wait between buses can sometimes be very, very long.) Prices are reasonable—essentially the same as those for second-class rail tickets. Buy your tickets from the ticket window at the bus station or directly from the driver on the bus. Long-distance buses can be full, so you might want to book a seat in advance; Čedok will help you do this. The only drawback to traveling by bus is figuring out the timetables. They are easy to read, but beware of the small letters denoting exceptions to the time given. If in doubt, inquire at the information window or ask someone for assistance.

By Car
Traveling by car is the easiest and most flexible way of seeing the Czech Republic. There are few four-lane highways, but most of the roads are in reasonably good shape, and traffic is usually light. The road can be poorly marked, however, so before you start out, buy one of the multilingual, inexpensive auto atlases available at any bookstore. The Czech Republic follows the usual Continental rules of the road. A right turn on red is permitted only when indicated by a green arrow. Signposts with yellow diamonds indicate a main road where drivers have the right of way. The speed limit is 110 kph (68 mph) on four-lane highways, 90 kph (56 mph) on open roads, and 60 kph (37 mph) in built-up areas. The fine for speeding is 300 Kč, payable on the spot. Seat belts are compulsory, and drinking before driving is absolutely prohibited.

Permits are required to drive on expressways and other four-lane highways. They cost 400 Kč and are sold at border crossings and some service stations.

Don't rent a car if you intend to visit only Prague. Most of the city center is closed to traffic, and you'll save yourself a lot of hassle by sticking to public transportation.

For accidents, call the emergency number (☎ 154 or 123). In case of repair problems, get in touch with the 24-hour **Autoturist Servis** (⊠ Limuzská 12, Prague 10, ☎ 02/773455). Autoturist (ÚAMK) offices throughout the Czech Republic can provide motoring information of all kinds.

By Plane

ČSA (Czech Airlines) no longer operates any internal routes in its home country. Small, private lines have filled some of the holes; one is **Air Ostrava** (Prague, ☎ 02/2403–2731), which links Prague, Ostrava, and Brno. ČSA still flies to Slovak destinations including Poprad (High Tatras) and Košice. Reservations can be made through Čedok offices abroad or ČSA in Prague (⊠ Revoluční 1, ☎ 02/2431–4271).

By Train

Trains vary in speed, but it's not really worth taking anything less than an express train, marked in red on the timetable. Tickets are relatively cheap; first class is considerably more spacious and comfortable and well worth the 50% increase over standard tickets. If you don't specify "express" when you buy your ticket, you may have to pay a supplement on the train. If you haven't bought a ticket in advance at the station, it's easy to buy one on the train for a small extra charge. On timetables, departures (*odjezd*) appear on a yellow background; arrivals (*příjezd*) are on white. It is possible to book sleepers (*lůžkový*) or the less-roomy *couchettes* (*lehátkový*) on most overnight trains. Since tickets are so inexpensive, most rail passes cost more than what you'd spend buying tickets on the spot. The European East Pass and the InterRail Pass—but not the EurailPass or Eurail Youthpass—are valid for unlimited train travel within the Czech Republic.

Contacts and Resources

B&B Reservation Agencies

Most offices of Čedok and local information offices also book rooms in hotels, pensions, and private accommodations. Travelers usually do not need to resort to reservation agencies and fare quite well by simply keeping a sharp eye out for signs reading ZIMMER FREI or UBYTOVÁNÍ. **In Britain:** Czechbook Agency (⊠ Jopes Mill, Trebrownbridge, near Liskeard, Cornwall PL14 3PX, ☎ FAX 01503/240629) arranges stays in B&Bs, self-catering apartments, and hotels.

Car Rentals

There are no special requirements for renting a car in the Czech Republic, but be sure to shop around, as prices can differ greatly. **Avis** and **Hertz** offer Western makes for as much as $500–$700 per week. Smaller local companies, on the other hand, can rent Czech cars for as little as $130 per week, but the service is of dubious quality and sometimes not worth the savings.

Customs and Duties

ON ARRIVAL

You may import duty-free into the Czech Republic 200 cigarettes or the equivalent in tobacco, 50 cigars, 1 liter of spirits, 2 liters of wine, and ½ liter of perfume. You may also bring up to 1,000 Kč worth of gifts and souvenirs.

If you take into the Czech Republic valuables or foreign-made equipment from home, such as cameras, carry the original receipts with you or register the items with U.S. Customs before you leave (Form 4457). Otherwise you could end up paying duty upon your return.

ON DEPARTURE

From the Czech Republic you can take out gifts and souvenirs valued at up to 1,000 Kč. Theft of antiques—particularly baroque pieces from churches—continues to despoil the Czech cultural heritage. Only antiques bought at specially appointed shops may be exported. If there's any doubt about a piece's history, it's likely to have been stolen.

Emergencies

Police (☎ 158). **Ambulance** (☎ 155). **Breakdowns** (☎ 154 or 123 [in some areas, 0123]).

Language

Czech, a Slavic language closely related to Slovak and Polish, is the official language of the Czech Republic. Learning English is popular among young people, but German is still the most useful language for tourists. Don't be surprised if you get a response in German to a question asked in English. If the idea of attempting Czech is daunting, you might consider bringing a German phrase book.

Mail

POSTAL RATES

Postcards to the United States cost 6 Kč; letters up to 20 grams in weight, 10 Kč; to Great Britain a postcard is 5 Kč; a letter, 8 Kč. You can buy stamps at post offices, hotels, and shops that sell postcards.

RECEIVING MAIL

If you don't know where you'll be staying, **American Express** mail service is a great convenience, available at no charge to anyone holding an American Express credit card or carrying American Express traveler's checks. The American Express office is at Václavské náměstí. 56 (Wenceslas Square) in central Prague. You can also have mail held *poste restante* (general delivery) at post offices in major towns, but the letters should be marked *Pošta 1,* to designate the city's main post office. The poste restante window is No. 28 at the main post office in Prague (✉ Jindřišská ul. 14). You will be asked for identification when you collect your mail.

Money and Expenses

CURRENCY

The unit of currency in the Czech Republic is the *koruna,* or crown (Kč), which is divided into 100 haléř, or halers. There are (little-used) coins of 10, 20, and 50 halers; coins of 1, 2, 5, 10, 20, and 50 Kč; and notes of 20, 50, 100, 200, 500, 1,000, and 5,000 Kč. The 1,000-Kč note may not always be accepted for small purchases, because the proprietor may not have enough change.

Try to avoid exchanging money at hotels or private exchange booths, including the ubiquitous Čekobanka and Exact Change booths. They routinely take commissions of 8%–10%. The best places to exchange are at bank counters, where the commissions average 1%–3%, or at ATMs. The koruna became fully convertible late in 1995 and can now be purchased outside the country and exchanged into other currencies. Ask about current regulations when you change money, however, and keep your receipts. At press time the exchange rate was around 27 Kč to the U.S. dollar, 19 Kč to the Canadian dollar, and 41 Kč to the pound sterling.

WHAT IT WILL COST

Despite rising inflation, the Czech Republic is still generally a bargain by Western standards. Prague remains the exception, however. Hotel prices, in particular, frequently meet or exceed the average for the United States and Western Europe—and are higher than the standard of facilities would warrant. Nevertheless, you can still find bargain private accommodations. The prices at tourist resorts outside the capital are lower and, in the outlying areas and off the beaten track, incredibly low. Tourists can now legally pay for hotel rooms in crowns, although some hotels still insist on payment in "hard" (i.e., Western) currency.

SAMPLE COSTS

A cup of coffee will cost about 15 Kč; museum entrance, 20 Kč–150 Kč; a good theater seat, up to 200 Kč; a cinema seat, 30 Kč–50 Kč; ½ liter (pint) of beer, 15 Kč–25 Kč; a 1-mile taxi ride, 60 Kč–100 Kč; a bottle of Moravian wine in a good restaurant, 100 Kč–150 Kč; a glass (2 deciliters or 7 ounces) of wine, 25 Kč.

National Holidays

January 1; Easter Monday; May 1 (Labor Day); May 8 (Liberation Day); July 5 (Sts. Cyril and Methodius); July 6 (Jan Hus); October 28 (Czech National Day); and December 24, 25, and 26.

Opening and Closing Times

Though hours vary, most banks are open weekdays 8–5, with an hour's lunch break. Private exchange offices usually have longer hours. Museums are usually open daily except Monday (or Tuesday) 9–5; they tend to stop selling tickets an hour before closing time. Outside the large towns, many sights, including most castles, are open daily except Monday only from May through September; and in April and October are open only on weekends and holidays. Stores are open weekdays 9–6; some grocery stores open at 6 AM. Department stores often stay open until 7 PM. On Saturday, most stores close at noon. Nearly all stores are closed on Sunday.

Passports and Visas

American and British citizens require only a valid passport for stays of up to 30 days in the Czech Republic. No visas are necessary. The seesaw situation for Canadian citizens seemed to come down in their favor when visa requirements for the Czech Republic were dropped on April 1, 1996. It's advisable to contact the Czech Embassy, however, for changes in the rules (⊠ Embassy of the Czech Republic, 541 Sussex Dr., Ottawa, Ontario K1N 6Z6, ☎ 613/562–3875, FAX 613/562–3878). U.S. citizens can receive additional information from the Czech Embassy (⊠ 3900 Spring of Freedom St. NW, Washington, DC 20008, ☎ 202/274–9100, FAX 202/966–8540).

Rail Passes

The **European East Pass** is good for unlimited first-class travel on the national railroads of Austria, the Czech Republic, Slovakia, Hungary, and Poland. The pass allows five days of travel within a 15-day period ($169) or 10 days of travel within a 30-day period ($275). Apply through your travel agent or through **Rail Europe** (⊠ 226–230 Westchester Ave., White Plains, NY 10604, ☎ 914/682–2999 or 800/848–7245). The **EurailPass** and **Eurail Youthpass** are not valid for travel within the Czech Republic. The **InterRail Pass** (£249), available to European citizens only through local student or budget travel offices, is valid for one month of unlimited train travel in the Czech Republic and the other countries covered in this book. For more information, see Rail Passes in Important Contacts A to Z and Smart Travel Tips A to Z.

Student and Youth Travel

In the Czech Republic, **CKM Youth Travel Service** (⊠ Žitná 12, Prague 1, ☎ 02/2491–5767) provides information on student hostels and travel bargains within the Czech Republic and issues IYH cards (200 Kč).

For general information about student identity cards, work-abroad programs, and youth hostels, *see* Student and Youth Travel *in* Smart Travel Tips A to Z.

Telephones

The country code for the Czech Republic is 42.

LOCAL CALLS

The few remaining coin-operated telephones take 1-, 2-, and 5-Kč coins. Most newer public phones operate only with a special telephone card, available from newsstands and tobacconists in denominations of 100 Kč and 190 Kč. A call within Prague costs 2 Kč. The dial tone is a series of short and long buzzes.

INTERNATIONAL CALLS

To reach an English-speaking operator in the United States, dial 00–420–00101 (**AT&T**), 00–420–00112 (**MCI**), or 0420–87187 (**Sprint**). For **CanadaDirect,** dial 00420–00151; for **B.T.Direct** to the United Kingdom, 00420–04401. The operator will connect your collect or credit-card call at the carrier's standard rates. In Prague, many phone booths allow direct international dialing; if you can't find one, the main post office (Hlavní pošta, ✉ Jindřišská ul. 14), open 24 hours, is the best place to try. There you can use the public phones in the lobby or ask one of the clerks in the 24-hour telephone room, to the left as you enter, for assistance. Twenty-four-hour fax and telex service is handled from the office to the right of the entrance. The international dialing code is 00. For international inquiries, dial 0132 for the United States, Canada, or the United Kingdom. Otherwise, ask the receptionist at any hotel to put a call through for you, though beware: The more expensive the hotel, the more expensive the call will be.

Tipping

To reward good service in a restaurant, round the bill up to the nearest multiple of 10 (if the bill comes to 83 Kč, for example, give the waiter 90 Kč); 10% is considered appropriate on very large tabs. If you have difficulty communicating the amount to the waiter, just leave the money on the table. Tip porters who bring bags to your rooms 20 Kč. For room service, a 20-Kč tip is enough. In taxis, round the bill up by 10%. Give tour guides and helpful concierges between 20 Kč and 30 Kč for services rendered.

Visitor Information

Čedok, the former state-run travel bureau, went private in 1995 and is now a travel agent rather than a tourist information office. It will supply you with hotel and travel information, and book air and rail tickets, but don't expect much in the way of general information.

Most major towns have a local or private information office, usually in the central square and identified by a lowercase "i" on the facade. These offices are often good sources for maps and historical information and can usually help visitors book hotel and private accommodations. Most are open during normal business hours, with limited hours on Saturday (until noon), and are closed on Sunday and holidays. Out-of-season hours are severely reduced. For individual centers, *see* Visitor Information *in* each of this chapter's A to Z sections, *above.*

3 Slovakia

Despite a long period of common statehood with the Czechs (which ended in 1993), Slovakia (Slovensko) differs from the Czech Republic in many aspects. Its mountains are higher and more rugged, its veneer less sophisticated, its folklore and traditions richer. Observers of the two regions like to link the Czech Republic geographically and culturally with the orderly Germans, while they put Slovakia with Ukraine and Russia, firmly in the east. This is a simplification, yet it contains more than a little bit of truth.

SLOVAKIA BECAME AN INDEPENDENT STATE on January 1, 1993, when Czechoslovakia—formerly composed of what is today Slovakia and the Czech Republic—ceased to exist. To the east of the Czech Republic, Slovakia is about one-third as large as its neighbor. Although the Slovaks speak a language closely related to Czech, they managed to maintain a strong sense of national identity throughout the more than 70 years of common statehood. Indeed, the two Slavic groups developed quite separately: Though united in the 9th century as part of the Great Moravian Empire, the Slovaks were conquered a century later by the Magyars and remained under Hungarian and Hapsburg rule. Following the Tartar invasions in the 13th century, many Saxons were invited to resettle the land and develop the economy, including the region's rich mineral resources. In the 15th and 16th centuries, Romanian shepherds migrated from Wallachia through the Carpathians into Slovakia, and the merging of these varied groups with the resident Slavs bequeathed to the region a rich folk culture and some unique forms of architecture, especially in the east.

By Mark Baker

Updated by
Timea Špitková

In the end, it was this very different history that split the Slovaks from the Czechs, ending the most successful experiment in nation building to follow World War I.

For many Slovaks, the 1989 revolution provided for the first time an opportunity not only to bring down the Communists, but also to establish a fully independent state—thus ending what many Slovaks saw as a millennium of subjugation by Hungary and the Hapsburgs, Nazi Germany, Prague's Communist regimes, and ultimately the Czechs. Although few Slovaks harbored any real resentment toward the Czechs, Slovak politicians were quick to recognize and exploit the deep, inchoate longing for independence. Slovak nationalist parties won more than 50% of the vote in the crucial 1992 Czechoslovak elections, and once the results were in, the end came quickly: On January 1, 1993, Slovakia became the youngest country in Europe.

The outside world witnessed the demise of the Czechoslovak federation in 1993 with some sadness; the split seemed just another piece of evidence to confirm that tribalism and nationalism continue to play the deciding role in European affairs. Yet there is something hopeful to be seen in the peaceful nature of the separation. Despite lingering differences about the division of the federation's assets, no Czechs or Slovaks have yet died in nationalistic squabbles. For the visitor, the changes may in fact be positive. The Slovaks have been long overshadowed by their cousins to the west; now they have the unfettered opportunity to tell their story to the world.

Most visitors to Slovakia head first for the great peaks of the High Tatras (Vysoké Tatry), which rise magnificently from the foothills of northern Slovakia. The tourist infrastructure here is very good, catering especially to hikers and skiers. Visitors who come to admire the peaks, however, often overlook the exquisite medieval towns of Spiš, in the plains and valleys below the High Tatras, and the beautiful 18th-century country churches farther east. (Removed from main centers, these areas are short on tourist amenities, so if creature comforts are important to you, stick to the High Tatras.)

Bratislava, the capital of Slovakia, is at first a disappointment to many visitors. The last 40 years of communism left a clear mark on the city, hiding its ancient beauty with hulking, and now dilapidated, futurist structures. Yet despite its gloomy appearance, Bratislava tries hard to project the cosmopolitanism of a European capital, bolstered by the fact that it is filled with good restaurants and wine bars, opera and art. The Old Town, though still needing more renovation, is beginning to recapture some of its lost charm.

Pleasures and Pastimes

Bicycling

Slovaks are avid cyclists, and the flatter areas to the south and east of Bratislava and along the Danube are ideal for biking. Outside large towns, quieter roads stretch out for many kilometers. A special bike trail links Bratislava and Vienna, paralleling the Danube for much of its 40-kilometer (25-mile) length. For the more adventurous bikers, the Low Tatras (Nízke Tatry) have scenic biking trails along the small secluded rivers surrounding Banská Bystrica. There is a hiking map of the Low Tatras, which includes routes for cyclists, available at the tourist office in Banská Bystrica. Not many places rent bikes, however; inquire at tourist information centers or at your hotel for rental information.

Boating and Sailing

Slovaks with boats head to the man-made lakes of Zemplínska Şirava (east of Košice near the Ukrainian border) or Orava (northwest of the Tatras near the Polish border). River rafting has been hampered in recent years by dry weather, which has also reduced river levels. However, raft rides are still given in summer at Çervený Kláštor, north of Kežmarok (☞ Eastern Slovakia, *below*).

Camping

There are hundreds of camping sites for tents and trailers throughout Slovakia, but most are open only in summer (May to mid-September). You can get a map of all the sites, with addresses, opening times, and facilities, from Satur; auto atlases also identify campsites. Camping outside official sites is prohibited. Some camping grounds also offer bungalows. Campsites are divided into Categories A and B according to facilities, but both have hot water and toilets.

Dining

Slovak food is an amalgam of its neighbors' cuisines. As in Bohemia and Moravia, the emphasis is on meat, particularly pork and beef. But you will seldom find the Czechs' traditional (and often bland) roast pork and dumplings on the menu. The Slovaks, betraying their long link to Hungary, prefer to spice things up a bit, usually with paprika and red peppers. Roast potatoes or french fries are often served in place of dumplings, although occasionally you'll find a side dish of tasty *halušky* (noodles similar to Italian gnocchi or German spaetzle) on the menu. No primer on Slovak eating would be complete without mention of *bryndzové halušky,* the country's unofficial national dish, a tasty and filling mix of halušky, sheep's cheese, and a little bacon fat for flavor (it seldom makes it onto the menu at elegant restaurants, so look for it instead at roadside restaurants and snack bars). For dessert, the emphasis comes from upriver, in Vienna: pancakes, fruit dumplings (if you're lucky), poppy-seed dumplings, and strudel.

Eating out is still not a popular pastime among Slovaks, particularly since prices have risen markedly in the past few years. As a result, you will find relatively few restaurants about; and those that do exist generally cater to foreigners or a wealthy business clientele. Restaurants known as *vináreň* specialize in serving wines, although you can order beer virtually anywhere. The Slovaks, however, do not have many bars equivalent to the Czech *pivnice* (beer hall).

Slovaks pride themselves on their wines, and to an extent they have a point. Do not expect much subtlety, though, for the typical offering is hearty, sometimes heavy, but always very drinkable wines that complement the region's filling and spicy food. This is especially true of the reds. The most popular is *Frankovka,* which is fiery and slightly acidic. *Vavrinecké,* a relatively new arrival, is dark and semisweet and stands up well to red meats. Slovakia's few white wines are similar in character to the Moravian wines and, on the whole, unexceptional.

Lunch, usually eaten between noon and 2, is the main meal for Slovaks and offers the best deal for tourists. Many restaurants put out a special luncheon menu, with more appetizing selections at better prices. Dinner is usually served from 5 until 9 or 10, but don't wait too long to eat. Cooks frequently knock off early on slow nights. The dinner menu does not differ substantially from lunch offerings, except the prices are higher.

CATEGORY	COST*
$$$$	over $20
$$$	$15–$20
$$	$7–$15
$	under $7

per person for a three-course meal, excluding wine and tip

Festivals and Seasonal Events

Many villages host annual folklore festivals, usually in late summer or early fall (☞ Festivals and Seasonal Events *in* Chapter 1). These frequently take place in the town center and are accompanied by lots of singing, dancing, and drinking. Every year, the Slovak Ministry of Economy puts out a calendar of events in English, available in travel agencies and tourist information centers. Try visiting Košice during June, when the International Folklore Festival is in full swing. Singing and dancing groups from all over show off their rich traditions and colorful costumes on the streets of this eastern Slovakia town.

Fishing

There are hundreds of lakes and rivers suitable for fishing, often amid striking scenery. Demanovská dolina, a picturesque valley near Liptovský Mikuláš in central Slovakia, offers some excellent places to catch trout. Some other freshwater fish include catfish, eel, pike, and carp. You should bring your own tackle or be prepared to buy it locally because rental equipment is scarce. To legally cast a line, you must have a fishing license (valid for one year) plus a fishing permit (valid for a day, week, month, or year for the particular body of water on which you plan to fish). Both are available from Satur offices.

Hiking

Slovakia is a hiker's paradise, with more than 20,000 kilometers (15,000 miles) of well-kept, marked, and signposted trails in both the mountainous regions and the agricultural countryside. You'll find the colored markings denoting trails on trees, fences, walls, rocks, and elsewhere. The colors correspond to the path marking on the large-scale *Soubor turistickych* maps available at many bookstores and tobacconists. The main paths are marked in red, others in blue and green; the least important trails are marked in yellow. The best areas for ambitious mountain walkers are the Low Tatras in the center of the country near Banská Bystrica and the High Tatras to the north. *Slovenský Raj,* or Slovak Paradise, in eastern Slovakia is an ideal place for hikers—a wild, romantic area where you'll see cliffs, caves, and waterfalls. If you have to stick closer to Bratislava, the Small Carpathians and the Fatra range in western Slovakia offer good hiking trails as well.

Lodging

Slovakia's hotel industry has been slow to react to the political and economic changes that have taken place since 1989. Few new hotels have been built, and many of the older establishments are still mostly owned by the state and often give shabby service. On the bright side, small, private hotels and pensions in beautifully renovated buildings have been springing up all over the country. While some may be a few rooms in someone's house, others provide the amenities of a hotel in a much more beautiful setting. Banská Bystrica's Arcade Hotel and Hotel Salamander in Banská Štavnica have both transformed 16th-century historical sites into stylish accommodations. The facilities in the Tatras remain good though a bit expensive, and Bratislava has added a few new hotels, but there still remains a shortage of good inexpensive accommodations. Elsewhere in the country, you'll find everything from a cheap fairy-tale-like villa, such as the 13th-century Arkada Hotel in Levoča, to a nightmarishly gloomy apartment building with tiny rooms and rude clerks, charging outrageous prices to foreigners.

In general, hotels can be divided into two categories: edifices built in the 1960s or '70s that offer modern amenities but not much character; and older, more central establishments that are heavy on personality but may lack basic conveniences. Hostels are understood to be cheap dormitory rooms and are probably best avoided. In the mountainous areas, you can often find little *chata* (chalets), where pleasant surroundings compensate for a lack of basic amenities. *Autokempink* (campsites) generally have a few bungalows available for visitors.

Slovakia's official hotel classification, based on letters (Deluxe, A*, B*, C), is gradually being changed over to the international star system, although it will be some time before the old system is completely replaced. These ratings correspond closely to our categories as follows: Deluxe or five-star ($$$$); A* or four-star ($$$); B* or three- to two–star ($$–$). We've included C hotels in our listings where accommodations are scarce or when the particular hotel has redeeming qualities. In any case, prices for hotels in Slovakia do not always mesh with the quality. As a rule, always ask the price before taking a room.

Slovakia is a bargain by Western standards, particularly in the outlying areas. The exception is the price of accommodations in Bratislava, where hotel rates often meet or exceed both U.S. and Western European averages. Accommodations outside the capital, with the exception of the High Tatras resorts, are significantly lower. Tourists can pay for hotel rooms in Slovak crowns, although payment in "hard" (i.e., Western) currency is still welcomed by some hotels.

The prices quoted below are for double rooms, generally not including breakfast. Prices at the lower end of the scale apply to low season. At certain periods, such as Christmas, Easter, or during festivals, there may be an increase of 15%–25%.

CATEGORY	COST*
$$$$	over $100
$$$	$50–$100
$$	$15–$50
$	under $15

All prices are for a standard double room, including tax and service.

Shopping

Among the most interesting finds in Slovakia are batik-painted Easter eggs, corn-husk figures, delicate woven table mats, hand-knit sweaters, and folk pottery. The best buys are folk-art products sold at stands along the roads and in Slovart or folk art stores in most major towns. There are also several Dielo stores, which sell paintings, some wooden toys, and great ceramic pieces by Slovak artists at very reasonable prices. The local brands of firewater—*slivovice* (plum brandy) and *borovička* (a spirit made from juniper berries)—also make excellent buys.

Skiing

Slovakia is one of the best countries in the region for downhill skiers, both amateurs and experts. The two main skiing areas are the Low Tatras and the High Tatras. The Low Tatras are more pleasant if you want to avoid crowds, but the High Tatras offer more reliable conditions (good snow throughout winter) and superior facilities, including places where you can rent equipment. The High Tatras are also blessed with high peaks such as Skalnaté Pleso (1,751 meters above sea level) and are host to several world championships. Lifts in both regions generally operate from January through March, though cross-country skiing is a popular alternative.

Exploring Slovakia

Slovakia can best be divided into four regions of interest to tourists: Bratislava, the High Tatra Mountains, central Slovakia, and eastern Slovakia. Despite being the capital, Bratislava, in the western part of the country, is probably the least alluring of these spots. The country's true beauty lies among the peaks of the High Tatras in the northern part of central Slovakia. The remainder of central Slovakia, also a striking mountainous region with great hiking trails, is rich in folklore and is home to fascinating medieval mining towns. Few tourists have yet discovered the eastern region, with its fairy-tale villages, castles, and wooden churches, or the caves, cliffs, and plateaus of the national park known as Slovenský Raj.

Great Itineraries

Although Slovakia is relatively small, its mountains and poor roads make it difficult to explore in a short period of time. Driving or taking the train from Bratislava to the eastern town of Košice will take you a minimum of seven hours. A more convenient option is to fly. From Košice, it's easy to explore the surrounding region, with the High Tatras less than three hours away. In 10 days you can travel through the country at a leisurely pace, exploring both the mountains in central Slovakia and the towns and villages of the eastern region. Unless you are flying, five days will allow you time in the High Tatras and a brief visit to a few historic towns in the surrounding area. If you only have three days, you can either stay in Bratislava and explore some of the vineyards and small villages in the outlying areas or get on the first plane headed for the High Tatras. Although the trip may be a bit rushed, the second option of a trip to the mountains will probably be far more rewarding, especially if the weather is pleasant enough for hiking.

IF YOU HAVE 3 DAYS
Numbers in the text correspond to numbers in the margin and on the maps.

If you only have a few days to see Slovakia, spend a maximum of a few hours walking through the Old Town and the castle in **Bratislava** ①–⑱, then head straight for the **High Tatras.** Once you get to the mountains, you can settle down in a comfortable hotel or a pension in one of the resort towns. 🏨 **Smokovec** ㉑ and 🏨 **Tatranská Lomnica** ㉓ are probably the most convenient places from which to explore the area and go hiking in summer or skiing in winter. You can also visit nearby **Ždiar** ㉔, a typical Slovak village high up in the mountains. If you can pull yourself away from the High Tatras on the second day, take a brief

Slovakia

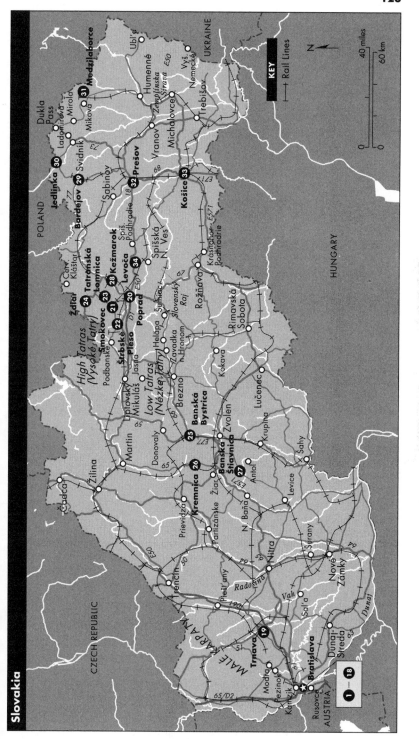

UKRAINE

KEY

—†— Rail Lines

N

40 miles

60 km

Ubľa

Medzilaborce **31**

Dukla
Pass

Ladomirová
Miroľa
Mikova

Vyš.
Nemecké

Humenné

Zemplínska
Šírava E50

POLAND

Jedlinka **30**

Svidník

Bardejov **29**

Vranov
Michalovce

Trebišov

E50

Prešov **32**

Sabinov

68

18

Košice **33**

I/3

Čer.
Kláštor

Ždiar **24**

Tatranská
Lomnica

Kežmarok **28**

Levoča **34**

Spiš.
Podhradie

Spišská
N. Ves

Krásnohor.
Podhradie

E571

Smokovec **21**

Štrbské
Pleso **22**

23

Poprad **20**

E50

High Tatras
(Vysoké Tatry)

Liptovský
Mikuláš

Podbanské

Jasná

Low Tatras
(Nízke Tatry)

Šumiac

Slovenský
Raj

67

Rožňava

Rimavská
Sobota

Helpa

Zavadka
n. Hronom

Brezno

Banská
Bystrica **25**

Kokava

Krupina

Donovaly

65

Martin

59

Žilina

Čadca

65

Kremnica **26**

Banská
Štiavnica **27**

E77

Zvolen

Lučenec

Šahy

Antol

I/51

Žiar

Prievidza

Partizánske

Levice

N. Baňa

50

E50

Trenčín

Piešťany

Radošina

I/61

19

Trnava

51

MALÉ KARPATY

Modra
Pezinok

Kamzík

Bratislava **1—18**

Rusovce

AUSTRIA

65/D2

Nitra

64

6

Šaľa

Váh

Šurany

Nové
Zámky

Dunaj-
Streda

63

Dunaj

75

CZECH REPUBLIC

HUNGARY

excursion slightly south to the beautiful Spiš town of 🏙 **Levoča** ㉞. Spend the night here, and on your last day, head back to Bratislava via **Poprad** ⑳ and **Banská Bystrica** ㉕.

IF YOU HAVE 5 DAYS
Do not linger too long in **Bratislava** ①–⑱ before heading out to 🏙 **Smokovec** ㉑ or 🏙 **Taranská Lomnica** ㉓, which offer easy access to the **High Tatras.** Spend your second day hiking in the mountains. On your third day, head east toward 🏙 **Levoča** ㉞, where you can spend the day (and the night). From here, you can also explore the Špis Castle and the caves and gorges in the area. The following day, head south toward 🏙 **Košice** ㉝. Take a look at some of the historic sights in the Old Town of this region's capital, and if there is still time, take an excursion to **Herľany Geyser,** about 20 miles outside the city. Overnight in Košice, and on your last day, make your way back home. From Košice, it's possible to fly to Bratislava or Prague or to take a direct day or night train to one of the two cities.

When to Tour Slovakia

Slovakia, which experiences all four seasons, is beautiful throughout the year. The High Tatras are loveliest in winter (January–March). However, the area does get crowded when thousands of skiers descend on the major resorts. A smaller summer season in the mountains attracts mostly walkers and hikers looking to escape the heat and noise of the cities. Because of the snow, many hiking trails, especially those that cross the peaks, are open only between June and October.

Bratislava is at its best in the temperate months of spring and autumn. July and August, though not especially crowded, can be unbearably hot. In winter, when many tourist attractions are closed, expect lots of rain and snow in the capital. Note that temperatures are always much cooler in the mountains. Even in summer, expect to wear a sweater or jacket in the High Tatras.

BRATISLAVA

Many visitors are initially disappointed when they see Europe's newest capital city, Bratislava—or "Blava" as it is affectionately known by residents. Expecting a Slovak version of Prague or Vienna, they discover instead a busy industrial city that seems to embody the Communists' blind faith in modernity rather than the stormy history of this once Hungarian and now Slovak capital. The problem, of course, is that Bratislava has more than its fair share of high-rise housing projects, faded supermodern structures, and less-than-inspiring monuments to carefully chosen acts of heroism. Even the handsome castle on the hill and the winding streets of the Old Town look decidedly secondary in their crumbling beauty.

The jumble of modern Bratislava, however, masks a long and regal history that rivals Prague's in importance and complexity. Settled by a variety of Celts and Romans, the city became part of the Great Moravian Empire around the year 900 under Prince Břetislav. After a short period under the Bohemian Přemysl princes, Bratislava was brought into the Hungarian kingdom by Stephan I at the end of the 10th century and given royal privileges in 1217. Following the Tatar invasion in 1241, the Hungarian kings brought in German colonists to repopulate the town. The Hungarians called the town Pozsony; the German settlers referred to it as Pressburg; and the original Slovaks called it Bratislava after Prince Břetislav.

When Pest and Buda were occupied by the Turks, in 1526 and 1541, respectively, the Hungarian kings moved their seat to Bratislava, which remained the Hungarian capital until 1784 and the coronation center until 1835. At this time, with a population of almost 27,000, it was the largest Hungarian city. Only in 1919, when Bratislava became part of the first Czechoslovak republic, did the city regain its Slovak identity. In 1939, with Germany's assistance, Bratislava infamously exerted its yearnings for independence by becoming the capital of the puppet Slovak state, under the fascist leader Josef Tiso. In 1945 it became the provincial capital of Slovakia, still straining under the powerful hand of Prague (Slovakia's German and Hungarian minorities were either expelled or repressed). Leading up to the 1989 revolution, Bratislava was the site of numerous anticommunist demonstrations; many of these were carried out by supporters of the Catholic Church, long repressed by the regime then in power. Following the "Velvet Revolution" in 1989, Bratislava gained importance as the capital of the Slovak Republic within the new Czech and Slovak federal state, but rivalries with Prague persisted. It was only following the breakup of Czechoslovakia on January 1, 1993, that the city once again became a capital in its own right. But don't come to Bratislava expecting beauty or bustle. Instead, plan to spend a leisurely day or two sightseeing before setting off for Slovakia's superior natural splendors.

Exploring Bratislava

If you want to discover the greater part of Bratislava's charms, you should travel the city by foot. Imagination is also helpful, as some of the Old Town's more potentially interesting streets are often covered with scaffolding or look as though they've recently gone through a war. Nevertheless, many areas have been reconstructed and are packed with interesting historical sights.

A Good Walk

Numbers in the text correspond to numbers in the margin and on the Bratislava map.

Begin your tour at the modern **Námestie SNP** (SNP Square) ①. SNP stands for *Slovenské Národné Povstanie* (Slovak National Uprising), an anti-Nazi resistance movement. In the middle of the square are three larger-than-life statues: a dour partisan with two strong, sad women in peasant clothing. From here walk up the square toward Hurbanovo námestie, where you can glance at the **Kostol svätej Trojice** ②. Across the road, unobtrusively located between a shoe store and a bookstore, is the enchanting entrance to the Old Town. A small bridge, decorated with wrought-iron railings and statues of St. Michael and St. John Nepomuk, takes you over a former moat, now blossoming with trees and fountains, into the intricate barbican, a set of gates and houses that comprised Bratislava's medieval fortifications. After passing through the first archway, you'll come to the narrow promenade of Michalská ulica (Michael Street). In front of you is **Michalská brána** (Michael's Gate) ③. Before going through the gate, you'll find the **Farmaceutické múzeum** (Pharmaceutical Museum). After a visit there, walk through the gate, and in an adjoining tower is a small museum, the **Múzeum zbraní a mestského opevnenia** (Museum of Weapons and Fortifications). You'll get a good view over the city from here.

Take a stroll down Michalská ulica. Many of the more interesting buildings along the street are undergoing renovation, but notice the eerie blue **Kaplnka svätej Kataríny** (Chapel of St. Catherine) at No. 6 on the left, built in 1311 but now graced with a sober classical facade. Opposite, at No. 7, is the **Renaissance Segnerova kúria** (Segner House),

126

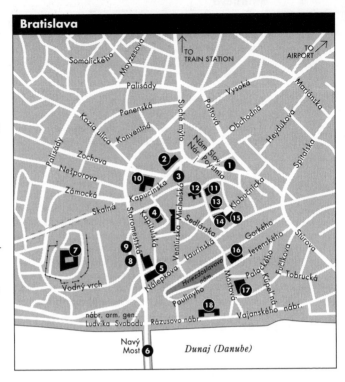

built for a wealthy merchant in 1648. Farther down on the right is the **Palác Uhorskej kráľovskej komory** (Hungarian Royal Chamber), a baroque palace that housed the Hungarian nobles' parliament from 1802 until 1848; it is now the University Library. Go through the arched passageway at the back of the building, and you'll emerge in a tiny square dominated by the **Kostol Klarisiek** (Church and Convent of the Poor Clares), which is now the Slovak Pedagogical Library.

Stretched along Farská ulica ahead of you is the 14th-century **Klariský kostol** (Klariský Church) ④. Follow Farská up to the corner and turn left on Kapitulská ulica (noticing the paving stone depicting two kissing lizards). This street could be the most beautiful in Bratislava, but its array of Gothic, Renaissance, and baroque buildings is in such disrepair that the effect is almost lost. Renovation has begun, and at No. 15 you can see that the remains of a wall painting have been uncovered on the stone facade. At the bottom of the street on the right is the late-Renaissance Jezuitské kolégium (Jesuit College), which has been a theological seminary since 1936. Ahead of you on the right is the side wall of the **Dóm svätého Martina** (St. Martin's Cathedral) ⑤, one of the more impressive churches in the city, despite the freeway built across its front doors in the 1970s.

As you leave the church and walk around to the front, the first thing you see is the freeway leading to the futuristic spaceship bridge, **Nový Most** (New Bridge) ⑥, formerly called Most SNP (Bridge of the Slovak National Uprising). When the highway was built, a row of old houses and a synagogue in the former Jewish quarter outside the city walls were destroyed. The only good thing to be said for the road is that its construction led to the discovery of remnants of the city's original walls, which have been partially restored and now line the free-

Your passport around the world.

- Worldwide access
- Operators who speak your language
- Monthly itemized billing

MCI Calling Card

415 555 1234 2244
J.D. SMITH

Use your MCI Card® and these access numbers for an easy way to call when traveling worldwide.

Austria (CC)♦†	022-903-012
Belarus	
From Gomel and Mogilev regions	8-10-800-103
From all other localities	8-800-103
Belgium (CC)♦†	0800-10012
Bulgaria	00800-0001
Croatia (CC)★	99-385-0112
Czech Republic (CC)♦	00-42-000112
Denmark (CC)♦†	8001-0022
Finland (CC)♦†	9800-102-80
France (CC)♦†	0800-99-0019
Germany (CC)†	0130-0012
Greece (CC)♦†	00-800-1211
Hungary (CC)♦	00▼800-01411
Iceland (CC)♦†	800-9002
Ireland (CC)†	1-800-55-1001
Italy (CC)♦†	172-1022
Kazakhstan (CC)	1-800-131-4321
Liechtenstein (CC)♦	155-0222
Luxembourg†	0800-0112
Monaco (CC)♦	800-90-19

Netherlands (CC)♦†	06-022-91-22
Norway (CC)♦†	800-19912
Poland (CC)✜†	00-800-111-21-22
Portugal (CC)✜†	05-017-1234
Romania (CC)✜	01-800-1800
Russia (CC)✜♦	747-3322
For a Russian-speaking operator	747-3320
San Marino (CC)♦	172-1022
Slovak Republic (CC)	00-42-000112
Slovenia	080-8808
Spain (CC)†	900-99-0014
Sweden (CC)♦†	020-795-922
Switzerland (CC)♦†	155-0222
Turkey (CC)♦†	00-8001-1177
Ukraine (CC)✜	8▼10-013
United Kingdom (CC)†	
To call to the U.S. using BT■	0800-89-0222
To call to the U.S. using Mercury■	0500-89-0222
Vatican City (CC)†	172-1022

To sign up for the MCI Card, dial the access number of the country you are in and ask to speak with a customer service representative.

MCI

http://www.mci.com

(CC) Country-to-country calling available. May not be available to/from all international locations. (Canada, Puerto Rico, and U.S. Virgin Islands are considered Domestic Access locations.) ♦ Public phones may require deposit of coin or phone card for dial tone. † Automation available from most locations. ★ Not available from public pay phones. ▼ Wait for second dial tone. ✜ Limited availability. ■ International communications carrier.

It helps to be pushy in airports.

Introducing the revolutionary new TransPorter™ from American Tourister® It's the first suitcase you can push around without a fight. TransPorter's™ exclusive four-wheel design lets you push it in front of you with almost no effort—the wheels take the weight. Or pull it on two wheels if you choose. You can even stack on other bags and use it like a luggage cart.

Stable 4-wheel design.

TransPorter™ is designed like a dresser, with built-in shelves to organize your belongings. Or collapse the shelves and pack it like a traditional suitcase. Inside, there's a suiter feature to help keep suits and dresses from wrinkling. When push comes to shove, you can't beat a TransPorter™ For more information on how you can be this pushy, call 1-800-542-1300.

Shelves collapse on command.

American Tourister®

Making travel less primitive®

©1996 American Tourister®

way on the right. Follow the steps under the passageway and up the other side in the direction of the castle.

Continue up the steps, through a Gothic arched gateway built in 1480, and climb up to the **hrad** (castle) ⑦ area. From the top, there is an excellent view over the Danube to the endless apartment blocks on the Petržalka side of the river. On a good day you can see over to Austria to the right. In the castle, you'll find the **Slovenské národné múzeum** (Slovak National Museum), which is worth a brief visit. Leave the castle by the same route, but instead of climbing the last stairs by the Arkadia restaurant, continue down Old World Beblavého ulica. Now home to stylish galleries and restaurants, this route to the castle was once one of the city's infamous red-light districts.

At the bottom of the street on the right is the **Múzeum umeleckých remesiel** (Handicraft Museum) ⑧. Next, go around the House at the Good Shepherd and continue along Židovská ulica (Jews' Street), marred by the freeway and dominated by a rash of buildings under construction. The street name recalls that this area was the former Jewish ghetto. You can visit the **Múzeum Židovskej Kultúry** (Museum of Jewish Culture in Slovakia) ⑨ in a Renaissance mansion, the only reminder that before World War II Jews made up more than 10% of Bratislava's population.

Continue on Židovská ulica until you come to a thin concrete bridge that crosses the freeway to the reconstructed city walls. Standing in the middle of this bridge, looking toward the river, you'll get one of the best views of the incongruous and contradictory jumble of buildings that make up Bratislava. Directly to the south is the Nový Most, surrounded by housing blocks; to the east (left) are the city walls, leading into St. Martin's Cathedral; to the west (right) are a little rococo house backed by construction and the towers of the castle. If you turn left and walk along the city walls, you will come, after negotiating a series of steps, to the main road, Kapucínska ulica.

Across the road on the left is the small, golden-yellow **Kostol kapucínov** (Capuchin Chapel) ⑩. Cross the street and take the steps leading down into the Old Town. Turn left at the bottom into little Baštová ulica. Go through the arch at the end, and you'll find yourself back at Michael's Gate. Continue straight along Zámočnícka ulica, which turns right heading in the direction of Františkánske námestie. To the left is the oldest preserved building in Bratislava, the **Františkánsky kostol** (Franciscan Church) ⑪. Across from the church is the beautifully detailed rococo **Mirbachov palác** (Mirbach Palace) ⑫, which today houses the Municipal Gallery.

Go across the Františkánske námestie, with its statues of little-known Slovak World War II heroes, onto the adjoining square, Hlavné námestie. The latter is lined with old houses and palaces representing a spectrum of architectural styles, from Gothic (No. 2), baroque (No. 4), and rococo (No. 7), to a wonderfully decorative example of art nouveau at No. 10. To your immediate left as you come into the square is the richly decorated **Jezuitský kostol** (Jesuit Church) ⑬. Next to the church is the colorful agglomeration of old bits and pieces of structures that make up the **Stará radnica** (Old Town Hall) ⑭. Walk through the arched passageway, still with its early Gothic ribbing, into a cheery Renaissance courtyard with romantic arcades and gables. Toward the back of the courtyard is the entrance to the **Mestské múzeum** (City Museum).

Leaving by the back entrance of the Old Town Hall, you'll come to the Primaciálne námestie (Primates' Square), dominated by the glorious palepink **Primaciálny palác** (Primates' Palace) ⑮, where you should take some time to explore. After you're done, walk down Uršulínska ulica and turn right at the bottom onto Laurinská ulica. If you continue to the left down Rybárska brána, you will emerge into the more modern part of the Old Town, with businesses and hotels stretched along the rectangular Hviezdoslavovo námestie (Hviezdoslav Square). To your right is the **Slovenské národné divadlo** (Slovak National Theater) ⑯, Bratislava's opera house. Behind the theater you can buy tickets to performances.

Across the Hviezdoslav Square, on the corner of Mostová ulica and Palackého ulica, is the **Reduta** ⑰, home to the Slovak Philharmonic Orchestra. If you can't make it to a concert, take a look inside. Continue down Mostová ulica to the banks of the Danube. To the right is the baroque onetime barracks, transformed by the Communists to house the modern **Slovenská národná galéria** (Slovak National Gallery) ⑱, which features a conglomeration of past and present works by Slovak artists.

Timing

If you get an early morning start, you can complete a leisurely walking tour of the Old Town in a day (make sure you have on comfortable shoes). With the exception of the Slovak National Gallery, which deserves some time, most of the museums are small and won't detain you long. If you have more than one day to explore Bratislava, save the Museum of Jewish Culture and the castle, two of the more interesting sights, for their own day. Avoid touring on Mondays, as many sights are closed. On other days, plan to break around lunchtime, because many museums close between noon and 1.

Sights to See

❺ Dóm svätého Martina (St. Martin's Cathedral). Construction of this massive Gothic church, with its 280-foot steeple twinkling beneath a layer of golden trim, began in the 14th century. The cathedral was finally consecrated in 1452, and between the 16th and 19th centuries it hosted the coronations of 17 Hungarian royals. Numerous additions made over the centuries were unfortunately removed in the 19th century, when the church was re-Gothicized. Nowadays, the three equal-size naves give an impression of space and light, but the uplifting glory found in Bohemia's Gothic cathedrals is definitely missing. ⊠ *Kapitulská 9,* ☎ *07/3309504.* ☉ *Weekdays 10–11:45 and 2–4:45, Sat. 10–noon and 2–4:45, Sun. 2–4:45.*

Farmaceutické múzeum (Pharmaceutical Museum). Housed in the barbican wall on the site of the former Red Crab Pharmacy, this small museum is worth visiting if only to see the beautifully carved wood shelves and imaginative pharmaceutical receptacles. Next to the museum, a small arched gateway topped with the symbol of a crab leads down through an apartment building to the moat-side garden, which has good views of the looming fortifications. ⊠ *Michalská ul. 26,* ☎ *07/5333596.* ▨ *10 Sk.* ☉ *Tues.–Sun. 10–4:30.*

⓫ Františkánsky kostol (Franciscan Church). Consecrated in 1297, this church was funded by the Hungarian king László IV to celebrate his victory over the Bohemian king Přemysl Otakar II at the Battle of the Marchfeld, near Vienna. Only its presbytery is still in early Gothic style, the rest having been destroyed in an earthquake in the 17th century and rebuilt in a mixture of baroque and Gothic. Just around the corner, built onto the church, is another quite different and much more stunning Gothic building, the 14th-century **Chapel of St. John the Evangelist,** the burial chapel for Mayor Jakub. Art historians believe that Peter Parler, architect of Prague's Charles Bridge and St. Vitus Cathedral, may have worked on this Gothic gem. You can take a look around before or after services at 7 AM and 5 PM. ⊠ *Frantíská nám.*

⑦ Hrad (castle). Bratislava's castle has been continually rebuilt since its foundations were laid in the 9th century. The Hungarian kings expanded it into a large royal residence, and the Hapsburgs further developed its fortifications, turning it into a very successful defense against the Turks. Its current design, square with four corner towers, stems from the 17th century, although the existing castle had to be completely rebuilt after a disastrous fire in 1811. Inside you'll find the **Slovenské národné múzeum** (Slovak National Museum), with exhibits featuring furniture, arts, folklore costumes, medieval warfare, and minting. ⊠ *Hrad, Zámocká ul.,* ☎ *07/5311444.* 🎟 *40 Sk.* ☉ *Tues.–Sun. 10–5.*

NEED A BREAK?	Snuggle up to a mug of beer or a glass of wine at **Judy's Gallery Bar** (⊠ Beblavého ul. 4, ☎ 07/516968) and contemplate the offbeat local art hanging from the walls. Judy's is open daily 4 PM to 1 AM.

OFF THE BEATEN PATH	**PETRŽALKA GARDENS –** On a balmy summer's day you can take a short ferry ride to this pleasant park on the water. However, if you'd rather spend more time cruising the Danube, stay on the ferry and enjoy the 10-kilometer (6-mile) ride up the river. The ferry operates between April and October and costs 10 Sk.; the ferry offices are on Fajnorovo nábrežie near the Slovak National Museum.

⑬ Jezuitský kostol (Jesuit Church). This church was originally built by Protestants who, in 1636, were granted an imperial concession to build a place of worship on the strict condition that it have no tower. The Jesuits took over the towerless church in 1672 and to compensate for its external simplicity, went wild with baroque detailing on the inside. ⊠ *Hlavné nám.* ☉ *Service at 4:30.*

④ Klariský kostol (Klariský church). This 14th-century church is simple but inspiring, with a wonderfully peaceful early Gothic interior. The small High Gothic steeple was added in an unusually secondary position at the back of the church during the 15th century; as a mendicant order, the Poor Clares were forbidden to build a steeple atop the church, so they sidestepped the rules and built it against a side wall. Unfortunately, the church is now a concert hall—and usually locked, but you may be able to get in for a concert or during rehearsals. ⊠ *Farská ul.*

⑩ Kostol kapucínov (Capuchin Chapel). A pillar of Mary, which commemorates the plague, stands in front of this small chapel, dating from 1717. The baroque chapel is of little artistic interest, but its peaceful interior is always filled with worshipers—something not often seen in Bratislava. You can sneak a peek inside the chapel before or after the services held early in the morning or in the evening 5–7. ⊠ *Kapucínska ul.*

② Kostol svätej Trojice (Church of the Holy Trinity). This golden-yellow baroque church has space-expanding frescoes on the ceiling, which are the work of Antonio Galli Bibiena in the early 18th century. ⊠ *Hurbanovo nám.* ☉ *Services at 9 AM and 6 PM.*

OFF THE BEATEN PATH	**DEVÍN –** Just west of the city atop a hill overlooking both the Danube and the Morava rivers is the ruined castle of Devín. The oldest section of the present castle dates from the 13th century, but most of the castle was destroyed by Napoléon's soldiery in 1809. A reconstructed basement of the Renaissance palace houses a small but interesting historical exhibition. Take Bus 29 from under the Nový Most to Devín and follow the

marked path up the hill to the castle. ⊠ *Devín*, ☎ *07/776346*. ▦ *10 Sk*. ☉ *Tues.–Fri. 10–5*.

❸ **Michalská brána** (Michael's Gate). This is the last remaining of the city's three original gates. The bottom part of the adjoining tower, built in the 14th century, retains its original Gothic design; the octagonal section was added in the early 16th century; and the flamboyant, copper onion tower, topped with a statue of St. Michael, is an addition from the 18th century. A small museum—**Múzeum zbraní a mestského opevnenia** (Museum of Weapons and Fortifications)—is housed in the tower. The museum itself is not really worth a lot of time, but the *veža* (tower) has a good view over the city. ⊠ *Michalská veža, Michalská ul. 24*, ☎ *07/5333044*. ▦ *5 Sk*. ☉ *Wed.–Mon. 10–5*.

⓬ **Mirbachov palác** (Mirbach Palace). This rococo palace with original stucco decor was built in 1770. Today it houses the **Municipal Gallery**, which has a small collection of 18th- and 19th-century Slovak and European art. ⊠ *Františkánske nám.*, ☎ *07/5331556*. ▦ *10 Sk*. ☉ *Summer, Tues.–Sun. 10–6; winter, Tues.–Sun. 10–3*.

★ ❾ **Muzeum Židovskej Kultúry** (Museum of Jewish Culture in Slovakia). This small but stirring museum is housed in a large, white mid-17th-century Renaissance mansion that's been reconstructed twice after fires in the 18th and 19th centuries. The exhibits celebrate the history and culture of the Jews living on the territory of Slovakia since the Great Moravian Empire. A section is devoted to the victims of the Holocaust in Slovakia. ⊠ *Židovská ul. 17*, ☎ *07/5318507*. ▦ *30 Sk*. ☉ *Sun.–Fri. 11–5*.

❽ **Múzeum umeleckých remesiel** (Handicraft Museum). In a baroque burgher house, this tiny museum displays a few nice works of arts and crafts from the 12th to 18th centuries, including ceramics, silverware, and furniture. ⊠ *Beblavého ul. 1*. ▦ *10 Sk*. ☉ *Wed.–Mon. 10–5*.

❶ **Námestie SNP** (SNP Square). The square, formerly known as Stalinovo námestie (Stalin Square), was and still remains the center for demonstrations in Slovakia.

OFF THE
BEATEN PATH

SLAVÍN MEMORIAL – This group of socialist-realist statues is a monument to the 6,000 who died during the Soviet liberation of Bratislava in 1945. You can get a dose of Communist Bratislava seeing this memorial. Even if you're not interested in the sculpture, the monument has fine views over Bratislava. Take a taxi for about 200 Sk.; or ride Bus 27, 43, 47, or 104 (from Hodžovo námestie up from Námestie SNP) to Puškinová, where you can climb the many steps to the top.

❻ **Nový Most** (New Bridge). Although it would make a splendid sight for an alien flick, the modern bridge is a bit of an eyesore for anyone who doesn't appreciate futuristic designs. The bridge is difficult to miss if you're anywhere near the Danube River.

NEED A
BREAK?

Unless you are squirmish about heights, have a coffee at the **Vyhliadková Kaviaren** (☎ 07/850042) on Nový Most. This spaceship-like café—reached via speedy glass-faced elevators for a minimal charge—is perched on top of pylons, 80 meters above the Danube River. One of Prague's English-language newspapers has dubbed the café's retro-Socialist interior "*Starship Enterprise*-gone-cocktail lounge." However you may feel about the architecture, it's not a bad place for a reasonable snack and an excellent view of the city. Be warned that during stronger winds the café does sway.

⓯ Primaciálny palác (Primates' Palace). This is one of the most valuable architectural monuments in Bratislava. Don't miss the dazzling Hall of Mirrors, with its six 17th-century English tapestries depicting the legend of the lovers Hero and Leander. In this room Napoléon and Hapsburg emperor Francis I signed the Bratislava Peace of 1805, following Napoléon's victory at the Battle of Austerlitz. In the revolutionary year of 1848, when the citizens of the Hapsburg lands revolted against the imperial dominance of Vienna, the rebel Hungarians had their headquarters in the palace; ironically, following the failed uprising, the Hapsburg general Hainau signed the rebels' death sentences in the very same room. ✉ *Primaciálne nám. 1,* ☎ *07/5331473.* 🎫 *10 Sk.* ☼ *Tues.– Sun. 10–5.*

⓱ Reduta. Bratislava's classical musical center, this extravagantly decorated building is home to the Slovak Philharmonic Orchestra. Built in neobaroque style but dating from 1914, the Reduta deserves a visit. ✉ *Medená ul. 3,* ☎ *07/5333351.*

⓲ Slovenská národná galéria (Slovak National Gallery). This gallery is in a conspicuously modern restoration of old 18th-century barracks. However you feel about the strange additions to the old building, the museum itself has an interesting collection of Slovak Gothic, baroque, and contemporary art, along with a small number of European masters. ✉ *Rázusovo nábrežie 2,* ☎ *07/5332081.* 🎫 *30 Sk.* ☼ *Tues.–Sun. 10–6.*

⓰ Slovenské národné divadlo (Slovak National Theater). You can see performances of Bratislava's opera, ballet, and theater at this striking theater, which was built in the 1880s by the famous Central European architectural duo of Hermann Helmer and Ferdinand Fellner. If you get a feeling of déjà vu looking at the voluptuous neobaroque curves, it's not surprising: The two men also built opera houses in Vienna, Prague, and Karlovy Vary, to name but a few. Don't bother trying to tour the theater; buy a ticket to a performance instead. ✉ *Hviezdoslavovo nám. 1,* ☎ *07/5330069 or 07/5321146.*

⓴ Stará radnica (Old Town Hall). One of the more interesting buildings in Bratislava, it developed gradually over the 13th and 14th centuries out of a number of burghers' houses. The imaginative roofing stems from the end of the 15th century, and the wall paintings from the 16th century. The strangely out-of-place baroque onion tower was a revision of the original tower. During the summer concerts are held here. You may want to stop in the **Mestské múzeum** (City Museum) here, which documents Bratislava's varied past. ✉ *Primaciálne nám. 3,* ☎ *07/5334742.* 🎫 *10 Sk.* ☼ *Tues.–Sun. 10–5.*

Dining

Prague may have its Slovak rival beat when it comes to architecture, but when it's time to eat, you can thank your lucky stars that you're in Bratislava. The long-shared history with Hungary gives Slovak cuisine an extra fire that Czech cooking admittedly lacks. Geographic proximity to Vienna, moreover, has lent something of grace and charm to the city's eateries. What does this add up to? You'll seldom see pork and dumplings on the menu. Instead, prepare for a variety of shish kebabs, grilled meats, steaks, and pork dishes, all spiced to warm the palate and served (if you're lucky) with those special noodles Slovaks call halušky. Wash it all down with a glass or two of red wine from nearby Modra or Pezinok.

The city's many street stands provide a price-conscious alternative to restaurant dining. In addition to the ubiquitous hot dogs and hamburgers (no relation to their American namesakes), try some *langoš*—flat, deep-fried, and delicious pieces of dough, usually seasoned with garlic.

$$$$ ✕ **Arkadia.** The elegant setting here, at the threshold to the castle, sets the tone for a luxurious evening. There are several dining rooms, ranging from intimate to more boisterous, all decorated with 19th-century furnishings. A standard repertoire of Slovak and international dishes, which include shish kebabs and steaks, is prepared to satisfaction. It is a 15-minute walk from the town center; take a taxi here and enjoy the mostly downhill walk back into town. ⊠ *Zámocké schody,* ☏ *07/5335650. Jacket and tie. AE, DC, MC, V.*

$$$$ ✕ **Rybársky cech.** The name means Fisherman's Guild, and fish is the unchallenged specialty at this refined but comfortable eatery on a quiet street by the Danube. Freshwater fish is served upstairs, with pricier saltwater varieties offered on the ground floor. ⊠ *Žižkova 1,* ☏ *07/5313049. AE, DC, MC, V.*

$$$ ✕ **Kláštorná vináreň.** In the wine cellar of a former monastery, this restaurant with its wine-barrel-shaped booths is pleasantly dark and intimate.
★ The Hungarian-influenced spiciness of traditional Slovak cooking comes alive in such dishes as *Cíkos tókeň,* a fiery mixture of pork, onions, and peppers; or try the milder *Bravcové Ražnicí,* a tender pork shish kebab served with fried potatoes. ⊠ *Františkanská ul.,* ☏ *07/5330430. No credit cards. Closed Sun.*

$$$ ✕ **Veľkí Františkáni.** Housed in a beautiful 13th-century building, this wine cellar has a menu and an atmosphere similar to that at the Kláštorná (☞ *above*). However, the Veľkí's expansive dining area, which includes a garden patio, nurtures a more raucous, giddy clientele. Try one of the local specialties, *Prešporská Pochúdka* (sautéed beef with vegetables and potato pancakes). ⊠ *Františkánske nám. 10,* ☏ *07/5333073. AE, MC, V.*

$$ ✕ **Korzo.** Here you'll find delicious Slovak specialties—try a shish kebab or spicy grilled steak—served in a clean, cozy cellar setting. After dinner take a stroll along the Danube, right next door. The Korzo's ground-floor café is a great spot for people-watching or writing postcards. ⊠ *Hviezdoslavovo nám. 11,* ☏ *07/5334974. No credit cards.*

$$ ✕ **Modrá Hviezda.** The first of a new breed of small, family-owned wine
★ cellars, this popular eatery serves old Slovak specialties from the village as well as some imaginative dishes; try the sheep-cheese pie. ⊠ *Beblavého 14,* ☏ *07/5332747. No credit cards. Closed Sun.*

$$ ✕ **Pekná Brána.** With more than 75 main-course meals to choose
★ from, this is not the place to go if you have trouble making up your mind. The menu includes Chinese and vegetarian dishes and traditional Slovak cuisine. You can also dine in the cellar, which is open until sunrise. The restaurant is open daily 9 AM to midnight. ⊠ *Obchodná ul. 39,* ☏ *07/5323008. AE, MC, V.*

$$ ✕ **Spaghetti and Co.** This local representative of an American chain serves good pizzas and pasta in a pleasant, tourist-friendly setting—a godsend if you're traveling with children. The adjacent food court, right out of your local shopping mall, has booths selling Greek, Chinese, and health foods. ⊠ *Gorkého l,* ☏ *07/5332303. No credit cards.*

$ ✕ **Gremium.** This trendy restaurant caters to the coffee-and-cigarette crowd and to anyone in search of an uncomplicated light meal. Choose from a small menu of pastries, sandwiches, and some local specialties including *brynzové halušky* (tasty noodles with goat cheese) and *pytliacky guláš* (creamy goulash with halušky topped with blueberries)— though a bizarre combination, it's scrumptious. The regulars are mostly students or, owing to the proximity of a ceramics gallery, Bratislava's self-styled art crowd. ⊠ *Gorkého 11,* ☏ *07/521818. Reservations not accepted. AE, MC, V.*

$ ✕ **Stará Sladovňa.** To Bratislavans, this gargantuan beer hall is known
★ lovingly, and fittingly, as *mamut* (mammoth). Locals come here for the
Bohemian brews on tap, but it is also possible to get an inexpensive
and filling meal. ⊠ *Cintorínska 32,* ☎ *07/5321151. No credit cards.*

Lodging

The lodging situation in Bratislava is improving, though not fast enough
to rid the city of some pretty shabby establishments. The few decent
hotels that do exist are very expensive; the cheaper hotels tend to be
rundown and utterly depressing. However, small, privately owned hotels and pensions continue to materialize and put the old establishments
to shame. Make reservations in advance or arrive in Bratislava before
4 PM and ask tourist information (☞ Bratislava A to Z, *below*) for help
finding a room. If all decent hotels are booked, consider renting an apartment. Beware of individuals offering apartments at train stations, or you
may be going back home with a much lighter load.

$$$$ ⊞ **Danube.** Opened in 1992, this French-run hotel on the banks of the
★ Danube has quickly developed a reputation for superior facilities and
service. The modern rooms are decorated in pastel colors; the gleaming public areas are everything you expect from an international hotel
chain. ⊠ *Rybné nám. 1,* ☎ *07/5340833,* FAX *07/5314311. 280 rooms
with bath. 2 restaurants, pool, sauna, health club, nightclub, conven-
tion center. AE, DC, MC, V.*

$$$$ ⊞ **Forum.** If creature comforts are an important factor, the Forum is
for you. Bratislava's most expensive hotel, built in 1989 right in the center of town, offers a complete array of services and facilities. The staff
is efficient and friendly, and the functional rooms are pleasantly, if in-
nocuously, decorated. ⊠ *Hodžovo nám. 2,* ☎ *07/348111,* FAX *07/314645.
219 rooms with bath. 2 restaurants, 2 bars, 2 cafés, indoor pool, beauty
salon, sauna, health club, casino, nightclub. AE, DC, MC, V.*

$$$ ⊞ **Bratislava.** This bland but suitably clean cement-block hotel in the
suburb of Ružinov has rooms with televisions and private bathrooms.
It offers few facilities beyond a standard restaurant and lounge, but
there is a large department store nearby where you can stock up on
supplies. From the city center take Bus 34 or Tram 8. Breakfast is in-
cluded. ⊠ *Urxova ul. 9,* ☎ *07/239000,* FAX *07/236420. 344 rooms with
bath. Restaurant, lobby lounge, snack bar. AE, DC, MC, V.*

$$$ ⊞ **Devín.** This boxy 1950s hotel set on the banks of the Danube has
managed to create an air of elegance in its reception area that doesn't
translate into much else, despite its five-star status. The furniture is poorly
arranged in the small rooms, and the service is on the gruff side. Nevertheless, the hotel is clean, with a variety of restaurants and cafés that
serve dependably satisfying food; breakfast is included. ⊠ *Riečna ul.
4,* ☎ *07/5330851,* FAX *07/5330682. 98 rooms with bath. 3 restaurants,
2 bars, café. AE, DC, MC, V.*

$$$ ⊞ **Hotel Pension No. 16.** This cozy pension in a quiet residential haven
★ close to the castle is a nice alternative to the big chain hotels—it pro-
vides all the conveniences, but with character. The apartments are suit-
able for families; breakfast is included. ⊠ *Partizánska ul. 16,* ☎ *07/
5311672,* FAX *07/5311298. 10 rooms with bath, 5 apartments. Kitch-
enettes. AE, MC, V.*

$$$ ⊞ **Perugia.** Finished in 1993, this stunning postmodern jewel is in a
renovated building in the center of Old Town. The light and airy in-
terior contrasts sharply with the dark, drab ones of many of the city's
buildings. The clean, colorful rooms are an eye-opener. Breakfast is included. ⊠ *Zelená 5,* ☎ *07/5331818,* FAX *07/5331821. 11 rooms with
bath. Restaurant. AE, DC, MC, V.*

$$ 🏨 **Hotel Echo.** This small, pink, modern hotel, not far from the center of Bratislava, looks more like a health club than a hotel, but it's a great place to stay, especially if you have a car. It has a friendly staff, large bright rooms—and a great breakfast, which is included in the price of a room. ✉ *Presovská ul. 39,* ☎ *07/329170,* FAX *07/329174. Restaurant. MC, V.*

Nightlife and the Arts

Nightlife

BARS AND LOUNGES

Bratislava doesn't offer much in the way of bars and lounges; after-dinner drinking takes place mostly in wine cellars and beer halls. Two of the former are **Kláštorná vináreň** or **Veľkí Františkáni** (☞ Dining, *above*), both in vaulted, medieval cellars. For beer swilling, the best address in town is the mammoth **Stará Sladovňa** (☞ Dining, *above*).

JAZZ CLUBS

Bratislava hosts an annual jazz festival in the fall, but the city lacks a good venue for regular jazz gigs. That said, **Mefisto Club** (✉ Panenska 24, no phone) occasionally features local jazz acts.

ROCK CLUBS

Bratislava's live-music and club scene is expanding; new bands, running the spectrum from folk and rock to rap, are constantly turning up. The venues are changing just as rapidly; check the English-language *Slovak Spectator,* a Bratislava-based newspaper with regular features on the city's cultural life, for the lowdown on the latest clubs. Dependable hot spots are the **Rock Fabrik Danubius** (✉ Komanárska ul. 3, no phone), featuring loud and sweaty Czech and Slovak acts nightly; and the **U Club** (✉ Pod Hradom ul., no phone), where hard-core rock can be fun if you're into that sort of thing.

The Arts

Bratislava does not have a roaring nightlife scene so stick to the classics. The celebrated **Slovak Philharmonic Orchestra** plays regularly throughout the year, and chamber-music concerts are held at irregular intervals in the stunning Gothic **Church of the Poor Clares.** In summer the Renaissance courtyard of the **Old Town Hall** is also used for concerts. Slovenské národné divadlo offers high quality opera and ballet performances at bargain prices. Call BIS or Satur (☞ Bratislava A to Z, *below*) for program details and tickets; the *Slovak Spectator* is another good source for information.

CONCERTS

The **Slovak Philharmonic Orchestra** plays a full program, featuring Czech and Slovak composers as well as European masters, at its home in the Reduta. ✉ *Medená 3,* ☎ *07/5333351. Buy tickets at the theater box office (*☉ *Weekdays 1–5).*

FILM

Most new releases are shown in their original language with Slovak subtitles. **Charlie Centrum** regularly shows American classics, in English, in a friendly, artsy environment. ✉ *Špitálska 4,* ☎ *07/363430.*

OPERA AND BALLET

The **Slovenské národné divadlo** (Slovak National Theater) is the place for high-quality opera and ballet. Buy tickets at the theater office on the corner of Jesenského and Komenského streets weekdays between noon and 6 PM or 30 minutes before showtime. ✉ *Hviezdoslavovo nám. 1,* ☎ *07/5321146.*

THEATER
Traditional theater is usually performed in Slovak and is therefore incomprehensible to most visitors. For non-Slovak speakers, the **Stoka Theater** blends nontraditional theater with performance art in a provocative and entertaining way. For details, contact the theater box office. ⊠ *Pribinova 1*, ☏ *07/364961.*

Shopping

Bratislava is an excellent place to find Slovak arts and crafts of all types. You will find plenty of folk-art and souvenir shops along **Obchodná ulica** (Shopping Street) as well as on **Námestie SNP.** Stores still come and go in this rapidly changing city, so don't be too surprised if some of the listed stores have vanished.

Antikvariat Steiner. This shop stocks beautiful old books, maps, graphics, and posters. ⊠ *Venturská ul. 20*, ☏ *07/52834.*

Dielo. This large store (☞ Pleasures and Pastimes, *above*) has designer jewelry and clothing in addition to very unusual and fun ceramic pieces and other works of art. ⊠ *Námestie SNP 12*, ☏ *07/5334568. Two smaller locations are:* ⊠ *Obchodná ul. 27*, ☏ *07/5334568, and* ⊠ *Obchodná 33*, ☏ *07/5330688.*

Folk, Folk. Here you'll find a large collection of Slovak folk art, including pottery, handwoven tablecloths, wooden toys, and dolls with Slovak folk costumes. ⊠ *Obchodná ul. 10*, ☏ *07/5334292.*

Folk Art. This spot has a nice selection of hand-painted table pottery and vases, wooden figures, and village folk clothing and numerous types of small corn-husk figures, which are dirt cheap and can be very beautiful, though not easy to transport. ⊠ *Námestie SNP 12*, ☏ *07/323802.*

Gremium Café. Try here for original pieces of art and pottery. ⊠ *Gorkého 11*, ☏ *07/51818.*

Bratislava A to Z

Arriving and Departing

BY BOAT
Hydrofoils travel the Danube between Vienna and Bratislava from April to December. Boats depart in the morning from Bratislava, on the eastern bank of the Danube just down from the Devín Hotel, and return from Vienna in the evening. Tickets cost $40–$70 per person and should be purchased in person at the dock.

BY BUS
There are numerous buses from Prague to Bratislava; the five-hour journey costs around 250 Sk. From Vienna, there are four buses a day from Autobusbahnhof Wien Mitte. The journey takes 1½–2 hours and costs about AS150. Bratislava's main bus terminal, **Autobus Stanica,** is roughly 2 kilometers (1¼ miles) from the city center; to get downtown, take Trolley (*trolej*) 217 to Mierové námestie or Bus 107 to the castle (*hrad*); or flag down a taxi.

BY CAR
There are good freeways from Prague to Bratislava via Brno (D1 and D2); the 325-kilometer (202-mile) journey takes about 3½ hours. From Vienna, take the A4 and then Route 8 to Bratislava, just across the border. Depending on the traffic at the border, the 60-kilometer (37-mile) journey should take about 1½ hours.

Although few international airlines provide direct service to Bratislava, **ČSA** (☎ 07/361042 or 07/361045), the Czech and Slovak national carrier, offers frequent connections to Bratislava via Prague. You can also fly into Vienna's Schwechat Airport, about 50 kilometers (30 miles) to the west, and proceed to Bratislava by either bus or train—a one-hour journey.

BY TRAIN

Reasonably efficient train service regularly connects Prague and Bratislava. Trains leave from Prague's Hlavní nádraží (main station) or from Holešovice station, and the journey takes five to six hours. The Intercity trains are slightly more expensive but faster. From Vienna, four trains daily make the one-hour trek to Bratislava. Bratislava's train station, **Hlavná Stanica,** is about 2 kilometers (1¼ miles) from the city center; to travel downtown from the station, take Streetcar 1 or 13 to Poštová ulica or jump in a taxi.

Getting Around

Bratislava is compact, and most sights can be covered easily on foot. Taxis are reasonably priced and easy to hail; at night, they are the best option for returning home from wine cellars and clubs.

BY BUS AND TRAM

Buses and trams in Bratislava run frequently and connect the city center with outlying sights. Tickets cost 5 Sk. and are available from large hotels, news agents, and tobacconists. Validate tickets on board (watch how the locals do it). The fine for riding without a validated ticket is 200 Sk., payable on the spot.

BY TAXI

Meters start at 10 Sk. and jump 10 Sk. per kilometer (½ mile). The number of dishonest cabbies, sadly, is on the rise; to avoid being ripped off, watch to see that the driver engages the meter. If the meter is broken, negotiate a price with the driver before even getting in the cab. Taxis are hailable on the street, or call 07/311311.

Contacts and Resources

EMBASSIES

United States: ✉ Hviezdoslavovo 4, ☎ 07/5330861. **British:** ✉ Grösslingova 35, ☎ 07/364420.

EMERGENCIES

Police: ☎ 158. **Ambulance:** ☎ 155.

ENGLISH-LANGUAGE BOOKSTORES

Several Slovak bookstores stock English-language titles. Try **Big Ben Bookshop** (✉ Michalská 1, ☎ 07/5333632) or the beautiful second-hand bookstore **Antikvariat Steiner** (✉ Venturská ul. 20, ☎ 07/52834). A small magazine shop at Laurinská 9 is a good source for English-language newspapers and periodicals. The well-stocked reading room of the U.S. Embassy (☞ *above*) is open to the general public Tuesday through Friday 9 to 2 and Monday noon to 5. Bring a passport.

GUIDED TOURS

The best tours of Bratislava are offered by **BIS** (☞ Visitor Information, *below*), although tours during the off-season are conducted in German and only on weekends. Tours typically take two hours and cost 270 Sk. per person. **Satur** (☞ Visitor Information, *below*) also offers tours of the capital from May through September. You can sometimes combine these with an afternoon excursion through the Small Carpathian Mountains, including dinner at the Zochová chata.

The pharmacy at Špitálska 3, near the Old Town, maintains 24-hour service; other pharmacies hold late hours on a rotating basis.

TRAVEL AGENCIES
Tatratur (✉ Bajkalská 25, ☎ 07/5233259 or 07/5211219, FAX 07/5213624) is a large, dependable agency that can help arrange sightseeing tours throughout Slovakia. Its office at Františkánske námestie 7 (☎ 07/335012) also acts as an official representative of American Express in Slovakia. **Satur** (☞ *below*) can also provide basic travel-agency services, such as changing traveler's checks and booking bus and train tickets to outside destinations.

VISITOR INFORMATION
Bratislava's tourist information service, **Bratislavská Informačná Služba** (BIS; ✉ Panská 18, ☎ 07/5333715 or 07/5334370), can assist in finding a hotel or private accommodation. The office, open weekdays 8 to 4:30 (until 6 in summer) and Saturday 8 to 1, is also a good source for maps and basic information. If you are arriving by train, the small **BIS** office in the station, open daily 8 to 8, can be very helpful.

The country's national travel agency **Satur Tours and Travel** (formerly known as Čedok; ✉ Jesenského 5, ☎ 07/367613 or 07/367624, FAX 07/323816; ⊙ Weekdays 9 to 6, Sat. 9 to noon) can help find accommodations in one of its hotels across the country and can book air, rail, and bus tickets.

SIDE TRIPS FROM BRATISLAVA

The Wine Country

Much of the country's best wine is produced within a 30-minute drive of Bratislava, in a lovely mountainous region that offers a respite from the noise and grime of the capital. Two neighboring towns, Pezinok and Modra, vie for the distinction of being Slovakia's wine capital.

Pezinok, the larger of the two, is home to the Small Carpathian vineyards, the country's largest wine producer. In this quaint, red-roofed town you can find enough to keep you busy for an entire day without ever stepping off its busy main street, Stefanika ulica. Take in the wine-making exhibits at the **Malokarpatksé muzeum** (Small Carpathian Museum, ✉ Stefanika ul.), closed Monday, and then head next door to the outstanding bakery. Leave some room for lunch at the **Zámocka wine cellar,** open daily 11–11, in the town's castle at the end of the street. The castle also serves as a winery; around the side you'll find a sales counter offering a variety of locally produced wines.

Modra is a typical one-horse town, with some pretty folk architecture and a few comfortable wine gardens. Combine a visit here with a night at the nearby Zochová Chata (☞ Dining and Lodging, *below*).

The Renaissance castle **Červený Kameň** (Red Rock) is a great hiking destination from Modra. You can begin the trail at Zochová Chata. On the prettier yellow-marked trail, the walk takes upwards of 2½ hours; on the blue-and-green trail, around 1½ hours. You can visit the most fascinating parts of the structure with a guide. These include the vast storage and wine cellars, with their movable floors and high, arched ceilings, and the bastions, constructed with an intricate ventilation system and hidden passageways in the middle of the thick slate walls. ✏ 10 Sk. ⊙ May–Oct., daily 11–3; Nov.–Apr., Tues.–Sun. 11–3. *Tours on the hr.*

Dining and Lodging

$$ ✕🏠 **Zochová Chata.** This attractive 1920s-style hunting chalet near
★   Modra, 32 kilometers (20 miles) outside Bratislava, is a comfortable al-
ternative to the latter's large luxury hotels. The rooms here are small but
very comfortable, and the food served in the adjoining tavern a few doors
down is top-rate. ⊠ *Modra-Piesok,* ☎ *070492/2956,* 🗏 *070492/2991.*
10 rooms with bath. Restaurant, wine tavern. No credit cards.

The Wine Country A to Z

ARRIVING AND DEPARTING

Infrequent buses link Bratislava with Modra and Pezinok; most leave
early in the morning, so contact **ČSAD** (Bratislava, ☎ 07/63213), the
national bus carrier, at least a day in advance. By car from Bratislava,
take Route 502, 4 kilometers (2½ miles) past the village of Jur pri
Bratislave, and turn right down a smaller road in the direction of the
villages Slovenský Grob and Viničné. At the latter, turn left onto Route
503 to reach Pezinok, a few kilometers beyond. Modra lies 4 kilome-
ters (2½ miles) farther along the same road.

Trnava

⑲ *45 km (28 mi) from Bratislava on the D61 highway.*

Trnava, with its silhouette of spires and towers, is the oldest town in
Slovakia; it received royal town rights in 1238. Trnava was the main
seat of the Hungarian archbishop until 1821 and a principal Hungar-
ian university center during the 17th and 18th centuries, until Maria
Theresa shifted the scholarly crowd to Budapest. That Trnava's "golden
age" coincided with the baroque period is readily apparent in its ar-
chitecture, beneath the neglected facades and pervasive industrial
decay. Look for the enormous **University Church of John the Baptist,**
designed by Italian baroque architects, with fabulous carved-wood al-
tars. Look for **St. Nicholas Cathedral,** which dominates the town with
its large onion towers.

Trnava A to Z

ARRIVING AND DEPARTING
Bratislava and Trnava are connected by frequent bus and train service.

CONTACTS AND RESOURCES
For tourist and lodging information contact the **Trnavský Informačný
Servis.** ⊠ *Trojičné nám. 1,* ☎ *0805/20203,* 🗏 *0805/42268.* ☉
June–Sept., weekdays 8–7, weekends 10–6; Oct.–May, daily 10–6.

THE HIGH TATRAS

Visiting the *Vysoké Tatry* (High Tatras) alone would make a trip to
Slovakia worthwhile. Although the range is relatively compact as
mountains go (just 32 kilometers, or 20 miles, from end to end), its
peaks seem wilder and more starkly beautiful than even those of Eu-
rope's other great range, the Alps. Some 20 Tatras peaks exceed 8,000
feet, with the highest Gerlachovský Štít at 8,710 feet. The 35 moun-
tain lakes are remote and clear and, according to legend, can impart
the ability to see through doors and walls to anyone who bathes in them;
however, they are also very cold, sometimes eerily deep, and swimming
is not permitted in the cold glacier lakes of the Tatras.

Humans are a relative latecomer to the Tatras. The region's first town,
Schmecks (today Starý Smokovec), was founded in the late 18th cen-
tury, and regular visitors began coming here only after 1871, with the
construction of a mountain railroad linking the resort to the bustling
junction town of Poprad. In the late 19th and early 20th centuries, with

the founding of Štrbské pleso and Tatranská Lomnica, the Tatras finally came into their own as an elegant playground for Europe's elite.

But the post–World War II Communist era was hard on the Tatras. Almost overnight, the area became a mass resort for the mountain-starved, fenced-in peoples of the Eastern bloc, prompting much development and commercialization. But don't despair: The faded elegance of these mountain retreats and spa resorts remains intact, despite the sometimes heavy winter- and summertime crowds.

Most of the tourist facilities in the High Tatras are concentrated in three neighboring resort towns: Štrbské pleso to the west, Smokovec in the middle, and Tatranská Lomnica to the east. Each town is pretty similar in terms of convenience and atmosphere, and all provide easy passage to the hills, so it makes little difference where you choose to begin you explorations of the mountains.

Finding a satisfying meal in the Tatras is about as tough as making the 1,000-foot climb from Starý Smokovec to Hrebienok, especially in the fall when some restaurants close completely. The good news is that a couple of entrepreneurs have recently jumped on the opportunity and created the best places to eat in the region. Don't leave the Tatras without eating in one of the restaurants with an open-face grill. An alternative to the restaurants are local grocery stores—try the one in Starý Smokovec—which stock basic sandwich fixings.

If you are looking to splurge on accommodations, you'll find no better place than the Tatras. In older hotels, ask to see several rooms before selecting one, as room interiors can be quite quirky. Prices are highest in January and February, when there is snow on the ground. They are lower during the off-season (late fall and early spring), but the mountains are just as beautiful.

Hiking

The best way to see these beautiful mountains is on foot. Three of the best Tatras walks (three to five hours each) are outlined below, arranged according to difficulty (with the easiest and prettiest first), although a reasonably fit person of any age will have little trouble with any of the three. Yet even though the trails are well marked, it is very important to buy a walking map of the area—the detailed *Vysoké Tatry, Letná Turistická Mapa* is available for around 20 Sk. at newspaper kiosks. If you're planning to take any of the higher-level walks, be sure to wear proper shoes with good ankle support. Also use extreme caution in early spring, when melting snow can turn the trails into icy rivers. And don't forget drinking water, sunglasses, and sunscreen.

Since the entire area is a national park, the trails are well marked in different colors. Mountain climbers who do not want a guide have to be members of a climbing club. There are climbs of all levels of difficulty (although Grade 1 climbs may be used only as starting points), the best are the west wall of **Lomnický Štít**, the north wall of the **Kežmarský Štít**, and the **Široká veža**.

Skiing

The entire region is crisscrossed with paths ideal for cross-country skiing. You can buy a special ski map at newspaper kiosks. The season lasts from the end of December through April, though the best months are traditionally January and February. Renting ski equipment is not much of a problem, and it is reasonably priced. Ždiar, toward the Polish border, has a good ski area for beginners.

Numbers in the margin correspond to numbers on the Slovakia map.

The High Tatras

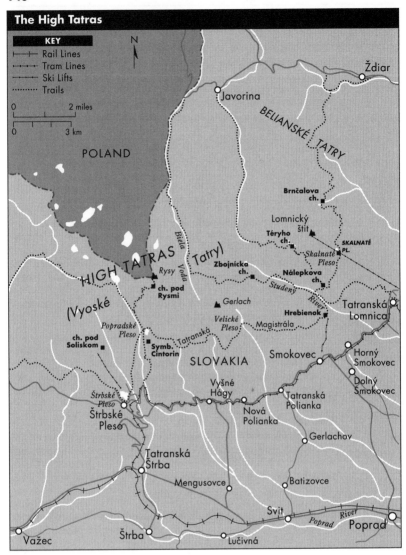

KEY
- ┼┼ Rail Lines
- ┼·┼· Tram Lines
- ·┼·┼ Ski Lifts
- ········· Trails

0   2 miles
0   3 km

POLAND

BELIANSKÉ TATRY

Ždiar

Javorina

Brnčalova ch.

Lomnický štít

Téryho ch.

SKALNATÉ PL.

Skalnaté Pleso

HIGH TATRAS

Biela Voda

Tatry

Rysy

Zbojnícka ch.

Nálepkova ch.

Študený River

ch. pod Rysmi

(Vyoské

Gerlach

Hrebienok

Tatranská Lomnica

Popradské Pleso

Velické Pleso

Magistrála

ch. pod Soliskom

Symb. Cintorin

Tatranská

SLOVAKIA

Smokovec

Horný Smokovec

Štrbské Pleso

Štrbské Pleso

Vyšné Hágy

Nová Polianka

Tatranská Polianka

Dolný Smokovec

Gerlachov

Tatranská Štrba

Mengusovce

Batizovce

Svit

Poprad River

Poprad

Važec

Štrba

Lučivná

Poprad

20   *329 km (204 mi) east of Bratislava along Highways E75 and E50.*

Poprad, the gateway to the Tatras, is a good place to begin exploring the region. But don't expect a beautiful mountain village. Poprad fell victim to some of the most insensitive Communist planning perpetrated in the country after the war, and as a result you'll see little more than row after row of apartment blocks, interspersed with factories and power plants. There's no need to linger here. Instead, drive or take the electric railroad to the superior sights and facilities of the more rugged resorts just over 30 kilometers (20 miles) to the north.

Dining and Lodging

$ ✕ **Slovenská Reštauracia.** If you have to spend a few hours in Poprad,
★ having a meal in this charming rustic restaurant is the best way of doing so. Try the brynzové halušky or *strapačky skapustou* (homemade noodles with sauerkraut). The English version of the menu translates some

of these delightful items as balls, bags, and pillows, but don't get frightened off—they really are delicious. ⊠ *Ul. 1 May 216,* ☎ *092/ 722870. No credit cards.*

$$ 🏨 **Gerlach.** This modern structure a couple of blocks away from the station is as dreary as Poprad itself. The rooms are cheerier than the public areas, but the bathrooms are only just acceptable. If you're not satisfied with your room, ask to see an apartment (about double the standard room price). One is attractively, if incongruously, decorated with antique furniture. ⊠ *Hviezdoslavova ul. 3,* ☎ *092/721945,* FAX *092/63663. 120 rooms, most with bath. Restaurant, café, barbershop. No credit cards.*

$ 🏨 **Europa.** This cozy little hotel is next to the train station. From the reception area to the modest, old-fashioned rooms (with neither bathrooms nor TVs), the place exudes a faint elegance. In season, the bar and restaurant on the ground floor buzz with activity in the evenings. ⊠ *Wolkerová ul.,* ☎ *092/721883. 50 rooms without bath. Restaurant, bar. No credit cards.*

En Route A kilometer and a half (1 mile) northeast of Poprad is the medieval hamlet of **Spišská Sobota,** now a suburb of Poprad but formerly one of the main centers of the historic Spiš Empire. Sobota's lovely old square features a Romanesque church, rebuilt in Gothic style in the early 16th century, with an ornate altar carved by master Pavol of Levoča. The Renaissance belfry dates from the end of the 16th century. The square itself is a nearly perfect ensemble of Renaissance houses. But the most impressive of all is the setting, a 16th-century oasis amid the cultural desert of socialist realism.

Smokovec

㉑ *32 km (20 mi) north of Poprad.*

The first town you'll reach by road or rail from Poprad is Smokovec, the undisputed center of the Slovak Tatras resorts and the major beneficiary of postwar development. Smokovec is divided into two principal areas, Starý Smokovec (Old Smokovec) and Nový Smokovec (New Smokovec), which are within a stone's throw of each other. Stay in Starý Smokovec if you want to be near grocery stores, bars, and the local Satur office. The town is also a good starting point for many mountain excursions (from here, for example, a funicular can take you the 4,144 feet up to Hrebienok and its many marked trails).

The Tatras are tailor-made for hikers of all levels. The best way to take in the scenery, of course, is on foot. **Starý Smokovec** is a great starting point for a trek that parallels a cascading waterfall for much of its three-hour length. From Starý Smokovec, walk out along the main road in the direction of Tatranská Lomnica for roughly 1 kilometer (½ mile). In Tatranská Lesná, follow the yellow-marked path that winds gently uphill through the pines and alongside a swift-running stream. In winter the walk is particularly lovely; the occasional burst of sunshine warms your cheeks and transforms the cold running water to a tropical blue-green.

Farther along there are red markers leading to the funicular at Hrebienok, which brings you back to the relative comforts of Starý Smokovec. However, if you're in good physical shape and there is *plenty* of daylight left, consider extending your hike by four hours. (The extension is striking, but avoid it during winter, when you may find yourself neck-deep in snow). Just before the Bilková chata, turn right along the green path and then follow the blue, red, and then green trails in the direction of windswept **Tery chata,** a turn-of-the-century chalet perched amid five lonely alpine lakes. The scenery is a few notches above dazzling. Once you reach the chalet after two strenuous hours of hiking, backtrack to Bilková chata and follow the signs to the funicular at Hrebienok.

A more adventurous and rigorous five-hour walk starts in Starý Smokovec behind and to the west of the Grand Hotel (☞ *below*). Begin by ascending to the tree line along the blue path. Thirty minutes of up-hill hiking will take you to the Magistrale Trail; follow the trail to the left, and after 20 minutes or so of moderate climbing, the trees thin out—leaving nothing but dwarf pines, rocks, and breathtaking peaks.

Sliezsky Dom, a 1960s cookie-cutter prefab (surely Slovakia's highest-elevation housing project), lies an hour down the trail. Forgive the building's architectural sins and head inside for a cup of tea and a bite to eat. The descent to Starý Smokovec along the green and then yellow trails is long and peaceful: Nothing breaks the silence save the snapping of twigs or, in winter, the crunch of snow underfoot.

Dining and Lodging

$$ ✕ **Restaurant Koliba.** This charming restaurant with rustic decor and
★ an open-face grill serves up tasty local fare. Try *kapustová polievka,* sauerkraut soup with mushrooms and sausage. If you're lucky, you may get serenaded by a local Gypsy band that plays here most nights. ⊠ *Starý Smokovec,* ☎ *0969/2204. No credit cards. Closed Sun.*

$$ ✕🏠 **Villa Dr. Szontagh.** Away from the action in Nový Smokovec, this
★ steepled little chalet offers mostly peace and quiet. The darkly furnished rooms and public areas are well maintained, and the courtly staff goes out of its way to please. The decent restaurant has an extensive wine cellar. ⊠ *Nový Smokovec,* ☎ *0969/2061,* 📠 *0969/2062. 11 rooms with bath. Restaurant, wine cellar. No credit cards. Closed Dec.*

$$$ 🏠 **Bellevue.** This modern hotel, just outside Starý Smokovec along the road to Tatranská Lomnica, lacks the atmosphere of the Grand (☞ *below*) but nevertheless offers top services and clean, functional rooms. However, you'll be a good 15-minute walk away from Starý Smokovec's grocers and bars. Breakfast is included with your room. For skiers and sports enthusiasts, a sporting-goods rental shop is right next door. ⊠ *Starý Smokovec,* ☎ *0969/2941,* 📠 *0969/2719. 110 rooms with bath. Restaurant, pool. AE, DC, MC, V.*

$$$ 🏠 **Grand Hotel.** Along with its sister hotel in Tatranská Lomnica
★ (Grandhotel Praha), this hotel epitomizes Tatra luxury at its turn-of-the-century best. The hotel's golden Tudor facade rises majestically over the town of Starý Smokovec, with the peaks of the Tatras looming in the background. The location, at the commercial and sports center of the region, is a mixed blessing. In season, skiers and hikers crowd the reception area, and the hallways are filled with guests and visitors alike. The rooms themselves are quiet. Breakfast is included. ⊠ *Starý Smokovec,* ☎ *0969/2154,* 📠 *0969/2157. 83 rooms with bath. Restaurant, café, pool, sauna. AE, DC, MC, V.*

Outdoor Activities and Sports

PARAGLIDING

Local sports shops provide equipment for many sports, including paragliding and paraskiing. The rates, surprisingly, are very reasonable. For information, consult the sporting-goods store, **Športcentrumin** (⊠ Pekná vyhliadka, ☎ 0969/2953), in Horný Smokovec. It's a 10-minute walk along the highway, to the east of Starý Smokovec.

SKIING

For renting equipment, try the **Sport Centrum** (☎ 0969/2953) in Horný Smokovec or the Ski Service in the **Švajčiarsky Dom,** next to the Grand Hotel (☞ *above*), open 8 to noon and 12:30 to 4. Arrive early—the equipment rents quickly when it snows. You can buy skis and equipment at the **Mladost'** department store in Starý Smokovec.

SLEDDING

If there's snow on the ground and the children are too young to ski, you'll find a good sledding slope at **Hrebienok,** just above Starý Smokovec. To get here, take the funicular from behind the Grand Hotel; you can rent sleds from the Ski Service near the Grand or purchase them for 200 Sk.–300 Sk. from local sporting-goods stores.

Shopping

The Tatras resorts are short on shopping places. Still, you'll find good-quality, reasonably priced hiking and camping equipment at several sporting-goods stores and at the **Mladost'** store in Starý Smokovec.

Štrbské Pleso

㉒ *18 km (11 mi) west of Smokovec.*

Štrbské pleso is the main center in the Tatras for active sports. As such, it's best suited for skiers and those who thrive on crowds and commotion. The best ski slopes are not far away, and the fine mountain lake is a perfect backdrop for a leisurely stroll—many excellent hiking trails are within easy reach, too. As for facilities, the town has not only the most modern hotels but also the most jarringly modern hotel architecture. This large resort presides over the finest panoramas in the Tatras. For a breathtaking view of the valley and mountains, head for the lawn of the town's sanatorium.

Dining and Lodging

$$$ ✕🏨 **Panoráma.** The architects of Štrbské pleso must have had a ball designing hotels. This one, built in the 1960s, resembles an upside-down staircase. The rooms are small and plain, with clean bathrooms. What is special, though, is the truly panoramic view of the High and Low Tatras. Nevertheless, the public areas are unimpressive, and the hotel is too expensive for what it offers. The cozy wine cellar, Cengálka, is worth a visit. ⊠ *Across from bus and rail station,* ☎ 0969/92111, ⅋ 0969/92810. *96 rooms with bath. Restaurant, bar. AE, DC, MC, V.*

$$$ 🏨 **Patria.** This modern, slanting pyramid on the shores of a mountain
★ lake has two obvious advantages: location and view. Ask for a room on a higher floor; those overlooking the lake have balconies, and the other side opens onto the mountains. The rooms are functional, bright, and clean. Sadly, the hotel managers have opted for darker interiors in the public areas (except for the top-floor restaurant), with thick blinds that block out the marvelous view. Don't bother trying the Slovenka tavern on the side of the hotel—both the food and the atmosphere are abominable. ⊠ *Štrbské pleso,* ☎ 0969/92591, ⅋ 0969/92590. *150 rooms with bath. 3 restaurants, café. AE, DC, MC, V.*

$$ 🏨 **Fis.** Right next to the ski jump, within easy reach of several slopes, this hotel is for young, athletic types. It makes no pretense to elegance, preferring a busy jumble of track suits, families with young children, and teenagers on the make. The rooms, each with a balcony, are pleasant if a little institutional. The hotel also has bungalows for rent. ⊠ *Štrbské pleso,* ☎ 0969/92221, ⅋ 0969/92422. *2 restaurants, pool, sauna, exercise room. No credit cards.*

Nightlife and the Arts

Despite the crowds, nightlife in the Tatras is usually little more than a good meal and an evening stroll before bed. The best option is an evening at one of the small rustic restaurants listening to a live Gypsy band. For discos, check out the **Patria** and **Panoráma** hotels (☞ *above*).

Outdoor Activities and Sports

SKIING

You can buy skis and equipment, plus a thousand other things, in the department store **Javor** (☎ 0969/92835). The **Patria Hotel** (☞ *above*) also rents skis.

SLEDDING

There is a gentle slope for sledding at the Hotel Fis (☞ *above*). Although there is no place to rent sleds, you can buy one (or an easily transportable rubber coaster) at any department store.

Tatranská Lomnica

㉓ *16 km (10 mi) southwest of Štrbské pleso.*

Tatranská Lomnica, on the eastern end of the electric rail line, offers a near-perfect combination of peace, convenience, and atmosphere. Spread out and relatively remote, the town is frequently overlooked by the masses of students and merrymakers, so it has been more successful in retaining a feel of "exclusivity" without being any more expensive than the other towns. Moreover, the lift behind the Grandhotel Praha brings some of the best walks in the Tatras to within 10 minutes or so of your hotel door.

If you want to brush up on the area's varied flora and fauna, visit the **Museum Tatranského Národného Parku** (Museum of the Tatras National Park). Children will love the startlingly realistic stuffed animals on the first floor. The upper floor documents the life of local peasants, who still wear vibrantly colored traditional dress in many villages.⊠ *Tatranská Lomnica,* ☎ *0969/96795.* 🎟 *10 Sk.* ☉ *Weekdays 8:30–1 and 2–5; weekends 9–noon.*

The **Magistrale,** a 24-kilometer (15-mile) walking trail that skirts the peaks just above the tree line, offers some of the best views for the least amount of exertion. A particularly stunning stretch of the route—which is marked by red signposts—begins in Tatranská Lomnica and ends 5 kilometers (3 miles) away in Starý Smokovec. The total walking time is three or four hours.

To start the walk, take the aerial gondola behind the Grandhotel Praha in Tatranská Lomnica to Skalnaté pleso—a 10-minute proposition. From here you can access the trail immediately; or if you are really adventurous, consider a 30-minute detour via cable car (25 Sk.) to the top of Lomnický Štít (8,635 feet), the second-highest peak in the range. Because of the harsh temperatures (be sure to dress warmly even in summer) you're permitted to linger at the top for only 30 minutes, after which you take the cable car back down.

Return to the cable-car station at Skalnaté pleso and follow the red markers of the Magistrale Trail to the right (as you stand facing Tatranská Lomnica below). The first section of the trail cuts sharply across the face of the Lomnický Mountain just above the tree line. Note the little dwarf pines to the right and left of the trail. The trail then bends around to the right and again to the left through a series of small valleys, each view more outstanding than the last. Finally, you'll begin a small descent into the woods. Continue by following the signs to Hrebienok.

Don't pass up the chance to have a snack and a hot or cold drink at the rustic **Bilková Chata** (☎ 0969/2266) in a little clearing just before you reach Hrebienok. This cozy cabin is a veritable oasis after the long walk. It's open 7 AM to 8 PM.

From Hrebienok, take the funicular down to Starý Smokovec. It runs at 45-minute intervals beginning at 6:30 AM and ending at 7:45 PM, but check the schedule posted at the Bilková Chata for any schedule changes. The funicular drops you off in the center of Starý Smokovec, just behind the Grand Hotel close to the electric rail, which connects all the resort towns and can take you back to Tatranská Lomnica.

Dining and Lodging

$$ ✕ **Zbojnická Koliba.** This stylish cottage restaurant serves up savory shish kebab made on an open-face grill in a romantic setting, though the portions are snack-size. Stock up on the tasty bread and cheese appetizers. ⊠ *Tatranská Lomnica*, ☎ *0969/967630. No credit cards. Closed Sun. No lunch.*

$$$ ✕▦ **Grandhotel Praha.** This large, multiturreted mansion, dating from
★ the turn of the century and resting in the foothills of the Lomnický Štít, is one of the wonders of the Tatras. Although it is no longer filled with the rich and famous, the hotel has managed to retain an air of relaxed elegance. The staff is polite and attentive. The rooms are large and nicely decorated—ask for a large corner room with a view of the mountains. Since the hotel is far from the action, the price remains reasonable for what's offered. If you're planning on eating in the restaurant—where more attention is paid to atmosphere than food—be sure to arrive well before the 9 PM closing, or you'll be hustled out the door. As an added compensation, the cable car to the peak is only a five-minute walk away. ⊠ *Tatranská Lomnica*, ☎ *0969/967941*, ℻ *0969/967891. Restaurant, sauna, health club, nightclub. AE, MC, V.*

Nightlife and the Arts

For a night out, there's live dance music and a floor show in the **Grandhotel Praha** (☞ *above*) nightclub.

Outdoor Activities and Sports

SKIING

Moderately challenging slopes are found at the **Skalnaté pleso,** above Tatranská Lomnica.

Ždiar

24 *17 km (11 mi) from Tatranská Lomnica. To reach the village, leave Tatranská Lomnica heading east on Route 537 and turn left at Route 67 along the road to the Polish border.*

This tiny traditional village where you can still find horse-drawn carriages, high up in the mountains, is a welcome respite from the stale resort towns. The village is noted for its unique folk architecture—mostly enchanting, vibrantly painted wooden houses built in traditional peasant designs. If you'd like to spend the night here, you can stay in one of the handful of private bed-and-breakfasts scattered along Ždiar's two streets. The population of Ždiar is Polish in origin (the Polish border is less than 16 kilometers [10 miles] away), but the people have long considered themselves Slovak.

Stop in one of the houses that has been converted into a small folk museum, the **Ždiarska Izba,** which is by the church. ☎ *0969/98135.* ☉ *Nov.–Apr., weekdays 9–4; May–Oct., weekdays 9–5, weekends 9–2.*

From Ždiar, you can continue along Route 67 and cross over to Poland to visit the village's twin, **Javorina,** also known for its unique folk architecture. Along the way you may want to stop in some of the outlying towns around Ždiar, which are good sources for lace and other types of folk arts and crafts.

The High Tatras A to Z

Arriving and Departing

BY BUS

Daily bus service connects Prague and Bratislava with Poprad, but on this run trains tend to be quicker and more comfortable. From Prague the journey will take 10 hours or longer, depending on the route.

BY CAR

Poprad, the gateway to the Tatras, is 328 kilometers (205 miles) from Bratislava, with a four-lane stretch between the capital and Trenčín and a well-marked, two-lane highway thereafter. The drive to Poprad from Prague takes the main east–west highway about 560 kilometers (350 miles) from the Czech capital in the direction of Hradec Králové. The eight-hour drive from Prague is relatively comfortable, very scenic, and can be broken up easily with an overnight stay in Olomouc, in the Czech Republic province of Moravia. The road is well marked, with some four-lane stretches.

BY PLANE

ČSA, the Czech and Slovak national carrier, offers service to the Tatras city of Poprad from Prague and Bratislava. The flight from Prague takes a little over an hour. Unfortunately, at press time ÇSA had temporarily halted its flights directly to Poprad and instead was flying passengers to Košice and shuttling them to Poprad, about two hours away. If ÇSA is still not flying to the High Tatras, try Air Ostrava, which offers direct flights from Prague to Poprad. On arrival, take a taxi to your hotel or to the Poprad train station, where you can catch an electric train to the Tatras resorts.

BY TRAIN

Regular rail service connects both Prague and Bratislava with Poprad, but book ahead: The trains are often impossibly crowded, especially in August and during the skiing season. The journey from Prague to Poprad takes about 10 hours; several night trains depart from Prague's Hlavní nádraží (main station) and from Holešovice station.

Getting Around

BY BUS

The bus network links all the towns in the High Tatras, but unless you are traveling to a town not directly on an electric rail route, the train service is faster.

BY CAR

Having a car is more of a hindrance than a help if you're just going to the High Tatras. Traveling the electric railway is much quicker than taking the winding roads that connect the resorts, and hotel parking fees can add up quickly. However, if you plan to tour the region's smaller towns and villages, or if you are continuing on to eastern Slovakia, a car will prove nearly indispensable.

BY TRAIN

An efficient electric railway connects Poprad with the High Tatras resorts, and the resorts with one another. If you're going only to the Tatras, you won't need any other form of transportation.

Contacts and Resources

Police: ☎ 158. **Medical emergencies:** ☎ 2444. **Car repair:** ☎ 2704.

From Poprad airport, **Slovair** offers a novel biplane flight over the Tatras region; contact the Satur office in Poprad (☞ *below*). The Satur office in Starý Smokovec (☞ *below*) is also helpful in arranging tours of the Tatras and surrounding area. In summer, Satur offers a bargain tour of Levoča, Kežmarok, and Markušovice on Wednesday.

Pharmacies (*lekárna*) are in all three major resorts and in the neighboring town of Ždiar. The pharmacy in Nový Smokovec (☎ 0969/2577) maintains late hours.

There are tourist information centers in all the resort towns listed above: **Starý Smokovec** (✉ Dom Služieb—House of Services, ☎ 0969/3440); **Štrbskě pleso** (✉ Športový Areál—Sport Hall, ☎ 0969/92824); and **Tatranská Lomnica** (✉ Múseum, ☎ 0969/967951). **Slovakoturist** (☎ 0969/2827), a half kilometer east of Starý Smokovec in Horný Smokovec, can arrange private accommodations, including stays in mountain cottages.

You'll find **Satur offices** in **Poprad** (✉ Námestie sv. Egídia 2950, ☎ 092/721740 or 092/721353, FAX 092/63619); **Tatranská Lomnica** (☎ 0969/967451); and **Starý Smokovec** (☎ 0969/2950), where you can change money, get hiking and driving maps, and find assistance in booking hotels (but not private rooms).

For more in-depth information on routes, mountain chalets, and weather conditions, contact the **Mountain Rescue Service** (✉ Horská služba, ☎ 0969/2820) in Starý Smokovec. This office can also provide guides for the more difficult routes for around 500 Sk. per day.

Few books or pamphlets on the Tatras are available in English. One good overview of the area, including a list of services, hotels, and restaurants, is provided in the hard-to-find booklet *Everyman's Guide to the High Tatras*. Look for it at hotel gift shops.

CENTRAL SLOVAKIA

Though generally overlooked by tourists, central Slovakia is the country's heart and soul. This is where the nation was born and where Slovak folklore and deep-rooted traditions continue to flourish. The people of the towns and villages of this mountainous region have been cut off from the world and continue to live in much the same way they have for hundreds of years. Not surprisingly, the people of central Slovakia are highly patriotic, and the region is home to the country's more nationalistic leaders as well as the Matica Slovenská, a less-than-liberal organization set up to protect Slovak language and culture.

Formerly a medieval mining town, Banská Bystrica lies at the heart of the region and is the ideal base from which to explore the towns and villages surrounding it. The city has been successfully reviving some of its former beauty, but as in the country's other large cities, it is unable to lose the rows of apartments and factories, which haunt an otherwise attractive landscape. The region's two other historical mining towns, Banská Štavnica and Kremnica, have remained more or less frozen in time since their glory days in the Middle Ages. Don't overlook the wooden churches in the villages; the most interesting is perhaps the large 17th-century church at Hronsek.

The beauty of central Slovakia, however, lies not so much in its architecture as in its inspiring natural landscapes. The region is not only home to the High Tatras (☞ *above*), it also contains the Low Tatras, the second-highest mountain range in Slovakia and largest by area. With a range stretching from Banská Bystrica and Ružomberok in the west to Poprad and Švermovo in the east, the area is largely undeveloped, with only an occasional isolated village with wooden houses. If you like to get away from the crowds, this is the place to do it. The thick pine forests that cover the lower slopes are populated by bears, lynx, and wolves. In winter, some of the best skiing slopes in the country can be found in the Low Tatras, which are mostly free from the hordes of tourists migrating to the High Tatras. In summer, the area offers wonderful hiking trails, caves, and scenic valleys.

Unfortunately, in central Slovakia you will also find some of the worst crimes against nature. In an effort to enrich the region in the 1950s, the Communist regime built many large steel- and tank-producing factories, which litter some of the most beautiful valleys in the country. Many of the worst can be seen while heading east from Banská Bystrica in the direction of Brezno, though to call them an eyesore would be an understatement. Some of the hills that surround the area are blackened with ash, and while the factories now operate at a fraction of their previous levels, breathing the region's air remains far from pleasurable. So unless you'd like to become a revolutionary environmentalist overnight, stick to exploring the area north and south of Banská Bystrica.

Banská Bystrica

㉕ *124 km (77 mi) southwest of Poprad, 205 km (128 mi) east of Bratislava.*

Banská Bystrica is handsome despite the rows of concrete apartments and factories that plague the outlying area and detract from the rolling hills that engulf the town. Surrounded by three mountain ranges—the Low Tatras, the Fatras, and the Slovak Rudohorie—Banská Bystrica is in an ideal starting point for exploring the beauty of the region. The town's historical sites are few and are mostly on the massive main square, which always brims with life.

Banská Bystrica has been around since the 13th century, acquiring its wealth from the nearby mines. Following the Tatar invasion in 1241, the Hungarian king Belo IV granted special privileges to encourage the immigration of German settlers, who together with the natives developed the prosperous mining of copper and precious metals. Once the mines had been fully exploited, Banská Bystrica became known in Slovakia for its role in the revival of the Slovak language and culture. In 1785, Slovak writers gathered here to found the first Slovak literary review. During the 19th century, the town was a major focus of Slovak national life, and it was from a school here that the teaching of the Slovak language originated and spread to the rest of the country.

The city is also famous as the center of the Slovak National Uprising during World War II. It was here that the underground Slovak National Council initiated the revolt on August 29, 1944. For some two months, thousands of Slovaks valiantly rose up against the Slovak puppet regime and their Nazi oppressors, forcing the Germans to divert critically needed troops and equipment from the front lines. Though the Germans eventually quashed the uprising on October 27, the costly operation is credited with accelerating the Allied victory and gaining Slovakia the short-lived appellation of ally.

You'll find reminders of the uprising (known in Slovak by the initials SNP) just about everywhere. The mecca for fans is the **Múzeum Slovenského Národného Povstania** (Museum of the Slovak National Uprising), which stands in a large field just outside the center of town, between Horný ulica and Ulica Dukelských Hrdinov. It's difficult to miss the monument's massive concrete wings—surprisingly evocative of a captive people rising up to freedom. The effect is particularly striking at night. The museum itself isn't of much interest, however. At press time, it was busily changing its commentary, which until recently was exceedingly dull and heavily biased toward a Communist perspective. More telling, perhaps, is the absence of Slovak visitors; since the locals are no longer required to visit, the corridors are often empty. More interesting are the historic planes and tanks parked on the museum's front lawn. ⊠ *Kapitulská ul. 23,* ☎ *088/723558.* ▨ *10 Sk.* ☉ *Tues.–Sun. 9–4 (summer 9–6).*

If you're partial to less recent history, head for the main square, the Námestie SNP, with its cheery collection of Renaissance and baroque houses. The most impressive is the **Thurzo House,** an amalgamation of two late-Gothic structures built in 1495 by the wealthy Thurzo family. The genuine Renaissance sgraffiti on the outside were added during the 16th century, when the family's wealth was at its height. Today the building houses the **City Museum,** which is more interesting for the chance to see inside the house than for its artifacts. ⊠ *Námestie SNP 4,* ☎ *088/725897.* ▨ *10 Sk.* ☉ *Weekdays 8–noon and 1–4, Sun. 9–noon and 1–4; in summer, until 5.*

Cross the main square in front of the leaning 16th-century Hodinová veža (Clock Tower) and venture up the Jána Bakoša ulica to see the **Parish Church of the Virgin Mary,** near the town walls. The church was built in 1255 by prosperous German mine owners. Inside the church, in **St. Barbara's Chapel,** you'll find the town's greatest treasure: a beautiful late-Gothic altar, another wooden masterpiece carved by Pavol of Levoča. At the altar's center stands the figure of St. Barbara, the patron saint of miners. The church forms a unit with the other surviving structures of the former castle complex: the Gothic royal palace and the Praetorium (the former city hall).

OFF THE BEATEN PATH	**ŠPANIA DOLINA –** One of the more beautiful areas in Slovakia, Špania Dolina is in a valley of the same name in the Low Tatras National Park. This village is renowned for its lace making, and if you're there in the summer, you can see older women making tablecloths and other lace articles on their front porches. Špania Dolina is 8 miles (13 kilometers) north of Banská Bystrica along Route 59.

Dining and Lodging

$$ ✕ **Starobystrická Pivnica.** Grilled food is the house specialty at this clas-★ sic wine cellar that features a spicy version of Slovak cuisine. Try an excellent pepper steak with spicy sauce, or if you want to go all out, call in a day ahead and treat yourself to an elaborate fondue meal. ⊠ *Námestie SNP 89,* ☎ *088/54326. AE, MC, V.*

$ ✕ **Slovenská Restauracia.** This homey restaurant serves hearty meals ★ in classic Slovak pottery in a village-style atmosphere. You can have the usual specialties—brinzové halušky or *strapačky plnene s kyslou kapustou*—but under no circumstances should you leave the restaurant without trying the *buchty na pare s kakaom.* This heavenly treat—plump, doughnut-size dumplings filled with fruit and covered with chocolate—is eaten as a main course, but feel free to have it as a dessert instead. ⊠ *Lazovná 18,* ☎ *088/53716. No credit cards.*

$$$ ✕▥ **Arcade Hotel.** This 16th-century building on the main square is
★   an ideal place to stay in Banská Bystrica. The rooms and apartments vary in size, comfort, and cost, but all are equipped with the basic creature comforts, including a fridge and satellite TV. Check out the bar for its bizarre interior, then head down to the beautifully designed stone wine cellar for a drink or a meal. ⊠ *Námestie SNP 5,* ☎ *088/702111,* ℻ *088/723126. Restaurant, bar, café, wine cellar, meeting room. AE, DC, MC, V.*

$$ ▥ **Lux.** On the edge of town, the Lux is one of the few successful high-rise hotels in Slovakia, managing to combine modernity with some semblance of style. The rooms (especially on the upper floors facing town) have a magnificent view over the mountains, enlivened at night by the Museum of the Slovak National Uprising glowing in the foreground. The elegant restaurant serves a good range of Slovak specialties. Breakfast is included. ⊠ *Nové nám. 2,* ☎ *088/724141,* ℻ *088/743853. 120 rooms with bath. Restaurant, bar, café. AE, DC, MC, V.*

$$ ▥ **Urpín.** Here you'll find clean rooms in an older, somewhat neglected hotel a block away from the city center. Breakfast is included. ⊠ *Ul. Jána Cikkera 5,* ☎ *088/724556,* ℻ *088/23731. 45 rooms, some with shower. No credit cards.*

$ ▥ **Motel Ul'anka.** This inexpensive motel, 6 kilometers (4 miles) outside town on the road to Ružomberok, is a good alternative for budget-minded travelers with a car. The surrounding mountain scenery is magnificent, but the rooms are only adequate. The motel has strict rules similar to a youth hostel. ⊠ *Ul'anská cesta,* ☎ *088/53657. 50 rooms without bath. No credit cards.*

Outdoor Activities and Sports

The mountainous region surrounding Banská Bystrica is ideal for all sorts of outdoor activities, from walking to skiing. In summer, the mountains have beautiful hiking and biking trails that link caves and natural lakes. The most attractive hiking trails are to the north of Banská Bystrica and in the area between Banská Bystrica and Kremnica. There is a hiking map of the Low Tatras, which includes routes for cyclists, available at tourist information (you can inquire here about bike rentals, too, since not many places rent them).

Nightlife and the Arts

The best bet for entertainment is seeing an opera or a ballet at the **Štátna Opera** (⊠ Národná 11, ☎ 088/724418) or seeing a puppet show at the **Bábkové Divadlo na Rázcestí** (⊠ Kollárova 18, ☎ 088/24567 or 088/193724). Another option is spending an evening in one of the city's wine cellars, listening to Gypsy music.

En Route   South of Banská Bystrica in the direction of Zvolen is the tiny village of **Hronsek.** This hamlet certainly warrants a stop—it has a wooden church built without a single piece of metal. The builders of this Protestant church, which was constructed at the time of the Counter-Reformation, abided by strict guidelines stipulating that wood was the only material to be used for building a church—even nails had to be made of wood!

Kremnica

②⑥   *Head south out of Banská Bystrica via busy Route 66. Bypass Zvolen, following the signs in the direction of Žiar, turning finally to the right on Route 65 when you see the sign to Kremnica. The drive through the mountains is about 50 km (31 mi) and can be done in under an hour.*

Kremnica, known as the Golden City, was one of the most famous mining towns in Slovakia and one of the richest gold mines in medieval Europe. But the city never developed any political or cultural ambitions, and most of the wealth generated here was carted away to build glorious structures elsewhere in the then-Hungarian kingdom. What you'll find today is a beautifully preserved medieval town, surrounded by sturdy walls and gates that guarded the gold once stored in Kremnica's vaults. You can enter the town through the impressive **Dolná Brána** (Lower Gate), dating from 1441. Past the gate you'll come to the grassy main square. Here you'll see some of the best-kept merchant houses in Slovakia.

You can learn about the town's 650-year history as a mining and minting center at the **Kremnica Museum.** For coin enthusiasts, the second floor has fascinating exhibits of coins in use in Central Europe from Celtic and Roman times to the modern day. The 30-minute English commentary on tape (ask the attendant), which booms throughout the museum as you walk from room to room, is helpful but hard to follow. ⊠ *Štefanikové nám. 10,* ☎ *0857/742696.* 🎟 *4 Sk.* ☉ *Tues.–Sat. 8– 4:30 (summer Tues.–Sat. 8:30–1 and 1:30–5; Sun. 9–1 and 1:30–3).*

The town square is dominated by the former **town castle,** dating from the 13th century and once used for storing gold. The castle is one of the finest in Slovakia and includes a late-Romanesque tower and a Gothic two-aisle church. At press time, parts of the castle were under construction. ⊠ *Hrad,* ☎ *0857/743968.* 🎟 *20 Sk.* ☉ *May–Sept., Tues.–Sun. 9–5; Oct.–Apr., Tues–Sat. 8:30–4:30.*

Dining

$ ✕ **Jelen.** For a delicious lunch or dinner, try this unassuming restaurant in the new part of town, outside the walls. Although it looks like any ordinary beer hall, the food is several notches above the usual fare. Start out with the delicious lentil soup, then try the roast beef with paprika sauce and dumplings. ⊠ *Dolná ul. 22,* ☎ *0857/744003.*

Banská Štiavnica

㉗ *42 km (26 mi) south of Kremnica, 45 km (28 mi) south of Banská Bystrica, along small but well-marked roads.*

Picturesque Banská Štiavnica is in a small valley among rolling hills. Since the 11th century, the town has earned its wealth from mining, and today it is essentially one large mining museum. German miners arrived here to exploit rich gold and silver deposits, and their success is apparent in some of the town's remaining monuments, such as the golden Trinity column and the impressive Lutheran church. The area surrounding the city, especially to the south, has some great hiking trails.

Built on the rocks above town, the **Old Castle** dates back to the early 13th century and has additions in practically every subsequent building style. It served as a fortress to protect the wealth of the local bigwigs against the Turkish invaders. After much reconstruction, it partially opened its doors to the public in May 1996. ⊠ *Starozámocká 11,* ☎ *0859/23103.* 🎟 *10 Sk.* ☉ *June–Aug., daily 8–4.*

The **New Castle** was built between 1564 and 1571 as part of an effort to strenghten fortification of the town against invasions from the Turks. The six-story Renaissance building was used as a watch tower and later it became the town's live clock—the exact time was announced every quarter hour by a trumpet. Inside you'll find historical exhibits of the Turkish invasions in the 16th and 17th centuries, including life-size statues of Turks dressed in full battle regalia. ⊠ *Novozámocká 22,* ☎ *0859/21543.* 🖃 *20 Sk.* ⊘ *May–Sept., daily 8–4; Oct.–Apr., weekdays 8–3.*

You can view some of the town's original mining buildings and machinery dating back to the early 13th century at the **Open Air Mining Museum.** There is also a tour of a mining shaft, which lets you see the conditions under which medieval miners worked. The museum is about 2 kilometers from town in the direction of Štavnické Bane. ☎ *0859/22971.* 🖃 *30 Sk.* ⊘ *May–Sept., Tues.–Sun. 8–4.*

OFF THE **CHATEAU AT ANTOL –** Don't miss this charming late-baroque château,
BEATEN PATH which was built in 1750 on the site of a 15th-century castle in the small
village of Antol, just outside Banská Štavnica. The château displays its
original furnishings and has an exhibition on hunting arms and game.
Take a look at the fresco paintings in the interior of the chapel. If the
weather's agreeable, walk through the park and see the giant sequoia
planted in 1878. ⊠ *Antol,* ☎ *0859/239.* ⊘ *May–Sept., Tues.–Sun.
8:30–4; Oct.–Apr., Tues.–Sat. 8–3.*

Dining and Lodging

$$ ✕🖬 **Antolský Mlín.** This small family-run pension, in a tiny village just outside Banská Štavnica near the château at Antol, is a pleasant place to overnight. The owners are so attentive you'll feel as if you're visiting a dear aunt or uncle. Though small, the rooms are modern and have new, clean bathrooms. The homey restaurant will serve anything you wish (within reason) according to your taste—that means local cuisine, of course, no burger and fries here! ⊠ *Antol,* ☎ *0859/621011. Restaurant. No credit cards.*

$$ ✕🖬 **Salamander.** This brand new hotel, in a beautifully renovated 16th-
★ century building, has everything you would expect from a first-class establishment, including impeccable service. The rooms are large and bright, and the public areas are decorated with antiques. Don't let the cheap price here fool you. This hotel draws many glamorous guests, including the president of Slovakia. ⊠ *Paláriková 1,* ☎ *0859/23992,* 🖷 *0859/621262, Restaurant, ice cream parlor, outdoor café, wine cellar. AE, MC, V.*

Central Slovakia A to Z

Arriving and Departing

Unless you have a car, the best means of arriving in Banská Bystrica is by rail. There are daily trains from Bratislava, and the journey takes almost three hours. The trip from Kosice to Banská Bystrica, one of the most scenic railway routes in the country (take the northern, not the southern, route), lasts about five hours.

Getting Around

For those without a car, Banská Bystrica is an especially convenient spot from which to discover the region, since it serves as a hub for the complex rail and bus system and allows for easier access to the smaller destinations.

Contacts and Resources

EMERGENCIES
Police: ☎ 158. **Ambulance:** ☎ 155.

GUIDED TOURS
The **Satur** office in Banská Bystrica (✉ Nám. Slobody 4, ☎ 088/742525) can book hotels and arrange tours at a reasonable cost.

VISITOR INFORMATION
Banská Bystrica: ✉ Nám. SNP 1, ☎ 088/54369. ☉ June–Aug., weekdays 7:30–6; Oct.–May, 7:30–4:30; **Kremnica:** ✉ Štefánikovo nám. 35/44, ☎ 0857/742856. ☉ Weekdays 9–5; **Banská Štavnica:** ✉ Radničné nám. 1, ☎ 0859/21859. ☉ Late May–early Sept., Mon.–Sun. 8–6; late Sept.–early May, weekdays 8–4.

EASTERN SLOVAKIA

To the east of the High Tatras lies an expanse of Slovakia that seldom appears on tourist itineraries. Here, the High Tatras' mountains become hills that gently stretch to the Ukrainian border, with few "musts" for visitors in between.

However, eastern Slovakia is an especial must for the outdoors enthusiast. The region is a veritable hiker's paradise. In addition to the offerings at Slovenský Raj, trails fan out in all directions in the area known as Spišská Magura, to the north and east of Kežmarok. Good outdoor swimming can be found in the lakes in Slovenský Raj and in Michalovce, east of Košice.

For 1,000 years, eastern Slovakia was isolated from the West; much of the region was regarded simply as the hinterland of Greater Hungary. The great movements of European history—the Reformation and the Renaissance—made their impact here as elsewhere on the continent, but in a muted and diluted form.

Isolation can have its advantages, however, and therein may lie the special charm of this area for the visitor. The baroque and Renaissance facades that dominate the towns of Bohemia and Moravia make an appearance in eastern Slovakia as well, but early artisans working in the region often eschewed the stone and marble preferred by their western counterparts in favor of wood and other local materials. Look especially for the wooden altars in Levoča and other towns.

The relative isolation also fostered the development of an entire civilization in medieval times, the Spiš, with no counterpart in the Czech Republic or even elsewhere in Slovakia. The territory of the kingdom, which spreads out to the east and south of the High Tatras, was originally settled by Slavonic and later by German immigrants who came here in medieval times to work the mines and defend the western kingdoms against invasion. Some 24 towns eventually came to join the Spiš group, functioning as a miniprincipality within the Hungarian monarchy. The group had its own hierarchies and laws, which were quite different from those brought in by Magyar or Saxon settlers. They also enjoyed many privileges denied to other cities and could choose their own count to represent them before the Hungarian king.

As the mines thrived, Spiš power and influence reached its height. But the confederation also had its bad times. In 1412, the Holy Roman Emperor Sigismund, king of Hungary, decided to sell 13 of the towns to his brother-in-law, the king of Poland, in order to finance a war with Venice. The split lasted until 1769, when the towns were reunited with one another. In 1876, the last of the Spiš towns lost its privileges, and the German speakers in the area were forced to learn Hungarian or emigrate—mainly to the United States. In 1919, when Slovakia became part of the new Czechoslovak state, the German speakers were again allowed to establish German schools, but in 1945 almost all of them were forced to leave the country because of their real or suspected collaboration with the Nazis.

Although the last Spiš town lost its independence 100 years ago, much of the group's architectural legacy remains—another fortuitous by-product of isolation, namely economic stagnation. Spiš towns are predominantly Gothic beneath their graceful Renaissance overlays. Their steep shingled roofs, high timber-framed gables, and brick-arched doorways have survived in a remarkable state of preservation. Gothic churches with imposing Renaissance bell towers are other major features of the area, as are some quite stunning altarpieces and exquisite wood carvings. Needless to say, Spiš towns are worth seeking out when you see them on a map; look for the prefix "Spišsky" in a town name.

Farther to the northeast, the influences of Byzantium are strongly felt, most noticeably in the form of the simple wooden churches that dominate the villages along the frontier with Poland and Ukraine. This area marks a border in Europe that has stood for a thousand years: the ancient line between Rome and Constantinople, between Western Christianity and the Byzantine Empire. Many churches here were built by members of the Uniat Church, Christians who acknowledge the supremacy of the Pope but retain their own organization and liturgy.

The busy industrial cities of Prešov and Košice, with their belching factories and rows of housing projects, quickly bring you back to the 20th century. Although these cities do bear signs of the region's historical complexity, come here instead for a taste of modern Slovakia, of a relatively poor country that is just beginning to shed a long legacy of foreign domination.

When visiting the region, keep in mind that more expensive does not necessarily mean better when it comes to food. Stay clear of the large hotels, some of which are state-owned, and instead, look to innovative, privately owned restaurants. Eastern Slovakia has successfully borrowed the best dishes and techniques from the Hungarians, the Ukrainians, and the Poles to create an original and delicious cuisine. Treat yourself to a some local specialties—try *palacinky* (crepes with fruit or jam stuffing) or *buchty* (puffy homemade doughnuts filled with fruit). You may gain a few pounds on your travels, but it's well worth it. Besides, hiking in the mountains will balance everything out.

Kežmarok

28 *15 km (9 mi) from Poprad driving northeast via Route 67, 320 km (199 mi) east of Bratislava.*

Kežmarok was once the great "second town" of the Spiš region. Founded by German settlers in the 12th century, the town for years competed—ultimately unsuccessfully—with Levoča to become the capital of this minikingdom. The main sights of Kežmarok today, however, have less to do with the Spiš tradition than with the town's later role within Greater Hungary.

You can't miss the enormous Gothic-Renaissance **Tokolyho hrad** (Tököly Palace), east of the main square. It was from here in the late 17th century that Count Imre Tököly launched his unsuccessful uprising against the Hapsburgs to form an independent Hungarian state in "Upper Hungary" (present-day Slovakia). The count initially enjoyed great success and soon united all of Upper Hungary, but he made the fateful decision to depend on the Ottoman Empire for support in his war. When the Turks were finally defeated by the Hapsburgs in 1683 at the city walls of Vienna, the Hapsburgs had the count condemned to death. Tököly escaped to Turkey, where he died in exile in 1705.

In the 19th century, the castle served as a barracks and was even used for a time as a textile factory. Today it houses a small museum of the town's history, with a cozy wine cellar in the basement. In summer, concerts are held in the castle chapel and courtyard. ⊠ *Hradné nám. 42,* ☎ *0968/2698.* ⊡ *28 Sk.* ☉ *Summer, tours every ½ hr, Tues.–Sun. 9– noon and 1:30–4; rest of yr, tours every hr, Tues.–Sat. 9–11 and 1–4.*

The **Kostol svätého kríža** (Church of the Holy Cross) is a Gothic structure with impressive netted vaulting that dates from the beginning of the 15th century. The designs on the 16th-century bell tower, with its tin crown, are characteristic of the so-called Spiš Renaissance style. The large and handsome main square, befitting Kežmarok's history as a leader among the Spiš towns, is just a couple of minutes' walk from the church. ⊠ *Nová ul.* ⊡ *Free.* ☉ *Weekdays 9–noon and 2–5.*

The wooden **Protestant Church** stands just outside the former city walls a few blocks west of the main square. The church owes its existence to a congress held in 1681 in Sopron, Hungary, where it was decided that Protestants living on then-Hungarian lands could have their own churches only if the churches were outside the town boundaries and were constructed completely of wood (without even iron nails or stone foundations). In 1717, Kežmarok's Protestants lovingly built this structure from red pine and yew, fashioning its gracious vaulting from clay. The church could accommodate some 1,000 worshipers. But the once idyllic setting has long since yielded to urban sprawl, and the church itself has been covered over in stone to protect the interior, so what you see today is something of a letdown. Still, next to the pompous pink-and-green Evangelical Church next door, built at the end of the last century in neo–*Arabian Nights* style, the church's elegant simplicity is still affecting. ⊠ *Hlavné nám.* ☉ *Daily 8–noon and 1–5.*

Dining and Lodging

$$ ✕⊡ **Hotel Club.** This bright, pinkish-blue hotel in the center of Kežmarok is a decent place to stay. The rooms are plainly furnished, but have modern bathrooms. Try the restaurant (look up to see the ornate carved-wood ceilings) or the cozy wine cellar, both of which serve good Slovak and Continental fare at reasonable prices. ⊠ *MUDr. Alexandra 24,* ☎ *968/4051,* ⅢX *968/4053. Restaurant, wine cellar. No credit cards.*

Bardejov

㉙ *88 km (55 mi) east of Kežmarok.*

Bardejov is a great surprise, tucked away in this remote corner of Slovakia yet possessing one of the nation's most enchanting squares. Indeed, Bardejov owes its splendors precisely to its location astride the ancient trade routes to Poland and Russia. It's hard to put your finger on exactly why the square is so captivating. Maybe it's the lack of arcades in front of the houses, which while impressive, can sometimes overburden the squares of Bohemian and Moravian towns. It could also be the pointed roofs of the houses, which have a lighter, almost comic effect.

The exterior of the Gothic **Kostol svätého Egídia** (St. Egidius Church), built in stages in the 15th century, is undeniably handsome, but take a walk inside for the real treasure. The nave is lined with 11 priceless Gothic side altars, all carved between 1460 and 1510 and perfectly preserved. Here you get pure Gothic, with no Renaissance or Baroque details to dampen the effect.

The most famous of the altars is to the left of the main altar (look for the number 1 on the side). The intricate work of Stefan Tarner, it depicts the birth of Christ and dates from the 1480s. Other noteworthy carvings are the figure of St. Barbara and the *Vir dolorum,* both to the right of the main altar, but in fact all of them are vividly detailed and merit close inspection. The Gothic pulpit, to the side of the nave, is as old as the church itself. The early baroque pews, with their sensuous curves, must have caused quite a sensation when they were added in about 1600. ⊠ *Radničné nám.*

The modest building with late-Gothic portals and Renaissance detailing in the center of the town square is the **town hall** (Radnice). Compared to the dark and imposing Gothic town halls in Bohemia and Moravia, this smaller, more playful structure is a breath of fresh air.

★ You may want to visit the pink **Šariš Icon Museum** on the south side of the main square to view its collection of 16th-century icons and paintings, taken from the area's numerous Russian Orthodox churches. The museum provides a fascinating look at the religious motifs of the surrounding area from between the 16th and 19th centuries. Pick up the short but interesting commentary in English (5 Sk.) when you buy your ticket. Many of the icons feature the story of St. George slaying the dragon (for the key to the princess's chastity belt!). The legend of St. George, which probably originated in pre-Christian mythology, was often used to attract the peasants of the area to the more abstemious myths of Christianity.

Take a close look at the icon of the Last Judgment on the second floor for what it reveals of this area's practices and fashions in the 16th century. The complex morality of the subject matter reflects quite sophisticated beliefs. Also on the second floor are models of the wooden churches that dot the surrounding countryside, the sources of many of these icons and paintings. ⊠ *Radničné nám. 13,* ☎ *0935/2009.* ⊠ *10 Sk.* ☾ *Tues.–Sun. 8:30–11:30 and 12:30–4:30 (summer 9–6).*

The **Rhody House** is Bardejov's best remaining example of Renaissance relief work. The structure, essentially Gothic but with reliefs added in the 16th century, was one of the few in the city center to survive the great fire of 1878. Continue down the Rhodyho to Na Hradbach to see the town walls, built in the middle of the 14th century. Some eight of the 23 original bastions are still standing, mostly along the south and east walls.

En Route Leave the Bardejov area along Route 77, heading north and east in the direction of Svidník. This is really where *eastern* Slovakia, with its strong Byzantine influence, begins. The colors seem wilder here; the villages also look poorer, reflecting the area's physical—and cultural—insularity. Both the Orthodox and Uniat faiths are strong in these parts, echoing the work of Byzantine missionaries more than a millennium ago.

Dining and Lodging

$ ✕▥ **Republika.** This depressing socialist-realist structure is an acceptable alternative for travelers without a car. The hallways are cluttered with mismatched furniture; and the rooms, though clean, show a similar lack of forethought. The big advantage is location: A couple of steps and you're in Bardejov's beautiful medieval square. ⊠ *Nám. Oslboditel'ov,* ☎ *0935/2721,* ▣ *0935/2657. 30 rooms, some with shower. Restaurant. No credit cards.*

Bardejovské Kúpele

6½ km (4 mi) north of Bardejov, off Route 77.

Though it is no longer the favorite haunt of Hungarian counts, this old spa town is still a pleasant enough place to stroll around and take in the fresh air from the surrounding hills. Don't expect lots of beautiful architecture unless you're a fan of "postwar modern." The town was built up rapidly after the war to serve as a retreat for the proletariat, and little of its aristocratic heritage remains. Be sure to walk behind the space-age colonnade to view a lovely wooden Russian Orthodox church from the 18th century along with some older wooden houses that form an open-air museum. The church was brought here in 1932 as a specimen of the "primitive" age. Ironically, the 226-year-old structure is holding up markedly better than the 20-year-old buildings from the "advanced" culture surrounding it.

Dining and Lodging

$$ ✕⊡ **Mineral.** Despite its location in a 19th-century spa town, this aging 1970s structure is fairly charmless. Yet as Bardejov lacks decent hotels, there aren't many choices. The rooms, some with a nice view over the spa area, are acceptably clean, and the restaurant serves a good breakfast. ⊠ *Bardejovské Kúpele,* ☎ *0935/724122. 50 rooms with bath. Restaurant, nightclub. No credit cards.*

Jedlinka

③⓪ *13 km (8 mi) north of Bardejov along the road to Svidník, 12 km (7½ mi) from Bardejovské Kúpele.*

The area's great delights are unquestionably the old wooden churches still in use in their original village settings. Like most, the one in Jedlinka dates from the 18th and 19th centuries and combines Byzantine and baroque architectural elements. Its three onion-domed towers rise above the west front. Inside, the north, east, and south walls are painted with Biblical scenes; the west wall was reserved for icons (many of which now hang in the icon museum in Bardejov). The churches are usually locked, and you'll need some luck to see the inside. If you happen across a villager, ask him or her (with appropriate key-turning gestures) to let you in. More often than not, someone will turn up with a key, and you'll have your own guided tour. If you see a collection plate inside, make a small donation—though there is no pressure to do so.

OFF THE **DUKELSKÝ PRIESMYK –** World War II buffs will want to complete the drive
BEATEN PATH north of Svidník to the Dukelský Priesmyk (Dukla Pass) on the Polish border. It was here in late 1944 that Soviet troops, along with detachments of Czech and Slovak resistance fighters, finally made their long-awaited advance to liberate Czechoslovakia from the Nazis. Most of the fighting took place between the town of Krajná Pol'ana and the border. Alongside the many war monuments, which are in odd juxtaposition to the tranquil loveliness of the wooden churches, you'll find bunkers, trenches, and watchtowers. The Germans mustered far more resistance than expected during the battle, and the number of dead on both sides grew to more than 100,000. Near the top of the pass, a great monument and cemetery commemorate the fallen Slovaks; their leader, General Ludvík Svoboda, went on to become president of the reborn Czechoslovak state.

En Route There are about a score of Uniat churches in the countryside north of Svidník, itself an uninteresting town destroyed during World War II and completely rebuilt in the 1960s. Consider seeking out the churches in the villages of **Ladomirová, Hunkovce,** and **Nižný Komárnik.** Venture off the main road to see more churches at **Bodružal, Mirol'a, Príkra,** and **Šemetkovce**—but be sure to take along a good map.

Medzilaborce

㉛ *40 km (25 mi) east of Svidník, 70 km (43 mi) east of Bardejov.*

The sleepy border town of Medzilaborce is quickly becoming the unlikely mecca for fans of pop-art guru Andy Warhol. It was here in 1991, near the birthplace of Warhol's parents, that the country's cultural authorities, in conjunction with the Andy Warhol Foundation for Visual
★ Arts in New York, opened the **Warhol Family Museum of Modern Art.** In all, the museum holds 17 original Warhol silkscreens, including two from the famous Campbell's Soup series, and portraits of Lenin and singer Billie Holiday. The Russian Orthodox church across the street lends a suitably surreal element to the setting. ⊠ *10 Sk.* ☉ *Daily 10–5.*

Prešov

㉜ *85 km (53 mi) southwest of Medzilaborce.*

Prešov is a lively town and the center of Ukrainian culture in Slovakia. Its other claim to fame is a little controversial now that the Communists have been ousted from power. It was here in 1919, from the black wrought-iron balcony at Hlavná ulica 73, that enthusiastic Communists proclaimed their own Slovak Soviet Republic in 1919, just 17 months after the Bolshevik Revolution in Russia. This early attempt at communism lasted three weeks. The balcony is still lit up at night, but in 1990 the name of the square—Slovak Soviet Republic (SSR for short)—was quickly changed back to Main Street.

Dining and Lodging

$$ ✕🏨 **Dukla.** Just down the main road from the center of town and right next to the theater, this hotel is a modern structure that works. The staff is friendly; the rooms, though nothing special, are comfortable and clean, with very immaculate bathrooms. Some rooms have balconies. ⊠ *Nám. Legionárov 2,* ☎ *091/22741–2,* 🖷 *091/32134. 89 rooms with bath. Restaurant, snack bar.*

$ ✕🏨 **Šariš.** Though it is a little removed from the city center, the Šariš has facilities—including bike rentals—that you do not often find at a budget hotel. The staff is friendly and helpful, and the rooms, though small, have refrigerators. The bathrooms, however, are a bit on the old and worn side. ⊠ *Sabinovská ul. 1,* ☎ *091/46351,* 🖷 *091/46551. 110 rooms with bath. Restaurant, bar. No credit cards.*

Košice

㉝ *30 km (19 mi) south of Prešov, 418 km (259 mi) east of Bratislava.*

In Košice you'll leave rural Slovakia behind. Traffic picks up, the smog settles in, and the high-rise apartment buildings of the suburbs suddenly seem to stretch out for miles. Though rich historically, Košice is a sprawling, modern city, the second largest in Slovakia after Bratislava. The city has always had an antagonistic relationship with the capital. No celebrations were held here when Slovakia became independent; the locals, who see themselves as more cosmopolitan, preferred the rule of Prague to that of Bratislava.

Positioned along the main trade route between Hungary and Poland, the city was the second largest in the Hungarian Empire (after Buda) during the Middle Ages. With the Turkish occupation of the Hungarian homeland in the 16th and 17th centuries, the town became a safe haven for the Hungarian nobility. Inevitably, however, it fell into economic decline as trade with Hungary came to a standstill. Relief did not come until 1861, with the advent of the railroad.

In this century the city has been shuttled between Hungary, Czechoslovakia, and now Slovakia. Sadly, Slovak efforts to eliminate Hungarian influence in Košice after World War II were remarkably successful. As you walk around, you'll be hard-pressed to find evidence that this was once a great Hungarian city—even with the Hungarian frontier just 20 kilometers (12 miles) away. Still, many of the older generation speak Hungarian, and the small Hungarian community in Košce is putting up a strong fight to retain Hungarian schools and maintain some of the diminishing government support for cultural activities. The city remains home to a popular Hungarian theater, as well as a successful Romany (Gypsy) theater, the only one of its kind in the world.

You won't see many Westerners strolling Košice's enormous medieval square, the **Hlavná ulica**; most of the tourists here are Hungarians on a day trip to shop and sightsee. The town square is dominated on its ★ southern flank by the huge tower of the Gothic **Dóm svätej Alžbety** (Cathedral of St. Elizabeth). Built in the 15th century and finally completed in 1508, the cathedral is the largest in Slovakia. First walk over to the north side (facing the square) to look at the famed Golden Door. The reputed friend of the sick and aged, St. Elizabeth stands in the middle of the portal. The reliefs above her depict her good works.

Inside the church is one of Europe's largest Gothic altarpieces, 35 feet tall. It is a monumental piece of medieval wood carving attributed to the master Erhard of Ulm. You can also pay a visit to the great Hungarian leader Francis Rakóczi II, most of whose remains (he left his heart in Paris) were placed in a crypt under the north transept of the cathedral. Although generally open to worshipers, the church is under renovation, and you may not be able to wander at will. ⊠ *Hlavná ul.* ☺ *Daily services at 7 PM.*

The **Urbanová veža** (Urbans' Tower), next door to the Cathedral of St. Elizabeth, is a 14th-century bell tower remodeled in Renaissance style in 1612. But much of what you see today isn't much more than 30 years old. In 1966 the tower burned and had to be rebuilt. It now houses a permanent exhibition of bell making, but don't waste your time climbing to the top unless you're interested in forging and casting techniques. The view is disappointing and can't compensate for the eight floors of bell and iron exhibits you'll be subjected to on your way there. ⊠ *Hlavná ul.* ☎ *5 Sk.* ☺ *Tues.–Sat. 9–5, Sun. 9–1.*

Kaplnka svätého Michala (St. Michael's Chapel) dates from around 1260. A relief on the portal shows the archangel Michael weighing the souls of the dead. On the east side of the town square is the **Dom Košického vládneho programu** (House of the Košice Government Program), which played an important role in the final days of World War II. It was from here that the Košice Program was proclaimed on April 5, 1945, announcing the reunion of the Czech lands and Slovakia into one national state.

The **Štátne divadlo** (State Theater), a mishmash of neo-Renaissance and neobaroque elements built at the end of the last century, dominates the center of the town square. The deliberate imitation of earlier architectural styles was all the rage in the Hapsburg Empire at the time; indeed, the building would be equally at home on Vienna's Ringstrasse. The theater's interior is elaborately decorated with plaster ornaments. Notice the paintings on the ceilings by Viennese artist P. Gastgeb. For a town this size, the quality of theater, ballet, and opera productions is very impressive. Tickets are reasonably priced and can be bought at the theater box office. ⊠ *Hlavná ul. 58,* ☎ *095/6221231.* ☉ *Weekdays 1–6, or 1 hr before performances.*

To the right of the State Theater, the impressive **rococo palace** at Hlavná ulica 59, which once housed the city's wealthiest nobility, was the unlikely site of a Slovak Soviet Republic congress in 1919, just a week before the revolutionary movement was aborted. The relief on the house has nothing to do with communism but recalls the stay here of the Russian commander Mikhail Kutuzov, who in 1805 led the combined Russian-Austrian forces in battle against Napoléon at Austerlitz.

On the main street between the theater and the cathedral is the **Music Fountain.** Water from this elaborate fountain springs in harmony with music (generally classical), accompanied by colored lights. It's worth a visit in the evening just to see all the pairs of lovers huddled around it.

NEED A
BREAK?   To feel like you've really stepped into turn-of-the-century Vienna, have a cup of coffee and dessert in the elegant art-nouveau confines of the **Café Slavia** (⊠ Hlavná ul. 63, ☎ 095/6224395).

Take a glance at the beautifully painted **Beggar's House** (⊠ Hlavná ul. 71). According to legend, the owner of the house, who was once a beggar, had a statue made of himself. Look to the top of the house, where he tips his hat to everyone who ever gave him money.

From the town square, take a right at E. Adyho ulica and continue to the end of the street to the town walls. In the 16th and 17th centuries, these bastions—which date from the 1200s—helped secure Košice as a safe haven for the Hungarian nobility; it was from here that they launched their attacks on the Turks occupying the Hungarian motherland.

The **Miklusova väznica** (Nicholas Prison), an old Gothic building used as a prison and torture chamber until 1909, now houses a museum with exhibits on Košice's history. The underground premises of the former torture chamber are open to the public. ⊠ *Pri Mikluśovej väznici 10,* ☎ *095/6222856.* ⊡ *20 Sk.* ☉ *Tues.–Sat. 9–5 (summer also Sun. 1–5).*

OFF THE
BEATEN PATH   **HERL'ANY GEYSER** – This geyser, with water shooting up nearly 130 feet for about 20 minutes, is an interesting day trip from Košice—it's about 30 kilometers (20 miles) from the city. The geyser has an eruption interval of 32 to 36 hours. Check with the **Satur** office in Košice (☞ Eastern Slovakia A to Z, *below*) for the expected eruption times. To get here, follow Route 50 east out of the city, making a right at Route 576 and following the signs.

KRÁSNA HÔRKA – Sitting on top of a hill, this fairy-tale castle can be seen from miles around. It is one of the best-preserved fortifications from the Middle Ages in Slovakia. The museum houses a valuable collection of paintings and a wide assortment of furniture and weapons from the 15th through 17th centuries. Below the castle is a beautiful art-nouveau mausoleum. To get here, head west on E57 in the direction of Rožnava and turn right at Krásnohradské Podhradie from where you can follow signs up to the castle; it takes about an hour from Košice. ⊠ *Krásnohradské Podhradie,* ☎ *0942/24769.* ☉ *Tues.–Sun. 8–5:30.*

Dining and Lodging

$ ✗ **Slovenská Reštauracia.** This tiny restaurant, decorated as an old country cottage complete with wooden tables, a pitchfork, and a picket fence,
★   serves mouthwatering local specialties. If you don't mind rolling out of the establishment, try one of the meals for two. You'll receive an

enormous plate piled high with various meats and either rice, mushrooms, and cheese or dumplings and red and white cabbage. ⊠ *Biela 3,* ☎ *095/6220402. No credit cards.*

$$$ ✕🏨 **Pensión pri Radnici.** This small pension is ideal for business travelers—modern apartments come with studies and fax machines. The upstairs restaurant is a bit upscale. If you want a quick lunch, try the buffet downstairs, which serves tasty local food at dirt-cheap prices. ⊠ *Bačíková 18,* ☎ *095/6228601,* ꜰᴀx *095/6227824. 3 apartments. Restaurant, beer garden, café, cafeteria. AE, MC, V.*

$$$ 🏨 **Hotel Cobra.** This hotel is a breath of fresh air when compared to ★ the concrete-block hotels that still plague much of Slovakia. The rooms are bright and the bathrooms pleasant. The hotel is outside the city center in a quiet residential area. ⊠ *Jiskrova 3,* ☎ *095/6225809,* ꜰᴀx *095/6225918. 10 rooms with bath, 3 apartments. Restaurant, bar, beer garden. AE, MC, V.*

$$$ 🏨 **Slovan.** This unsightly high-rise surprisingly does many things well— the English-speaking staff is attentive, and the decor here is tasteful. Choose a room on one of the upper floors for a beautiful view of Košice's main square, just a few minutes' walk from the hotel. Breakfast is included. ⊠ *Hlavná ul. 1,* ☎ *095/622–7378,* ꜰᴀx *095/622–8413. 212 rooms with bath. Restaurant, café, minibars. AE, DC, MC, V.*

Nightlife and the Arts

NIGHTLIFE

If you're looking for a lively evening, **Jazz Club,** a cozy basement bar, is a popular hangout for locals. The name is a bit misleading, though, as the club features not only live and taped jazz music, but disco, country, and rap music as well. ⊠ *Kováčská 39.*

Levoča

★ ㉞ *From Košice travel via Route 547, following the signs in the direction of Spišská Nová Ves. The road quickly turns hilly, offering beautiful panoramas over several central Slovak ranges. Follow Route 547 to Spišské Podhradie, turning left on Route 18 in the direction of Levoča.*

You'll enter Levoča, the center of the Spiš kingdom and the quintessential Spiš town, through the medieval Košice Gate. A few hundred yards beyond the gate you come to the beautiful main square, surrounded by colorful Renaissance facades. Some are in appalling disrepair, and others are undergoing renovation, but this detracts little from the honest Old World feel. This medieval capital of the Spiš region was founded around 1245 and flourished between the 14th and 17th centuries, when it was an important trade center for art and crafts.

Today, Levoča and the surrounding area continue to follow many of the old traditions. Thousands of people come every year to a pilgrimage held in the first week of June. The worshipers take a long walk up the Mariánska Hora, where they pray to Virgin Mary, who is said to have appeared on the mountain.

The main sights in the town are lined along and in the middle of the square. Take a closer look at the golden sgraffiti-decorated **Thurzo House** (at No. 7), named for the powerful mining family. The wonderfully ornate gables are from the 17th century, though the sgraffiti were added in the 19th-century. At the top of the square is the **Small Committee House** (No. 60), the former administrative center of the Spiš region. Above the doorway, in sgraffito, is the coat of arms of the Spiš alliance. The monumental classical building next door, the **Large Committee House,** was built in the early 19th century by Anton Povolný, who was also responsible for the Evangelical Church at the bottom of the square.

★ The most impressive sight in town is the **Kostol svätého Jakuba** (St. Jacob Church), a huge Gothic structure begun in the early 14th century but not completed in its present form until a century later. The interior is a breathtaking concentration of Gothic religious art. It was here in the early 16th century that the greatest Spiš artist, Pavol of Levoča, created his most unforgettable pieces. The carved-wood high altar, said to be the world's largest and incorporating a truly magnificent carving of the Last Supper in limewood, is his most famous work. The 12 disciples are in fact portraits of Levoča merchants. Two of the Gothic side altars are also the work of master Pavol. The wall paintings on the left wall are fascinating for their detail and inventiveness; one depicts the seven deadly sins, each riding a different animal into hell. For 2 Sk., a tape recording in an iron post at the back of the church gives you detailed information in English. ⊠ *Nám. Majstra Pavla.* 🎟 *20 Sk.* ◷ *Tues.–Sun. 8:30–4.*

Mestská radnica (town hall), with its fine example of whitewashed Renaissance arcades, gables, and clock tower, was built in 1551 after the great fire of 1550 destroyed the old Gothic building along with much of the town. The clock tower, which was added in 1656, now houses an excellent museum, with exhibits of guild flags and a good collection of paintings and wood carvings. Here you can also look at the 18th-century *Lady in White,* painted on a doorway through which, as legend has it, she let in the enemy for a promise of wealth and a title. For this act of treason, the 24-year-old beauty's head was chopped off. ⊠ *Nám. Majstra Pavla,* 🕿 *0966/2449.* 🎟 *10 Sk.* ◷ *May–Oct., Tues.–Sun. 9–5; Nov.–Apr., Tues.–Sun. 8–4.*

The wooden cage **Klietka Hamby** (the Cage of Shame), which sits beside Evangelical church, is not much to look at, but has an interesting history. In the 16th century, single women were placed in here if they were caught wandering outside after 10 PM. Additionally, if a woman was caught in flagrante delicto with a man she wasn't married to, she was put in the cage for everyone to look at, the man was tied to a pole (no longer there), and the two were then married and banished from the town forever.

OFF THE BEATEN PATH

SPIŠSKÝ HRAD (Spiš Castle) – A former administrative center of the kingdom, this is the largest castle in Slovakia (and one of the largest in Europe). Spiš overlords occupied this site starting in 1209; the castle soon proved its military worth by surviving the onslaught of the Mongol hordes in the 13th century. The castle later came under the domination of the Hungarians. Now, however, it's firmly in Slovak hands and in season is open to the general public. The museum has a good collection of torture devices, and the castle has a beautiful view of the surrounding hills and town. From Levoča, it's worth taking the short 16-kilometer (10-mile) detour east along Route 18 to this magnificent spot. ⊠ *Spišský hrad,* 🕿 *0966/512786.* 🎟 *30 Sk.* ◷ *May–Oct., Tues.–Sat. 9–6.*

En Route   From Levoča, head south on Route 533 through Spišská Nová Ves, continuing along the twisting roads to the junction with Route 535. Turn right onto Route 535, following the signs to Mlynky and beyond, through the tiny villages and breathtaking countryside of the national park known as **Slovenský Raj** (Slovak Paradise). It is a wild and romantic area of cliffs and gorges, caves and waterfalls. Once the refuge for Spiš villagers during the Tatar invasion of 1241–42 and now a national park, the area is perfect for adventurous hikers. The gorges are accessible by narrow but secure iron ladders. The main tourist centers are Čingov in the north and Dedinky in the south.

Dining and Lodging

$ ✕ **U Janusa.** This family-owned restaurant is the perfect place to get a taste of Slovak culture as well as cuisine. Here you'll have no choice but to try one of the local specialties such as homemade sausage or dumplings with goat cheese. In summer, you can enjoy the garden patio. ✉ *Kláštorská 22,* ☎ *0966/4592. No credit cards.*

$$ ✕🏨 **Arkada Hotel.** Arkada, with large, bright rooms, is one of the few
★ near-perfect hotels in the country. This hotel is housed in a 13th-century building that in the 17th century became the first printing shop in the Austro-Hungarian Empire. ✉ *Nám. Majstra Pavla 26,* ☎ *0966/ 512255,* 🖷 *0966/512372. Restaurant, café, wine cellar. AE, MC, V.*

$$$ 🏨 **Hotel Satel.** Levoča should win an award for having two of the best
★ hotels in the country. This beautiful 18th-century mansion is built around a picturesque courtyard. The rooms are large and bright, though some of the furniture, especially the peach-colored sofa chairs, are a bit gaudy. The glossy modern lobby area can be disappointing too, but it's all made up for in the service, which is impeccable. ✉ *Nám. Majstra Pavla 55,* ☎ *0966/512943,* 🖷 *0966/514486. Restaurant, bar, wine cellar. AE, MC, V.*

Eastern Slovakia A to Z

Arriving and Departing

BY BUS

Daily bus service connects Prague and Bratislava with Košice, but on this run, trains tend to be quicker and more comfortable.

BY CAR

Poprad, a good starting point for a tour of eastern Slovakia, lies on Slovakia's main east–west highway about 560 kilometers (350 miles) from Prague in the direction of Hradec Králové. The seven- to eight-hour drive from Prague can be broken up easily with an overnight in Olomouc. The drive from Bratislava to Poprad is 328 kilometers (205 miles), with a four-lane stretch from Bratislava to Trenčín and a well-marked two-lane highway thereafter.

BY PLANE

ČSA offers regular flights from Prague and Bratislava to Košice at reasonable prices.

BY TRAIN

Trains regularly connect Košice with Prague (12 hours) and Bratislava (six hours), but book in advance to ensure a seat on these sometimes crowded routes. Several night trains make the run between Košice and Prague's main stations Hlavní nádraží and Holešovice.

Getting Around

BY BUS

Most of the region is reachable via the extensive bus network. The only exceptions are some of the smaller towns in northeastern Slovakia. Most buses run only on weekdays; plan carefully or you may end up getting stuck in a small town that is ill equipped for visitors.

BY CAR

A car is essential for reaching some of the smaller towns along the tour. Roads are of variable quality. Try to avoid driving at night, as routes are not well marked. A good four-lane highway links Prešov with Košice.

Regular trains link Poprad with Košice and some of the other larger towns, but you'll have to resort to the bus to reach smaller villages.

Contacts and Resources

EMERGENCIES
Police: ☎ 158. **Ambulance:** ☎ 155.

LATE-NIGHT PHARMACIES
Lekárna (pharmacies) take turns staying open late and on Sunday. Look for the list posted on the front door of each pharmacy. For after-hours service, ring the bell; you will be served through a little hatch door.

TRAVEL AGENCIES
The **Satur offices** in eastern Slovakia are the best—and sometimes the only—places providing basic assistance and information. They offer tours of the region and can book you a room at one of their hotels. There are branch offices in the following towns: **Košice** (✉ Rooseveltová ul. 1, ☎ 095/6223123 or 095/6223847); **Prešov** (✉ Hlavná ul. 1, ☎ 091/724041); and **Kežmarok** (✉ Hlavné nám. 64, ☎ 0968/3121).

VISITOR INFORMATION
There are offices in the following towns: **Košice** (✉ Hlavná ul. 8, ☎ 095/186); **Prešov** (✉ Hlavná ul. 67, ☎ 091/722594), **Kežmarok** (✉ Hlavné nám. 46, ☎ 0968/4046); **Levoča** (✉ Nám. Majstra Pavla 58, ☎ 0966/3763); and **Bardejov** (✉ Radničné nám. 21, ☎ 0935/551064).

SLOVAKIA A TO Z

Arriving and Departing

By Bus
There is no direct bus service from the United Kingdom to Slovakia; the closest you can get is Vienna. **International Express** (✉ Coach Travel Center, 13 Lower Regent St., London SW1Y 4LR, ☎ 0171/439–9368) operates daily in summer.

By Car
Hoek van Holland and Ostend are the most convenient ferry ports for Bratislava. From either, drive to Cologne (Köln) and then through Dresden or Frankfurt to reach Bratislava.

By Plane
At press time, few international airlines provided direct service to Bratislava, hence the best airports for traveling to Slovakia remain Prague's **Ruzyně Airport** and Vienna's **Schwechat Airport. ČSA,** the Czech and Slovak national carrier (in the U.S., ☎ 718/656–8439), offers regular service to Prague from New York's JFK Airport, Chicago, Los Angeles, and Montréal. Many of these flights have direct connections from Prague to Bratislava ($60–$75 each way); the trip takes about an hour. ČSA also offers regular air service between Prague and Košice. Vienna's Schwechat Airport is a mere 50 kilometers (30 miles) west of Bratislava. Four buses a day stop at Schwechat en route to Bratislava; the journey takes just over an hour. Numerous trains and buses also run daily between Vienna and Bratislava. From New York, a flight to Bratislava (with a stopover in Prague) takes 11–12 hours. From Montréal it is 8½ hours; from Los Angeles, 17 hours.

British Airways (in the U.K., ☎ 0171/897–4000) has daily nonstop service to Prague from London; **ČSA** (in the U.K., ☎ 0171/255–1898) flies five times a week nonstop from London. Numerous airlines offer service between London and Vienna.

By Train

There are no direct trains from London. You can take a direct train from Paris via Frankfurt to Vienna (and connect to another train or bus), or from Berlin via Dresden and Prague (en route to Budapest). Vienna is a good starting point for Bratislava. There are several trains that make the 70-minute run daily from Vienna's Südbahnhof.

Getting Around

By Bus

S.A.D. (Slovenská autobusová doprava; Bratislava, ☎ 07/7211667), the national bus carrier for Slovakia, maintains a comprehensive network in Slovakia. Buses are usually much quicker than the normal trains and more frequent than express trains, though prices are comparable with train fares. Buy your tickets from the ticket window at the bus station or directly from the driver on the bus. Long-distance buses can be full, so you might want to book a seat in advance; any Satur office will help you do this. The only drawback to traveling by bus is figuring out the timetables. They are easy to read, but beware of the small letters denoting exceptions to the times given.

By Car

Slovakia has few multilane highways, but the secondary road network is in reasonably good shape, and traffic is usually light. Roads are poorly marked, however, so an essential purchase is the *Auto Atlas SR,* which is inexpensive and available at bookstores throughout Slovakia.

Slovakia follows the usual Continental rules of the road. A right turn on red is permitted only when indicated by a green arrow. Signposts with yellow diamonds indicate a main road where drivers have the right of way. The speed limit is 110 kph (70 mph) on four-lane highways; 90 kph (55 mph) on open roads; and 60 kph (40 mph) in built-up areas. The fine for speeding is roughly 300 Sk., payable on the spot. Seat belts are compulsory, and drinking before driving is prohibited.

To report an accident, call the emergency number (☎ 155); in case of car failure call rescue service (☎ 154 or 124) in Poprad.

By Plane

Despite the splintering of the Czechoslovak federation, **ČSA** maintains a remarkably good internal air service within Slovakia, linking Bratislava with Poprad (Tatras) and Košice. Reservations can be made through Satur offices abroad or ČSA in Bratislava (☎ 07/311205).

By Train

Trains vary in speed, but it's not really worth taking anything less than an "express" train, marked in red on the timetable. Tickets are relatively cheap; first class is considerably more spacious and comfortable and on full trains well worth the 50% increase over the price of standard tickets. If you don't specify "express" when you buy your ticket, you may have to pay a supplement on the train. If you haven't bought a ticket in advance at the station, it's easy to buy one on the train for a small extra charge. On timetables, departures appear on a yellow background; arrivals are on white. It is possible to book *couchettes* (sleepers) on most overnight trains, but don't expect much in the way of comfort. The European East Pass and InterRail Pass are valid for all rail travel within Slovakia.

Contacts and Resources

Car Rentals

There are no special requirements for renting a car in Slovakia, but be sure to shop around, as prices can differ greatly. **Hertz** offers Western makes for as much as $1,000 per week. Smaller local companies, on the other hand, may rent local cars for as low as $130 per week.

The following agencies are in Bratislava: **Auto Danubius** (⊠ Trnavská 31, ☎ 07/273–754); **Hertz** (⊠ Hotel Forum, ☎ 07/533–4441); and **Recar** (⊠ Svetoplukova 1, ☎ 07/5266436).

Europcar InterRent (⊠ Ivanka Airport, ☎ 07/522–0285; ⊠ Hotel Danube, ☎ 07/534–0841 or 07/534–0847).

Customs and Duties

You may import duty-free into Slovakia 250 cigarettes or the equivalent in tobacco, 1 liter of spirits, 2 liters of wine, ½ liter of perfume, and up to 1,000 Sk. worth of gifts and souvenirs.

As with the Czech Republic, if you take into Slovakia any valuables or foreign-made equipment from home, such as cameras, it's wise to carry the original receipts with you or register the items with U.S. Customs before you leave (Form 4457). Otherwise you could end up paying duty upon your return.

Language

Slovak, a western-Slavic tongue closely related to both Czech and Polish, is the official language of Slovakia. English is popular among young people, but German is still the most useful language for tourists.

Mail

POSTAL RATES

Postcards to the United States cost 6 Sk.; letters, 11 Sk. Postcards to Great Britain cost 4 Sk.; a letter, 6 Sk. Prices are due for an increase in 1997, so check with your hotel for current rates.

RECEIVING MAIL

If you don't know where you'll be staying, you can have mail held *poste restante* (general delivery) at post offices in major towns, but the letters should be marked Pošta 1 to designate a city's main post office. You will be asked for identification when you collect mail. The poste restante window in Bratislava is at Námestie SNP 35.

Money and Expenses

CURRENCY

The unit of currency in Slovakia is the crown, or koruna, written as Sk., and divided into 100 halierov. There are bills of 20, 50, 100, 200, 500, 1,000, and 5,000 Sk., and coins of 10, 20, and 50 halierov and 1, 2, 5, and 10 Sk.

At press time, the rate of exchange was around 30 Sk. to the American dollar, 21 Sk. to the Canadian dollar, and 46 Sk. to the pound sterling.

SAMPLE COSTS

A cup of coffee, 15 Sk.; museum entrance, 10 Sk.–30 Sk.; a good theater seat, from 60 to 750 Sk. (some theaters, including the Slovak National Theater, charge foreigners a hefty fee and locals pay only a margin of this price); a half liter (pint) of beer, 15 Sk.; a 1-mile taxi ride, 100 Sk.; a bottle of Slovak wine in a good restaurant, 100 Sk.–150 Sk.; a glass (2 deciliters, or 7 ounces) of wine, 25 Sk.

National Holidays

January 1; Easter Monday; May 1 (Labor Day); July 5 (Sts. Cyril and Methodius); August 29 (anniversary of the Slovak National Uprising); September 1 (Constitution Day); and December 24, 25, and 26.

Passports and Visas

American and British citizens do not need a visa to enter Slovakia. A valid passport is sufficient for stays of up to 30 days. Questions should be directed to the Slovakian Embassy (✉ 3900 Linnean Ave. NW, Washington, DC, ☎ 202/363–6315). Canadian citizens must obtain a visa (C$50) before entering the country; for applications and information contact the Slovak Embassy (✉ 50 Rideau Terrace, Ottawa, Ontario K1M 2A1, ☎ 613/749–4442).

Telephones

INTERNATIONAL CALLS

The country code for Slovakia is 42. Dial ☎ 00–420–00101 (AT&T) or ☎ 00–420–00112 (MCI) to reach an English-speaking operator who can effortlessly connect your direct, collect, or credit-card call to the United States.

Otherwise, you can make a more time-consuming and expensive international call from Bratislava's main post office (✉ Nám. SNP 36) or for an even larger fee, at major hotels throughout the country.

For international directory inquiries call 0149; call 0139 for information on international services and rates.

LOCAL CALLS

For local directory assistance call 120. Call 121 for directory inquiries in Slovakia that are outside the city from which you're calling. Not all operators speak English so you may have to ask a hotel clerk for help.

Tipping

To reward good service in a restaurant, round up the bill to the nearest multiple of 10 (if the bill comes to 86 Sk., for example, give the waiter 90 Sk.). A tip of 10% is considered appropriate in expensive restaurants or on group tabs. Tip porters 20 Sk. For room service, a 20-Sk. tip is sufficient. In taxis, round up the bill to the nearest multiple of 10. Give tour guides and helpful concierges 20 Sk.–30 Sk.

Visitor Information

Satur Tours and Travel Agency (formerly known as Čedok) has remained the official travel bureau for Slovakia. With offices in almost every city throughout the country, it will supply you with hotel and tour information and book air, rail, and bus tickets, but do not expect much in the way of general information. For Satur addresses and telephone numbers, *see* Visitor Information *in* specific region A to Z sections, *above*.

4 Portraits

History at a Glance: A Chronology

Further Reading

HISTORY AT A GLANCE: A CHRONOLOGY

ca. 400 BC Bohemia, the main region of the Czech Republic, is settled by the Celtic Boii tribe, from which the area gets its name.

ca. 500 Closely related Slavic tribes begin to settle in the regions that make up the Czech Republic and Slovakia.

AD 846–94 The Great Moravian Empire under princes Ratislav and Svätopluk unites Bohemia, Moravia, and most of Slovakia, and extends into Poland and Hungary. Byzantine missionaries Cyril and Methodius—credited with the creation of the Cyrillic alphabet—translate Christian liturgy into Slavonic and convert much of the region.

892 German king Arnulf asks the help of the Magyars to fight Moravia.

907 Slovakia is conquered by the Magyars, beginning a thousand years of subjugation by Hungary.

965 Polish prince Mieszko I marries a Czech princess, marking the start of "official" Polish history. He introduces Christianity and unifies most of Poland from the Baltic Sea to Kraków. Mieszko's son, Bolesław I the Brave, expands the empire to both Prague and Kiev.

1029 Czech princes aligned with the Holy Roman Empire shift the center of power from Moravia to Bohemia. Moravia is annexed by Bohemia.

1348 Charles University, the first university in Central Europe, is built in Prague.

1355 Czech prince Charles IV, known as the "Father of the Country," is named Holy Roman Emperor. Prague becomes a cultural center of Europe as well as capital of the empire.

1415 Czech religious reformer Jan Hus is burned at the stake, but the Czech Reformation, or Hussite movement, continues.

1526 Ferdinand I of Hapsburg inherits the crown of Bohemia. Hapsburgs rule the Czech region, with few brief interruptions, until 1918.

1918 The Republic of Czechoslovakia is formed; Tomaš Garrigue Masaryk, who led the independence movement, is named its first president.

1920 In the Versailles settlement Czechoslovakia receives Slovakia and Ruthenia, the country adopts its first democratic constitution, and national elections are held.

1938 The Munich Pact formed by Germany, Italy, Britain, and France allows Hitler to annex the German–Czech border area known as the Sudetenland.

1939 Slovakia, led by Catholic priest Father Josef Tiso, declares its independence. Two days later Slovakia becomes a protectorate of Nazi Germany and remains a semi-independent state throughout the war. Seventy thousand out of 95,000 Slovak Jews are exterminated by the end of the war. Bohemia and Moravia are proclaimed protectorates of Nazi Germany.

1945 Prague is liberated by the Soviet army, giving the Soviet Union an important political victory in Czechoslovakia.

1946 The Czechoslovak Communist Party wins its first postwar national elections but does not receive a majority.

1968 After several years of demands for political liberalization, Slovak political reformer Alexander Dubček is named the first secretary of the Czech Communist party, ushering in the Prague Spring. Dubček tries to create "socialism with a human face," calling for multiparty democratic elections. In August, Soviet and other Warsaw Pact troops invade Czechoslovakia.

1969 Czech student Jan Palach sets himself on fire to protest the forced ending of the Prague Spring; Palach's martyrdom becomes an important motivation for the revolution of 1989.

1977 Czech intellectuals, including playwright Václav Havel, sign Charter 77, a declaration of grievances with the hard-line Communist government.

1989 Demonstrations in Prague in honor of the 20th anniversary of the death of Jan Palach lead to sweeping political and economic reforms, including free elections. Czech police beat protesters at a rally in Prague and at least one student is reportedly killed. This proves to be the catalyst for the most rapid revolution in Eastern Europe. Two days later the organization Civic Forum is created by Václav Havel and others. A day after that, 200,000 people pack Wenceslas Square and demand democracy. On November 24, Alexander Dubček returns to Prague for his first public appearance there since 1969 and addresses a mass demonstration. The Communist Party relinquishes its "leading role" on November 29. Václav Havel replaces Husák as president on December 29. Dubček is named speaker of the national parliament.

1990 Under pressure from Slovak Nationalists, Czechoslovakia changes its name to the Czech and Slovak Federative Republic. Czechoslovakia holds its first free democratic elections since 1946. Civic Forum and its counterpart in Slovakia, Public Against Violence, win convincingly in races against as many as 21 parties. President Bush is the first American president to visit Prague.

1991 Czechoslovakia sends 200 troops to the Gulf War, signaling its support of the Western cause. The Czech Civic Forum party splits into free-market and social-democratic factions, while the leading Slovak party, Public Against Violence, splits along pro- and antiseparatist lines.

1992 Parliamentary elections in Czechoslovakia lead to a deeper split between the Czech and Slovak republics. Newly elected Czech premier Václav Klaus and Slovak Nationalist leader Vladimir Mečiar fail to agree on terms for a common government and direct their respective parliaments to develop guidelines for the establishment of separate governments. Unwilling to preside over the dissolution of the nation, Václav Havel resigns the presidency in July.

1993 Failing to find a compromise, Czech and Slovak leaders split the 74-year-old Czechoslovak federation on Jan. 1, 1993. The Czech Republic and Slovakia become fully sovereign and separate countries. Václav Havel is elected by Parliament to be the new Czech president; the Slovaks appoint former banker Michael Kováč.

1994 Prague hosts the NATO summit, the first time the alliance has ever met behind the former Iron Curtain, and U.S. President Bill Clinton unveils to regional leaders the "Partnership for Peace" plan that allows former Eastern bloc countries to cooperate with NATO.

Clinton relaxes by playing saxophone—passably—with a band in a Prague jazz club. The most developed Central European nations begin the process of applying for, and obtaining, associate status in the European Union, a precursor to eagerly awaited full membership.

1995   Former Communists, now running as Western European–style Socialists, sweep back into governments across Central and Eastern Europe. The Czech Republic's right-wing government loses some ground in elections the following year, but is not knocked from power. In Slovakia, politics remain caught up not in left-versus-right struggles, but in years of fighting between allies of the country's moderate president and followers of its Nationalistic prime minister, Vladimir Mečiar.

FURTHER READING

Eastern and Central Europe

Since the revolutions of 1989–90, a number of leading journalists have produced highly acclaimed books detailing the tumultuous changes experienced by Eastern and Central Europeans and the dramatic effects these changes have had on individual lives. Timothy Garten Ash's eyewitness account, *The Magic Lantern: The Revolution of '89 Witnessed in Warsaw, Budapest, Berlin, and Prague,* begins with Václav Havel's ringing words from his 1990 New Year's address: "People, your government has returned to you!" Winner of both a National Book Award and a Pulitzer Prize, *The Haunted Land* is Tina Rosenberg's wide-ranging, incisive look at how Poland, the Czech Republic, and Slovakia (as well as Germany) are dealing with the memories of 40 years of Communism.

Also essential reading is *Exit into History: A Journey Through the New Eastern Europe,* in which Eva Hoffman returns to her Polish homeland and five other countries—Hungary, Romania, Bulgaria, the Czech Republic, and Slovakia—and captures the texture of everyday life of a world in the midst of change.

Forty-three writers from 16 nations of the former Soviet bloc are included in *Description of a Struggle: The Vintage Book of Contemporary Eastern European Writing,* edited by Michael March. Focusing on novels, poetry, and travel writing, the *Traveller's Literary Companion to Eastern and Central Europe* is a thorough guide to the vast array of literature from this region available in English translation. It includes country-by-country overviews, dozens of excerpts, reading lists, biographical discussions of key writers that highlight their most important works, and guides to literary landmarks.

Czech Republic and Slovakia

With the increased interest in the Czech Republic, English readers now have an excellent range of both fiction and nonfiction about the country at their disposal. The most widely read Czech author of fiction in English is probably Milan Kundera, whose well-crafted tales illuminate both the foibles of human nature and the unique tribulations of life in Communist Czechoslovakia. *The Unbearable Lightness of Being* takes a look at the 1968 invasion and its aftermath through the eyes of a strained young couple. *The Book of Laughter and Forgetting* deals in part with the importance of memory and the cruel irony of how it fades over time; Kundera was no doubt coming to terms with his own forgetting as he wrote the book from his Paris exile. *The Joke,* Kundera's earliest work available in English, takes a serious look at the dire consequences of humorlessness among Communists.

Born and raised in the German–Jewish enclave of Prague, Franz Kafka scarcely left the city his entire life. *The Trial* and *The Castle* strongly convey the dread and mystery he detected beneath the 1,000 golden spires of Prague. Kafka worked as a bureaucrat for 14 years, in a job he detested; his books are, at least in part, an indictment of the bizarre bureaucracy of the Austro–Hungarian empire, though they now seem eerily prophetic of the even crueler and more arbitrary Communist system that was to come. Until recently, most of his works could not be purchased in his native country.

The most popular Czech authors today were those banned by the Communists after the Soviet invasion of 1968. Václav Havel and members of the Charter 77 illegally distributed self-published manuscripts, or *samizdat* as they were called, of these banned authors—among them, Bohumil Hrabel, Josef Škvorecký, and Ivan Klíma. Hrabel, perhaps the most beloved of all Czech writers, never left his homeland; many claim to have shared a table with him at his favorite pub in Prague, U Zlatéyho tygra. His books include *I Served the King of England* and the lyrical *Too Loud a Solitude,* narrated by a lonely man who spends his days in the basement compacting the world's greatest works of literature along with bloodied butcher paper into neat bundles before they get carted off for recycling and disposal. Škvorecký sought refuge and literary freedom in Toronto in the early 1970s. His book *The Engineer of Human Souls* reveals the double censorship of the writer in exile—censored in the country of his birth and unread in his adopted home. Still, Škvorecký did gain a following thanks to his translator, Paul Wilson—who lived in Prague in the 1960s and '70s until he was ousted for his assistance in dissident activities. Wilson also set up 68 Publishers, which is responsible for the bulk of Czech literature translated into English. Novelist, short story writer and playwright Ivan Klíma is now one of the most widely read Czech writers in English; his books include the novels *Judge on Trial* and *Love and Garbage,* and *The Spirit of Prague,* a collection of essays about life in the Czech Republic today.

Václav Havel, one-time dissident playwright and now president of the Czech Republic, is essential nonfiction reading. The best place to start is probably *Living in Truth,* which provides an absorbing overview of his own political philosophy and of Czechoslovak politics and history over the last 30 years. Other recommended books by Havel include *Disturbing the Peace* (a collection of interviews with him) and *Letters to Olga.* Havel's plays explore the absurdities and pressures of life under the former Communist regime; the best example of his absurdist dramas is *The Memorandum,* which depicts a Communist bureaucracy more twisted than the streets of Prague's Old Town.

A new wave of young writers pick up where the dissident writers leave off. Among the most prominent are Jáchym Topol, whose *A Visit to the Train Station* documents the creation of a new Prague with a sharp wit that cuts the false pretenses of American youth currently occupying Prague.

CZECH VOCABULARY

English	Czech	Pronunciation

Basics

English	Czech	Pronunciation
Please.	Prosím.	**pro**-seem
Thank you.	Děkuji.	**dyek**-oo-yee
Thank you very much.	Děkuji pěkně.	**dyek**-oo-yee **pyek**-nyeh
You're welcome (it's nothing).	Není zač.	neh-nee **zahtch**
Yes, thank you.	Ano, děkuji.	**ah**-no **dyek**-oo-yee
Nice to meet you.	Těší mě.	**tye**-shee myeh
Pardon me.	Pardon.	**par**-don
Pardon me (formal)	Promiňte.	**pro**-meen-teh
I'm sorry.	Je mi líto.	yeh mee **lee**-to
I don't understand.	Nerozumím.	**neh**-rohz-oom-eem
I don't speak Czech very well.	Mluvim česky jen trochu.	**mloo**-vim **ches**-ky yen **tro**-khoo
Do you speak English?	Mluvíte anglicky?	**mloo**-vit-eh ahng-**glit**-ski
Yes/No	Ano/ne	**ah**-no/neh
Speak slowly, please.	Mluvte pomalu, prosím.	**mloov**-teh poh-**mah**-lo **pro**-seem
Repeat, please.	Opakujte, prosím.	**oh**-pahk-ooey-teh **pro**-seem
I don't know.	Nevím.	**neh**-veem

Questions

English	Czech	Pronunciation
What . . . What is this?	Co . . . Co je to?	**tso** yeh toh
When . . . When will it be ready?	Kdy . . . Kdy to bude hotové?	g'**dih** toh **boo**-deh **hoh**-toh-veh
Who . . . Who is your friend?	Kdo . . . Kdo je váš přítel?	g'doh yeh vahsh **pshee**-tel
How . . . How do you say this in Czech?	Jak . . . Jak se to řekne česky?	yak seh toh **zhek**-neh **ches**-kee
Which . . . Which train goes to Bratislava?	Ktery . . . Ktery vlak jede do Bratislavy?	k'**tair**-ee vlahk **yeh**-deh doh **brat**islavee
What do you want to do?	Co chcete dělat?	tso kh'**tseh**-teh **dyeh**-laht
Where are you going?	Kam jdete?	kahm **dyeh**-teh

This material is adapted from the Living Language™ Fast & Easy series (Crown Publishers, Inc.). Fast & Easy "survival" courses are available in 15 different languages, including Czech, Hungarian, Polish, and Russian. Each interactive 60-minute cassette teaches more than 300 essential phrases for travelers. Available in bookstores, or call 800/733-3000 to order.

What is today's date?	Kolikátého je dnes?	**ko**-li-kah-**teh**-ho yeh d'nes
May I?/I'd like permission (to do something)	S dovolením, prosím.	s'**doh**-voh-leh-**neem pro**-seem
May I . . . ?	Smím . . . ?	smeem
May I take this?	Smím si to vžít?	**smeem** see toh v'**zheet**
May I enter?	Smím vstoupit?	smeem v'**sto**-pit
May I take a photo?	Smím fotografovat?	smeem **fo**-to-gra-fo-vaht

Numbers

Zero	Nula	**noo**-la
One	Jeden, jedna, jedno	ye-**den**, **yed**-nah, **yed**-no
Two	Dva, dvě	dvah, dvyeh
Three	Tři	tshree
Four	Čtyři	ch'**ti**-zhee
Five	Pět	pyet
Six	Šest	shest
Seven	Sedm	**sed**-oom
Eight	Osm	**oh**-soom
Nine	Devět	**deh**-vyet
Ten	Deset	**deh**-set
Eleven	Jedenáct	yeh-deh-**nahtst**
Twelve	Dvanáct	dvah-**nahtst**
Thirteen	Třináct	tshree-**nahtst**
Fourteen	Čtrnát	ch't'r-**nahtst**
Fifteen	Patnáct	paht-**nahtst**
Sixteen	Šestnáct	shest-**nahtst**
Seventeen	Sedmnáct	**sed**-oom-**nahtst**
Eighteen	Osmnáct	**oh**-soom-**nahtst**
Nineteen	Devatenáct	deh-**vah**-teh-**nahtst**
Twenty	Dvacet	**dvaht**-set
Twenty-one	Dvacet jedna	**dvaht**-set **yed**-nah
Twenty-two	Dvacet dva	**dvaht**-set dvah
Twenty-three	Dvacet tři	**dvaht**-set tshree
Thirty	Třicet	**tshree**-tset
Forty	Čtyřicet	ch'**ti**-zhee-tset
Fifty	Padesát	**pah**-deh-**saht**
Sixty	Šedesát	**sheh**-deh-saht
Seventy	Sedmdesát	**sed**-oom-deh-saht
Eighty	Osmdesát	**oh**-soom-deh-saht
Ninety	Devadesát	deh-**vah**-deh-saht
100	Sto	sto
1,000	Tisíc	**tee**-seets

Common Greetings

Hello/Good morning.	Dobry den.	**dob**-ree den
Good evening.	Dobry večer.	**dob**-ree **ve**-chair
Goodbye.	Na shledanou.	Na **sled**-ah-noh

Title for married woman (or unmarried older woman)	Paní	**pah**-nee
Title for young and unmarried woman	Slečno	**sletch**-noh
Title for man	Pan	**pan**
How do you do?	Jak se vám daří?	yak seh vahm **dah**-zhee
Fine, thanks. And you?	Děkuji, dobře. A vám?	dyek-oo-yee **dobe**-zheh a vahm
How do you do? (informal)	Jak se máte?	yak se **mah**-teh
Fine, thanks. And you?	Děkuji, dobře. A vy?	**dyek**-oo-yee **dobe**-zheh ah vee
What is your name?	Jak se jmenujete?	yak se **men**-weh-teh
My name is . . .	Jmenuji se . . .	**ymen**-weh-seh
I'll see you later.	Na shledanou brzo.	na **sled**-ah-noh **b'r**-zo
Good luck!	Mnoho štěstí!	m'**no**-ho **shtyes**-tee

Directions

Where is	Kde je	g'deh yeh
Excuse me. Where is the . . . ?	Promiňte, prosím. Kde je . . . ?	**pro**-meen-teh **pro**-seem g'deh yeh
Where is the bus stop?	Kde je autobusová zastávka?	g'deh yeh **ow**-to-boos-oh-vah zah-**stahv**-kah
Where is the subway station, please?	Kde je stanice metra, prosím?	g'deh je **stah**-nit-seh **meh**-trah **pro**-seem
Where is the rest room?	Kde jsou toalety, prosím?	g'deh so twa-**leh**-tee **pro**-seem
Go	Jděte	**dye**-teh
On the right	Napravo	**na**-pra-vo
On the left	Nalevo	**na**-leh-vo
Straight ahead	Rovně	**rohv**-nyeh
At (go to) the end of the street	Jděte na konec ulici	**dye**-teh na **ko**-nets **oo**-lit-si
The first left	První ulice nalevo	**per**-vnee **oo**-lit-seh **na**-leh-vo
Near	Blízko	**bleez**-ko
It's near here.	Je to blízko.	yeh to **bleez**-ko
Turn	Zahnete	**zah**-hneh-teh
Go back.	Jděte záptky.	**dye**-teh z'**paht**-ky
Next to	Vedle	ved-**leh**

Shopping

| Money | Peníze | pen-**ee**-zeh |
| Where is the bank? | Kde je banka? | g'deh yeh **bahn**-ka |

I would like to change some money.	Chtěla bych si vyměnit peníze.	kh'**tyel**-ah bikh see vih-myen-it pen-**ee**-zeh
Please write it down.	Napište to, prosím.	**nah**-peesh-tye toh **pro**-sim
What would you like?	Co si přejete?	tso see **pshay**-eh-teh
I would like this.	Chtěl bych tohle.	kh'**tyel** bikh **toh**-hleh
Here it is.	Tady to je.	**tah**-dee toh yeh
Is that all?	To je všechno?	toh yeh **vshekh**-no
Thanks, that's all.	Děkuji. To je všechno.	**dyek**-oo-yee toh yeh **vshekh**-no
Do you accept traveler's cheques?	Přijímáte cestovni šeky?	pshee-yee-**mah**-teh **tses**-tohv-nee **shek**-ee
Credit cards?	Kredit Karty?	**cre**-dit **kar**-tee
How much?	Kolik?	**ko**-lik
Department store	Obchodní dům	**ohb**-khod-nee **doom**
Grocery store	Potraviny	**poh**-trah-**vin-ee**
Pastry shop	Cukrárna	tsoo-**krar**-na
Dairy products shop	Mlekárna	mleh-**kar**-na
I would like a loaf of bread and rolls.	Chtěla bych chléb a rohlíky.	kh'**tyel**-ah bikh khleb ah **roh**-hleck-ee
Milk	Mléko	**mleh**-koh
A half kilo of this salami	Půl kilo tohoto salámu	**pool kee**-lo **toh**-ho-toh sah-**lah**-moo
This cheese	Tento syr	**ten**-toh seer
A kilo of apples	Kilo jablek	**kee**-lo **yah**-blek
Three kilos of pears.	Tři kila hrušek.	tshree **kee**-la h'**roo**-shek
Women's clothing	Dámské odévy	**dahm**-skeh **oh**-dyeh-vee
Men's clothing	Pánské odévy	**pahn**-skeh **oh**-dyeh-vee
Souvenirs	Upomínkové předměty	**oo**-poh-**meen**-koh-veh pshed-**myeh**-tee
Toys and gifts	Hračky a dárky	h'**rahtch**-kee ah **dar**-ky
Jewelry and perfume	Bižutérie a voňavky	**bizh**-oo-teh-ree-yeh ah **voh**-nyahv-kee

At the Hotel

Room	Pokoj	**poh**-koy
I would like a room.	Chtěl (Chtěla) bych pokoj.	kh'**tyel** (kh'**tyel**-ah) bikh **poh**-koy
For one person	Pro jednu osobu	pro **yed**-noo **oh**-so-boo

For two people	Pro dvě osoby	pro dveh **oh**-so-bee
For how many nights?	Na kolik nocí?	na **ko**-lik **note**-see
For tonight	Na dnešní noc	na **dnesh**-nee notes
For two nights	Na dvě noci	na dveh **note**-see
For a week	Na tyden	na **tee**-den
Do you have a different room?	Máte jiny pokoj?	**ma**-teh **yee**-nee **poh**-koy
With a bath	S koupelnou	s'**ko**-pel-noh
With a shower	Se sprchou	seh **sp'r**-kho
With a toilet	S toaletou	s'twa-**leh**-to
The key, please.	Klíc, prosím.	kleech **pro**-seem
How much is it?	Kolik to stojí?	**ko**-lik toh **stoy**-ee
My bill, please.	Účet, prosím.	**oo**-chet **pro**-seem

Dining Out

Café	Kavárna	ka-**vahr**-na
Restaurant	Restaurace	res-toh-**vrat**-seh
A table for two	Stůl pro dva	stool pro dvah
Waiter, the menu, please.	Pane vrchní! Jídelní lístek, prosím.	**pah**-neh **verkh**-nee **yee**-dell-nee **lis**-tek **pro**-seem
The wine list, please.	Líst vin, prosím. (or, vinny listek).	leest vin **pro**-seem **vin**-nee **lis**-tek
The main course	Hlavní jídlo	**hlav**-nee **yid**-lo
What would you like?	Co si přejete?	tso see **psheh**-yeh-teh
What would you like to drink?	Co se přejete k pití?	tso seh **psheh**-yeh-teh k'**pit**-ee
Can you recommend a good wine?	Můžete doporučit dobré víno?	**moo**-zheh-teh **doh**-por-oo-cheet **dohb**-zheh **vi**-noh
Wine, please.	Víno, prosim.	**vi**-noh **pro**-seem
Pilsner beer	Plzeňské pivo	**pil**-zen-skeh **piv**-oh
What's the specialty of the day?	Jaká je dnešní specialitá?	**ya**-ka yeh **dnesh**-nee spet-sya-lih-**tah**
I didn't order this.	Tohle jsem neobjednal.	**toh**-hleh sem **neh**-ob-yed-nahl
That's all, thanks.	Děkuji, to je všechno.	**dyek**-oo-yee to yeh **vsheh**-khno
The check, please.	Učet, prosím.	**oo**-chet **pro**-seem
Is the tip included?	Je záhrnuto zpropítně?	yeh **za**-her-noo-toh **zpro**-peet-nyeh
Enjoy your meal.	Dobrou chut'.	**doh**-broh khoot
To your health!	Na zdraví!	**na** zdrah-vee
Fork	Vidlička	**vid**-litch-ka
Knife	Nůž	noozh

Spoon	Lžíce	l'**zheet**-seh
Napkin	Ubrousek	**oo**-bro-sek
A cup of tea	Šálek čaje	**shah**-lek **tcha**-yeh
A bottle of wine	Láhev vína	**lah**-hev **vi**-nah
One beer	Jedno pivo	**yed**-noh **piv**-oh
Two beers, please.	Dvě piva, prosím.	dveh **piv**-ah **pro**-seem
Salt and pepper	Sůl a pepř	sool ah pepsh
Sugar	Cukr	**tsook**-rr
Bread, rolls, and butter	Chléb, rohlíky a máslo	khleb **roh**-hlee-ky ah **mah**-slo
Black coffee	Černá káva	**chair**-na **kah**-va
Coffee with milk	Káva s mlékem (or, Bílá káva)	**kah**-va s **mleh**-kem **bee**-la **kah**-va
Tea with lemon	Čaj se citrónem	tchai se **tsi**-tro-nem
Orange juice	Pomerančovy džus	po-mair-**ahn**-cho-vee dzhoos
Another (masc., fem., neuter)	Ještě jeden (ještě jednu, ještě jedno)	yesh-**tyeh** ye-**den** (yesh-**tyeh** yed-**nu,** yesh-**tyeh** yed-no)
More	Ještě	yesh-**tyeh**
I'd like more mineral water.	Chtěl bych ještě minerálku.	kh'**tyel** bikh yesh-**tyeh** min-eh-**rahl**-ku
Another napkin, please.	Ještě jeden ubrousek, prosím.	yesh-**tyeh** jeh-**den** **oo**-bro-sek, **pro**-seem
More bread and butter	Ještě chléb a máslo	yesh-**tyeh** khleb ah **mah**-slo
Not too spicy	Ne příliš ostré	neh **pshee**-leesh **oh**-streh
I like the meat well done.	Chci maso dobře upečené (or, Chci propečené).	kh'tsee **mah**-so **dobe**-zheh **oo**-petch-en-eh kh'tsee **pro**-petch-en-eh
May I exchange this for . . .	Mohl bych tohle vyměnit za . . .	**mole** bikh **to**-hleh **vee**-myen-it zah

Telling Time

What time is it?	Kolik je hodin?	**ko**-lik yeh **ho**-din
Midnight	Půlnoc	**pool**-nohts
It is noon.	Je poledne.	yeh **po**-led-neh
Morning	Ráno, dopoledne	**rah**-no, **doh**-po-led-**neh**
Afternoon	Odpoledne	**ohd**-po-led-**neh**
Evening	Večer	**veh**-chair
Night	Noc	nohts
It is 9:00 AM.	Je deset hodin dopoledne.	yeh **deh**-set **ho**-din **doh**-po-led-neh

It is 1:00 PM.	Je jedna hodina odpoledne.	yeh yed-**na ho**-din-ah **ohd**-po-led-**neh**
It is 3 o'clock.	Jsou tři hodiny.	so tshree **ho**-din-y
It is 5 o'clock.	Je pět hodin.	yeh pyet **ho**-din
5:15	Pět patnáct	pyet paht-**nahtst**
7:30	Sedm třicet	**sed**-oom **tshree**-tset
9:45	Devět čtyřicet pět	**deh**-vyet ch'**ti**-zhee-tset **pyet**
Now	Teď	tedj
Later	Později	poh-**zdyay**-ee
Immediately	Hned	h'ned
Soon	Brzo	b'**r**-zo

Days of the Week

Monday	Pondělí	**pon**-dye-lee
Tuesday	Úterý	**oo**-teh-ree
Wednesday	Středa	**stshreh**-da
Thursday	Čtvrtek	ch't'v'**r**-tek
Friday	Pátek	**pah**-tek
Saturday	Sobota	**so**-boh-ta
Sunday	Neděle	**neh**-dyeh-leh

Months

January	Leden	**leh**-den
February	Únor	**oo**-nor
March	Březen	b'**zhe**-zen
April	Duben	**doo**-ben
May	Květen	k'**vyet**-en
June	Červen	**chair**-ven
July	Červenec	**chair**-ven-ets
August	Srpen	s'**r**-pen
September	Září	**zah**-zhee
October	Říjen	**zhee**-yen
November	Listopad	**list**-o-pahd
December	Prosinec	**pro**-sin-ets

At the Airport

Airport	Letiště	**leh**-tish-tyeh
Arrivals	Přílety	**pshee**-leh-tee
Where are the taxis?	Kde jsou taxíky?	g'deh so **tak**-seek-ee
Is there a subway?	Je tady metro?	yeh **tah**-dee **meh**-tro
Is there a bus?	Je tady autobus?	yeh **tah**-dee **out**-oh-boos
Stop here, please!	Zastavte tady, prosím!	**zah**-stahv-teh **tah**-dee pro-seem
What is the fare to downtown?	Kolik to stojí do středu města?	**ko**-lik toh **stoy**-ee doh st'**shreh**-doo **myes**-tah
Have a good trip!	Šťastnou cestu!	sht'**shast**-no **tsest**-oo

At the Train Station

Train station	Nádraží	**nah**-drah-zhee
I'd like a ticket, please.	Chtěl bych lístek, prosím.	kh'**tyel** bikh **list**-ek **pro**-seem
A one-way ticket	Jednoduchy lístek	**yed**-no-**dookh**-nee **list**-ek
A return ticket	Zpátečni lístek	**zpah**-tetch-nee **list**-ek
A local train	Osobní vlak	**oh**-sobe-nee vlahk
An express train	Rychlík	**rikh**-leek
Do you have a timetable?	Máte jízkní řád?	**mah**-teh **yeezd**-nee zhahd
Is there a dining car?	Je ve vlaku jídelní vůz?	yeh veh **vlah**-koo **yee**-dell-nee vooz
A sleeping car	Spací vůz	**spa**-tsee vooz
Where is this train going?	Kam jede tenhle vlak?	kahm **jeh**-deh **ten**-h-leh vlahk
What time does the train leave for . . . ?	V kolik hodin odjíždí vlak do . . . ?	v'**ko**-lik **ho**-din **ohd**-yeezh-dee vlahk doh
What time does the train arrive from . . . ?	V kolik hoden přijíždí vlak z . . . ?	v-**ko**-lik ho-**din pshee**-yeezh-dee vlahk z
From what platform does the train leave?	Z kterého nástupiště vlak odjíždí?	z'k'tair-**ay**-ho **nah**-stoo-pish-tyeh vlahk **ohd**-yeezh-dee
The train arrives at 2:00 PM.	Vlak přijiždí ve čtrnáct hodin.	vlahk **pshee**-yeezh-dee veh ch'tr-**nahtst** ho-din
The train is late.	Vlak ma zpoždění.	vlahk mah z'**poh**-zhdyeh-nee
Can you help me, please?	Mohl byste mi pomoci, prosím?	**mole** bis-teh mee **poh**-moh-tsee **pro**-seem
Can you tell me, please?	Mohl byste mi říci, prosím?	**mole** bis-teh mee **zhee**-tsee **pro**-seem
I've lost my bags.	Ztratila jsem zavazadla.	z'**tra**-tih-lah sem **zah**-vah-zahd-lah
My money	Peníze	**peh**-nee-zeh
My passport	Pas	pahss
I've missed my train.	Zmeškal jsem vlak.	z'**mesh**-kahl sem vlahk

At the Post Office

Post office	Pošta	**po**-shta
Stamps, please.	Známky, prosím.	**znahm**-kee **pro**-seem
For letters or for postcards?	Na dopisy nebo na pohlednice?	na **doh**-pis-ee **neh**-bo poh-**hled**-nit-seh

To where are you mailing the letters?	Kam posíláte dopisy?	kahm **poh**-see-**lah**-teh **doh**-pis-ee
To the United States	Do Spojenych Států	doh **spoy**-en ikh **stah**-too
Airmail	Letecky	**leh**-tet-skee
The telephone directory	Telefonní seznam	te-le-**fon**-nee **sez**-nahm
Where can I go to make a telephone call?	Odkud mohu telefonavat?	**ohd**-kood **moh**-hoo te-le-**fo**-no-**vaht**
A telephone call	Telefonní rozhovor	te-le-**fon**-nee **rohz**-ho-vor
A collect call	Hovor na ůčet volaného	**ho**-vor na **oo**-chet **voh**-lah-**neh**-ho
What number, please?	Jaké číslo, prosím?	**yah**-keh **chee**-slo **pro**-seem
May I speak to Mrs. Newton, please.	Mohl bych mluvit s paní Newtonovou. prosím.	**mole** bikh **mloo**-vit **spah**-nee **new**-ton-oh-voh **pro**-seem
The line is busy.	Je obsázeno.	yeh ob-**sah**-zen-**oh**
There's no answer.	Nehlásí se.	**neh**-hlah-see seh
Try again later.	Zkuste to poszději.	**zkoo**-steh toh po-**zdyay**-ee
May I leave a message, please?	Mohla bych nechát vzkaz, prosím?	**moh**-hla **bikh** **neh**-khaht v'**zkahz** **pro**-seem

INDEX

Index

185

WHEREVER YOU TRAVEL, *H*ELP IS NEVER FAR AWAY.

From planning your trip to providing travel assistance along the way, American Express® Travel Service Offices are always there to help.

Czech Republic

BVV Fair Travel (R)
Starobrnenska 20
Brno
5/42-217-7445

Incentive Travel Service (R)
Vridelni 51
Karlovy Vary
17/32-25-317

American Express Czech Republic Ltd.
Vaclavske Namesti 56
Prague
2/24-219-992

Slovakia

TatraTour (R)
Frantiskanske Nam 3
Bratislava
7/52-11-219

TatraTour (R)
Winterova 28
Piestany
838/25-305

TatraTour (R)
Alzbetina 6
Kosice
95/622-1334

TatraTour (R)
Nam. Sv. Egidia 9
Poprad
92/63-712

TatraTour (R)
Marianske Namestie 21
Zilina
89/47-529

Travel

http://www.americanexpress.com/travel

Fodor's Travel Publications

Available at bookstores everywhere, or call 1–800–533–6478, 24 hours a day.

Gold Guides
U.S.

Alaska

Arizona

Boston

California

Cape Cod, Martha's
Vineyard, Nantucket

The Carolinas & the
Georgia Coast

Chicago

Colorado

Florida

Hawai'i

Las Vegas, Reno,
Tahoe

Los Angeles

Maine, Vermont,
New Hampshire

Maui & Lāna'i

Miami & the Keys

New England

New Orleans

New York City

Pacific North Coast

Philadelphia & the
Pennsylvania Dutch
Country

The Rockies

San Diego

San Francisco

Santa Fe, Taos,
Albuquerque

Seattle & Vancouver

The South

U.S. & British Virgin
Islands

USA

Virginia & Maryland

Washington, D.C.

Foreign

Australia

Austria

The Bahamas

Belize & Guatemala

Bermuda

Canada

Cancún, Cozumel,
Yucatán Peninsula

Caribbean

China

Costa Rica

Cuba

The Czech Republic
& Slovakia

Eastern &
Central Europe

Europe

Florence, Tuscany
& Umbria

France

Germany

Great Britain

Greece

Hong Kong

India

Ireland

Israel

Italy

Japan

London

Madrid & Barcelona

Mexico

Montréal &
Québec City

Moscow, St.
Petersburg, Kiev

The Netherlands,
Belgium &
Luxembourg

New Zealand

Norway

Nova Scotia, New
Brunswick, Prince
Edward Island

Paris

Portugal

Provence &
the Riviera

Scandinavia

Scotland

Singapore

South Africa

South America

Southeast Asia

Spain

Sweden

Switzerland

Thailand

Tokyo

Toronto

Turkey

Vienna & the Danube

Fodor's Special-Interest Guides

Caribbean Ports
of Call

The Complete Guide
to America's
National Parks

Family Adventures

Gay Guide
to the USA

Halliday's New
England Food
Explorer

Halliday's New
Orleans Food
Explorer

Healthy Escapes

Kodak Guide to
Shooting Great
Travel Pictures

Net Travel

Nights to Imagine

Rock & Roll Traveler
USA

Sunday in New York

Sunday in
San Francisco

Walt Disney World,
Universal Studios
and Orlando

Walt Disney World
for Adults

Where Should We
Take the Kids?
California

Where Should We
Take the Kids?
Northeast

Worldwide Cruises
and Ports of Call